American Alchemy

**Cultural Studies
of the United States**

Alan Trachtenberg, editor

EDITORIAL ADVISORY BOARD

Michele Bogart

Karen Halttunen

Mae Henderson

Eric Lott

Miles Orvell

Jeffrey Stewart

American Alchemy

The California Gold Rush and Middle-Class Culture

Brian Roberts

THE UNIVERSITY OF NORTH CAROLINA PRESS

CHAPEL HILL & LONDON

© 2000 The University of North Carolina Press
Designed by April Leidig-Higgins
Set in Monotype Bulmer by Keystone Typesetting, Inc.
Manufactured in the United States of America

The paper in this book meets the guidelines for
permanence and durability of the Committee on
Production Guidelines for Book Longevity of the
Council on Library Resources.

Library of Congress Cataloging-in-Publication Data
Roberts, Brian, 1957– American alchemy : the California
gold rush and middle-class culture / by Brian Roberts.
p. cm.—(Cultural studies of the United States)
Includes bibliographical references (p.   ) and index.
ISBN 0-8078-2543-3 (cloth: alk. paper)
ISBN 0-8078-4856-5 (pbk.: alk. paper)
1. California—Gold discoveries—Social aspects.
2. Frontier and pioneer life—California. 3. Frontier
and pioneer life—West (U.S.) 4. Pioneers—California—
History—19th century. 5. Pioneers—Northeastern
States—History—19th century. 6. Middle class—
California—History—19th century. 7. Middle class—
Northeastern States—History—19th century.
8. California—Social conditions—19th century.
9. Northeastern States—Social conditions—19th
century. I. Title. II. Series.
F865.R64 2000   979.4'04—dc21   99-048082

04 03 02 01 00   5 4 3 2 1

For my mother, Margaret Cardoza,
and in memory of my father, Don Roberts

Contents

A section of illustrations
follows page 142.

Acknowledgments

About a year ago we, meaning myself and my "better half," were driving cross-country, heading west to new jobs in Sacramento. "Ho for California!" I screamed at the top of my lungs each morning as we approached the car and the long day's drive. About the time we crossed into South Dakota we began to notice something: we were surrounded by motorcycles. As luck would have it, our trip corresponded with the last days of South Dakota's famous Sturgis Rally, the largest gathering of bike enthusiasts on the planet. The participants were not just enthusiasts, their machines not mere motorcycles. Most of the rally-goers were rough-looking men, bearded and dangerous Hell's Angel types. Their bikes were "choppers," great and thundering beasts. What man and beast seemed to be saying was this: "HEY PERFESSOR, WE ARE GONNA . . . KICK! YOUR! ASS!" Later on we faced the unavoidable meeting with these ruffians, for they occupied every cafe, campground, motel, service station, and restroom in the state. It turned out that most of these men were lawyers, stockbrokers, or college professors. For hours I babbled incessantly over this discovery, and all my babblings made the same point: "IT'S MY BOOK! IT'S MY BOOK COME TO LIFE!"

This is what happens to a person who has been working on a book for eight years. All becomes the book. The book becomes all. For eight years this book has taken over my life. Many people and institutions have stood by while this was happening and many have actually helped the process along. I am responsible for all the errors here, the errors of fact, interpretation, and judgment. But they are going to have to take responsibility for something, maybe for helping me, maybe for not telling me to stop.

Research for this project was supported by a fellowship from the

Graduate School at Rutgers University along with the Rutgers Department of History. I also benefited from the kindness and friendship of Stephanie Williams, who let me sleep on her floor while I did research in San Francisco and Berkeley. Later, a fellowship from the Charlotte Newcombe Foundation allowed me to write, to make revisions, and to begin the process of turning a rather unwieldy dissertation into something more readable. Still later, a National Endowment for the Humanities–sponsored fellowship from the American Antiquarian Society provided me with time and space to make some final revisions on the manuscript, and to gather together its illustrations.

As well, I owe a great debt to the archivists and staff members of several libraries. I am eternally grateful for the patience, expertise, and overall willingness to help of staff members at the Bancroft Library, the California State Library, the California Historical Society, the New-York Historical Society, the New York Public Library, Yale's Beinecke Library, and the Alexander Library Archives at Rutgers. I am particularly grateful for the support and help of my friends at the American Antiquarian Society: Gigi Barnhill, Joanne Chaison, Tom Knowles, John Hench, Caroline Sloat, Marie Lamoureux, Sara Hagenbuch, and Laura Wasowicz. Throughout my stay at the American Antiquarian Society, Thomas Doughton was both a good friend and a wise mentor. I have him to thank for inspiring much of the commentary on gold rush reenactments in the conclusion of this book.

In the early years of this project, I benefited from a stimulating and challenging environment at Rutgers. Suzanne Lebsock and Bonnie Smith helped get the project started, mostly by not laughing when I came to them with the idea of writing about the gold rush, or at least about the women who remained in the East during the rush. My old grad school clique—Suzanne Kaufman, Scott Sandage, and Carol Helstosky—helped me survive those years. Scott passed several extremely useful sources my way. Carol gave me a title for the project. As for Suzanne, she challenged all my ways of thinking and being in the world. Without her support and critical insights into my writing and myself, I would certainly never have written this book. Other colleagues at Rutgers who must be listed as enablers include Matt Berger, Jonathan Nashel, Rebecca Brittenham, Kurt Spellmeyer, and Richard Miller.

Several scholars read portions of my manuscript, and several others read nearly the whole thing; all offered helpful advice. Alice Kessler

Harris and Myra Jehlen read early versions of each chapter, and both greatly influenced my understandings of gender, women's work, and the ideological uses of language. Malcolm Rohrbough read early versions of Chapters 1–3, and his comment that they seemed written "from Mars" helped urge me to be more clear in my arguments. Ken Owens did the same for Chapter 5. As readers for the University of North Carolina Press, Karen Halttunen and John Mack Faragher probably did more to turn this project into a real book than anyone else. When it comes to readings, advice, and help, my greatest debts are to Jackson Lears and James Livingston. They shaped this book from beginning to end. They supported me when I was down, at times expressing more confidence in this project than I was able to maintain myself.

David Hyde has provided me with a sense of scholarly community and camaraderie. For the last eight years, we have had one long conversation about practically all the themes of this book. When I have been facile, he has pushed me to complicate my thinking. Whenever I have been satisfied that I finally "got" some point of historical contention, he has reopened the issue. Whenever I have been off track, he has reminded me of how to do cultural history. In all, he is that rarest of individuals: a colleague and a true friend.

Finally, I owe much to my editors at the University of North Carolina Press, for their patience, their good humor, and their ability to decipher my handwriting. Sian Hunter resurrected my manuscript, suggested or supported countless revisions, and talked me through the process of making a book. For at least two years she has been the best of editors, always urging me on, always promising a light at the end of the tunnel. More recently, Ron Maner and Kate Lovelady have offered help with copyediting and final revisions. If, as someone once told me, "God is in the details," I am without God. Luckily for me, they are not.

Without a doubt, my greatest debt is to Barbara Cutter. Of course, she is neither mine nor better nor a half; that was just for style. She is a scholar in her own right, a writer, a teacher, and a professional historian. She has also been my editor, seer, soothsayer, co-conspiracy theorist, and closest colleague. Many times she has borne the burden of my ramblings as this book has taken over my life. Yet through it all, she has taken time out of her own busy schedule to listen, to offer critical insights, to add her ideas to the mix and nuance mine, and in every way to make this a better book. I can never really thank her enough. With this book out of the way, however, I can go back to what I do best: cleaning house, cooking dinner, and, as one of the protagonists of this book might have put it had she lived in a different time, "lightening her burden by all those little acts that a househusband has at his control, and that he is prompted to exercise for the well-being and happiness of those he loves."

American Alchemy

Introduction

If there is one work that best sets the context for the northeastern experience of the California gold rush, it is undoubtedly Herman Melville's "Bartleby the Scrivener." Melville first published this story in 1853; yet its main characters, the isolated slave to the inkstand and the plodding white-collar gentleman, had been around for some years. The story's setting is the quintessential New York City clerk's office, described as a "snug retreat" by the narrator, nightmarishly dreary to the reader, a dusty second-floor chamber surrounded by the taller buildings of Wall Street, a space of hard wood surfaces, screens, and partitions. Two windows merely add to its aura of claustrophobia: one opens to an interior air shaft, the other frames a wall across the alley, a square of brick "black by age and everlasting shade." Within this melancholy space, a gentleman lawyer, the story's narrator, works with two scriveners who spend their days engaged in the dry task of copying legal documents. Pressed by business, the lawyer hires a third copyist. This is Bartleby, a clean, polite, and quiet individual, a mild man whose complete lack of spark matches the requirements of the position. At first, the newcomer seems the perfect clerk: unquestioning and diligent, fastidious in appearance and penmanship. Soon the narrator finds that there is something seriously wrong with this fellow.

For Bartleby suffers from a strange and "incurable disorder," an illness not of body but of soul. From the first, there are small signs of this illness. Each time he is asked to perform any office task aside from mere copying, he responds with a polite but firm refusal, saying only "I would prefer not to." Disarmed by his clerk's otherwise mild character, the narrator seems incapable of doing anything about this strange behavior. Eventually the scrivener's preferences expand: he would "prefer not" to perform any editing of documents. He would "prefer not" to run errands. Soon he declares that he will do no work at all, saying only that he would "prefer not to." Nor for that matter will he leave the office, instead standing silent and motionless within his screened cubicle, staring at the darkened brick wall beyond the window above his desk. At last, unable to confront his now ghostlike employee, trapped between feelings of pity for his clerk's obvious soul-sickness and frustrated outrage at his refusals, the narrator moves his business to another office. The chamber's new tenants have Bartleby hauled off to jail. There, he eventually dies of starvation while staring at the thicker and darker walls of New York City's famous prison, "The Tombs."[1]

Melville's characters are representative men. The narrator seems the epitome of early Victorian propriety: inwardly, he wrestles with the issue of whether to pity his clerk or to fire him; outwardly, he remains stiff and dignified, so fearful of making a scene that he is tyrannized by the scrivener's polite refusals and silent presence. Bartleby, meanwhile, is the quintessential white-collar clerk. He is clean and neat in his behavior and dress, respectable and polite in manners and tone. He is a brain-worker, alienated from physical labor, a man for whom the office, the desk, and the cubicle have become the whole of existence. All in all, Melville's characters fit nearly perfectly into the mold of America's emerging middle class as historians have defined it. They are refined, respectable, and repressed. They are dignified, fearful of confrontation and intimate social contact. They are white-collar professionals, willfully cut off from the chaotic and vulgar world outside of their walls.[2] And yet, the story raises a crucial question that many of these historians have overlooked: where is the vaunted social power of the middle-class in this picture of isolated and repressed respectability?

The answer, of course, is that membership in such a one-dimensional middle class is not a position of power. What Bartleby's story suggests is something that everyone knows but few discuss. It suggests that even at the historical moment of class formation, there were limits to respectability; that refinement, self-control, and politeness—while fine in their place—might be problems for individuals who had to make their way in a real world of business, competition, and social confrontations. It indicates, in other words, that the very qualities historians have associated with the middle class might actually leave its members cut off and almost completely powerless. Above all, it suggests that there was another dimension to middle-class culture, some other set of qualities that lay outside the realm of politeness and respectability, some other chapter in its formation that would take its adherents beyond the darkened brick walls of the office district.

Between 1849 and the mid-1850s, this other dimension would be provided by the California gold rush. The general narrative of the gold rush is well known, for it has been repeated hundreds of times by hundreds of historians, and nearly always in the same general way. The story begins with James Marshall's accidental discovery of gold on the north fork of the American River in early 1848. It continues with the rapid spread of "gold fever," first through California, then through the rest of the nation. This first madness spread to become a mass exodus of men (for the most part) bound for the new Eldorado, some 80,000 in 1849, about half of whom came from the American Northeast. Little is known about these men. If we believe the standard narrative of the gold rush, they revealed little about themselves, still less about their former lives and social ties. One thing seems clear, however; based on what we know about the repressed bourgeoisie, they could not have been middle class in origin.

For many Americans in the mid-nineteenth century, there were few characters so comical or pathetic as the overcivilized easterner. Bartleby was one of these characters; Jeremiah Saddlebags was another. The protagonist of one of America's first comic strips, Saddlebags made his appearance in eastern booksellers' stalls in 1849. Then as now, he was an immediately recognizable figure. His creators pictured him as the essential urban dandy, a social upstart whose every cent goes toward outfitting himself in the accouterments of the "man of fashion." He spends much of his time practicing for this role: standing before a mirror in his tiny boarding-house room, straightening his silk cravat, tightening his white kid gloves, making exaggeratedly feminine scrapes and bows to an imagined audience of the city's best residents. By day he works as a low-paid clerk, by night he courts his fiancée, wooing her with the stiff parlor manners of middle-class etiquette manuals. All of this would be hilarious enough. But luckily for the history of comedy, Saddlebags's creators removed this foppish young man from his comfortable station: they had him join the California gold rush. His experience is a series of idiotic missteps. Upon learning that the miners collect gold with "rockers," the milksop clerk buys an infant's cradle and straps it to his back. He is so frightened of Indians that he shaves his head, figuring this will make his scalp less attractive. He is so out of place in the mining camps that a group of the region's miners threaten to thrash him for posturing. Finally, he is forced to flee

California for his life, returning to the safety of parlor society a grotesque figure: head shaved and nicked, body emaciated and covered with scars. The message of Saddlebags's creators was clear: the affected bourgeois was no forty-niner.[3]

Indeed the American West as a whole seems completely divorced from anything that might be remotely concerned with the middle class. From the historical moment of its appearance, the mid-nineteenth-century middle class has been characterized by ideals and values that filter "real life" through prescriptive literature stressing hard work, postponed gratification, repressive manners, and, above all, respectability. The American middle class, in other words, is largely a cultural phenomenon: from its rise to prominence its assumed goals, to borrow the still resonant words of H. L. Mencken, were to get ahead and "punish the man with the superior capacity for happiness."[4] The American West, in contrast, has long been understood as a place of stark oppositions to middle-class values, an arena for manly self-testing, self-expression, lawlessness, and violence.[5]

If there is one expression of this popular version of the West, it is undoubtedly the California gold rush. Consisting of equal parts democratic epic and drunken debauch, the gold rush has been characterized as a period of freedom and raw experience unfiltered by the dictates of culture. California during the flush times was a place of disputed claims, shoot-outs, gambling halls, and prostitution. It was a place where an antiaristocratic national character could express itself, unfettered by the niceties of bourgeois respectability. Finally, it was a place populated by the most liberated of men: the California forty-niner. Few figures in lore and history have been portrayed as more ardently opposed to respectable values. "But they were rough," wrote Mark Twain in perhaps the most powerful and lasting commentary on this figure: "They fairly reveled in gold, whiskey, fights, and fandangos, and were unspeakably happy." Among them there were few "simpering, dainty, kid-gloved weaklings," nor would they long put up with the "sleepy, sluggish-brained sloths" occupying the musty offices and merchant's exchanges of New York, Boston, and Philadelphia.[6] For 150 years, the forty-niner has remained a happy figure, a symbol of freedom from bourgeois restraint. The gold rush continues to be interpreted as a reversal of middle-class standards, as a rebellion against a cultured elite and "culture" itself, as perhaps the last and greatest example of the masculine and liberated West.

This book is a cultural history of the California gold rush. It is also a social history of the California forty-niner. As cultural history, its goal is to explore myths and ideologies, to analyze and unpack them for their statements about American values and conceptions of a national character. As social history, its goal is to focus on average people, to explore the realities of their daily lives. As a result of these approaches, this study raises a couple of possibilities that many readers will doubtlessly find startling. From the standpoint of culture, this narrative focuses on two of the central myths of the California gold rush. One is the myth of the lone, male forty-niner, the independent man without past, connection, or moral conscience. The other is the myth of a fixed, unchanging, and hopelessly repressed eastern middle class. That both of these subjects are in fact mythical is borne out by one of the gold rush's central social realities: a large percentage of northeastern forty-niners either were or aspired to become members of America's emerging middle class. At its most basic level, the argument of this narrative is this: the gold rush was a rebellion against certain middle-class values; this revolt, in turn, was largely carried out by middle-class individuals.

From an analytical perspective that looks only west, the forty-niners typically appear as unattached bravos, the very seed and model of antibourgeois rebellion and working-class identity. They were poor, or at least so it is assumed; for the gold regions of California were on public lands, claims were free for the taking, and all the gold seeker needed was a pick and a pan. And they were vulgar, embracing a style of expression associated with the authentic "b'hoys" of the working class, trampling the dictates of bourgeois propriety with bawdy songs, cursing, drinking, and fighting.[7] With a turning of this lens to the East, the forty-niner looks different. First, he was rarely poor. In fact, he could not afford to be, for the cost of getting to California was often more than a year's pay for the average American. Most fell into three broad occupational categories, roughly split between artisans, farmers, and white-collar workers, the new breed of clerks, shopkeepers, and professionals who had emerged with industrialization. Second, he was almost never unattached. The eastern forty-niner was often married, usually respectable, and almost always connected to family and community. Finally, he was rarely a vulgarian. Nearly all the forty-niners of this study were brought up and surrounded in the East by the moral codes they would trample in California, bred and educated in the values the gold rush would come to stand against.

On further review, in other words, Jeremiah Saddlebags *does* fit the mold of the forty-niner. So does William Prentiss. Prentiss was one of the leading citizens of Davenport, Iowa. Although a newcomer to the community, having migrated in the mid-1840s from the Northeast, by 1849 he had become one of the town's most respected medical doctors. He was a member of several fraternal and reform associations, a temperance man and an Odd Fellow. He seemed to be settled in life, a good husband to his wife, Elizabeth, a good father to his two children. Yet toward the end of 1849 Prentiss's neighbors began to hear some strange talk from the good doctor: he was thinking about joining the rush to California. "I cannot help thinking that you have overlooked the advantages of this location," wrote one in warning, "when you prefer going to California (in search of glittering gold which never yet gave happyness) to locating yourself where there is a prospect of doing good business and where you can enjoy the privileges of a *Christian* and the protection of civil laws."[8]

The assumption of Prentiss's neighbors is clear from this passage: respectable Christian gentlemen, men with families and reputations, did not go to California to search for gold. Prentiss went anyway. So did thousands of others like him. "It seems as if the Atlantic Coast was to be depopulated," noted George Templeton Strong at the time, as he watched what he called "the most remarkable emigration in the history of man" from his New York City office. What made the emigration remarkable, according to a writer in *Godey's Lady's Book*, was the fact that these men were not the usual pioneering types. Thousands were going, noted one of the magazine's writers, "who have never dug a rood of garden in their lives, and never slept out of the home."[9] Stranger still, few of these emigrants seemed willing to abandon their moral codes, and many freely admitted that the whole venture was wrong, at least morally. Theological school graduate and clerk Caspar Hopkins left for California from Vermont in 1849, just after discovering, as he later put it, that "the love of money is the root of all evil." Another clerk, Stephen Wing of Yarmouth, Massachusetts, left home for the gold regions a short time later, fully admitting that the "allurements of that 'Root of all Evil'" could be deadly to young men like himself. Benjamin Martin left two children and a wife in Chelsea, Massachusetts, writing back in his first letter from California that he had found his object, that "gold, the root of all evil, is to be seen here in great quantities."[10]

Each of these self-questioning northeasterners was a forty-niner. And none would be unusual, or even particularly out of place, in gold rush–era California. This study focuses on the experiences, perceptions, and writings of more than 150 individuals, nearly all of whom came from the northeastern region of the United States, nearly all of whom may be termed "forty-niners." Of these individuals, twenty-seven were women, and most of these were wives who remained in the East. These women too had a gold rush, even though most never went to California. The rest were men, most of whom traveled by sea to California during the years 1849–52. More than half of these forty-niners were married or engaged to be married. Most were over the age of twenty-five. All were literate; many were highly literate and college educated. All had strong ties to families, communities, and institutions in the East. Among those whose occupations can be ascertained from the available evidence, the vast majority held what may be termed "white collar" callings or professions. Economically, these individuals represent a mixed group. At the time they joined the rush, some were struggling to get by, while more than a few were quite affluent. Yet nearly all shared a background in and a commitment to the period's emerging middle-class standards of success, self-control, morality, and respectability.

These findings complicate what many historians have said about the American middle class; they also change the standard narrative of the gold rush. Certainly, the American middle class as it appears in this narrative is a far cry from the group of stiff Victorians who have appeared elsewhere, the gold rush much more than a quixotic explosion of marginal desires. In this narrative, the recognition that so many forty-niners were middle class in background, coupled with an analysis that takes this background seriously, has altered the rush and its meanings in three major ways. First, it calls for a much greater emphasis on the importance of gender, and women, to the gold rush experience. Second, it raises the importance of literacy, and the use of language, in the making of the rush, both *by* the forty-niners and *for* their eastern audiences. And finally, it necessitates a certain amount of rethinking about the process of class formation in Jacksonian-era and antebellum America. The argument here focuses not so much on what the gold rush was, but what it reveals. What this argument suggests is that there is another chapter in the historical process of middle-class formation, a chapter that both builds on previous analyses and goes much further in explaining the cultural and social power of this class in American thought, life, and patterns of behavior.

For many readers, perhaps the most radical difference between this narrative and others will be its focus on women in the East as active participants in the gold rush. Northeastern women have generally been left out of gold rush narratives, or, at best, shunted to the margins of the experience. Traditional histories of the event depicted them as the "women left behind," as abandoned "grass widows" waiting patiently for their husbands to return. These women were important primarily for their absence. For without their "civilizing presence" and "refined graces," the flush times of California quickly descended into a chaotic bachelor culture of greed and debauchery, lawlessness, and violence.[11] More recent historians have followed a "politics of inclusion" approach to the history of women in the gold rush. Women were there, they claim of the gold regions, as wives, reformers, laundresses, prostitutes, and even as gold miners. Welcome as these studies are for getting a few northeastern women involved in the event, they have said very little about the majority.[12] Most women from the eastern seaboard did not go to California in 1849. These women remain situated as having been left behind, as women who "did nothing" either for or in the event.

In a sense, both traditional and revisionist treatments of women in the gold rush have eclipsed the northeastern woman's experience of the event. Both seem mired in problematic assumptions about gender and class, actually strengthening the stereotypes that middle-class women were prisoners in the home, or that the eastern home was a refuge from work, a place where nothing of any real importance happened. The focus in this study should break down these assumptions. Few of these women were left behind. Instead they were central to the experience: as partners who ran businesses in their husbands' absences, as audiences for men in California, as key figures in negotiating the meanings of the event. Many of these women were forty-niners, if by that term we mean people who experienced the gold rush, individuals who helped make it an event of wide-ranging social and cultural significance.

The shift in focus of this study, its turning of the lens away from men acting alone to men acting within the context of the family and finally to women, reveals an alternate history of the gold rush. As well, it provides key insights into the actual workings of the early middle-class home and family. First of all, this focus reveals that women, even middle-class women, continued to do an extraordinary amount of work, and that the home, despite the tenets of domesticity, was not a refuge from cash transactions and commodity exchange. It also reveals the survival of female-directed networks of kin and credit, the intricate exchanges of goods, services, and promises that once dominated women's lives and put their economic functions on nearly equal footing with those of men, well into the nineteenth century.[13] By the 1840s, these networks had gone underground, buried beneath ideologies of self-made manhood and female purity. Yet as soon as the husbands of this study left for California, these female networks resurfaced—they did not appear out of nowhere but were there all along.

In fact, some of the letters exchanged between forty-niner husbands and wives indicate that the transition to middle-class ways of thinking actually meant more work for women than ever before. Many of the men considered in this study trusted their wives more than anyone else, including and perhaps especially their employees. Thus as middle-class standards of privatization would have it, when they joined the rush they placed their businesses in the care of their wives. Such cases reveal that forty-niner wives also had a gold rush. They did not just wait passively for their husbands to return. Indeed, if we measure the rush by material standards, according to who made the most money and who conducted the most paying business, many of these wives were more successful than their husbands.

In the end, the work of these women, along with their participation in the gold rush as audiences, readers, and writers, would all but disappear from historical accounts of the event, eclipsed by analyses that rarely looked beyond California. There are reasons, of course, for this shift in focus. Some are frankly ideological, based on the assumption that women are always homebound, and never involved in the making of history. Others seem less overtly political, such as the seemingly commonsense assertion that what happened out in California between 1849 and 1852 was simply more exciting than what happened back home. During the rush, women's letters from home reflected serious concerns: work, caring for families, and dealing with creditors. They are dull, in other words, or "about nothing." The letters, diaries, journals, and published accounts of men, in turn, are a lot more fun, and certainly they are about something: long and arduous voyages, new and exotic sights, the sinking of good men into a morass of immoral behaviors. And in the end they are about perseverance, noble suffering, and heroic manhood.

Seemingly natural as they are, these last distinctions between men's and women's letters are also ideological. As well, they raise the subject of this narrative's second major shift in analysis, its focus on the importance of literacy and language to the making of the gold rush. For these distinctions are primarily literary, distinctions made not merely on the basis of "what happened" or on competing sets of facts, but on the basis of taste, style, and the imposition of cultural meanings on social events. The standard approach to the gold rush has been to accept forty-niner journals, diaries, and letters as unvarnished fact, as direct windows onto events and social contacts, free from pretense or literary style. This approach has had two major results. One has been the publication of hundreds of "eyewitness" accounts, all purporting to finally reveal the true facts of the rush, the leaden realities of one man's experience reflecting the experience of all. Another has been the event's fall from favor as a subject for serious analysis, its decline from once epic status to what is now generally understood, at least in higher academic circles, as a series of hackneyed anecdotes from the likes of "Old Kentuck" and "Pike County Jess."[14]

This shift toward experiential reality, in other words, has produced an opposite effect. It has moved the gold rush closer than ever to fiction, even further from serious study. One reason for this problem is obvious: to write from the perspective of "Old Kentuck" takes considerable literary skill, skill that the roistering bravos of many accounts should have lacked, but that middle-class forty-niners possessed in abundance. The individuals on which this study focuses were the most likely to write about their experiences and impressions of the gold rush. They were not simple people; nor were they lacking in literary pretense. Almost all were educated and most were avid readers, their accounts framed by literature and imagination, filled with literary references and elements of style. During the rush, gold was both "root" and "evil," even though factually it was neither; failure was "seeing the elephant." Certain deeds in California and places along the way were always "dark," Mexicans were nearly always "gamblers," Indians "sneaky savages," and women "angels." Much of the experience, in turn, would be written in a kind of "eye dialect," accented in tones having no real geographical basis or origin, but that looked authentically western or rustic to the reader's eyes. Thus friends became "pards," dry mines "diggins," and many of the skilled writers of these accounts became lone prospectors, authentic 'niners from Pike County, no matter their refined and educated backgrounds.

The approach here has been to treat forty-niner writings, along with the writings of observers in the East, as literary creations. Some of these writings are obvious literary documents: poems, short stories, novels, and recollective accounts. Some are not. Yet all contain elements of style, writers' decisions on metaphor, tone, and subject, attentiveness to audiences imagined and real. In part, this approach reflects an analytical linguistic turn. In larger part it is a turn toward historical accuracy. For from beginning to end, the main characteristic of written gold rush experiences, that is, the social reversal of eastern norms and behaviors, was itself a literary formula. Again, the formula required skill and knowledge, knowledge of the standards the accounts reversed, skill at playing between largely semantic binaries of east and west, repression and expression, female and male, and light and dark. In these documents the male forty-niner had the skill to assign characteristics to people and places: the feminized East, the violent West, and the exotic South; the patient wife, the passionate Mexican, and the redemptive woman. And finally, they had the skill and the power to re-create themselves as lone and rugged miners, as men who were free to move between these people and places, liberated to draw upon all their characteristics.[15] Once these stories were anecdotes. Here they reveal the working of language and power, along with the remaking of the middle class.

This narrative's focus on class, and on the importance of the gold rush to class formation, reflects perhaps its major analytic shift, its most controversial departure from standard historical interpretations. Certainly, in its efforts to take the relationships between the gold rush and middle-class culture seriously, this study immediately departs from most previous works on the event. Within this broad expanse of literature, two approaches dominate the field. Both date from the period of the gold rush itself, and neither sees class as a factor. One is the approach mentioned above, an approach based on the reprinting of "eyewitness" accounts and presenting the rush as an example of primary or firsthand experience, ungarnished by eastern myths or literary pretensions. The other approach has long portrayed the gold rush as a democratic epic, an example of America's commitment to social equality, rush-era California as a classless society characterized by the event's vaunted freedom of expression and rough frontier egalitarianism.[16] If the middle class appears at all in this literature, it is primarily as a gray and lifeless background against which the colorful history of the frontier, the gold rush, and true democracy would play itself out.

More recently, historians have taken notice of a middle-class element in the gold rush–era population of California. Yet apart from this notice, the middle class remains separate from the flush times. Social historians Peter Decker, Rodman Paul, and Ralph Mann have each found significant white-collar populations among the early immigrants to the region and state. Yet at least according to their analyses, such immigrants were not forty-niners. Instead, they were a different type altogether: family men, propertied, respectable, and serious. As former members of a northeastern middle class, they were entrepreneurial in their values, willing to take risks, but above all committed to bringing order to California.[17] For Paula Mitchell Marks, middle-class gold seekers were mutineers to their class, abandoning their bourgeois backgrounds, values, and prescriptions along the trail to California as they would gold rockers and extra supplies of food and clothing. The West changed them, turning them into authentic and isolated "stampeders," no matter their backgrounds, no matter their pasts. For Malcolm Rohrbough, middle-class types simply disappeared into the anonymous and diverse population of the gold camps. And although, as he puts it, the rush was America's "most significant event in the first half of the nineteenth century," it said nothing about the nation's larger context of class formation, industrialization, or its transformation to modern capitalist social and economic relations.[18]

Ultimately, the number of historians who have placed the rush in this context may be counted on one hand. In fact, they may be counted on two fingers. These recent studies, one by David Goodman, the other by Susan Johnson, identify a large percentage of gold seekers as middle class in attitude and origin. Both see class as a major factor in the making of the event, and both have attempted to take seriously the ways that middle-class prescriptions for behavior, along with its members' attitudes toward race, gender, and morality, contributed to the event. These studies are welcome additions to the event's historiography and will undoubtedly go a long way toward rescuing it from its current decline into anecdotalism. Yet both of these scholars stick to the idea of a fixed and repressive middle class. For Johnson, bourgeois forty-niners were in the middle of the flush times, getting dirty, fighting, baiting bears, and engaging in homosexual relations. Yet through it all, their seemingly innate bourgeois interiors remained untouched, stainlessly white and proper, so bloodlessly respectable they seemed incapable of realizing what fun they were having. Instead they waited for the fun to stop, so they could return to their mundane order. For Goodman, the middle-class man's center could not hold in California. His central core of moral codes fell apart, crumbling before the region's constant play of greed, gambling, and violence. As a result, the gold rush was a transitory moment, as the country moved from moral rigidity to liberalism, from tradition to modernity.[19]

The forty-niners in the present study are not the class mutineers of Marks and Rohrbough. They are neither Johnson's repressed bourgeoisie nor Goodman's liberal "outriders of modernity." Instead, they are complicated people, leading complicated lives during a period in which ethical traditions increasingly met with liberal yearnings and neither tradition nor yearning was likely to go away. At the moment of the rush, their time was not "flush"; their place was not California. Instead, theirs was a time of rapid change, of class formation and market revolution. Their place was the American Northeast. Most were products of the economic boom following the War of 1812. Most were children of the 1820s, and as children had witnessed the massive building of roads, the construction of canals, the arrival of the "Age of Steam," and with it factory towns and cities that seemed to have sprung up overnight.

As adolescents or young adults, most of these people had witnessed great changes in production, labor, and employment: the rise of factory work and wage labor, the institution of training and standards for professions once inherited as vernacular callings. Many had seen great changes in family structures, as fathers increasingly worked outside of the home and mothers took over responsibilities for childraising, as former apprentices and household members moved away to become seldom-seen laborers from another side of town.[20] By 1849, many of these individuals believed, whether it was true or not, that they occupied a far more complicated world than that of their parents. This was a world of increased competition and pressures, one in which a young man could not expect to inherit his father's calling but had to strike out on his own, one in which getting ahead in business might require a few false claims, a bit of lying and cheating.

Up to a point, many of the individuals in this study followed a trajectory that historians have identified with a rising middle class. Their lives—as children, as young adults, and as married couples—had to a large extent been devoted to acquiring the tastes, manners, and morals increasingly codified as markers of middle-class status. Most came from areas burned by the fires of religious revivals, from towns visited by itinerant ministers, sometimes by Charles Finney himself. With these visits, they became awakened to a new awareness of sin and the promise of salvation through good works and better behavior. Almost all had been affected by the reform associations and new standards that had come out of these revivals, by the rhetoric of temperance, widows and orphans societies, and even abolitionist meetings. Virtually all of these individuals had witnessed an enormous rise of shame during their lives. They learned that good men and women were ashamed of the body's functions and fluids. They learned that the "better sort" did not drink or swear, that they did not make public scenes, eat with their fingers, or beat their children. They learned that the proper man's wife did not work (even if middle-class wives did). Most important, they learned that the central value of the middle class was respectability. Respectable men did not cheat. Respectable women did not raise their sons to be liars. They were honest and responsible, fathers and husbands upon whom wives and children could rely, wives and mothers who made the home a haven of nurturance and security. Respectable people did not pull up stakes to go gold hunting.

The result of these lessons was not what we might expect. For without these standards, without their eventual spread throughout the United States, the gold rush would have very little meaning, and much less charm as a series of moral reversals. Up to a point perhaps, this emphasis on respectability as a means to class status was fine. But by 1849, if not before, these lessons had become problems. By 1849, the market revolution had nearly been won; what remained was a cataclysmic civil war to cement its victory, a bloody victory for capitalism and wage labor over the nation's confederate stronghold of slavery and household economy. Then as now, apologists for capitalism who could see beyond the gathering clouds of this coming conflict could look ahead to a bright future. Yet to themselves and perhaps to their wives if no one else, few would deny that getting ahead in this new world of intensified competition required an ability to cheat, lie, and sometimes steal, an ability to get dirty, to shamelessly promote passions and appetites for the sake of profits. According to most historians of this period, members of the emerging middle class had few doubts and anxieties. They rarely looked back to the age of kinship and household economy. They rarely noticed the inconsistencies between their own moral standards and what was necessary to get ahead in a competitive economy. Instead, they buckled under to their work ethic. They channeled whatever doubts they had into reform associations, social control, and self-repression.[21] Yet many of the people considered here had anxieties that could not be so easily contained.

The cult of respectability had taken them a long way, separating them from the presumed squalor of common laborers, creating new hierarchies of taste and manners as older ones of birth and property broke down. Still, many felt trapped, as overly refined as Jeremiah Saddlebags, as isolated as Bartleby the scrivener.

These people were not idiots. They knew that characters like Bartleby did not represent positions of power. They were smart enough to recognize the limits of respectability, the limitations that refinement, politeness, and proper morals would place on an individual's efforts to get ahead. They were aware that the necessities of getting ahead might—and probably would—raise threats to their moral standing. And so in 1849, many of these people either left for California or watched from a distance as loved ones departed, sometimes complaining, more often supporting the venture as best they could. They joined the rush for a variety of reasons: for gold, to be sure, but also to escape this new world of competition, the stultifying walls of moral codes and lawyers' offices. In California and along the way, many would rebel against their class, but their rebellion would be short-lived. Many would be liberated, for a time at least, but they would not become liberals. Instead they would enact and write another chapter in the process of class formation, a chapter written sometimes unconsciously, with no set design or plan, but one that always built on their respectable pasts and positions. In the process they would remake themselves as individuals capable of mutiny, but always holding on to the very standards that provoked the mutiny. They would also remake the middle class, as something they were and were not, in part as a social category, a grouping in which they belonged, in part as a myth, a fixed and unchangingly repressed identity against which they could rebel. The result would be a class empowered with the ability to rebel against itself, daily, repeatedly, and, as long as its members defend the myth of bourgeois repression, seemingly without end.

One

California Gold and Filthy Lucre

In 1848, Edward Neufville Tailer was living in New York City, working as a clerk in a dry goods store. Although only twenty years old, he seemed well on his way toward a successful business career. His white-collar employment, while not highly paid, was clean and steady. From his store, he could walk out along Pearl Street, passing new mercantile ventures and shops. Turning down Whitehall Street or Fulton or Broad, he would arrive at the city docks. There he would have seen the masts of great ships lining either side of the City Battery, piles of off-loaded goods stacked the length of South Street and West. More would be coming up the East River or down the Hudson from the Erie Canal, eventually to be transported for sale at stores like his own. Everywhere, it must have seemed, was proof of a rapidly growing economy, evidence that his clerking future was bright. In December, however, Tailer began to see signs that the great ships had brought something else to the docks. A virulent new sickness had arrived in the city. This was a strange illness: its early manifestations were marked by a "flush" of excitement, its later stages by "feverish" visions. Less deadly than cholera, it killed few people outright, but it changed them, attacking their organs of self-control, forcing them to behave in bizarre ways. The sickness was "gold fever."

News of the fever's spread worried the young clerk. For it seemed frightfully catching. "The thirst for California gold," he noted in his diary, "appears to be unabated and young men are enticed away from their business haunts, and daily occupations, for the sake of acquiring the filthy lucre." They would soon, he thought, realize their mistake. From a distance he admitted the gold seemed "glittering and enticing," the visions of California like "lofty castles," but what were these things compared with home, family, friends, and "a quiet but sure and productive situation?" "All is not gold that glitters," he reminded himself; and despite the fact that many of his own friends were joining the exodus, Tailer decided his course: he would not go to California. In this situation, the best a respectable man like himself could do was to warn others "against all thoughts of going to the El Dorado of America, unless they wish to make an uncivilized part of the world their home, and to live and subsist like savages."[1]

Nearly everything about Tailer smacks of the resolute bourgeois character. He was committed to an emerging work ethic, to a slow and steady career path marked by the cautious acquisition of affluence and success. He valued family and friends over wealth and gold. As a prudent Yankee, he knew that promises of easy wealth were most frequently bubbles anyway. He was a clean man, and he wanted no part of the vulgarity of physical labor or proximity to laborers themselves. These types were "uncivilized"; they lived like "savages." Above all he was *respectable*. Like others among his class, his inner being contained a profound sense of propriety and dignity along with a deep reservoir of moral maxims. Together, these teachings would maintain his resistance to California's promises. For him, visions of easy wealth meant little. The gold from the pacific glittered without substance. It was "filthy lucre," wealth made sordid by its separation from the time and energy necessary for its real production. Presumably, all of these character traits should have placed Tailer somewhere outside of the California gold rush.[2] He would not find himself in this position.

For Tailer, there was nothing very special about the discovery of gold in California. Northeastern Americans had heard about gold rushes before, in Georgia and Alabama. To most, these western tales probably seemed little more than the stuff of juvenile fiction: believable, perhaps, to country rustics and vulgar rubes but scoffed at by more sophisticated urban readers. In fact, even in California gold discoveries had long been met with casual nods and blithe indifference. Native Americans, Spanish, and later Mexicans all knew that gold flecked the streams of the lower Sierra Nevada, long before 1848. The difficulty of finding enough of it, however, coupled with the success of mines in lower Mexico, kept interest low.[3] But the gold rush was a phenomenon, a ritual, not merely an event or discovery. Before the ritual could begin, a sense of "eventicity" had to be created, made appealing to a buying public, nurtured into existence by the imagination.

This production, in turn, proceeded within the dynamics and tensions of class formation and market transformation. Its best descriptive term resonates with the con-artistry and ethos of a modern consumer culture: from the beginning the gold rush was "Barnumesque." In January 1848, a transplanted New Jerseyian, James Marshall, found some gold flakes in the tailrace of a sawmill being constructed for Johan Sutter's New Helvetia Colony in California. An imaginative leap later, Phineas T. Barnum had yellowish paint slapped on a rock, displayed it as a "twenty-five pound lump of gold," and positioned a real live miner (fresh from California) next to it at his American Museum on Broadway. Crowds went to see the exhibit, drawing connections, perhaps making plans. Along with observers at the time, historians have pointed out the "remarkable coincidence" that Marshall's discovery came just as California became a United States territory.[4] More important, perhaps, it occurred just when such an "event" could become a consumer object.

Following Marshall's discovery, much happened in California before people in the northeastern United States took notice and made the search for gold a national obsession. Mexicans, mostly from the northern state of Sonora, South Americans from Chile, and a few deserting soldiers from the Mexican-American War went prospecting into the gold country. Some actually found substantial amounts of the metal. Limited in scope and visibility, this brief period from Marshall's discovery through the end of 1848 was about all there was to the vaunted "poor man's rush" of many historical accounts. During this time fortunes might be made with minimal investment. For most of this year, however, few along the Atlantic shore paid much attention to California. Eastern newspapers expended precious little ink on the gold reports, maintaining that if indeed the metal had been found, the amounts cited from the California sheets were typical western exaggerations. In a small aside printed in October 1848, the *New York Sun* reported some gold discoveries, but again it framed the report with a resistant aphorism: "all is not gold that glitters."[5] Undoubtedly, clerks like Edward Tailer and Philadelphia's Samuel Upham read these reports; but certainly, with these kinds of warnings, they remained skeptical. "When the news of the discovery reached the Atlantic States," recalled Upham, "I held a somewhat lucrative situation in the counting house of a mercantile firm in the city of Brotherly Love. The early reports were of so vague a character as scarcely to be credited by the most enthusiastic, and were pronounced by the skeptical as visionary—schemes gotten up by the powers at Washington to encourage emigration to California and Oregon."[6] While these prudent Yankee voices would remain throughout the period of the gold rush, by the end of the year they would be muted beneath a mass of official statements and elevated rhetoric. Led by the United States government and echoed by a variety of publications, the new word was that the reports from California were authentic. The gold was real.

On 5 December 1848, President James Polk announced in his outgoing address to Congress that the abundance of gold deposits on the West Coast "would scarcely command belief were they not corroborated by the authentic reports."[7] Government spokesmen added to this corroboration, announcing and elevating the importance of the first gold shipment to Washington. Sent on to the United States mint, the gold elicited a one-word seal of approval. Immediately, the word became a headline: "GENUINE." In the welter of symbol manipulation, especially after Secretary of War William Marcy added that the shipment would be melted down to make military medals for the war with Mexico, it could probably be overlooked that the amount came to a paltry $4,000. The president's address and Marcy's statements accomplished their purpose: the reports had been authenticated, the gold from the Pacific was genuine, its magical, even heroic qualities confirmed in the ritual of a medal ceremony.

Soon after Polk's message, articles from California began appearing in eastern newspapers, often lifted word for word from western sources without thought of corroboration, sometimes side by side with warnings against gold bubbles and filthy lucre. "The whole country, from San Francisco to Los Angeles and from the sea shore to the base of the Sierra Nevada, resounds with the sordid cry of '*gold*! GOLD!! GOLD!!!'" read a typical report from the San Francisco *Californian*. "As to the richness of the mines," another article from the paper added, "were we to set down half the truth, it would be looked upon in other countries as a 'Sinbad' story, or the history of 'Aladdin's Lamp,' which required that its possessor should but wish, and his wishes should be accomplished. Many persons have collected in one day, of the finest grade gold, from three to eight hundred dollars, and for many days together averaged from 75 to $150."[8] Obviously, the tone of such articles was still exaggerated. And just beneath the claims there remained hints of a real estate deal. California was a good investment, read a typical addendum. "Her unparalleled gold mines, silver mines, iron ore and lead, with the best climate in the world, and the richest soil, will make it the garden spot of creation."[9] After December, however, these reports increasingly had the imprimatur of approval from more respectable sources. "There is no longer any doubt about the fact that gold in immense quantities has been found in California," read an article from *Hunt's Merchant's Magazine and Commercial Review* in early 1849. By then, even this usually sober-toned journal appeared drunk with metaphors of abundance. California's gold, it claimed, lay in plain sight: "sparkling in the sun," it "glittered" from the bottom of the region's streams and "glowed" from the summits of its mountains. The rumor of California's riches, once "indefinite and vague," had now burst forth "like the sun . . . through obscuring mists . . . into a vivid and golden reality." And yet, warned the article's writer, as with the sun, readers should only stare into this reality at their peril, for "it overpowers, almost more than pleases, by excess of light."[10]

Many northeastern readers were already dazzled. During the first few months of 1849, references to California's riches began appearing everywhere along the eastern seaboard. Advertisements headed by shouts of gold, meanwhile, were used for pills, cure-alls, sarsaparilla, just about anything. A useful symbol for desires and promises of fulfillment, genuine, liquid enough to melt into several meanings, the ore flowed into the focal points of a still-rising consumer culture. Immediately advertisers grasped its malleable qualities and put them to use. "Gold! Gold!" announced one message in a Morristown, New Jersey, paper. The attracted eye might quickly descend the column, only to find an advertisement for T. & E. Ayres Store, a pitch announcing the "most durable roofing ever used," a building material that was "equal to gold, without going to California and running any risks of life or money."[11] Morristown readers would later find a similar lure under a banner usually announcing a ship to the gold country: "Ho for California." For a moment, imaginative fires may have been kindled; but the "Bound for the Sacramento" journey turned out to be toward the shop of local dry goods merchants. One connection here seems clear: consumer yearnings could be the object of gold rush rhetoric; California gold might be the solvent for resistance to vulgar accumulation. The dry goods merchants explained another; they were, as the advertisement put it, offering their wares "at such prices as to enable their customers to purchase, though they should not be loaded with yellow dust."[12]

Many of these published announcements actually did advertise places on California-bound ships. But these places were not for just anyone. According to the papers and broadsides, northeasterners had two choices of travel to the gold country. The first and most common in the early days of the rush involved joining a "mining and trading association." The prospective gold seeker had to invest some $300 to $700 in company stock, the money to be used in purchasing a ship, supplies, and a berth on board. The second required booking steamer passage to the Colombian Isthmus of Panama, arranging passage across the isthmus to pick up a ship or Pacific Mail packet on the other side. The prices quoted for this passage were cheaper—usually between $200 and $400—but often did not include the costs of baggage transport or the isthmus crossing. By 24 January 1849, a Newark paper reported the formation of some forty-seven companies of gold seekers in the New York area. Typical of calls for members was one for a company that would sail on the bark *Griffon* from New York Harbor. The advertisement listed the initial required cost at $500 per person. Another call, for men to fill the bark *Palmetto*, listed the same price if the reader wanted to join the "California Mining and Trading Company" of New York.[13]

At a time when the average American's yearly wage was between $200 and $300, the costs quoted in these announcements represented something on the level of high finance. These costs, in turn, reveal a fact of western migration often buried beneath perceptions and myths. Envisioning the frontier, many writers then as now portrayed it as a place for the rootless and purseless. While this may have been true of certain locales, the western trek itself was expensive. Only the more stable and solvent could afford it.[14] Faced with these advertisements, men like Tailer and Upham found that they could not step outside of the rush, no matter their skeptical attitudes, no matter their reservoir of resistant adages. For the company broadsides and sailing notices had been directed toward men like themselves, their audience not freebooting types, but substantial individuals with money to invest. That is, if men like Tailer refused to go to California, very few would go at all. Still a question remained to be answered: certainly, these men could afford the voyage to California, but would their internalized codes of respectability allow them to go?

Throughout the period of the gold rush, this question would dominate much of the public discourse surrounding the event. Soon enough, observers and writers realized that this apparently simple question was much more complex than it first appeared. For just beneath it lay other issues and anxieties, larger questions about relationships between status and success, the individual and wealth. In effect, the arrival of gold fever in the Northeast unleashed a host of long-developing questions concerning the position of the middle class in the American marketplace. Could the respectable middle class remain and thrive in an increasingly amoral marketplace? Could it blend propriety with the vicissitudes of competitive accumulation? Ella Rodman's short story combining the gold rush with domestic duty, which under the title of "Going to California" appeared in the first 1849 issue of *Peterson's Magazine*, is a clear example of such anxieties.

As Rodman's tale implied, the outlook for any affirmative answers to these questions was doubtful. Her story centers on a young and would-be middle-class couple, George and Susan Brendall, whose near giving in to the lure of California gold threatens to undo their proper privatizing impulses. George works as a clerk in a "flourishing business," a humdrum type of brain work but one that, if followed with proper patience and careful planning, "gave promise of wealth in after years." His wife takes care of their two children in their moderate home. There, she has plenty of time to dream of silver tea sets, plush furniture, and decorated vases. Longing for these accouterments of middle-class status, she envisions a proper haven for them: "in the country," far from the gloomy counting room in which her husband was to earn the wealth that would someday "act the part of Aladdin's lamp, and effect this wonderful change." George, seeing evidence of more efficient magical qualities in reports of gold from California, one day announces his intention of joining the rush.

His reasons are both financial and physical. Proclaiming his desire for wealth, his fatigue with a partitioned-off, Bartlebylike existence, and his boredom with his "stay-at-home life," he decides to take a "pleasure jaunt" to the gold country. His intention, while it promises to collapse the distance between present desires and future riches, also threatens to collapse his modest but secure domestic hearth. Susan responds in the coin of domestic rhetoric; for her, the morally lax frontier is not the place to build a respectable family life. "I suppose I must have humble views," she warns her husband, "but I own that I prefer a cheerful home, an affectionate husband, lovely children, and the creature comforts of life to any fascination which may be discovered in this rather dismal picture."[15]

With this vivid portrayal of the perceptual chasm between masculine scheming and domestic contentment, George's intentions begin to weaken. Yet it is only for a moment, and as he glances again at a letter containing the gold reports—"the serpent," according to the author, "which fascinated him"—his resolve returns. He dangles luxurious lures of his own, conjuring up the fine paintings, the statuary, the carriages, even the diamonds that will be Susan's if she will only relent and support his venture. Slowly these seedlings of desire begin to grow. Thinking of "how splendidly a diamond tiara would gleam in her sunny tresses," Susan at last relents. But only, she avers, if she can go along with her husband. Here Rodman's tale arrives at the climactic meeting point of opposite forces: George refuses to take his bride with him; Susan proclaims her intention of going anyway, as a missionary for the redemption of California's immorality. Respectability and desires for wealth meet in hostile suspension; the Brendalls need money to confirm their status as a middle-class couple, yet neither their domestic security nor Susan's femininity, we are led to conclude, will survive the vicissitudes of frontier life. Suddenly, and out of nowhere, a resolution of these tensions comes with a contrived plot twist: an unknown uncle dies, leaving George $20,000. He cancels his voyage, wealth works its magic, and the Brendalls "were soon settled in a delightful country dwelling."[16]

At the time, the proverbial rich uncle was a common device in middle-class short fiction, a convenient deus ex machina for quick and happy endings. As well, these figures have been identified as vehicles for avoiding the realities of class conflict and poverty. Appearing at the last minute, they assured readers that even the poorest characters had never really been poor, that they really, and naturally, belonged in the more elevated stations of society all along.[17] In the case of Rodman's story, however, the issue to be avoided seems not just conflict but contact. All in all, Rodman's couple seems cut off from the real world, curiously adrift in unfulfilled yearnings. They long to embrace the luxuries of industrial capitalism. Unabashedly materialistic, or so it seems, they are ready to seek worldly pleasures. Yet a chasm between desire and realization remains. With its looming presence throughout Rodman's story, gold has a solidity lacking in the Brendall's magical world of commodities. And although it rests in the granite crevices of faraway California, it seems a far more real source of wealth than the mysterious unknown uncle. Still, the precious element cannot be embraced and cannot even be sought without reducing the Brendall home to fragments. Stalled in their pursuit of wealth by a need for respectable distance from the lawlessness of California and the harsh physicality of manual labor, the Brendalls appear caught between twin and conflicting necessities of middle-class formation.

Rodman's characters are bent on separating production from the home, motivated by their desire to create and maintain a private haven, secure from the vulgarity of market relations. As many historians have pointed out, this development of a nuclear family—fully cut off from the scene of production and virtually outside of market forces—was one of the key elements in the formation of the mid-nineteenth century middle class. The key to this development may be seen in the great social and economic shifts during this period. Historians are fond of locating great change at practically any given moment. But to the period from about 1830 to the Civil War there has been attached a telling sobriquet: "the Market Revolution." This was the time of America's first wave of industrialization, its transition from social and economic relations based largely on face-to-face contacts and community to the more competitive and anonymous settings of the modern market. Technological revolutions in transportation laid the foundations for these rapid changes in life and thought. Beginning with the completion of the Erie Canal in 1825 and continuing through the development of railroads, these new technologies webbed goods to markets, producers to merchants to consumers, on a heretofore unimaginable scale.[18] Factories sprang up along this water and steel network, "magically," or practically overnight according to many observers. Communities like Utica, Troy, and Rochester in New York and Lowell, Worcester, and Lawrence in Massachusetts became mill towns, small but bustling and growing urban centers of trade.

Prior to this great transformation, much of the American economy was dominated by household production. A typical model for the earlier period's business establishment might be a two-story building. Downstairs, at street level, the artisan-merchant had his factory and shop. There, he worked side by side with sons, apprentices, and laborers. Upstairs, he had his living quarters, along with quarters for his family and workers. Here this diverse household slept, ate, talked, and lived together as a type of extended family. Thus, before the 1830s, home and work were not geographically separate; the "family" was likely to contain several laborers, their spiritual, social, and economic well-being dependent on the patriarchal head of the household.[19] In the 1830s and 1840s, the traditional ties of this corporate family structure underwent a slow process of fragmentation. Traditional conceptions of a wider, extended family broke down, to be replaced by new standards emphasizing privatization and the separation of work, along with workers, from the home. Merchants and artisans increasingly located their shops away from their homes. New types of employment, for clerks and managers, were located in business districts to which white-collared workers walked from homes several blocks away. Laborers moved away from their former masters, creating a social geography in industrializing cities and towns based on separate neighborhoods for a nascent middle class and a forming laboring class.[20]

By the time of Rodman's story, these social and economic distinctions had done much to establish class boundaries. Still, having separated themselves geographically from physical laborers, many middle-class writers and thinkers worked to create distinctions between middle-class and laboring-class values as well. The result was a mass proliferation of prescriptive literature for proper behavior, the rise of a genteel "polite culture" centered on reform, respectability, and self-control. Culturally as well as physically, merchants, skilled artisans, and laborers went their separate ways. Those on one side donned the white collar of well-mannered affectation, those on the other the stained apron of the factory worker. One side gravitated toward better neighborhoods, toward well-appointed outposts of propriety and privacy; the other remained beyond urban or western frontiers, occupying the teeming streets of urban slums or the lazy backwaters of country farms and villages. According to these standards, the middle classes would coalesce around standards of refinement and a commitment to a work ethic characterized by mental labor and incremental success. Its members, both male and female, would retreat as far as possible from the outside world, maintaining the home and the nuclear family as a private haven against the vulgarity of the laboring classes, the teeming streets, and the competitive chaos of the marketplace as a whole.

These values formed the context of Rodman's story, and within this context she appears to have found it impossible to envision a way to allow a respectable man like George Brendall to go to the gold regions. The problem for her, it appears, was that a stress on polite culture and refinement, combined with ideals of domesticity and the nuclear family, simply could not be squared with the envisioned moral laxity and physical labor of life in California. Undoubtedly, individuals like Tailer would agree with this conclusion. And yet, what is interesting about Rodman's story is the idea that these same individuals might be tempted by visions of wealth in California, the possibility that lucre, even filthy lucre, might be enticing. As Rodman's readers must have known, the real life process of becoming middle class was not simply a matter of waiting for rich uncles to die. Becoming middle class was a complicated process. At the very least it involved venturing outside the home.

Another young clerk provides a good example of these complexities. Franklin A. Buck hailed from the town of Bucksport, a small and somewhat isolated village situated on Maine's central coast. Descended from the town's original founders, Buck's roots were deeply embedded in the region's soil, his background that of an older, more traditional class of landowners and farmers. Yet this group too was making a transition to new middle-class standards. In the mid-1840s, Buck's father sent him away to school, to Phillips Academy in Andover, Massachusetts. There he received a solid education, a firm moral foundation, and what must have been more than a few lessons in applying these skills to a wider field. For upon completing his degree he did not return to Bucksport but instead left for the greater opportunities of the city. He arrived in New York City in 1846. A youth who prided himself on his ability to adjust to new experiences, he immediately set about making his own way in the world. To do so, he had to make the transformation to the standards of the new middle class.

This transition would be as difficult as it was exciting. For many observers of the time, the city was a dangerous place, particularly for recent arrivals from the country. According to reformers, it was a place of dizzying temptations, a confusing matrix of shadows and light. Good and proper neighborhoods, the well-lit streets near Broadway and the bucolic residential areas of Brooklyn, seemed a bit too close to the darker mysteries of the Five Points District and the Bowery. These largely working-class districts were filled with dangerous urban toughs, pimps, and prostitutes, with shifty merchants plying trades from bodily desires and with drunkards giving in to them. But they also contained what more than a few moral reformers recognized as enticements: friendly and cheap oyster cellars, inexpensive theaters and music halls, the romance of lively streets filled with hawkers, match boys, and muscular Irish firefighters. To naive newcomers such characters might seem charming, poor but decent "b'hoys" and "g'hals" straight out of the pages of juvenile fiction. The city's older residents knew better. As respectable city dwellers, they knew enough not to cross into these neighborhoods. Country immigrants did not; thus, at least according to popular literature, they were in constant danger of being beaten, robbed, or, worse, becoming corrupted by the districts' dazzling array of cheap amusements and urban pleasures.[21]

For Franklin Buck, New York City was just the place for a young man on his way to forging his own success. As for its temptations, he had connections enough to assure that he stuck to the proper urban pathways. "Here is the place to find business of all kinds," he wrote his sister Mary soon after arriving, "and as my friends here interest themselves for me I think there is a prospect of my doing something." While admitting that there was "quite a change" between this urban environment and Bucksport, he made his preference clear: "I like a city best," he added, "I shall make New York my home for the present." Within a year, he had found a good job as a clerk. He had also found a decent place to live, a side street boardinghouse a few steps from Broadway. In the meantime, his letters indicate that he followed a conscientious path toward self-improvement. Early on, his friends introduced him to Italian opera. "I always supposed that the Italian singing was all affectation," he wrote, "but I must confess that in spite of myself . . . I never heard such music in my life." Inspired by this first introduction to the culture of a better sort, he took it upon himself to acquire other elements of sophistication and respectability. By the fall of 1848, he had joined a "musical society" and had acquired his first pair of white kid gloves. Later in the year, he would begin taking lessons in dancing and French. He continued to attend the theater, but he also went to balls where he practiced his dancing lessons along with the niceties of polite conversation. By this time, he felt that he was well on his way to polishing his rough country edges: "I have to adapt myself to all classes of men and women," he wrote to Mary, "but always move in the first society if you can, that is my motto."[22]

Buck's "first society" was a key repository for the development of middle-class standards of behavior. And, as his letters indicate, its measures of refinement and respectability had to be carefully learned, even more carefully practiced and maintained. Accordingly, we can assume that in addition to his other lessons, he acquired much of his parlor manners from etiquette guides. These guides proliferated wildly in the middle decades of the nineteenth century. Easily available, sold not just in stores but through direct mail and by traveling salesmen, they were extremely popular and widely read. As for why they were read, there seems to have been a variety of reasons. Some people undoubtedly received them as gifts, for they were popular presents, only to leave them unopened, adorning parlor tables and bookshelves. Others may have read them merely to mock their contents, scoffing along with satirists and foreign observers at their pretentious efforts to codify gentility and good taste.[23]

The majority of their readers probably took them seriously. The point of the etiquette guide was the acquisition of self-control. Most scholars, in turn, have depicted them as repressive mechanisms, focusing on their discipline of behavior and bodily functions. Undoubtedly, this was true in many cases. Indeed, many manuals imposed a host of rules on bodily functions previously taken for granted, from eating to coughing, laughing, spitting, scratching, and nose blowing. Loud laughter, some proclaimed, was vulgar, as was unrestrained coughing and sneezing. All needed to be suppressed, along with excessive emotionalism or physical display. Suppression, dignity, and politeness, meanwhile, were all hallmarks of good breeding.[24] At the same time, the guides' valorization of "polite culture" had its advantages to many Americans. By placing a great emphasis on humanitarianism, they contributed to the rise of temperance societies along with the growth of labor reform movements and abolitionist associations. Their emphasis on "feminine" models for the consideration of others and polite sensibility made women guardians of morality, elevating their status in society and allowing them entrance into wider fields of political activity.[25] Perhaps their most important function, however, was to map the way to middle-class status.

For young men in transition, like Buck, these guides were often required reading, studiously pored over for their illumination of boundaries between vulgarity and refinement, laboring-class or country rudeness and urban civility. Indeed, many were quite clear on boundaries between classes; they are among the first documents in American letters to specifically mention and codify the meaning of the term "middle class." As readers soon discovered, this position required a double boundary, a separation not merely from the vulgarity of the common laborer, but also from the excesses of the wealthy. "There is no ornament so becoming as a polite address," admonished one 1837 manual, for it "affords a ready passport to those circles which the *merely* rich never enter." The "highest classes," it went on to say, were overly solemn, marked by a "grave and almost diplomatic stiffness of manners," too occupied with "wealth and ambition." The "lower orders" were "ignorant from want of means of instruction," too preoccupied by a love of amusements. "It is, therefore," this guide concluded, "to the middle class almost exclusively that we must look for good society; to that class of society which, enjoying the *aurea mediocritas* of Horace, has not had its ideas contracted by laborious occupations, nor its mental powers annihilated by luxury."[26]

Despite the jarring sound of this description to modern readers, individuals like Franklin Buck probably found this "air of mediocrity" agreeable. Within this prescribed state, they could envision themselves as relatively free to draw upon the behaviors of the "first society" even while enjoying—in proper moderation—the amusements of the city's earthier elements. Certainly Buck's letters suggest this pattern. While he attended the opera, he also took in his share of minstrel shows. And while he embraced many of the requisites of parlor culture, including kid gloves, white cravats, and playing whist, he remained aware that these things were "affectations." Desirous of moving within the city's first society, he remained critical and mocking of its wealthy "upper ten-thousand," the "snobs" as he described them, who went everywhere in ostentatious carriages, and who seemed to take polite culture to extremes of stiffness and posturing. But there was another important element in advice manuals that may have left upwardly mobile young men like Buck a bit uncomfortable, if not confused.

For there was a major tension within this prescriptive literature, particularly when it came to the subjects of individual success and wealth. On one hand, many guides made success in business a key rationale behind the acquisition of, as one put it, "those principles of good breeding which every man should be 'wax to receive and marble to retain.'" The point of good manners, as this guide had it, was the same as doing business. Both were based on appearances, on pleasing a buying public. "An ordinary man," it proclaimed, "can never gain that place in life for which his talents and his merits fit him, unless he is acquainted with that style of behaviour which the world insists on observing." On the other hand, these same guides frequently warned readers against the excesses of the business world, especially its selfishness, its ambition, and its promotion of unbridled appetites. Often the business rationale for propriety and warnings against the dangers of doing business existed in the same text. "It must not be denied," continued the same guide in a later chapter, "that to all men, and to young men in particular, society is full of dangers." These dangers came from the selfish nature of business dealings, its temptations and pleasures; these, it concluded, "unless tasted with the utmost temperance," might be found fatal.[27]

Thus the tenets of middle-class prescriptive literature evinced at least an implied hostility to the necessities of doing business. From the outset, in fact, its central tenet may have been difficult for business-men to follow. This stricture was simply "The Golden Rule," and it appeared—somewhere and in some form—in practically every man-ual. As one of the earliest guides had it, the rule was the very founda-tion of genteel carriage. The seeking of "honour, profit, and pleasure" posed serious problems for the man of character, it proclaimed; all were "sufficient to draw a soul off from God, and ruin it for ever." In response to these problems, its author offered the model of good Christianity, strict temperance and sobriety, and especially the Golden Rule: "As a trader keep that golden sentence of our Saviour's ever before you—'whatever you would that men should do unto you, do also unto them.'" Through the 1830s and 1840s, the rule remained at the core of polite culture, following the would-be respectable individ-ual from childhood through maturity. "The principles of good breed-ing are founded in generosity," read the text of one canon, while another for juveniles urged its young readers to "be as polite and amiable at home, as if you were among strangers. You need not learn the art from masters; the observance of the Golden Rule will make you polite: for it will teach you to prefer the happiness and comfort of others to your own, even in the most trifling particulars."[28]

Undoubtedly, Franklin Buck received these lessons, if not during his stay in New York City, then certainly during his education at Phillips Academy. Whether or not he was aware of their contradic-tions, he soon would be. At the beginning of 1848, he could clearly indicate that he had arrived in the middle class. "I have found out," he wrote, "that it is altogether better to get an honest living and live in a parlor and wear kid gloves than live in a camp and haul cord wood, a life which I once thought would suit me."[29] By the end of that year he was rethinking this position. Like others in his situation, news of the gold rush interrupted Buck's upward trajectory toward the higher stations of refinement. "Have you read the account from there about the Gold?" he wrote his sister in Bucksport, "I have seen letters from Captains whom I know, who write that their men have all run away and are digging up $20 a day, PURE GOLD, for some of it has been sent home. It has created a real fever here." At first, Buck had thought the news was "all humbug, gotten up to induce people to emigrate." By mid-December, however, he was "fully convinced"; the proof, he felt, was in the reports of the president and Secretary Marcy, in the gold sent back from the West, and even in the fact that many other young and respectable men were preparing to depart for California. "There is," he wrote, "something about it—the excitement, the crossing the Isthmus, seeing new countries and the prospect of making a fortune in a few years—that takes hold of my imagination, that tells me 'Now is your chance. Strike while the iron is hot!' "[30] By then he had made up his mind: he was going to California.

And so Franklin Buck, white-collar clerk, refined and respectable member of a new urban middle class, had decided to join the gold rush. Despite these qualities, he was not unusual. By the second week of January 1849, an editorial in the *New York Herald* noted that the gold seekers were "educated, intelligent, civilized, and elevated men, of the best classes of society."[31] A week later, another editorial in the same paper repeated the observation. The emigrants were "men of energy and enterprise," its writer claimed, lamenting that in this case, at least, the West was not working as a safety valve. "It is a character of the emigration," the article went on to say, "that we do not (as we willingly would) get rid of the worst part—the idle, the rowdies, the vagabonds—of our population; but we lose—with regret we say it— the finest portion of our youth, and in all cases such as possess some means—such as are not impelled to emigrate by want."[32]

Membership rolls in eastern stock companies, the "mining and trading associations" forming at this time, support this observation. "Farmer" was the most commonly listed occupation on these rolls, usually followed closely by "clerk." They frequently mentioned several other white-collar occupations, including merchant, lawyer, and doctor. But skilled tradesmen made up by far the greatest percentage of company members. There were eighteen farmers and nine clerks in the Bunker Hill Trading and Mining Company, formed to sail from Boston aboard the ship *Regulus*. There were also five carpenters, four shoemakers, three painters, and a selection of skilled craftsmen who listed occupations such as baker, pianoforte maker, bookbinder, lithographer, paper maker, harness maker, cabinet maker, tinsmith, cigar maker, blacksmith, and weaver. The *Emma Isadora* sailed out of Boston with seven farmers and four clerks on board. Also treading its decks were four blacksmiths, three merchants, a minister, a glass blower, and a marbleworker, among many other craftsmen.

What these passenger lists reveal is that the gold seekers were not unattached young men without established occupations. The high cost of the voyage and provisions required economic solvency; and, because the venture necessitated the raising of a large amount of cash, it required men with connections in their communities. Many of these forty-niners were young men, but the rolls indicate that there were nearly as many in their mid-thirties—or even in their forties—as there were younger men who sailed to California. Thirty-three of the fifty-nine members of the Salem Company were over twenty-seven years old. These older men frequently had economic ties through marriage. There were twenty-five married men and three widowers in the same company.[33] A member of the New England and California Company, which left Boston in early February aboard the ship *Lenore*, recorded that there were thirty-one married members out of a total of eighty-eight men.[34]

A closer look at the formation of one of these companies provides more details concerning their prohibitive high costs along with the respectable origins of many gold hunting expeditions. In early January 1849, an article in the *New York Herald* noted that a company was forming in the town of New Brunswick, New Jersey. It would, claimed the announcement's writer, be composed of "several scores of men of means." Indeed, as a local newspaper put it, the "New Brunswick and California Mining and Trading Company" included the town's "most respectable and enterprising citizens."[35] Its president, Augustus Fitz Randolph Taylor, was a college graduate and a town doctor. Forty years old in 1849, he was also the town's mayor. James Spader, a clerk and the company's agent, sold stock in the association. These bonds conferred membership and reserved a place for the voyage to California, at $600 per share. A later surcharge of $100 for those making the trip brought the initial cost of the venture to $700 per man. By February, the company's capital stock totaled over $30,000. Included in this accounting was the bark *Isabel*, purchased by company funds for $11,250, and stocked at greater expense with provisions for the voyage.[36]

In its membership and high costs, the New Brunswick Company shared characteristics with other eastern expeditions. Like others, its members included many men whose hands were more frequently ink-stained than callused. Yet if these company rolls indicate that the gold rush was at least a cross-class phenomenon, the records of individuals who actually wrote about the event suggest the extent to which respectable types would frame the rush and its meanings. For among the men whose writings have been most frequently used by historians, middle-class professions predominate. This is certainly the case of the nearly 100 individuals whose letters, diaries, and recollective accounts constitute much of the evidence for this study. Among these gold seekers, sixty out of the sixty-five whose occupations can be discerned from the evidence held white-collar occupations. Seventeen of these men were clerks, ten were journalists or writers, nine were merchants, and thirteen were doctors, lawyers, or clergymen. Six others were students, either in college or freshly graduated and in search of white-collar positions. Only five of these individuals referred to themselves as "farmers." Three of the five, on closer inspection, appear to have been at best part-time farmers. One was looking for a clerking position at the outset of the rush. Two others had been raised in farming families and preferred to think of themselves as farmers, but by the time of the rush both had broken with this family tradition: one had become a doctor, the other had opened a printing shop and was pursuing a career as a songwriter. Thirty of these men—again, about one-third of the whole—were definitely married prior to the rush. All had solid social, economic, and family moorings in the East.

Statistics revealing that a high percentage of gold seekers had firm economic ties, that many were married or came from white-collar or skilled occupations, may not be true indicators that they were members of a solid middle class. Occupation was a fluid concept at this time, and frequently not a measure of economic or social position. Many of the men who listed artisanal trades as their occupations might have already made a transition to middle-class status, becoming employers of shoemakers rather than cobblers themselves. Yet they might still think of themselves—and list themselves in city directories— under their old trades. Other members of this group, engaged in outdated trades, might have seen their status slipping, without the ability to fall back on old networks of interdependency and kinship.[37] In addition, the preponderance among forty-niners of occupations such as carpenter or blacksmith may have indicated hopes rather than actual experience. Much in demand in California, these skills were extremely well paid; anyone who could pound a nail or a bit of heated iron might list such talents out of a desire for lucrative employment.

Among the old artisan class, too, personal finances were likely to be marked by increasing debt. Caught in a changing economy, craftsmen frequently sought creditors to help them maintain traditional callings. In Nantucket, for example, where declines in the whaling industry had increased debts among whalemen, some 600 islanders joined the gold rush. Although the list of these gold seekers reads, according to one local historian, "like a register of the leading island families," these individuals were likely to be very insecure in their class status.[38]

And yet, of the men who were most likely to write about their California ventures, one thing is clear: they were closer in identity to Franklin Buck, and even Edward Tailer, than they were to the unattached young men of many gold rush historians. Nearly all of their writings show evidence of at least some training in the emerging middle-class standards of refinement, self-control, and morality. In this respect, Buck was typical. So was David Hewes. When news of California's gold reached the eastern seaboard, Hewes had just graduated from Yale College. His schoolboy letters, in turn, reveal a solid middle-class background: strong family ties, desires for self-improvement, and a refined sense of morality. They indicate that his family raised him right. And, as his sabbath school teacher reminded him, he was obliged to be thankful: "not only that you have these privileges but . . . that God has so early inclined your heart to improve them; for we must remember 'tis God who enables us to overcome sin or even think a good thought." Later, family and teachers urged him to strive against "sin and temptation," warning him to be humble, to watch his motives, to march forward toward "victory [over] sinful pleasure."[39] From Yale, Hewes wrote home to inform his mother of the college's "high tone of religious piety, & the life giving and soul cheering assurance which it gives to all that it is a lover of virtue & protector of good morals."[40] Less than two years after writing this, his ultimate victory over sin and temptation may have seemed in doubt, and he no longer seemed so inclined to think good thoughts. Instead, he was thinking about joining the gold rush.

John Beeckman and William Prince may be the best examples of the more affluent forty-niners. Beeckman was a New York City lawyer. He was also a man with important political connections. In January 1848, he married Margaret Gardiner. The ceremony took place at the Virginia home of Margaret's sister Julia, the wife of former president of the United States John Tyler. Beeckman was also a keen speculator, his plan in going to California simple but ambitious: buy land while prices were low, sell high when the gold seekers finally realized the advantages of locating permanently in California. Then, when natural leaders like himself organized the territory into a state, he would be in position to contend for public office.[41] A graduate of Princeton College, William Prince owned a booming nursery business on Long Island. He too saw the rush as a business affair. He would invest over $2,500 dollars in the voyage, paying his own passage along with that of two employees who would work for him at the gold diggings. He also planned to take more than $1,000 to invest in land and goods.

Forty-niners of more moderate means included men like Cornelius La Tourette, Eri Hulbert, and Samuel Adams. Frequently, men like these were reluctant gold seekers, respectable individuals whose positions within a new market economy of wildly fluctuating fortunes left them little choice but to grasp the economic opportunities presented by the reports from California. La Tourette was a farmer from Bound Brook, New Jersey. Following a series of setbacks that included the death of his brother and the destruction of the family barn during a lightning storm, he faced a difficult decision: he could accept a clerking position at a New York City bank or go to California. He decided to join the rush.[42] Hulbert, who suffered serious reverses in Chicago and in Oswego County, New York, made his plans for similar reasons. A building contractor, he had lost a large investment of time and money when the state of New York refused to pay him for the work he had done on the construction of the Erie Canal. By 1849 he was heavily in debt, and so he decided to join the rush in the hopes of paying off his creditors. "I can hardly bear the thought," he wrote his father about leaving his family behind, but he added that the risks were nothing "when compared with the thought of poverty in old age and having a family destitute when I am dead and gone."[43] Adams, originally from Winthrop, Maine, but working as a clerk in a Brooklyn counting house, was not the adventurous type. Just as the reports of gold reached the East, however, his company's store burned down. Suddenly out of work, he claimed to have been forced to join the rush. Married with three children, he had "little disposition," as he put it, "to travel abroad and a strong attachment for the peace, comforts and enjoyments of Home and the dear ones who make life pleasant and desirable."[44]

All of these men were married, and, as their writings indicate, all had adopted middle-class standards of respectability and refinement. But here is where they faced a serious problem. For according to many observers of the time, gold seeking was not an activity for respectable men, and California was no place for the refinement of parlor culture. As one article in a Newark paper described it, "vice of every kind, and in the most horrible forms" prevailed throughout the gold country. There, claimed the article's author, the easy availability of wealth had unleashed a cycle of greed and debauchery. The pattern would become familiar with repetition: typical miners, in this case "runaway sailors," were gathering gold dust, returning to town, paying eight dollars per bottle of liquor, having sprees, going broke, and returning to the foothills to start the process again. Another article in the same paper noted the incongruous fact that 100 lace veils had been sent to the Pacific. The only purpose they might serve, its writer maintained, would be as gold-washing sieves: for "unless the senoritas of California have much improved of modesty of late, they will not be much in demand for the purpose for which they were made."[45]

Even before these men could depart, in other words, many observers envisioned California as a place of vulgar men, immodest women, and immoral behaviors. At the root of these visions was gold. For if doubts over the existence of this gold were increasingly muted beneath an official corroboration of its abundance, criticisms of gold seeking were not. Gold remained filthy lucre. Immediately, moralizers brought forth a host of long-standing adages: "All that glitters is not gold" became a standard refrain, as did statements that it was "the root of all evil." As for respectable men tempted by reports of its abundance, they needed to be reminded of lessons learned at school, warned one source: for "the history of King Midas, which most of them read there, teaches that the possession of gold is not happiness." Reports from California, claimed one writer for the *New York Herald*, had set "the public mind almost on the highway to insanity." They had generated a sort of national crossroads, declared another, opening "a new era, a fresh crisis in the history of commerce, and even of civilization."[46] All of this reflected a type of "moral insanity," recalled Josiah Royce several decades later; the crisis was an ethical crisis. The quest for gold itself, he wrote, "was at all events an unmoral one." According to him, as many observers, the "daily and most sober business" of the forty-niner would be "at best dangerously close to gambling."[47]

These warnings appeared with particular frequency in periodicals that have been identified as forming the "women's literature" of the time. There, they might at times reflect the usual admonitions against greed and luxury or, as with Ella Rodman's story, the detrimental effect gold would have on happiness and domesticity. "Wed Not for Gold," declared the title of one poem from the pages of the *Knickerbocker*, offering a tale to illustrate the maxim:

Scarce one short year ago, a youthful pair
Plighted their troth, and swore through life to share,

Whether through weal or woe, their mutual lot;
But wealth came limping by, and she forgot
Her faith, his love: alas! poor girl, she sold
His earthly happiness, her heaven, for gold.[48]

At other times, however, these warnings spoke to more specific concerns raised by the temptations of gold and California. "Gold fever," according to a March 1849 article in *Godey's Lady's Book*, had given rise to "unhealthy feelings and extravagant projects." Yet it was not a new disease, it declared; one had only to look to what for many nineteenth-century Americans was the world center of luxury and dissipation to see its sordid roots. This center was, of course, Paris. There, readers would find the *maison-de-jeu*, the typically French gambling hall, filled with green tables and glittering coins, along with false smiles, fevered brows, mocking smirks, and, especially, desperate hopelessness: the "wretched calmness of the resolved suicide" and the "remorseful anxiety of those whose doom is yet suspended." The truth behind the gold delirium, in other words, lay in the "premeditated recklessness of the gambler." Thus forty-niners would have to give into desires that could only be described under the epithet of "French."[49]

This sort of warning applied specifically to men on the rise. Gold, as this article claimed, would make them "yellow slaves," colored by the metal's sickly hue, jaundiced by their own corrupt yearnings for easy wealth and easier morals. This bizarre metaphor of the yellowed individual would reappear in *Godey's* pages some months later in an article titled "A Dreamy Hour in the Gold Regions." Borrowing liberally from Dickens, this little fable had as its main character a Scrooge-like merchant, a "hard" and wealthy man by the name of Mr. Tot. Yet its most memorable and frightening character is a spirit who approaches Tot in a dream. "His face was very yellow," proclaimed the author, "and seemed so hard that it might have been cast in metal. His hands were also of the same hue, and his dress was made of scraps of printed paper, which as Mr. Tot thought they resembled bank notes, caused his inclination to be rude to the stranger to diminish gradually." Tot is clearly attracted to the figure, more so when he learns the spirit's identity: for this, according to the author, was the "Genius of Gold." Following this meeting, the genius leads Tot to the source of wealth, down into the bowels of the earth. Actually, Tot discovers two sources of wealth in these lower regions. One is the "Rock of Labor," from which a "small but beautiful" stream of pure gold springs forth to fall gently over the ridges of "Industry, Talent, and Perseverance." The other is a rather obvious metaphor for California, a "noisy, swollen, and tempestuous flood," a torrent of gold mixed with baser, more noxious metals. Stunted and withered trees line the banks of this river, on their branches the skewered heads of Tot's fellow merchants. "Hideous, wrinkled, cunning and spiteful," they cry in unison, "Hurrah! we have another chum to taste our splendid misery." When asked to choose between streams, Tot does not hesitate. He opts for the flood: " 'What matters it' thought he, 'if these people are ugly, and the stream is noisy; there is more gold here than in the little river.' " Through the rest of the story he learns his mistake. The genius leads him on a gold-water rafting expedition through the flood's rapids, past a series of horrors: the counting houses of corrupt and deformed money lenders, the parlors of merchants who sell their own children for a fast profit. At last Tot comes to realize his error: "I see, now, that I've been a fool." "Worse, mortal," answers the genius, "You've been a bad man."[50]

Here then was the voice of polite culture, the apparently natural response of the Golden Rule when faced with the temptations of actual gold. If these represented "feminine" critiques of gold fever (which is doubtful, considering that some men surely read parts of these publications, and wives, mothers, and sisters surely showed them to husbands, sons, and brothers), they were by no means out of line with the general prescriptions of the period. "Do not be in a hurry to get rich," warned one self-education manual for young men and women, adding that "gradual gains are the only natural gains, and they who are in a haste to be rich, break over sound rules, fall into temptations . . . and generally fail of their object." One New England minister described the gold fever as a "pestilence . . . more terrific than the Cholera." Another warned that the metal's sudden abundance would have the same effect on America that it had on Spain in an earlier age, leading to a decline in frugality, industry, and civilization. From Concord, as influential an observer as Ralph Waldo Emerson looked at the departing emigrants and was appalled: the "search after the great," he noted, was the most "serious occupation of manhood." But, he added, "we are put off with fortune instead."[51]

Undoubtedly, fewer prospective gold seekers read Emerson than read the *Knickerbocker* or the *Herald*. Fewer still would have been likely to read the more abstract prose of Herman Melville. And yet, here too, in Melville's 1849 novel, *Mardi*, the pervasive debate surrounding the wisdom and morality of treasure hunting found voice. *Mardi* resonates with two of these themes: the connection between California and hell, and the personification of wealth in a "yellow" individual. But the book also raised another criticism, arguing in effect that the search for gold would be a colossal waste of time and energy. In *Mardi*, Melville's unnamed protagonist, along with his fellow voyagers Yoomy and Babbalanja—one a mystic, the other an exotic eastern philosopher—engage in a meandering and fruitless search for "Yillah," the protagonist's dream woman. They never find her. They do, however, encounter a ship of gold hunters, who sing a gold-hunting song. Their chorus is so strange, so evocative of the historical moment, that it bears quoting at length:

> We rovers bold, To the land of gold,
> Over bowling billows are gliding:
> Eager to toil, For the golden spoil,
> And every hardship biding.
>
> .   .   .   .
>
> All fires burn a golden glare:
> No locks so bright as golden hair!
> All orange groves have golden gushings!
> All mornings dawn with golden flushings!
> In a shower of gold, say fables old,
> A Maiden was won by the god of gold!
> In golden goblets wine is beaming:
> On golden couches kings are dreaming!
> The Golden Rule dries many tears!
> The Golden Number rules the spheres!
> Gold, gold it is, that sways the nations:
> Gold! gold! the centre of all rotations!
>
> .   .   .   .
>
> But joyful now, with eager eye,
> Fast to the Promised Land we fly:
> Where in deep mines,
> The treasure shines;
> Or down in beds of golden streams,
> The gold flakes glance in golden gleams!
> How we long to sift,
> That yellow drift!
> Rivers! Rivers! cease your going!

Sand bars rise, and stay the tide
'Till we've gained the golden flowing;
And in the golden haven ride!

Perhaps no other statement, during the gold rush or since, would so effectively capture the comic dementia associated with gold fever.

But if Melville's portrayal of this illness was particularly vivid, so was his critique of where it would lead these hunters. "No Yillah there!" utters Babbalanja, as he watches the ship pass. Yoomy, meanwhile, has a vision: on the rovers would go, "over forest, hill and dale, and lo! the golden region! After the glittering spoil, by strange river margins, and beneath impending cliffs, thousands delve in quicksands; and sudden, sink in graves of their own making: with gold dust mingling their own ashes. Still deeper, in some solid ground, other thousands slave, and pile their earth so high, they gasp for air, and die; their comrades mounting on them, and delving still, and dying— grave pile on grave! Here, one haggard miner murders another in his pit; and murdering, himself is murdered by a third. Shrieks and groans! cries and curses! It seems a golden Hell!" In the end, these gold seekers too would see their mistake. Once again, visions of easy wealth and California gold would lead men away from home and family, down into the bowels of hell. To Melville and his characters the lesson behind this episode was clear. "Ah! home! thou only happiness," Yoomy has the gold hunters say at last, "better thy silver earnings than all thy golden findings. Oh, bitter end to all our hopes, we die in golden graves."[52]

Despite these warnings, Franklin Buck prepared to depart for California in January 1849. Others had already finished their preparations and sailed. Still more would follow, some 40,000 individuals by the end of the year, some 800 ships, barks, brigs, schooners, and steamers from northeastern ports.[53] Of these forty-niners, the vast majority would be men, and among them would be many who saw themselves as respectable, middle-class men. Along with other historians, we might assume that in choosing to go these men also chose to ignore many warnings and middle-class prescriptions. Undoubtedly a few did, and these simply disappeared over the horizon, consciously abandoning wives, children, and businesses along with their moral codes. Yet the vast majority would do no such thing, and for them, the lure of gold and warnings against its immoral pursuit would remain in constant oscillation. "What fools we are," wrote one during the voyage, "to leave *good* society, good homes, good enjoyments, in pursuit of a shadow that can make no one contented or happy." Others would refer as Edward Tailer did to California gold as "filthy lucre," even as they pursued it. Not long after sailing, John Beeckman would admit to his wife that he passed his time "drawing pictures of future years when our golden dreams perhaps realized we would laugh as we talked over our adventures in search of the root of evil."[54]

Edward Tailer did not go to California. We might assume that he did not because he was too respectable, that his was a typical reaction on the part of a drab middle class to the excitement and excess of the gold rush era, or to genuine and spontaneous behaviors of any sort. And yet, if Tailer was typical of his class, it may not have been in this respect. For if we follow his diary, we find a familiar pattern. On one hand, his diary is the record of a rising individual; in it Tailer recorded his climb in the world of business along with his marriage in 1852. On the other, it contains occasional forays into a "darker" world of temptation. In September 1853, the successful clerk traveled away from home, away from his wife, on a business trip to Boston. That night he wrote this in the diary: "I met with several interesting adventures this evening, having set out for the purpose of studying the depravity of human nature, when the passions are permitted to have full sway."[55] We will never know what depravities Tailer studied that night, or whose passions he permitted full sway. But one thing seems sure: this expression, combined with his moral criticism of gold seeking, would place him squarely within the domain of the forty-niner. And, as his mode of expression along with theirs clearly reveals, there would be much more to the emergence of middle-class culture than the embrace of respectability.

Two

Gold Fever as a Cure

For Caspar Hopkins, the gold rush would be the primary experience of his life. It would mark his transition to manhood, his entrance into the world of business, his turning point toward a successful and lucrative career. A native of Pittsburgh who had moved to Burlington, Vermont, in an unsuccessful attempt to start his own newspaper, Hopkins opted to join the rush at age twenty-three. Even at this age he already possessed the qualities of a respectable middle-class man. He was, as he recalled, a young man of "singular" intelligence and "powerful" organizational abilities, "gifted with eloquence, distinguished by a great versatility, strong will, indomitable industry, entire self-reliance & aesthetic tastes." And if as this self-image indicates he was not always modest, his immodesty made a crucial point. For the clearest memory he retained was that these virtues had nearly barred him from joining the California argosy. Like many men on their way to embracing middle-class standards of refinement and good taste, Hopkins confronted a serious problem: these very qualities would make it difficult to engage in an increasingly competitive marketplace predicated on the trade in desires.

In the most dramatic passage of his recollections, Hopkins recounts a conversation with an agent for a California-bound ship on which he hoped to reserve a place. The agent was a certain "Mister B." The dialogue took place at a shipping house across from the New York City docks. Even some thirty years later he claimed to remember every word of it. "Said Mr. B.," he recalled, "you are going to California to make money are you not?"

Mr. H. Yes Sir.
Mr. B. If when you get to San Francisco you find you can make

> more money at selling rum by the glass than at anything else will you sell rum by the glass?
>
> Mr. H. Decidedly not. Sir.
>
> Mr. B. If when you get there you find you can make more money by keeping a gaming table than at anything else will you keep a gaming table?
>
> Mr. H. No Sir.
>
> Mr. B. If when you get there you find you can make more money on Sunday than on any other day will you work Sunday?
>
> Mr. H. Not anything absolutely necessary.
>
> Mr. B. Then Sir, I fear your education has ill fitted you for success as a business man. We shall have no occasion for your services.[1]

Rejected by this particular agent, Hopkins would continue his search for a passage to California. Eventually he found one, and he arrived in the gold country later in 1849. There he made a fortune underwriting fire insurance, got married, and fathered thirteen children. His goal in writing this interview with Mr. B may have been to point out that there were respectable men in California, even during the gold rush, and that some of these men at least did not give in to the region's temptations. What it does, however, is reveal his innermost fears about his bourgeois aspirations.

For many mid-nineteenth-century readers, Hopkins's Mr. B would have been a recognizable character. In fact, he appears under the same name in one of the period's most popular novels: Samuel Richardson's *Pamela*. Here too he personifies temptation, this time imperiling the sexual virtue of the novel's title character.[2] Mr. B, as Hopkins implies and many readers certainly knew, was the devil. The problem for young men like Hopkins was that by 1849 these characters seemed to be everywhere. For in his earthly incarnation the devil was a businessman, his place not merely the offices of California agents, but also the counting houses, mercantile firms, sales rooms, and even the factory floors of a burgeoning market economy. What Hopkins's passage illustrates, in other words, is not the victory of respectability over the gold rush. Instead it suggests that at the particular moment of the gold rush both respectability, as the formative ethos of a rising middle class, and competition, as the organizing ethos of the American marketplace, had become real sources of anxiety. At issue for men like Hopkins was the tension between status and success. The first demanded good morals and respectability, the second something darker and more devious, such as selling rum by the glass or working on a Sunday. Their fear was that an ethos of respectability would leave them cut off, separated from the real world in which they could best—and perhaps only—get ahead through a willingness to break their own moral codes. The gold rush was an example of these tensions. It would also contain their cure.

The problem with the gold rush, according to an anonymous writer for the *Southern Quarterly Review*, was the problem of America's market revolution as a whole. Both, that is, had generated a "rapid growth of wealth," along with a "passion for gain." Both had gone a long way toward destroying "the sense of duty and the sense of right." Both would eventually snap the cords of "reciprocal affections, the intricate and delicate springs of relative regards." And finally, both had released dark forces on the land. In Europe the liberalism of the market had raised up the masses to compete with their betters, unleashing their passions, fueling the revolutions of 1848. In America, it had unleashed the gold mania. "The spell of modern civilization," concluded the article's author, "has evoked a devil, which it is powerless to lay, and which yields not to its exorcisms. Like the luckless conjurers in Arabian story, the fancied magicians of our own time tremble before the genii whom they have raised, but whom no incantations will charm to their bidding, and no Abracadabra drive back to the darkness whence they came. The lid has been removed from the Caldron; the giant has swelled to his huge and terrible proportions."[3] On one hand this article may have struck readers as another in a growing list of southern critiques of northern industrialization and free-labor ideology, another defense of a slaveholding culture based on strict hierarchy, patriarchal duty, and forced labor that its defenders could not afford to admit was forced. On the other hand, they probably found much in this argument with which they could agree. Certainly many moralists who opposed the gold rush would agree. They too believed in this devil: from the beginning of the rush they had equated going to California with going to hell, the gold region with devilish temptations.

Perhaps more interesting, however, is the fact that even many northern businessmen might have agreed with this view of the market and the emergence of the competitive social relations of modern capitalism. The new world of mid-nineteenth-century business, according to *Hunt's Merchant's Magazine*, contained "an undercurrent of deception, selfishness, and dishonesty." It had become far more competitive, far more cutthroat in its daily transactions. In fact, the article claimed it had become "impossible to have aught to do with business transactions without encountering those who, by an air of candor and justice, succeed in duping those of their fellows not yet initiated in the mysteries of deceiving." Business had become a competitive game, but one without rules or restrictions. Few could play and remain unsullied by its daily deceptions; and, the article concluded, few seemed to care: "to say, there is an honest man, is to say there is a very strange man."[4]

Yet, as the existence of this critique indicates, many Americans did care. And many were decidedly uneasy. Indeed, critics realized that the expansion of capitalism from economic to social relations had created what one reformer called an "anxious spirit of gain" in the country, a sense that in this new marketplace of commodified pleasures and corrupt schemes, honesty was not its own reward. "The scheming speculations of the last ten years have produced an aversion among the young to the slow accumulations of ordinary industry, and fired them with a conviction that shrewdness, cunning, and bold ventures, are a more manly way to wealth," wrote Henry Ward Beecher, three years before the gold rush began. "While trade is destined to free and employ the masses," wrote business reformer Henry Bellows a year earlier, "it is also destined to destroy for the time much of the beauty and happiness of every land."[5]

The period of the 1830s and 1840s has long been depicted as a time of great confidence, an era when people wrote poetic paeans to the power of steam, when newspaper editors could speak—apparently without self-suspicion—of "Young America" and its "manifest destiny to overspread and to possess the whole of the continent."[6] Situated in the context of the market revolution such statements seem more like whistling in the dark than evocations of the period's overall feeling of confidence. When, beginning in the mid-1820s, the Second Great Awakening swept through the northeastern states, and when Charles Grandison Finney's religious revivals stopped off at Utica and Rochester on the way to New York City, these underlying anxieties exploded into the public arena. Down in front of the revival meetings the "guilty bench" was frequently crowded with merchants and civic leaders, ready to express their sins.[7] They had good reasons to feel guilty. One undoubtedly came from these perspectives of the marketplace, the idea, that is, that success in business required a certain amount of false claims, lying and cheating.

Another reason was the widespread perception that the advent of market relations was leading to rampant social fragmentation, that the new emphasis on self-made individualism and competition was undermining older values of home ties and kin relations. Beginning in 1837, a series of nationwide panics, bankruptcies, bank closures, and credit squeezes contributed to an overall sense that the market was a place of chaos and disorder. By this time, success had become an ever-growing obsession, failure an ever-growing fear. Northeastern as well as southern observers of this business environment frequently came to an alarming conclusion: the rise of competition was destroying the American family.

During the 1820s and 1830s, the market revolution had definitely destroyed one version of this family, the bonds of kinship, which existed—or which many believed existed—between merchant and live-in laborers prior to this period. By the mid-1840s, it seemed to threaten even the nuclear family of the middle-class household. To many it appeared that all responsibilities for child raising within this type of family had fallen to women. As for men, the "absorbing passion for gain, and the pressing demands of business," left them little time to impart ethical or moral lessons to their children. By the time of the gold rush, these men appeared to be providing models of behavior that were decidedly unethical, possibly immoral, and certainly hostile to family harmony. An article in *Godey's Lady's Book* was prepared to admit the worst: observing "the extraordinary facility with which men have left accustomed pursuits, local obligations, and family altars," the writer could only lament the accuracy "of De Tocqueville's declaration, that the ties of home and kindred are essentially loose in a mercantile republic."[8]

In the years, or even decades, leading up to the gold rush, these types of expressions appeared with some frequency. Their existence, in turn, suggests that the commonly held idea that middle-class Americans welcomed the market revolution is at best an oversimplification. In fact, for all the lamentations among historians about middle-class philistinism and the lack of socialism in America, the gold rush period was marked by more socialist experiments than any other. Only a few years later, reformer John Humphrey Noyes would cite the existence of some seventy socialist or communist societies during this time. These communities, from New Harmony to Oneida and the Northampton Association, from Brook Farmers to Mormons, Rappites, Owenites, Fourierites, and Shakers, drew many of their growing list of converts from disillusioned members of the middle class. For Noyes, their widespread popularity indicated a change in the "heart of the nation; and that a yearning toward social reconstruction has become a part of the continuous, permanent, inner experience of the American people."[9] For many new middle-class followers, it seems likely that these experiments offered a last chance to resurrect the ideal of a wider and more closely interconnected family.

Home and family, according to these critics of the marketplace, would provide a point of resistance to social and moral fragmentation. "No truly conscientious, Christian parent," concluded *Hunt's* investigation into the lack of integrity among businessmen, "will allow one of his children to leave him until he feels he will be safe 'in the world's broad field of battle.' "[10] To young men like Caspar Hopkins, this response to the immoralities of the marketplace was a thorny solution. For if indeed the world of business was a field of battle, and home the only place where a respectable moral code might not be met with derisive laughter, then it seemed they might never be able, or even allowed, to make the transition from home to this new world at all.

Certainly the home, increasingly dominated by women, increasingly separate from the market, was not a very good place for young men to learn the battle strategies of the marketplace. According to Elisha Crosby, a lawyer working and living in New York City at the outset of the gold rush, this transition from home to business world was among the most difficult moments of his life. Although he was over thirty years old at the time, his trip to the city to start a law career remained a painful memory. Home, as he remembered it, was a place of "kindness and motherly endearments," leaving its refuge the "strongest pressure we ever experience." In fact, far from preparing him for the world of the market, home and mother had done the opposite, leaving him a "sensitive boy" faced with a "battle of life," surrounded only by "self-ish and unfriendly faces."[11]

Other prospective forty-niners would have agreed, and their writings suggest similarly difficult transitions. Even as he departed for California, New York merchant Isaac Halsey began a diary of his voyage with a poem that he titled "Home of my Childhood." Two stanzas suffice to indicate his frame of mind as he began his adventure:

How dear to Mem'ry is the spot
Where oft I danced in childish mirth;
The spot where want and care came not
To the paradise of earth

Happy, O happy then was I
My heart was gay, my step was light;
Would childhood's day had ne'er gone by,
And I had ne'er felt sorrow's blight[12]

Another gold seeker, Alonzo Hill of Spencer in Worcester County, Massachusetts, reflected on parallel sentiments in a letter to his sister. "Tis past and we no more may meet," he wrote soon after sailing, "For years perhaps for ever / But memory's records Sad and Sweet / Can lose their influence never."[13] Even among older forty-niners, the thought of leaving the "endearments of home" might be difficult to contemplate. This was certainly the case for prospective miners like Hiram Dwight Pierce of Troy, New York. Pierce was a church elder, a city alderman, and the president of the local volunteer fire department. A blacksmith with seven children, he joined the California exodus at the age of nearly forty. And, as he prepared for his departure, yet another ode to home came to mind: "We seek too high for things close by / And lose what nature found us; / For life has here no charmes so dear / As Home & friends around us."[14]

This tension between home and the outside world of business was everywhere apparent in mid-nineteenth-century American bourgeois culture. Increasingly trained by their mothers to be good sons in the home, educated in the intricacies of polite conversation and table manners, young men especially but older ones too undoubtedly experienced a sense of loss when faced with the rougher culture of the streets. Some turned to the rising gentleman's sport of boxing, toughening themselves up for the battle of life, if only as spectators. Others felt partitioned off from the outside world; more than a few, like Elisha Crosby, with Bartleby the scrivener, would probably have "preferred not" to join it. New Brunswick's town doctor and mayor, Augustus Fitz Randolph Taylor, may not have appeared a Bartleby type in public, but his private thoughts show evidence of similar feelings of loss and isolation. On the surface he cut a confident figure. With a large barrel of a body, full whiskers, and thick spectacles, he had an air of stolid weight and studiousness. His earliest diary entry, however, reveals a deep ambivalence toward the masculine world of competition. "I have procured this book," he wrote at age twenty-nine, "to record from day to day my experience of men & things in general—my joys & sorrows—the sorrows will far-far outweigh the joys—the pleasures of life are far between."[15] This figure of success, as it turns out, was a heavily burdened man.

Others who were less burdened by their own perspectives of the marketplace might still chafe under the constraints of family and community. Like Caspar Hopkins, James Barnes was nearly denied access to the gold rush. For Barnes, however, the barrier of respectability came not from his own qualities but from those of his parents. Originally from Blooming Grove, New York, Barnes was probably a student when the first gold reports reached the East. A victim of the cholera epidemic sweeping the region, he seems to have been sent away from home to recover. While away, he decided that he could best effect his cure with a journey to the Pacific. In October 1849, he informed his parents of his intention, adding that he needed to borrow money for the voyage, along with the hope that they would "rais no objections to my going when I come home." He was disappointed on both counts. His parents did raise objections. They would neither support his scheme nor lend him money. Like other good Christians of their class, they wanted him to stay at home.

Because Barnes did not save their letters, the precise wording of his parents' objections may never be known. Their general substance, however, is clear from his response, in which he makes every attempt to convince them of his preparedness to safely enter a world of immorality. "I hope you dont think that I intend to spend my substance in [riotous] living," he wrote a second time, adding that since finishing his first letter he had taken down his Bible and strengthened his resolve with the fifteenth chapter of Luke. Still, he seems to have known that his parents would never allow him to go. Finally, he closed the letter with a tone of desperation: "Mother o mother, why do you still resist my going my mind is made up to go why o why cant you let me go with a cheerful heart[?] I do not intend to return as the prodigal did but I hope to return and say father father here is your 200 dollars and the interest also."[16] For the moment, at least, Barnes had been cut off in his effort to join the gold rush, denied entry to a world of temptation by a code of respectable morality. Eventually, he found a source to fund his passage. His father may have even relented and loaned him the money. Still, he remained bitter over his parents' refusal to support his efforts to break with the ties of home. "I have not been home sick nor heart sick since I left," he wrote from Panama. Reading this letter, his parents would certainly have been hurt, if not properly chastised for their overly respectable fears.

For many Americans then, the period preceding the gold rush was a time of mounting tensions between the dictates of polite culture and the necessities of the marketplace. To some the problem was the market, its basis in the distinctly impolite behaviors of dishonest dealings. To others the problem was respectability, its grounding in a golden rule of polite and honest exchange that seemed hopelessly out of line with market realities. For many if not most, both perceptions generated anxieties. At the high-water mark of these tensions would be two major developments in American culture: the explosion of creative literature that has come to be called the "American Renaissance" and the California gold rush. Both would be characterized by these tensions, by strange and lively discourses between strict morality and forbidden behavior, between a centering ethos of respectability and the fragmenting force of the market, and between binaries of reason and appetite, light and dark, East and West. Both would also be literary events, framed by wild fantasies, dominated by yearnings for escape and experimentation with social and cultural alternatives to a bourgeois way of being.

This literary context for the gold rush, while often ignored or simply denied, is every bit as important as the political, social, and geographical contexts of manifest destiny, the West, or California. For the market revolution was also a print revolution, and a mass increase in reading and writing would frame the gold rush as much as economic necessity or a spirit of western expansion. Indeed, one of the elements that makes the California gold rush stand out from other rushes is the sheer volume of writing produced by the California gold seekers. Emigrants to California rarely left home without notebook, quill pen, and ink. The result, according to one historian, was an unparalleled "explosion of vernacular autobiography."[17] What is so striking about this literature is the frequency with which its accounts are well written. The gold rush was a good story. One reason it has remained a good story is the fact that many forty-niners, as well-read men, knew how to imbue it with elements of adventure, romance, and sentiment.

Through the 1820s and 1830s, one would most likely find few books, and fewer libraries, in the homes of average Americans. While literacy was widespread at this time, especially in the Northeast, books remained expensive, their ownership limited to a wealthy few at the higher end of the economic scale. By the middle years of the 1840s, printed material had become more available: the expansion of transportation networks along with the invention of steam-driven roller presses resulted in far cheaper methods of production and distribution and major reductions in price for pamphlets, almanacs, and story collections. In addition, these developments allowed for the rise of cheap daily newspapers, weekly magazines, and monthly journals. Editors frequently fleshed out these publications with serializations of novels, offering weekly literary supplements for their readers from the works of Dickens, Thackeray, and Longfellow, along with later serials of adventure stories, sensational literature, and sentimental fiction penned by a rapidly growing number of American authors. By 1840, with some 1,500 of these publications appearing throughout the country, a New York newspaper could announce that a "golden age of periodicals" had arrived. As for books, the development of the cylinder press in 1847 allowed publishers to create inexpensive editions of older titles and to flood the market with cheap adventure novels. By this time, Americans, particularly middle-class Americans, were reading to an unheard-of extent; some were even beginning to amass small libraries.[18]

Northeastern forty-niners were clearly caught up in this trend; in fact, they may have been driving it as consumers. Frank Buck could not imagine going to the gold region without a large stock of books. He planned to purchase some 100 volumes before his departure and actually did buy a whopping total of 58 from a New York store for a mere $9.44. The ship *Edward Everett*, which sailed from Boston in 1849, was just one of many that carried an on-board library, but its collection, judging from its notoriety, appears to have been particularly large and impressive. Frank Marryat, an English participant in the gold rush, was amazed at the amount of reading and writing that went on in California. Even in 1849, he cited the existence of seven newspapers in San Francisco alone, with additional "weekly sheets" in practically every mining town and foothill village. "Apparently," he noted, "every Californian can read." And, as he added with reference to the 50,000 letters carried from the Pacific every two weeks, "we may presume that there are few among them that cannot write."[19] As for the types of books these men were reading, according to Marryat they were overwhelmingly novels. His own stock included works by Fielding, Smollet, Defoe, and Goldsmith. At a typical "thriving" bookstore in San Francisco, the "importations" consisted "for the most part of novels[, which] find a ready sale in the mining regions." Other observers would note the popularity of romance and adventure novels in the gold country, from works by Dumas and Defoe to Ned Buntline, along with verse collections by Shakespeare, Spenser, Shelley, and Byron.

For men who thought about California during these anxious times, much of this literature offered a way out of the impasse between respectability and the marketplace. For if there is one major theme in the popular literature at the time of the gold rush and in the texts that forty-niners took with them to California, it is escape from both. Among these texts, undoubtedly the most popular was Daniel Defoe's *Robinson Crusoe*. This should not be surprising. First published in England in 1719, by the 1840s Defoe's classic tale of captivity turned to advantage was reaching the zenith of its popularity. Enjoyed by young boys and girls alike, its text was frequently lifted for inclusion in penny press literary supplements and bowdlerized for the pages of dime novels.[20] There were good reasons for its popularity, for the novel offered a prescient exploration of the problems of modern middle-class identity, particularly the problem of effecting a balance between status and success, respectable ethicality and the competitive pursuit of luxury.

From the Protestant Reformation through the eighteenth century, practically every book or pamphlet addressing the issue of material abundance portrayed it as conducive to sin. Nearly all took a moral stance against luxury and the embrace of physical appetites. *Robinson Crusoe* did not.[21] As generations of readers found, Crusoe's was a strange captivity, a blend of Christian and aesthetic resistance to savagery and a materialist engagement with the luxuries of nature, leading to an eventual and perfect mastery over both poles of being. Never during his thirty-year marooning does he allow his Protestant sensibilities to drop: he refuses to go naked in the tropical heat; he works continuously, building fortresses, sowing crops, penning wild animals. At the same time, this apparent resistance to the charms of savagery and nature is undermined by a curious admission: from his Caribbean island the castaway can actually see the South American mainland. It seems, in other words, he can escape whenever he wants. Instead, it is obvious that Defoe wanted him to stay and luxuriate. So did Defoe's readers. Marooned on his island, stuck in a magical economy of tropical abundance that he must master to survive, Crusoe's captivity could be read as a type of freedom. Far from the questionable deceptions of the marketplace, conveniently apart from a self-limiting code of temperance and moderation, he is free to surround himself with elements of abundance: tame goats, talking birds, a personal manservant, and at least two intricate and intriguingly well-appointed island homes.[22]

Defoe's story, as several historians have noted—even while banning literary pretense from the rush—was an "inspiring myth" of the California venture. " 'The idea of a life in the mines,' " wrote one gold seeker, " 'had about it a smack of Robinson Crusoe.' "[23] Forty-niners mentioned the story frequently, partly because the actual island of Juan Fernandez (on which the true marooning of Scotsman Alexander Selkirk had supplied Defoe with the idea) was on the Cape Horn route, partly because, as one recalled, "I had listened to these stories of adventure as many another child had listened to fairy tales. The magical isle . . . became to my young mind a commingling of fact and fancy—a dream island whereon my father and Robinson Crusoe had been exiled together."[24] For one forty-niner the island was "the most fascinating spot . . . on the face of the globe! . . . what New England boy but has imagined himself a castaway on this very island." Others preferred a shorter visit to the carefree spot, "where Robison Cruso [*sic*] spent so many days of dancing with goats and cats," where "our youthful fantasies had gone with so keen and lively an interest along with Robinson Crusoe and his man Friday." When they did visit the island, they followed, as one put it, "the footsteps of my hero, in imagination at least." They stood before the castaway's cave, communing with the descendants of his tamed goats, expressing kinship with his desires. As Crusoe had inspired their games as children, so would he inspire a dream at the heart of the aspiring middle-class gold seeker: "I say," said one in a reflective moment, "to be thus liberated is a source of almost exquisite pleasure."[25]

If Defoe gave these yearnings for freedom optimistic direction, projecting them onto a perfect space apart from the concerns of the real world, another favorite forty-niner reading, Lord Byron's *Childe Harold's Pilgrimage*, described them more in terms of an aimless quest, a romantic disdain for everyday existence. Published in four cantos from 1812 through 1818, the poem was Byron's most popular work in America. As with Defoe's, Byron's theme is flight from social restraints. His goal, however, is not blameless self-assertion, nor assertion of any kind; rather, it is complete self-dissolution. For Byron was the poet of the modern middle-class aesthetic, his popularity a reflection of the growing idea that manly artistic genius involved losing one's self to the point of destruction, that it required the immersion of the individual in an oceanic flood of immediate sensation.[26]

There is "pleasure in the pathless woods," muses Childe Harold in a typical romantic moment, "rapture on the lonely shore." But in the competitive hum of "human cities," there was only "torture."[27] In such pithy lines, Byron struck a chord with a society in violent transition, with men who had similar doubts. And so, they would follow Harold in his escape, away from this industrial hum, moving "o'er vales that teem with fruits, romantic hills," into exotic places wrapped in rich vowel sounds: from Leucadia's far projecting rock of woe to Ambracia's gulf, from Illyria's vales, bleak Pindus, Acherusia's lake to Monastic Zitsa and the glittering minarets of Tepalen. In these places were exotic peoples, mystical exemplars of oriental passion: Turks, Greeks, Albanians, Moors, and, more glamorous still, the great "Ali Pacha," the "Chimariot," "Illyrian," and "dark Suliote!" Many forty-niners could quote Harold's yearnings line and verse; a very large percentage would sprinkle their journals with Byronic images, with "adieus" to their native shores, with depictions of themselves as eternal wanderers, gloomy outcasts moving from the controlled rigidity of city and office to a liberating immersion in nature, in oceanic sensual pleasures.

Byron would seem an unlikely hero for men bent on middle-class assertion, unlikelier still as the muse of the gold rush. He was the greatest libertine of the age, a man whose prime object, according to Harriet Beecher Stowe, was the absolute destruction of virtue. He lived in a gothic castle and dressed in black clothing. He had long hair, a purposely emaciated body, and dark and brooding eyes that flashed wickedness, free thought, and melancholic self-indulgence. Often associated with diabolical forces if not the devil himself, his veins coursed with illicit desires—bisexuality, incest, fetishistic license—and with equally illicit opium. But as other mid-nineteenth-century critics commonly averred, Byron was also the "poet of youth and enthusiasm, of the natural emotions of the heart."[28] He was the model class mutineer, living and writing to shock the staid aristocracy and *epater les bourgeois*. Properly shocked, his largely middle-class audience loved him, embracing Childe Harold's vices as its not-so-secret titillations and desires, again revealing their yearnings to escape, to educate the senses not merely with a controlling respectability but also with passion and free play with exoticism and erotica.

Much of the literature surrounding and preceding the gold rush, which formed its context and framed its individual experiences, followed directions established by Defoe and Byron. It moved readers along specific pathways: away from the home, outside of the market, into imagined spaces where one might meet the devil apart from the self-limiting dictates of moral restraint or the Golden Rule. Some of this literature led inward, into the impulses of the subconscious where traditional distinctions between right and wrong, good and evil, might be broken down in romantic transcendence. Such was the direction established by Ralph Waldo Emerson. "What have I to do with the sacredness of traditions?" asked the Concord seer in "Self Reliance," declaring that he preferred to live "from within," by impulse, even base impulse: "if I am the devil's child, I will live then from the devil."[29] Other writers took readers across urban borders, plumbing the depths of urban demimondes and working-class neighborhoods to expose the "secret life" of the city's libertines and laborers. Here, in best-selling works such as George Lippard's *The Quaker City* (1844) and George Foster's *New York by Gas-Light* (1850), devils proliferated wildly in the shadows and corners of the darkened city. These devils were most frequently successful businessmen: "aristocratic blacklegs," as Foster referred to them, the "pious and devout hypocrites, libertines, gamblers, fancy men, high flyers and spoonies" who by day engaged in "magnificent falsehood" and "sublime mercantile swindling," by night in orgiastic revels, loosening the reins of their "prurient tastes and manners" to engage in riots of "confusion, drunkenness and profanity." "I say gentlemen, shall we make a night of it," reads the first line from one of Lippard's *Quaker City* characters, "shall we elevate— the devil along Chesnut Street, or shall we subside quietly to our homes?" In 1844, readers, especially middle-class readers, knew what answer to expect: for the devil's elevation, if it was feared, would also, they knew, lead to some sensational and gruesome adventures.[30]

Working-class neighborhoods, as they appeared in this literature, were filled with far superior types. Here, middle-class readers could reembrace—in imagination at least—their old family members from the pre-market household economy. By this time these former cohabitants had taken on more colorful hues, becoming matchboys, newspaper hawkers, bootblacks, and, above all, the working-class characters of Moze and Lize, the Bowery "b'hoy" and "g'hal." Characterized by "sturdy frame" "unyielding sinews and reckless daring," Moze, according to Foster's *New York Gas-Light*, was the very soul of authentic self-expression. He was a common laborer, his bread earned by honest sweat. If he was loud, boisterous, and even a bit vulgar in his speech, he was always cheerful and hearty in disposition. And if he was unschooled in the niceties of polite society, or "book-larnin'," as he was apt to put it, he had his own kind of street smarts. These were marked, above all, by "his open abhorrence of all 'nonsense.'"

In fact, despite the tendency among social historians to label the "b'hoy" a working-class character, Foster referred to him as the model for a rising middle class, a perfect balance between the stiffness of New York's upper-class elite and the self-expressive physicality of the Bowery's street culture. Whether working class or middle class, the character of Moze undoubtedly had great appeal to middle-class boys and young men, particularly in his western manifestation as Davy Crockett. A large part of this appeal most likely came from his disdain for the isolating elements within middle-class culture itself. For as Foster and others pointed out, Moze despised all examples of affectation and snobbery. Always ready for a fight or a frolic, freed by his class position from the prescriptions of parlor culture, by his poverty from the necessities of the marketplace, the b'hoy was the yearned-for opposite to the refined young gentlemen of polite society. To Moze, added Foster, these latter types were the "plodding slaves of the inkstand," the "milk hearted sucklings of foppery and fashion."[31]

Written by middle-class authors for a largely middle-class audience, much of this literature suggests the emergence, by the mid-1840s, of two extremely important cultural contexts for the gold rush. One was an emerging pattern of reaction against the moral strictures of polite culture, a growing distaste for the foppish trappings of the parlor, a feeling so strong it often took the form of bourgeois self-hatred. The other was a rather bitter disdain for the daily grind and isolation of white-collar office work. These contexts seem particularly clear in perhaps the most common form of the period's adventure literature, the short stories, novels, and serialized books that drew readers out of the home and into the open spaces of the American West.

In much of this western literature, one point is made above all others: there is nothing so contemptible and pathetic as an over-civilized easterner. Indeed, as a story in William T. Porter's sporting journal the *Spirit of the Times* suggested, the West had no use for the lisping of parlor manners or the minced steps of refinement, and out on the prairies these affectations would provide little more than comic relief. The protagonist of this story, a citified dandy who has gone west to join a buffalo hunting party, is completely out of place. While he does manage to kill a buffalo, his achievement is hardly heroic. The toothless animal, nearly dead of old age, wobbles right up to the dude, presenting him with a stationary target. He fires his rifle six times, and misses. Finally, on the seventh shot the decrepit animal falls, likely from exhaustion. Later, when he brags of his achievement, we see the eastern dandy at his most hilarious. "Oh gracious, gracious, gracious!" the writer has the tinhorn say, "Oh I had such battle! . . .

a regular chef d'ouevre magnifique. (Our language not being rich enough, he was in the habit of trimming up his sentences here and there with French.) Gracious, gracious, but he was terrible. He was so fat as to make my mouth water; regularly l'eau en vient a la bouche . . . six shots I made at him, still he showed game. Ma foi! says I, this is regularly ouvrage de longue halaine—terrible! bad! horror! gracious! I shall not forget the risk I ran—jamais!"[32] Here was the slave of the inkstand, the milksop clerk who had risen to the pinnacle of middle-class refinement only to find himself the subject of scorn and mockery. Undoubtedly, eastern readers laughed at this vignette. At the same time, Porter's *Spirit of the Times* was a self-styled gentleman's paper, and its readers could not laugh without the suspicion that the joke was on them.

By the time of the gold rush, the out-of-place bourgeois had become an object of derision, an immediately recognizable stock character of satirical literature, minstrel shows, comic plays, and popular songs. At the same time, if some examples of western literature pictured this fig-ure as the butt of jokes, others offered escape from his isolated position and surrounding laughter. Among these works, the most resonant with forty-niner desires may have been Richard Henry Dana's *Two Years Before the Mast* and Francis Parkman's *The Oregon Trail*. Dana and Parkman had much in common. Both were descended from old New England stock, and as was to be expected of such young men, both studied at Harvard College, Dana in the 1830s, Parkman a decade later. Both found the sedentary Brahmin existence to be chafing, the brain-work of college numbing to body and mind. Finally, both attempted to escape their humdrum lives through physical experience, by journey-ing into the American West.[33] Dana went to sea on a California-bound sealing vessel in 1834, leaving, as he put it, out of an "anxiety to escape from the depressing situation of inactivity at home," in hope that the hard life of the common sailor would cure him of an eye affliction suffered from too much reading.[34] Parkman sojourned onto the far western prairies a decade later, in a similar effort to escape. Compared to the wilderness, civilization seemed to him "flat and stale." "Its plea-sures," he added, "are insipid, its pursuits wearisome, its conventional-ities, duties, and mutual dependence alike are disgusting."[35]

Dana's voyage seems to have cured him. His 1840 account of his voyage and work in California would later provide the forty-niners with a guide to the Cape Horn route to the Pacific and serve as a model for man-making adventure. Along the way west, at least according to his story, he was able to bond with his authentic working-class crew-mates, sharing in their hard work, wormy food, and cramped living conditions, winning their acceptance by trimming topmasts in high winds and heaving the hearty hoes of pulling songs. By narrative's end, he returns to Boston Harbor rejuvenated. Called down from the masts to meet a fellow Harvardian come to greet him, he swings down nimbly: to his friend's astonishment, "there came down from aloft a 'rough alley' looking fellow, with duck trousers and red shirt, long hair, and face burnt as black as an Indian's. He shook me by the hand, congratulated me upon my return and my appearance of health and strength, and said my friends were all well."[36]

Parkman's case was more difficult, and although he suffered from the same bookish myopia as Dana, his physical decline was far more advanced. His was a composite illness: it was untreatable, its origins mysterious, its manifestations terrible. He experienced periods of blindness. His body was racked by bowel and digestive disorders that shared all the characteristics of cholera but instead of passing or killing him lasted a lifetime. He entered the vast solitude of the prairie seeking a cure for this illness of overcivilization, evincing, with Byron as his conscious model, what by then had become an almost traditional romantic yen for an oceanic dissolution of the self. The result was his publication of *The Oregon Trail*, which first appeared in serialized form in the 1847 issue of the *Knickerbocker*. Like Dana's, his narrative pictures the West as a place of rejuvenation, characterized by the freedom of buffalo hunts, wild and violent chases in which Parkman, despite his illness, somehow manages to take part. "Here," he wrote, "society is reduced to its original elements, the whole fabric of art and conventionality is struck rudely to pieces."[37]

Parkman is never quite cured of his afflictions, even in this healthy environment of unconventionality and freedom. He does, however, manage to find, and at moments bond with, two alternatives to a bourgeois way of being. One is manifested in the figure of Henry Chatillon, his rugged mountain man guide, the other by the ardent physicality of the Ogalala Sioux. Of Chatillon he wrote: "I defy the annals of chivalry to furnish the record of a life more wild and per-ilous." The Sioux, meanwhile, represented his main reason for going west. He had come "with a view of observing their character." But it was their life he wanted: "to accomplish my purpose, it was necessary to live in the midst of them, and become, as it were, one of them."[38] Living with these examples of peerless manhood, Parkman manages, for a few moments at least, to forget his illness and his overcivilized background.

These writings, along with this mid-nineteenth-century explosion of literature, had major effects on the American middle class and provided its growing membership with important lessons. The lesson of these writings seems clear: polite culture had its limitations, and nature, or the West, was a utopian space in which one could escape the stiffness of bourgeois respectability. What these literary works reveal, in other words, is that at a certain point in the process of middle-class formation, many respectable individuals were ready for the gold rush, or something like it. By the 1840s, they imagined that their bodies were becoming softer, weakened by the acquisition of table manners and parlor etiquette. The market, meanwhile, was becoming harsher. It demanded not manners but strength and shiftiness—the physical strength necessary to compete, the moral shiftiness necessary to meet the devil, deal with him on his own ground, and win one's way to success.

The effect of this literature on class formation is more theoretical. As the gold rush reveals, it may have provided middle-class forty-niners with a mode of production, *literary* production, that few class analyses have taken into account. Its access dominated to a large degree by well-read men with equally developed imaginations and literary skills, this mode of production would give middle-class individuals the power not only to make class distinctions, but to effectively deny these distinctions by moving beyond them. Simply put, the greatest power of middle-class forty-niners was their ability to make their experiences believable. They would not do so by merely recording experiences and events as they happened. Instead, they would give these experiences meaning; they would color events with metaphor. Readers at home, they would become writers in California and along the way. As writers they would have power, power to turn their experiences into life-transforming moments, power to recreate themselves as authentic b'hoys and stampeders. In actual fact, of course, it is possible for a refined gentleman to voyage across oceans and continents in search of gold and still remain a refined gentleman. The power of the gold seekers would be their ability to make the readers of their imaginative accounts forget this fact, to make them fully believe that men bound for the new Eldorado had stepped out of their former existences, that they had fully stepped away from the walls, boundaries, and privileges of their class and their pasts.

Gold fever would be characterized by these elements of escapist literature and utopian experimentation. For as much as they centered on gold schemes and the pursuit of wealth, the visions and fantasies of the gold rush would be overtly literary and frankly utopian. In fact, they make far better sense in this literary and utopian context than they do within a timeless context of greed and economic necessity. The goals of the period's many socialist utopias included the reduction of want through an enforced scarcity of resources, the breakdown of class distinctions, the substitution of harmony for competition. The goal of western literature was evasion and nostalgia: it offered alternatives to respectability, escape from the marketplace, and the denial of class distinction in favor of reembracing family members from a preindustrial past. California offered all of these promises.

Few documents did more to establish these promises than *Three Weeks in the Gold Mines* by Henry Simpson. A self-styled firsthand account of mining and a guide to the gold regions, this little pamphlet began appearing in northeastern bookseller stalls by the end of 1848. Purportedly written by a colonel of the New York Volunteers, a military outfit in California at the time of the first gold discoveries, it sold for twelve-and-a-half cents per copy, or twenty-five cents with a map of the gold country and travel routes to the Pacific. The guide was worthless in any practical sense. Yet for a while at least, it did booming business. Josiah Royce called it a "lying document"; a later historian would refer to it as "the first gold rush hoax." These views are correct. For as it turns out, there was no Henry Simpson. The guide's actual author was George Foster, New York bohemian, avowed supporter of Fourierite socialism, and extremely prolific writer of semi-pornographic sensationalist literature.[39] Foster rarely traveled west of Philadelphia. But armed with imagination, a felicitous pen, and a few early reports from California, he managed to create a western utopia filled with every fantasy that the anxieties of the time produced.

The guide's text, according to Royce, was "very persuasive and plausible," and as such, it led many men "to death in the wilderness." In part, this was a result of its simplicity. Foster had only three main points to make about California: first, gold was everywhere, and finding it was easy; second, the region's miners were good companions, not competitors; and third, the life in the gold camps was "perfectly happy."[40] The source for these findings, in turn, may not have been California so much as the yearnings of a certain class of men. Foster had an acute sense of class consciousness, and his finger was firmly on the pulse of middle-class desires. He made a point of directing his text toward readers who simultaneously felt a need for social distinctions and a yearning to step away from them, to embrace or even become authentic working-class b'hoys. Among the characteristics of the gold country, accordingly, was a "perfect familiarity" between classes. On one hand Foster depicted this familiarity as a problem, and the guide urged readers of the better sort to come settle the region, to provide the "necessary distinction . . . among the various classes." On the other, the region's want of distinction was an attraction, for another of the guide's points was that class, conflict, and competition need not exist in California.

According to the guide, the region's countryside was bucolic, to say the least, characterized by gently rolling hills, an "extreme fertility of soil," meandering and transparent streams "sparkling in the sunshine," all refreshed by "soft breezes . . . laden with perfume." All of the streams, and most of the hills, were rich in gold. The only problem one faced was deciding on the richest; this, as the guide had it, was about all there was to prospecting. Indeed, the reason the guide covers the experiences of three weeks, apparently, is that Simpson's company faces precisely this problem. In the meantime its members spend their time in a leisurely search, pausing occasionally to drink from gurgling brooks and to count the "sparkling grains of gold" that inevitably collect in the bottoms of cups. Simpson meets with the region's natives and finds them to be docile, innocent, and conveniently ignorant as to the value of gold: one trades him a seven-ounce nugget for a handkerchief. Most important, he makes connections with seasoned miners.

Here is where class distinctions break down, along with competition among men: for these miners, while they are authentic mountain men and hard-working types, are extremely convivial fellows. Among them, promised the guide, new comers to the region would find "much hospitality and good feeling, without a symptom of jealousy." For that matter, it continued, "there is but little need of anything like selfishness, for the field of enterprise seems inexhaustible." Soon after making this observation, the guide reached its climax. While out prospecting with these authentic miners, the narrator has one of them point goggle-eyed "to a small sparkling stream which ran limped [sic] at his feet." He turns "to examine . . . what had so affected him," and there, in the guide if never quite in the actual gold region, was a sight that must have stirred more than a few souls to feverish yearning: "*The stream, for several yards, apparently ran over a bed of gold.*" The gentle washing of the water, added Foster, as if he needed to add anything, had "acted as a sort of polisher," exposing "the glittering heap in all its richness."[41]

The idea that merchants, clerks, and other educated professionals actually believed this fantastic concoction may seem an example of hopeless naiveté. Throughout the period of the rush, however, there were observers who did question these claims. Some magazines, including *Godey's Lady's Book*, remained particularly troubled by their economic logic: "indeed," claimed a March 1849 *Godey's* article, "it requires but little sagacity and a limited knowledge of history to perceive—that the financial worth of the precious metals diminishes in the exact ratio of their abundance."[42] Even if, in other words, these visions were true, and, as Simpson's guide proclaimed, gold "welled up volcanically in the Sierras," making the range one enormous mine, it merely meant that gold would soon be worthless as a supposedly precious metal backing for paper money. Yet hope and not naiveté seems to have been the main force at work; and what needs to be taken into account is the extent to which men, perhaps especially these white-collar types, desperately needed to believe in California's abundance.

Their publication of preference, *Hunt's Merchant's Magazine*, supported the claims. The goal of this magazine, as one of its writers proclaimed, was to get at the "leading facts" behind the reports from California. These facts did little more than lend solidity to Foster's guide, this time with the weight of numbers and statistics. One article even cited *Three Weeks in the Gold Mines* as proof of the region's riches, along with another report claiming that the region's miners were digging up an average of $1,000 worth of gold per day. "To give you some idea of the quantity of 'dust' produced," wrote another of the magazine's on-the-scene reporters, "people are daily arriving from the gold region with from 10 to 100 pounds of the gold dust, worth here $192 per pound, or say from $1,920 to $19,200; and some trading concerns have brought down $25,000 worth at once."[43]

Statistics like these probably did as much as Foster's guide to inspire dreams and fantasies. "I now saw these numbers printed in glowing ciphers," wrote George Payson, a member of an old Boston Brahmin family, "with all the lifelike, seductive reality of a lottery placard." The glowing numbers were simply these: "$2,000 certain, $20,000 probable, $100,000 possible." This flashing placard silenced his own misgivings about joining the rush, along with the warnings of family and friends. They only increased yearnings for adventure and camaraderie, especially among readers of adventure novels and sensational literature. Even more than wealth, these numbers offered escape, an entry into a world formed by adventure stories and youthful fantasies. His fellow gold seekers, claimed Payson, pictured the gold regions as an abundant West laced with "placid streams, flowing gently between green banks," where the miners would drift along, shooting abundant game when they were hungry, and occasionally "digging out a peck of nuggets like so many clams." "It was a most seductive picture," he added, "glowing like an Eastern tale, or the stories of those old buccaneers rifling a Spanish galleon—how the word seems to roll in riches—and aroused our desires to go a gold hunting in the same privateering fashion."[44]

As for the problematical economic logic within the gold reports, the writers at *Hunt's* simply swept logic aside. The abundance of California might make gold cheaper, admitted one, but this would only lead to more baubles, ornaments, and gold-gilded eating utensils. "More gold then, say we," added another, "it brings its temptations; it brings also the means of great good, of glorious results." In response to older aphorisms the editors at *Hunt's* offered a new one. "The only gold is not that which glitters," they claimed, implying that all forms of material wealth might be gathered under the rubric of gold, and that, conversely, none arose from base impulses. After all, they concluded, times had changed: "Those who dwell upon the commonplace and out of place warnings applicable to other times and circumstances, mistake the spirit and men of the age."[45]

The "spirit of the age" to which *Hunt's* referred may have been capitalism. And yet, like Foster's guide, the thinking behind the spirit seemed informed by socialist visions. "The laborer is now the capitalist in California," claimed one *Merchant's Magazine* writer, adding that since one needed only a few tools, "a bush arbor to sleep in," and a minimum of experience in order to mine, there was "no room for the exclusiveness and monopoly of capital." Accordingly, California embraced all classes of men equally, from lawyers, editors, and printers to sailors and army deserters. "All distinctions indicative of means have vanished," wrote one observer, for the "only capital" that the forty-niner needed was "muscle and honest purpose." The fact that the abundance of gold had "entirely obliterated all social distinctions," added another, was an example of its "wondrous influence."[46]

Thus Foster's point was echoed by others: California would have the same basic result as a New Harmony or a Fourierite phalanx. Both ideals, that is, promised a kind of anticompetitive social leveling, one through the denial of wealth, the other through an embrace of wealth in such abundance that social distinctions no longer mattered. Forty-niner Lewis Carstairs Gunn saw the possibilities within each promise. An individual of varied careers, Gunn began as a farmer, became a teacher, and in the 1830s found moderate success first as an apothecary and then as a doctor. In 1842 he embraced Millerism and gave away all of his possessions. This utopian Christian sect, which was based on the denial of worldly goods in preparation for an end-of-the-world second coming of Christ set to occur between 21 March 1843 and 21 March 1844, never quite worked out. The day of reckoning came and went, and the cult fell apart. But five years later, Gunn seems to have been ready for a social experiment of a different sort. In March 1849, he joined the gold rush, moving from the leveling scarcity of Millerism to the leveling plenty of California. Here he was more successful, resuming his trade as a doctor, becoming a noted reformer, and later returning east as an antislavery editor for the *Philadelphia Times* and a Republican Party leader.[47]

In fact, the claims about the abundance of gold in California were outlandishly extravagant. And certainly, historians might reasonably cite them as evidence of gold rush–era dementia. By January 1849, these yearnings had taken on strange new forms. Northeastern newspapers carried magical appliances for finding gold, generating new meanings for the metal and resurrecting old ones linking gold with physical desires. One of these appliances was "Signor D'Alvear's Goldometer," a device that promised to detect the "magnetic influence" of gold, and that sold for the "remarkably low price of THREE DOLLARS." Another was "California Gold Grease." This product sold for some ten dollars a tin, but if its directions were any indication, it was worth the money. All the erstwhile prospector had to do was carry a tin to California, climb the nearest gold country hill, strip naked, rub the grease over his body, and roll to the bottom. The result, since gold "and nothing else" would stick to the product, had more than a little resonance with Walter Raleigh's yearned-for "shining suit of gold" from an earlier age.[48]

These feverish productions begin to make sense, however, if viewed as arising out of fears of competition and longings for escape. As much as they would later stress their independence, most gold seekers depended on one thing above all: that California's plenitude would make competition, along with the fear of failure and humiliation, go away.

"Mr Atherton's Gold Lecture at the Tabernacle," published by the Washington *Globe*, was the most reassuring: "the supply of gold was absolutely inexhaustible; . . . *one hundred thousand persons* could not exhaust it in *ten* or *twelve years*."[49] Isaac Halsey, a New York City merchant, noted the "incredible stories" in the newspapers. He gave them physical, even sexual, resonance, again revealing linkages between California gold and physical desires. "The larger lumps, some of them weighing Several Tons would be taken possession of by their lucky finders," he claimed, ill concealing his passion; "mounting their huge proportions," the gold seekers would thus remain "astride their vast fortunes."[50]

These might be public fantasies, but they could be acted out, especially if they were projected west. There, the bourgeois could own the very desires denied by a crippling stress on respectability and solid work habits. Like others of his class, New York City physician James Tyson frequently extolled the virtues of hard work and earned success. Yet in 1849 he began to dream of a West "where precious metals were picked up with scarcely an effort." The region's assumed abundance lured him on, as he put it, to "take the wings of the morning and fly to the uttermost parts." Once there, he would find rest "in the midst of this earthly paradise." Another physician invoked the liberating qualities of California's wealth: he was going, he wrote, to "try for awhile the life of liberty and unrestrained indulgence; the future will show the result." Meanwhile, having long held the conception that life was a "battle," Elisha Oscar Crosby now reported that the air around him "seemed filled with a golden halo." The moment one of his law firm's clients, the Pacific Mail Steamship Company, offered to send him to California to check on the validity of the gold reports, he leapt at the chance to leave his humdrum employment.[51] No more than a few blocks away, and at about the same time, Frank Buck was busy trading his kid gloves and parlor manners for a shovel and tent. "Labor is capital out there," he wrote his sister, "I am assured by persons that have lived there that it is a fine country, perfectly healthy and room enough for us all."[52]

At the outset of 1849, these utopian visions were having their effect even on the most formerly skeptical and conservative. "It was agreed," exclaimed Boston's Garrett Low, "that a man of average strength and ability should be able to clean up a thousand dollars in thirty days, that is the first thirty days." For Low this amount was a "conservative figure"; but it was only a start, and he thought that the "second month and all thereafter should return much more."[53] These visions were also changing the gold seekers. As modern-day Jasons, they were about to become rich, or so onlookers assumed. And so they merited a grand send-off. The citizens of New Brunswick feted Doctor Taylor and his New Brunswick Mining and Trading Company in January, holding a "complimentary supper" for them at the end of the month.

Elsewhere, crowds gathered at city docks, hoping to get a look at these men as they sailed. These well-wishers were "composed of men women and children," noted one gold seeker, "Husbands wives, fathers, Mothers, Sons and Daughters, Uncles, Aunts, Cousins from first to forty second, besides numerous friends and acquaintances." All had been brought together by the "gold excitement." "It beats all! . . . this California fever," exclaimed Buck as he gazed at the throng: "The docks are crowded with fathers and mothers, brothers and sisters and sweethearts, and such embracing and waving of handkerchiefs and 'I say Bill! If you send me a barrel of Gold Dust don't forget to pay the freight on it!' One fellow who went in the Brooklyn, threw his last five dollar piece ashore. Says he: 'I'm going where there is plenty more!' "[54] For young men like Caspar Hopkins, the cult of respectability might still be a problem, the market might still be filled with devils. For others like Franklin Buck and New York's Joseph Chaffee, these anxieties had suddenly disappeared. Chaffee had no last-minute doubts concerning the outcome of his venture. He mingled with the crowd at his hotel near the wharves of New York City, thoroughly enjoying the scene. "We are all bound for the land of promise," he wrote his parents, "and according to all accounts there is enough for us all, So Hurrah!! for California!!"[55]

Finally, all of this talk of gold seemed to be transforming its meanings. On 14 January 1849, the Reverend Samuel Worcester came to the Tabernacle Church in Salem, Massachusetts, to address the members of the Naumkeag Mutual Trading and Mining Company before their departure. The Reverend was a bit uncomfortable. He knew his listeners were not, as he put it, "embarked on a religious enterprise," and that their "immediate object" was "pecuniary." In fact, he added, "I have never been very forward to speak in praise of wealth; for I have esteemed wisdom better than gold. And I have never thought it prudent for any man to be 'in haste to be rich': for there is the greatest danger, that 'he will not be innocent in so doing.' "

And yet the Reverend felt different about this enterprise. One difference was historical: why was it, he asked his listeners, that the Spanish, "so ferocious and blood thirsty in their search and rage for gold," had never discovered California's treasures? "It must certainly be that God has a purpose," he exclaimed. A second difference lay in the varied meanings of gold. Certainly, it was the "root of all evil." But this was not its only meaning, he noted: for gold had been mentioned in the Scriptures, once in connection with the Garden of Eden, "before the fall of man," again in a description of heaven, where it had served as pavement in the City of God.[56] Here indeed was the beginning of a great transformation. Gold would still on many occasions be "filthy lucre" and the "root of evil." But now, in addition, it had become pavement in the City of God, imbued with spiritual and utopian elements, and offering possibilities for escape, perhaps even for salvation.

Three

Husbands and Wives

In the midwinter of 1849, Harriet Dunnel ventured down to the New York City docks to watch her husband depart for California. Despairing but mindful of appearances, she had her carriage stop at an adjacent pier where she watched the departure from a distance, giving vent to her emotions in private, away from the boisterous crowd of spectators and well-wishers. John Dunnel's ship sailed. Harriet drove home, where in her words she "did little in the Afternoon but endeavor to compose myself." Later, in a letter to John, she wrote that although she felt that her "spirit" was with her husband, she scarcely trusted herself "to look across the bed at night for fear that I shall realize more fully my loneliness."[1] At about the same time, in Maine, Leah Rebecca Nash witnessed her husband's departure with a similar sense of despair. Returning to her home in Addison, she sat for the rest of the day with her two babies in her arms, "weeping bitterly" with the thought that her husband might never return.[2] Like thousands of women, Harriet Dunnel and Leah Nash were left in the East by their forty-niner husbands. They would not be left out of the experience.

Much of the focus on women's experience in the gold rush has been on the relatively few women who went to California, the rough and ready types who transgressed social conventions by entering a presumably male world of romantic adventure.[3] Far more commonly, women of the gold rush were like Harriet Dunnel and Leah Nash. They were on the perceptual margins of the event; left in the "states," they waited, suffered, and worked; but they were still in the home, and the home, according to the standard view of things, was a place where very little of importance or interest could possibly happen. These one-dimensional, binary images—fixed, dependent females contrasted with roving, independent males—are precisely the images that current historians of women would like to leave behind. These historians, particularly those working within the auspices of the New Western history, have urged a focus on women who left their eastern homes to go west, on women who *did something*, who were neither silent nor marginal to active experience, and who were real rather than fixed images of the masculine imagination.[4]

Certainly such an approach should be welcomed as a corrective to studies of the West that leave women out of the picture. As it applies to the gold rush, however, shifting the focus from the home to the West would remove all but a few northeastern women from the story. This approach also seems to bar these women's experiences and writings from cultural formation, implying that they had no role in the construction of frontier ideologies. And finally, while the goal of this approach may be to break down assumptions of separate male and female spheres along with ideological images of female passivity and male activity, it actually seems to confirm them. By focusing on women who went west, or who ventured out of the home as heroic models of female agency, it merely reconfirms the idea that the home was a place where nothing happened. Thus in the case of the gold rush, a return to the concept of the frontier as a dialogic process rather than a fixed locality might be in order.

All in all, the gold rush seems almost tailor-made to fit the pattern of separate male and female spheres. Truly, here is a seemingly clear case in which women were in the home and men in the world. These appearances are deceiving. Closer examination illumines extensive overlappings of interest and experience between men and women. A study of the dialogues between husbands and wives, women and men, indicates that men could not simply act as free individuals and take off for the gold country. Instead, they had to negotiate departures. These negotiations and dialogues brought women, along with the home, to the center of the experience.

The gold rush was a blend of imagination and action: an event framed as much by perspectives in the East as adventures in the West. From the first stirrings of the rush in the East, many observers envisioned this relationship as a gendered dialogue. As one poem that appeared in a Newark paper at the end of January 1849 illustrated it, this would be a dialogue between male adventure and female suffering, masculine yearnings for utopian brotherhood and wealth versus feminine ideals of duty, self-sacrifice, and sentimental love.

Away with the anvil, the hammer, the pen,
Their niggard assistance w'ell seek not again,
   Our western Golconda exploring;
For the magical touch of Midas we pine,
Though our hearts grow as hard as the metal we coin,
Its glittering beauty adoring.

This stanza of the poem portrays the gold seeker as a hard-hearted rebel against the work ethic of the marketplace and middle-class prescriptions against greed, the utopian promise of California as offering a space in which the characteristics and tools of opposing classes might be combined. In opposition to this manly exuberance, the poem then places this seemingly classless character within the context of the privatized home:

Ah! many a cherished home will fall,
And many a maiden's cheek grow pale,
   For one still this home-love forsaking;
Though missives of love to the wanderer are sent,
And many a message of seeming content,
While the heart that indicts them is breaking.[5]

For many observers, this dialogue would frame the gold rush from beginning to end. What made the rush so interesting, in other words, was the fact that the forty-niners were not unattached young men. Instead, the imagined gold seeker had a home; he had a family, a mother, a sister, a wife or mistress. All were forsaken for the love of gold and adventure. And yet, all would be a major part of the drama: they would be watched for their reactions, scrutinized for their shock and dismay at the forty-niners' behavior. Within this context, each example of forty-niner excess, every anecdote of his trampling of bourgeois moral codes, carried an extra frisson of excitement. In actual fact, the real forty-niner seems to have been little different. While probably no more than 30 percent of forty-niners were married, a far higher number would experience the rush through a prism of gender. If they did not have wives, they had mothers, sisters, daughters, and other female connections "back home." And it was to them, and for them, that they would most frequently write their letters and tell their tales of adventure. Through these communications, both men and women would negotiate the meanings of the event.

First, however, these family men had to negotiate their departures, and these negotiations were often fraught with difficulties. Undoubtedly, many women saw the lure of easy wealth and visceral male experience embedded within the imagined gold rush as a threat rather than an opportunity. Envisioned as an adventure, the voyage to California, not to mention the life in the gold fields, was too filled with risk and elements of irresponsibility to be supported within the dynamics of the privatizing family. That the rush was so often conceived in escapist terms no doubt contributed to women's reservations, particularly those of wives. For many, the gold country was an incomprehensible distance from the eastern seaboard. It could only be reached through a long and difficult sea voyage or a trek spanning the entire distance of the Overland Trail. This distance, coupled with the fact that the only real knowledge forty-niners had of these routes was that they were extremely dangerous and costly, meant that the vast majority of wives could not expect to go along with their husbands.

Yet, while the voyage to California meant a two-year separation from husbands or loved ones, women had reasons for supporting it as a business venture. They had their own aspirations for success. They were not averse to the things gold could buy; nor for that matter were all immune to the attractions of risk and adventure. "I really envy you reconnoitering the coast of the Pacific," wrote one grown-up daughter of an affluent New Hampshire gold seeker to her father, while another urged him on in the pursuit of wealth. "Do make a splendid fortune if it is possible," she wrote. "Every year I live I see how important money is to happiness. I no longer believe the twattle of poverty and happiness—poverty pulls down the best and noblest while wealth makes them comfortable."[6] In their negotiations over the departure of the forty-niners, these women revealed that they too envisioned wealth and independence as central elements of middle-class status. As well, they appear to have seen this status as the product of partnership rather than as a strictly male measure.

Constrained by mid-nineteenth-century domestic ideology, women had to negotiate the terms of this partnership carefully. Certainly the ideology is everywhere in the gender dialogues prior to the departure of men for California. Like a patchy fog, it enshrouds the negotiations, obscuring certain possibilities—such as the idea that women might actually accompany their husbands—while at the same time revealing others. Adhering to the widely disseminated domestic virtues of piety, purity, and submissiveness, forty-niner wives took care to recognize boundaries between male and female interests and identity. Still, constraint is not the same as denial of voice, nor is the recognition of boundaries the same as complicity with disempowerment. For many women, these boundaries might at times be welcomed as well as lamented. Knowledge of gender boundaries carried the knowledge of where they might be crossed or reconfigured. And if an ideology of separate spheres limited women's exercise of power over men, the actual separation of the gold rush threw women together. In the home they had the companionship of other women, a sense of independent self-worth, a measure of power over domestic affairs, and an idea of the juncture between these affairs and the presumably outside world of business activity.[7]

For all of its limitations, gender ideology did not relegate middle-class women to the margins either of the gold rush or of the marketplace as a whole. Female domesticity, as middle-class doctrine, reveals many of the contradictions pervading a social group trying to combine respectability with a competitive drive for success. On one hand, ideologues urged women to be content in the home. There, they would be on a pedestal. Cut off from the real world of cash and commodity exchange, they would be kept clear of the dirty world of male competition. On the other hand, the same writers urged them to make the home a place of bourgeois comfort and a showplace of status within an increasingly acquisitive culture. Thus domestic ideology created egresses from the home as well as boundaries for women. Although the rhetoric of domesticity drew lines, the walls of the domestic fortress could not be solid; they had to be permeable, allowing for the entrance of goods, commodities, and luxuries from the outside world.

For many women, this apparent contradiction undoubtedly created splits in attitudes toward the rush. Where gold rush rhetoric took the language of flight and escape, it generated uneasiness. Some articles in women's magazines evinced particular hostility to gold fever and those who dared give in to it. Few of these articles portrayed the gold seeker's home or wife as anything but happy, warm, and affectionate. Few saw any rationale for leaving this haven, holding instead that the only reasons for doing so were entirely irrational: abandonment, escape, or sheer madness.[8] The disturbing possibility that their men *were* running away from responsibility could bring women into direct conflict with their husbands' plans. Sometimes these confrontations worked. Mary Jane Hayden, who wanted to go with her husband but whose most recent child was too young to stand the journey, met her husband's plans with the threat of divorce. "We were married," she told him upon hearing his scheme, "to *live together* . . . under these circumstances *you have no right* to go where I cannot, and if you do, you need never return for I shall look upon you as dead."[9] Faced with this logic, her husband agreed to put aside his plans for a year.

Just as frequently, however, such tests of power did not end to the woman's advantage. Bitter scenes of departure could only have been preceded by bitter dialogues. These rancorous debates, however, might simply conclude with the assertion of the rights of patriarchy. As one observer described a son's leave-taking of his desperate mother, women could be frustrated at every attempt to forestall men's plans. This wealthy woman, the observer noted, followed her son to the wharves, where "with all the persuasions of a mother's eloquence and tears, [she] besought him not to leave her alone, offering him any sum of money he desired, to the amount of $20,000." In the end, however, her efforts fell on deaf ears, and the young man went his way. As the observer put it, "the love of adventure prevailed over a mother's tears and entreaties."[10]

If women were to support the gold rush, and thereby avoid such desperate scenes, they had to renegotiate motivations away from a "love of adventure" and toward a more equitable arrangement based on shared duties. This shift in thinking allowed them to join the gold rush as shared business partners. For them, the gold rush was best spoken of as a business enterprise, less as a romantic adventure than as a capital venture to which they could be full partners. These dialogues, in turn, contributed much to the motivations behind participation in the rush. For while containing desires for flight from the market, the constraints of polite culture, and the suffocating environment of the home, these motivations would also, as it turned out, contain elements of respectability and high purpose.

These elements are particularly evident in the organization of eastern mining and trading associations, the stock companies that in the early days of the rush represented the most popular means of travel to the Pacific. Membership in these companies, it must be remembered, could be tremendously expensive, and their advertisements were thus directed toward individuals with means and solid connections. Aware that prospective applicants had to justify going to California to wives and family members, company agents stressed that their enterprises represented the serious activities of respectable men. Presenting the

venture as something serious, even wholesome, they typically advertised the names of the "better sort" who joined their roles. One Philadelphia company, for example, continued to use the name of a leading
citizen to lure applicants so long after this merchant had changed his
mind about going that he complained. Claiming that he had "entirely
given up the notion of going to California," he added: "I would rather
you would not put my name in the paper any more; as it is necessary
for me to tell the people that I am not going, and the advertisements
contradict my assertions."[11]

Andrew Cochran, the man to whom this complaint was addressed,
was a Walnut Street merchant who recognized a business opportunity
when it came his way. Knowing the power of a good endorsement, he
left the advertisement unchanged, at least until he filled his company's
ship. Cochran's activities also indicate just how careful companies
could be in avoiding any members who lacked proper means. He
required references from younger applicants along with signed se-
curities from businessmen that these prospective members were finan-
cially solvent.[12] As with other agents, Cochran's most important task
was indeed, as the falsely advertised member put it, "contradicting
assertions." Among the assertions about the West was that it was a
place of raw lawlessness. Included in perceptions of potential company members was the idea that they were abandoning wives and
steady positions for the pursuit of ill-gotten lucre.[13]

These perceptions posed problems for potential gold seekers and
observing public alike: for while escape from gloomy counting houses
was one thing, complete loss of self-control was another. Company
organizers like Cochran attempted to deal with these perceptions in
their "Articles of Association." Ardently respectable in tone, blending
"masculine" purposefulness with "feminine" tenderness, these regulations for behavior appeared to have been designed to appeal not so
much to the young men in transition but to older forty-niners, men
who had to justify their plans to wives and families. In fact, these
bylaws appear to reflect precisely the prescriptions for the "ideal husband" of many mid-nineteenth-century marriage manuals. Like the
manuals, company articles typically warned against idleness, drinking,
smoking, gambling, swearing, and "licentiousness in every form." One
simply forbade all acts that were "unbecoming a Christian and a gentleman." Another offered a strict proscription against "intoxicating
liquors of any kind, except in case of emergency." Almost all established strict rules for duty and order during the voyage and in Califor-

nia, identifying and naming company officers from director to treasurer, bookkeeper, and secretary.

In an age that has been characterized as an "Era of Associations," perhaps none of this is very surprising. What may be more surprising is the extent to which these articles stressed that the gold rush might be joined in the name of moral reform, that it might actually make men better behaved, and that it offered a chance for a socialist reform of the competitive marketplace. On one hand, these documents stressed the serious, businesslike aspects of the voyage to California. One, for example, referred to the opportunity "now offered for active, enterprising young men to enrich themselves on our Western shores." On the other hand, they stressed communalism and sharing. As one article from New York's Perseverance Mining Company's contract stated: "It is agreed, and we hereby pledge ourselves, to support and protect each other in case of emergency and sickness, and in all cases to stand by each other as a band of brothers." In the words of one historian, the language of the articles reflected "idealistic and moralistic codes of conduct, and the concept of a socialistic brotherhood." As one forty-niner said at the time: "We were a commune—a socialistic order—who believed in the old Spartan division of all spoils. The sick, and the weak, were to be on one common level with the strong and well." Some company bylaws might even resonate with the intimacy and shared duties of a middle-class marriage contract. As the contract of the Bunker Hill Company of Salisbury, Massachusetts, stated: "we the undersign[ed] . . . members of said Association have mutually agreed to support each other for better or for worse."[14]

Typically, articles of association contained provisions for payments to wives and families in case of a forty-niner's death. Many companies had their articles published as broadsides, and they could also be taken home and shown to mothers, wives, and family members, serving as advertisements, calming fears of wilderness-inspired overindulgence and moral slippage. Thus company agreements altered at least some of the motivations for joining the California migration, frequently combining desires for escape with the elements of moral reform and a sense of duty. The "high purpose" of the rush, encoded in the rhetoric of duty, may have been at least partly a result of women's influence on the negotiations for departure.[15] As well, it may have allowed women to lend their support to the Californian venture.

Certainly, this seems to have been the case with Sabrina Swain. A highly religious woman who lived with her husband, William, on their family farm near Buffalo, New York, Sabrina worried constantly about the moral effects that gold seeking might have on her partner. Yet she tried to be supportive, at least for a time, especially after hearing that William had joined up with an overland association from Michigan. Mindful of the burden of responsibility that would be her share of the rush, she continued, however, to remind him of their separate but equally important duties. She consulted with him before he left on the drawing up of his will. She exacted the surety that he would be returning, as he put it, "with a pocketful of rocks." For his part, William Swain left with "the joyful reflection," as he later wrote from the Overland Trail, "that the separation is only temporary & that we are both in the line of duty."[16] This same rhetoric of duty may have allowed the more stay-at-home husbands among the forty-niners to join the rush. Brooklyn's Samuel Adams, for example, devoted his journal to his wife, Philomela, and his three children. In fact, he seems to have framed the entire experience as a measure of his devotion. "The wife that all are praising," he wrote in one of the first pages of his journal,

is not the wife for me
Too many eyes are gazing
   for love of purity
But I've a wife in yonder home
   whose love and charms are *mine* alone
So dearly do I love her
   Oh thats the wife for me[17]

Regardless of whether women could exact such professions of duty from husbands or loved ones, they might still recast the motivations of men to gain entry to the experience and to fit it to their purposes. Lucretia Prince, of New London, Connecticut, whose extremely close relationship with her brother Ephraim reveals that mid-nineteenth-century gender studies cannot be limited to relations between husbands and wives, transformed her brother's experiences into services to the family. Writing to another brother in New York, Lucretia noted Ephraim's promise to care for her along with her intention to someday join him in California. As for his gold hunting, she admitted that it was a "grate [*sic*] risk to run." Yet she remained hopeful: "he has got to run such a risk, in order to know, whether he can make anything or not . . . and I am in hopes it will all be for the best." Content for the moment to stay at home, Lucretia counted on Ephraim's gold to lift the Prince family—which along with Lucretia included Ephraim's father, who, she noted, had a difficult time staying sober—into the realm of respectability. Turning his motivations to suit her own needs and the well-being of the family, she solaced herself with the expectation that his activities offered "the hope of seeing better days."[18] Even as Ephraim Prince remained silent as to his motivations for joining the rush, Lucretia produced a rationale that fit her wishes.

For sheer excitement, companionate duty cannot match love of adventure as an organizing principle of the gold rush. Compared to the ritualistic fervor of the forty-niners, women's approaches to the undertaking seem strikingly serious. In certain rare contexts, however, duty and love might be transformed into a game of errant knights and towered ladies. Indeed, this seems to have been the case for Enos Christman and his fiancée, Ellen Apple, a young couple from West Chester, Pennsylvania. Envisioning the adventure and the difficulties of the voyage as trials to be faced in winning each other's esteem, both worked to combine gold seeking with romance. For his part, Enos pictured himself as a knight-errant, spending much of his time before departure discussing "the terrors of Cape Horn and the danger of long sea voyage" with his sweetheart, writing soon after that "no danger must be met half way, every difficulty should be met with manly fortitude, and my intention is to meet them in such a manner that I need never be ashamed." Ellen, meanwhile, wrote her wanderer with teasing accounts of other suitors. She reminded Enos that "I would have no objections to your returning with your pockets full of gold." In other letters, she playfully built upon the motif, disdaining the stay-at-home boys of West Chester as unworthy of her affections. Enos, after all, had gone to California on a dangerous and worthy quest: not merely for gold, but for Ellen's heart.[19]

This type of imaginative play was less available to married women. Perhaps because mid-nineteenth-century gender dynamics forced wives to express their desires in the idiom of domesticity, and because "duty" was a *mot clef* of this language, many of the dialogues prior to departure reflect the drawing of opaque screens between male and female experiences of the gold rush. The rhetoric of women does seem more serious than that of men. Yet when the record of these dialogues is more detailed, it is clear that there was a lot more to these negotiations of companionate duty than can be categorized under binaries of male jollity and female seriousness.

One of the key issues within these negotiations is that of power.

Some women had more power than others; and some, it appears, had more of a certain type of power than their husbands. The negotiations between Margaret and John Beeckman, for example, could only have proceeded with her as an equal if not senior partner. John Beeckman went to California with great plans: once there, he told his wife, he would invest in land and run for office. Yet it was Margaret who had the better political connections as sister-in-law to President John Tyler. Furthermore, she controlled the money. John's plans, from the cost of his voyage to the capital he took with him to buy land, were nearly entirely funded by Margaret's mother.[20] Similar arrangements characterized the efforts of other eastern gold seekers. Cornelius La Tourette, for example, farmed with his wife, Margaret, within the township of Bound Brook, New Jersey. The land they farmed, however, was on her ancestral homestead. To both La Tourettes this arrangement was something of a problem. Margaret's large family sometimes made the homestead a difficult place; it seemed entirely wanting in the necessities of privacy and peacefulness. Both envisioned the gold rush as a chance to purchase a farm of their own. And while Cornelius would take the more visible part in this partnership, he could not have followed his dream without the financial support of his wife and her kinship connections.[21]

Other wives had less power over their husbands. The experience of Mary Louisa Walker Hulbert, for example, seems to fit within a more patriarchal configuration of gender relations. Her husband, Eri, would define the meaning of duty alone. Mary had been with her husband, and had taken care of their three sons, through good times and bad. By 1849, the family was in the direst of straits. Having failed as a building contractor in the East, Eri had moved to Chicago, where he hoped to restart his construction business. Finally, with these plans stalled and his debts climbing, he decided to take the risk of going further west. "I can never extricate myself here," he wrote from Chicago, "because a man that has no means to do business with, can not more than support his family, and hardly that, particularly if harassed all the time with old debts."[22] By this time his fortunes had recovered, but only to a limited extent. Although he had built a store in Chicago and was running it, he was obviously still in debt; and while he could support his family after a fashion, middle-class ideals of masculinity required that he do more.

The negotiations for departure within the Hulbert family reveal that a sense of manhood, a willingness to take the risks necessary to do more than just "get by," was as important as money in the minds of the gold seekers. At the same time, if the seeking of wealth was understandable, the man-making side of the forty-niners' constellation of desires may have appeared inscrutable to wives and family members. Mary Louisa Hulbert thought her husband had become "almost crazy." It was a "desperate idea," she later recalled: "none but God will ever know how stunningly the first announcement of his determination fell upon me—I begged, I prayed, I besought—But all in vain. He said my dear wife God only knows the trial it is to me to go and leave you and my children—But duty requires it."[23] This admission that "none but God" knew how stunned she was may indicate that despite her admitted pleadings, she withheld some of her reservations and eventually lent her support to Eri's plans. Yet, as she sewed her savings into a money belt that she later bestowed upon her husband, she may have been wondering what he had meant in his reference to "duty." For women like Mary Hulbert, overpowered by their husbands, silenced by their grand plans, the gold rush would frequently be experienced through feelings of abandonment and loss.

At the same time, it would be unwise to assume that patriarchal power framed all dialogues between men and women, even in 1849. Mid-nineteenth-century gender relations were characterized by conceptions of romantic love and intimacy as much as they were by separate spheres and male dominance. Within the discourse of romantic love, women could exercise power over men, requesting reciprocal and equal expressions of emotion, sincerity, and compassion. In requesting the love of women, that is, men had to express their emotions and admit their dependence. In withholding this love, women could make demands and exercise power. Thus romantic love might serve to ameliorate power relations between women and men, even within an ideology of domesticity.[24] In certain cases, such as Enos and Ellen's, the ideal of romantic love seem to have worked this way.

In others, it did not. As it was used by Henry Billington Packer, the rhetoric of romantic love seems to have actually contributed to his power to create truths about the gold rush and to silence his fiancée's reservations about his departure. Like many ambitious young men in the mid-nineteenth century, Packer was highly mobile and open to new ideas in his search for business opportunities. A lapsed Quaker, at age twenty-six he moved from his hometown of Pittsburgh to Illinois just prior to the gold rush. There, while making a meager living lecturing on the curative powers of hypnosis, or "magnetism," he met Mary

Elizabeth Judkins, another recent immigrant to the Midwest, from Vermont. Frequently away while he magnetized people on his lecture circuit, he began courting Mary in letters. In doing so he followed the proper dictates of romantic courtship, consciously eschewing an elevated writing style in favor of true expression and emotion. He urged Mary to express herself in a similar manner, warning her away from stilted prose and the exaggerated language of propriety. "Such a style," he wrote, "I cannot sanction." Instead, he told her that both should adopt "the principle of perfect candor and confidence." "I wish the phraseology and real meaning to perfectly harmonize," he explained, "making use of no words or phrases which would be likely to convey to the person addressed, an impression or idea differing in the least, from that which is really *felt* by the writer. . . . I feel like keeping a little below, rather than getting above, the reality."[25]

While Mary's letters do not survive, it is likely that this assertion allowed for a large degree of reciprocal intimacy and shared feelings. At the same time, this rhetorical device could elevate the content of Henry's missives, giving his emotions additional power. In Henry's woo-pitching, such emotional power would come in handy, lending his "Lines on the Presentation of a Parasol to a Lady Friend," included in the same letter, a certain cachet that the rhyme might otherwise lack.

When summer's genial Suns
On Earth with fervor beam,
How pleasant then, to seek the shade
Beside some cooling stream.

How pleasant then with those we *love*
To while away the time,
In pleasant groves and sylvan shades,
That art and nature thus combine.

When thou'rt obliged to walk the streets,
On errand of mercy or friendly call,
And canst not keep to shady groves
Then please to use the parasol.

If fortune says I'm n'er to meet,
with thee—thou friendly—M.E.J.
Permit me now to sign myself
Thy friend, and brother—H.B.P.[26]

Given this missive's introductory remarks, it is likely that Mary read these lines with pleasure. Yet the intimacy and emotional charge that could raise this example of Victorian distance into an expression of love might also serve to confirm the emotions leading Henry to join the rush to California. "Symptoms of the California fever are pretty strongly manifested sometimes," he wrote toward the end of 1849. Deciding to join the migration, he expressed his decision to Mary; here, the intimacy of his professed desire to depart along with his expressed frustration with his work may be considered a demand for her support. The travel involved in lecturing, he explained, pleased him "first rate." At the same time, midwestern audiences, composed, as he put it, of "religious biggots, superannuated old dotards and block-heads," did not always cotton to his newfangled science of magnetism. His competitors among the more traditional healers were skeptical for better reasons, and worse, their skepticism was bad for business. "In this town is a little bullet headed Doctor, who thinks he knows everything," he wrote Mary while on his lecture circuit, "I think it would puzzle him to know beans from shot."[27] Henry's intimate exposure of frustration may have left Mary little room in which to argue against his gold-seeking plans. Certainly, California had more to offer than this dismal picture. Thus, even within a discourse of romantic love, Henry dominated the negotiations over his departure, and Mary was silenced.

The same dynamic cannot be said to exist in the negotiations between Alfred and Chastina Rix. Nowhere, perhaps, is there a more detailed example of dialogues between forty-niner wives and their husbands than can be found in this couple's remarkable diary. Born in Canada in 1822, Alfred Rix moved to Vermont as soon as he finished college. By 1841 he had founded a school in Wolcott, a small town in the isolated north-central region of the state. There, he immediately met and fell in love with one of his older students, Chastina Walbridge. Two years Alfred's junior, by 1843 she had joined him as a fellow teacher. The couple married in 1849, moving to Peacham, another small town near Alfred's school. From the outset, their marriage reflected a bond of partnership. The day of their marriage, they began a diary, warning the world, in its first entry, "from this day forth to address us as Mr. & Mrs. and also, especially, to kick every dog that barks at us."[28] As might be garnered from this entry, the diary is a playful document. It is all the more unique in that Alfred and Chastina

filled it with alternate entries. Forming what may be read as an intimate conversation fully within the middle-class discourse of romantic
love, these entries provide insight into the private dynamics of mid-
nineteenth-century marriage and bourgeois aspiration. Most of all,
they reveal that the pressures to succeed and the motivations that led
men to join the gold rush could be shared concerns.

In many respects, the Rix diary reflects a clear contrast between
Alfred's attempts to get ahead in the public world of the market and
Chastina's activities in the private sphere of the home. In several of her
entries, Chastina recorded that much of her time was taken up in
washing. By 1851, she was busy with the care of a newborn child, referred to as "bub." She spent much of her time with other women,
often joining them in Peacham's "reading circle." Her husband, having
cut back on his teaching in search of more remunerative work, was
often away from home in his new capacity as an adding machine sales-
man. Many of Chastina's activities, however, were within Peacham's
cash and credit network. Still operating, although in difficult straits,
the school was the couple's primary shared concern. In February 1850
they noted that enrollment had fallen to forty-three students. Despite
the declining number of students, Chastina continued as a teacher of
drawing and writing classes. In addition to her activities in the class-
room, she had time to engage with Alfred in debates concerning slavery, Thaddeus Stevens, and the "free soilers." During Alfred's absences, she also took care of the couple's business dealings. She often
recorded the receipt of "dunning letters," along with the regular sending of similar letters to neighbors and merchants.[29]

By May 1850, there were financial worries in the Rix household.
Commenting on the increasing needs of the family with the birth of
their child, Chastina added that "we are rather poor now days." Two
days later the first mention of the gold rush appears in the diary. "Saw
some Calafornia gold sent home by John [May]," wrote Alfred, du-
biously adding that a letter accompanying the souvenir had warned
"any one who wants to come to Calafornia to stay at home."[30] Despite
this advice, Alfred was interested. He must have checked further into
the news from the Pacific, for two weeks later he had corrected his
spelling of California.

In August, the Rixes celebrated their first wedding anniversary.
"Within the year which is now gone," began Alfred's poem to mark the
occasion,

Let's see, Chastina, what's been done.
First we have slept from 9 till 6!
Quite unbecoming thee and Rix!
Bright mornings passing, while in bed.
A young, strong pair lie stretched stone dead!
Shame, Shame upon you! Get you out
Betimes and stir yourselves about,
Or Bed bugs, lice and moths will crawl
Upon you and devour you all.

Next we have spent in fun and laughter
And in the scraps that follow after,
Two hours each day—a loss of time
I cannot reckon quite a crime
For I have thought and still am thinking
That fun will keep a man from drinking.[31]

Alfred's poem, while partly a charming celebration of sex and leisure, ironically linked the couple's uncertain economic status with a lack of ambition. Although playful, it contained a serious call for concerted economic activity, and it came at a time when both were increasingly on the lookout for an opportunity. Not immune to the bruit of hucksters and advertisers, they turned their sights and ambitions to the gold country. In June 1850, Alfred noted California's admission as a state. Chastina, meanwhile, averred her satisfaction that it had entered as part of the "free soil" contingent. For some time, the couple had continued to receive letters from John May, a fellow Peachamite who apparently, despite his earlier reports, was doing well in California.[32] As 1850 drew to a close, Alfred and Chastina saw increasing numbers of their neighbors depart for the Pacific. In January 1851, the couple loaned a friend, referred to only as "Hale," some money for the trip. Watching as he left, "all in a puff for California," Alfred remarked wistfully that while "we may be anxious to see our brothers & friends well off as to gold, . . . I wish to Heaven every noble and big hearted young man like Hale could find honorable & comfortable homes without running such risks as he runs."[33]

Yet even as they admitted that Hale was taking a great risk, Alfred and Chastina seem to have been feeling growing compulsions to try similar measures. Leading up to Alfred's decision to join the rush, the Rix diary provides evidence of a typical pattern: for it contains all the anxieties and tensions regarding the limiting constraints of respectability, perceptions of the market as a space dominated by devils, and fears of being isolated from the outside world. Peacham was a small town, yet it was not isolated from the pervasive talk of gold, nor was it devoid of prescriptions for proper behavior. Even there, in other words, the couple appears to have shared a perception that their energies were being stifled by hypocritical admonitions to accept their lot, to be respectable, and to avoid the mammon-seeking schemes of the younger generation.

Meanwhile, spring had come and Alfred, seeing perhaps his last chance to join the rush while gold seemed plentiful and easy to find, had grown tired of these "stale" sermons. He surmised that their church was being taken over by the will of overly respectable old men. "We have no sympathy with such operations," he wrote. He maintained that these attempts at social control reflected "at best a foolish mockery—to call on the youth who has just come to the age of feeling & excitability to unite with a lot of old hard hearted hypocrites & bury his fun & police his [love] of life in the grave of empty devotions." Chastina, too, was becoming fatigued with the couple's humdrum affairs: "Cook, cook, cook, & eat is my business," she complained, "I am just about tired out." And, in what is possibly a reference to the news and conversation that finally settled the matter, she added that she and Alfred had "heard from Hale. He is well."[34]

Undoubtedly liberals by choice, but also by the contingencies of their status as a young couple in search of opportunity, Alfred especially, but Chastina as well, bridled under the cult of a respectable "middle station." By the early summer of 1851, they had made up their minds: Alfred would go to California to make his fortune. Equating respectability not with middle-class virtue but with poverty, Alfred mused that if "a poor man dies, nobody has a word to say against him if he has kept clear of the State Prison—while if a rich man dies he is cursed anyhow & sent to hell if he has not acted in all things like a saint. This is unjust. Give Satan his due & rich men too."[35] Desirous of more than respectability, by September Alfred was prepared to beat the devil and break with the past. "A man with gumption goes by it," he declared in the diary, "one without any goes where his father did."

Chastina was less willing to make such a drastic break. If Alfred seemed intent on forging new paths to success, she was determined that he should take at least some of the family with him. There is nothing in the Rix diary to suggest that the couple ever discussed the possibility of Chastina going to California. Their child, after all, was not quite two years old and probably could not have withstood the voyage. At the same time, when preparations are discussed, they are done so in terms of a family venture. As we might assume from these entries, it was only within this context that Chastina could lend her support. Alfred would go to California with a party that included his brother Sidney, from Peacham, another brother, Oscar, from Boston, and Chastina's brother Dustan Walbridge. Chastina still had her doubts, both about the risk Alfred would take and her ability to fend alone for herself and their child. She noted, at the end of September, that her husband was "doing up his business as fast as possible, I dont know what will become of poor me when [he] goes." Still, as a member of the family prospecting party, she willingly opened her house to, and appears to have taken part in, meetings to discuss the costs and preparations involved in the expedition.[36]

Two days before Alfred's departure, the Rixes shared their last night out together. In a setting as quaint as it was resonant with their hopes, they talked about Alfred's voyage while visiting a rolling panorama of the Garden of Eden. If Chastina had any bitterness about her husband's impending departure, she kept it to herself, or at least out of the diary. The next night, while Alfred packed, she recorded the callings of relatives, mentioning only what a "sore trial" it was "to think of parting with a husband for so long a time." Despite her misgivings, the next day, at one-thirty in the morning, she awoke to help Alfred in his early start. The party left at dawn. Suddenly faced with the loneliness that her support required, Chastina at last gave vent to her feelings. "It is hard," she wrote, "to part with a friend when the hand of death is laid upon them. And hard too it is to part with one where danger lies in their track. Never shall I forget our parting; if it be the last there is sweet consolation in the thought that we were & ever have been the happiest of the happy in each others society. He has gone! The hours are days. Lonely and sad am I. & and our little boy he misses his papa."[37]

The Rix diary appears to contain surprisingly equitable power relations, at least according to many assumed dynamics of mid-nineteenth-century marriage. At the same time, if Chastina's voice was unusually clear in the couple's negotiations for departure, it was still constrained by dominant gender expectations. Her role in the gold-seeking venture was to stay at home, to take care of the couple's child, to maintain the family's domestic business. Much of her experience of the rush would be through imagining Alfred's adventures. "This afternoon Alfred sailed for Calafornia," she mused three days after his departure, "while I am at home with our boy by my side, he is borne onward and away on briny sea." Each of her entries for the following week would be a commentary on loneliness. "If I could only know," she wrote, "how & where Alfred & the rest of our friends were it seems as though I could feel some better."[38] In the long days waiting for Alfred to return with the gold that would raise the couple's fortunes, Chastina might also discover what it was to be a middle-class woman. She was not alone in her dependency. She missed her husband terribly, but he, too, as she found, depended on her for emotional and financial support. She would have to keep the Rix home intact, to stave off creditors and send out dunning letters, until he could send some money. Alfred and Chastina needed each other; and in this respect their close ties, along with their liberality of expression, were entirely characteristic of other middle-class gender arrangements during the gold rush.

The lines of mutual reliance connecting the Rixes seem especially clear. Similar reciprocal needs evidenced in the communications between forty-niner wives and their husbands give lie to narrow conceptions of nineteenth-century gender in terms of independent, active men and dependent, passive women. Certainly, the aspiring middle-class men of the gold rush had the preponderance of visible and experiential activity. Written communications between husbands and wives indicate, however, that if anything the forty-niner husbands relied on their wives more than their wives depended on them. This evidence calls for a repositioning of women away from the margins to a place between the home and the West. Many researchers have noted the incredible amount of writing done by the forty-niner men; a few have correctly pointed out that they wrote with an audience in mind.[39] Even in their personal journals, the gold seekers' primary audience was their wives. These wives were more than willing readers; they were also editors and confidantes. As one miner concluded his journal: "you will see that I have made a blunder in writing this as is usual when I have not got you to show me how . . . you must fix it to suit you if you can for I cannot."[40] The accounts these women would help frame would be concerned with more than an exposition of male independence and female passivity.

For mid-nineteenth-century men, independence was measured by one's powers as a provider. The more people depended upon the male head-of-household, in other words, the more independent and masculine he became. Male conceptions of independence, in effect, required an assumption of female dependency.[41] If, however, forty-niner calls for help are any indication, as it was expressed in the gold rush this independence was shaky at best. Although free to move in the outside world, they were not free of the pain of loneliness. "About two thirds are married men that go to Cal.," wrote one gold seeker, and if his statistics were exaggerated, his conclusions were not: for they looked, as he put it, "rather sorry . . . when they think of their wives and children dear."[42] At the moment of departure many of these men faced a truth that notions of male independence denied. In that "dreaded moment," as one forty-niner wrote while pulling out of New York Harbor, "we feel an anguish that words fail to express or pen convey, in a moment like this, we feel and feel Keenly, the sacrifice made in this voluntary Exile from Home."[43]

Having seen the forty-niners off for the gold fields, crowds in the East awaited letters as first installments in a series of visceral adventures. In the letters the gold seekers sent back for publication, the crowd got what it wanted. What many wives received, however, were private missives of regret, tacit admissions of a fool's errand. At home in Addison, Maine, Leah Nash may have been surprised at her husband's first report. Jared, she read, was having a "trying time." Surrounded by "sickness and death," he could only report his desire to "wish himself at home." In upstate New York, Sabrina Swain read that her husband's mind was filled not with buffalo herds or waves of prairie grass, but with visions of home and "emotions that require my greatest self control to suppress." "Indeed my dear!" he added, "I have . . . only learned the strength of my feelings by separating myself from those I love." In New Jersey, Francis Alexander read her husband's declaration that he could "never Eat, sleep nor Drink" without thinking of home.[44]

Many forty-niner wives appear to have been waiting for these first letters to give some kind of structure to the event. Sara Pierce wrote soon after her husband left Troy, New York, that she was so shocked by his going through with the venture that for a time "I did not know . . . what I was about—it seem[ed] like an ugly dream." Sabrina Swain echoed these feelings, writing her husband that when she thought "of the separation for a moment it seems like a dream."[45] What the receipt of the forty-niners' first letters may have revealed to women, however, was that their husbands were in over their heads. The venture was going to be a lot more difficult than had been imagined. Having negotiated their husbands' departures in terms of companionate duties, these women read that their work would be real and recognized. In turn, the burden of responsibility, at least until their husbands could make it through to California and start sending bank drafts home, would be theirs.

Faced with the admission that their husbands were counting on them to provide, it may have taken a while for women to respond to their husbands' needs or fully realize their new positions. To Elizabeth Martin, of Chelsea, Massachusetts, the whole business seemed downright unbelievable. Accordingly, she wrote her husband that she would have sent more letters but thought he would abandon his efforts when he came to his senses. "Every one thought you would sell the vessel down the Coast," she wrote, referring to her conversations with other Chelsea company wives, "and I had more hopes of your coming home than of your going to San Francisco."[46] Granted, before their departures, most husbands willingly conveyed their expectations that wives would handle their business affairs.[47] But this was only theory. With the news that their husbands would be a while in remitting any money, and that in the meantime only women's work at home could contribute to the venture's success, many women found themselves in the curious position of being recognized masters of home *and* the business world.

Here then was a dramatic inversion of gender expectations. Women were seen, men unseen; wives were at work, husbands were off doing very little but complaining, for the time being at least. Even stranger, some husbands seemed willing to recognize that usual gender relations had somehow been turned upside down. "I think every day of the responsibilities thrown upon you by my absence," wrote one forty-niner to his wife, "I earnestly hope & pray you may be sustained and guided by the Almighty in the arduous duties."[48] Mary Locke, of Summerville, Massachusetts, read her husband's admission that "I saw more plainly than ever when I left the difficulties attending your situation." And if he added his hope that "your courage will not fail," she could also note his recognition of her strength: "it is not as through you never had any trials to cope with." Nine months after leaving home Jonathan was still counting on Mary's courage, hoping that she could make her supply of coal last "till you get something from me which I hope will not be long."[49]

Between 1849 and 1852, thousands of eastern men left their homes and families for the gold country. A very high percentage of these men had to negotiate the terms of their departure with wives and loved ones. In the process, both sides frequently engaged in unavoidable renegotiations of gendered lines of work and duty. While these negotiations might not significantly alter the actual work of women, they did contain a certain amount of rethinking of what this work would mean. Gold rush wives would have to take on responsibilities for the upkeep of the home and business. Forty-niner husbands would have to recognize, and count upon, their wives' creativity, strength, and abilities. These were not new responsibilities; maintaining the home had never separated most of these women from regular engagement with business, credit, or cash exchange. What was new was the admission that they could do it alone.

Dependent as they were on their loved ones' abilities to get by, above all, married gold seekers relied on their wives to maintain lines of communication. As Rebecca Nash read in one letter, her husband did not know when he would be able to send any money. At the same time, however, he urged her to "take the best care" of the family, and to "write to me at every opportunity and let me know how you get along, and what takes place." Another forty-niner apologized for not sending anything home but promised that he would "try to make some money to send you as soon as I can." He concluded with an admission of his need: "you must write often I would give anything I have to get a letter."[50] Thus, left in demanding situations and urged to communicate their experiences, California widows received an invitation to explore their creativity and self-expression. Prior to their husbands' departures, many had negotiated lines of separate duties; now, they were about to find that their own part in these duties might be much greater than they had imagined.

Throughout the period of the gold rush, departures would continue to constitute much of the romance and imagery of the event. For the most part, these leave-takings have been portrayed according to the seemingly natural rights of patriarchy, as monologues, the noisy and rugged independence of the gold seeker on one side, the silent and self-sacrificing passivity of forty-niner wives on the other. Certainly, men frequently depicted them in this manner at the time, even in women's magazines. The epigraph to Park Benjamin's poem "The California Gold-Seeker to His Mistress" stated that the forty-niner man heard a voice that a woman could not hear, saw a hand that she could not see. Voice and hand pointed to wealth and gold, along with yearnings for adventure. Once the poem had denied women access to these yearnings, the rest was the usual stuff of flight and fantasy:

FAREWELL, dear heart, awhile farewell!
   I go o'er land and sea;
For wealth I brave the billows' swell
   Afar from love and thee.
The vessel waits—the gathered crew,
   With hope and vigor bold,
Impatient long for regions new
   That teem and burn with gold.

Free as a bird that cleaves the air
   On pinions never slow,
An onward, upward course I dare,
   Nor pause to look below.
And oh! believe if adverse fate
   Shall pierce my faithful breast,
It ne'er will own another mate
   Nor find another nest.

Then dash away the tears that shade
   Those fond, expressive eyes;
Thy cheeks' red roses shall not fade
   Ere I obtain the prize.
Give courage to my heart, and be
   My light and leading star,
That with confiding trust to thee
   I still may turn from far.[51]

In April 1849, many of *Godey's* readers probably found this bit of male sentimentalism charming; some may have even blinked back a few tears. Many forty-niner wives, in turn, may have read it with different feelings, and blinked in disbelief. For they were never quite so deaf to the voice of wealth and gold, never quite so blind to the hand that pointed to California. Few were so powerless and passive when faced with husbands' and loved ones' gold-seeking plans. In fact, urged to be creative in men's absence, urged to write every feeling in letters, they might discover their own means to produce experience through literature. These productions might not be so sentimental.

Of the writers of "sentimental" literature who came to dominate the women's fiction of the mid-nineteenth century, it was E.D.E.N. Southworth who actually experienced the departure of her husband for

California during the rush. But it was Fanny Fern's 1854 novel, *Ruth Hall*, that included perhaps the best women's version of gold rush departure fantasies. One of the novel's supporting characters is a husband, Mr. Skiddy, who constantly dreams of going to California. Mrs. Skiddy halts his plans at every turn. Finally Skiddy escapes, literally fleeing his "hen-pecking" wife for the freedom of the gold regions. About a year later, he writes home: he has failed in the gold regions, his life in California has been dominated by ill luck, and he needs his wife to send him money for the passage home. And here, we may see what would be the result of at least one woman's creativity. Mrs. Skiddy had been abandoned by her husband, but she had not been left out of the gold rush. For in the end, she would make his experience what it was. According to Fern, she examined the letter, drew from "her pocket a purse well filled with her own honest earnings," rolled the coins between her fingers, and, with her teeth set, hissed "like ten thousand serpents" one extremely powerful word: "N-e-v-e-r!"[52]

Four

Numberless Highways to Fairy Grottos

In the mid-nineteenth century the middle-class man stood on the shores of a sea of temptation. Metaphors of respectability stressed rigidity and stiffness: the good man firmed himself up to retain prescriptions against forbidden behaviors, he "steeled" himself against the ebb and flow of carnal desires. Sin, in turn, was very fluid. As the Reverend Lyman Beecher described it in 1826, intemperance threatened these shores of respectability "like a flood; and if anything shall defeat the hopes of the world, . . . it is that river of fire." By 1834 masturbation had become such a common indulgence that it called forth an even more alarming metaphor: in the words of one reformer, it threatened to sweep "a widespread tide of desolation, over our land and the world." By the 1840s, it seemed to some observers that the proper Anglo-European character was about to be inundated: Americans by a "deluge" of Irish immigrants, the rest of the civilized world by a flood carrying all the dark flotsam of the orient: Hungarians, Muscovite "hordes," "Japhetic Races," and Panslavism.[1] Along the edges of this swirling maelstrom, the good man's goals might be summed up in three simple admonitions: stay dry, remain always on shore, do not go near the waters of temptation. In the midst of these warnings, some 40,000 northeastern forty-niners took to the ocean in pursuit of what they freely admitted was the root of evil. Many would—for a moment at least—allow themselves to be swept away by this sea.

From January 1849 through the end of the year, the emigration that would become known as the gold rush was at "swell tide." By the end of this period, *Hunt's Merchant's Magazine* had counted nearly 800 ships, barks, brigs, and schooners leaving from North American ports: 214 from New York City, 151 from Boston, the rest from smaller mar-

itime centers like Philadelphia and New Bedford along with the southern ports of Baltimore and New Orleans. This was a strange and varied
armada. Many of these were recently built three- or four-mast ships
manned by capable crews. Others were worm-eaten brigs or former
whalers relegated to dry dock but bought and hurriedly reequipped
for one last voyage. By January 1850, the office of the harbormaster at
San Francisco would estimate the total number of these shipboard
emigrants at nearly 40,000, the vast majority from the American
Northeast. Most of these individuals—about two-thirds of the total
number—would travel a route 13,328 miles long, sailing around Cape
Horn in a voyage usually lasting from 150 to 200 days. Others would
take a shorter route by steamer via the Colombian Isthmus of Panama,
yet still cover prodigious distances in their 30 to 90 days at sea.[2]

Argonauts all, these men were reversing a moral trend, voyaging
into uncharted waters, entering dark and unethical territories. There
were elements of "unrighteousness" and "ungodliness" in this undertaking, proclaimed the Reverend Samuel Worcester in a warning to his
California-bound listeners at Salem's Tabernacle Church. And yet, he
added, like the "Mayflower Pilgrims," they might bring civilization to
the wilderness of California—if, that is, they could resist the sea of
temptations along the way. They would have to be careful, guarding
their identities, watching themselves at all times. In order to fend
against the idleness that might lead to these temptations, he told them
to "keep a diary, or a journal."[3] A month later, at sea aboard the
schooner *Edward Everett* out of Boston, the Reverend Joseph Augustine Benton urged his listeners to similar self-awareness. The object of their quest, he told them, was not merely gold but a new linkage
between the spirit and the body. Even if the desire was material and
bodily, he maintained, "the desire accomplished is sweet to the soul."[4]
He too urged his listeners to keep up their diaries.

A very large number of forty-niners, it seems, did try to keep idle
hands busy by writing journals. Many had purchased notebook, pen,
and ink prior to departure; most recognized that this would be the
greatest adventure of their lives. Yet here they faced a problem: once
out on the ocean, the sky might be empty, the sea a blank and seemingly endless circle of blue, nothing on the horizon, no sound except
the creak and groan of a ship and the wind in the sails. A world of
competition was behind them; a utopia of abundance lay ahead. In the
meantime, during this long moment between, when nothing seemed to
be happening, what were they going to write about?

Historians continue to be amazed at the sheer volume of these writings, and somewhat confused about what to make of them. Among scholars of the gold rush the most common approach to forty-niner journals has been to portray them as "pure" or "unmediated" narratives of events. Presented as unvarnished by literary pretense or creative sentiment, these accounts are supposed to represent a kind of antiliterature, a direct window onto external stimuli, written in a language of authentic and immediate experience. This approach, it would appear, has worked for overland diaries. Here, forty-niner narratives may be followed across a varied landscape: the vast prairies stretching from Saint Louis, the Rocky Mountains, the sun-blasted salt flats of Utah and Nevada, the snowbound passes of the Sierras. Along the way came adventures: encounters with buffalo, Indians, and Mormons; scenes of heroic perseverance: storms raged, wagons overturned, horses and oxen died in their traces, and still the pioneers struggled to reach California. The approach has worked far less well for the journals of seagoing gold seekers. Most of these accounts evince a bland sameness of experience, a repetitious record of weather phenomena, miles traveled during the day, the times of sunrise and sunset. The result, according to one historian, is that "scores of such documents are all but indistinguishable from one another." The "element of common experience was large," adds another, "and the repetitions from diary to diary are striking."[5]

The problem here may not be the documents but the approach. For having defined these journals against literature and creativity, having valorized external experience over internal sentiment, these historians have missed, or dismissed, much of their content. Indeed, very little actually happened along the sea route to break the monotony of the long voyage. What did happen often occurred with rhythmic sameness: there were storms off Cape Horn, occasional passing ships, more storms on the high seas, more ships, more storms. Many accounts are filled with little more than day-to-day records of weather and mileage. Frequently however, this lack of stimuli contributed an imaginative depth to diaries. The tedious rhythms of the sea voyage threw forty-niners onto their internal resources. And within the interstices between weather reports—sometimes displacing them entirely—one finds precisely the elements many historians say should not be there: wild flights of fantasy, efforts at literary style, experiments with metaphor and identity. Perhaps above all else, these are literary documents, records not of events but feelings, sentiments, and impulses. As such, they provide unique insights into nineteenth-century creativity. This creativity, in turn, would be characterized by play, by imaginative constructions of a utopian world apart from the rigid boundaries of life on shore, apart from the dictates of respectability and the requirements of the marketplace. Out on the ocean, many forty-niners shuffled off the rigid coil of dry respectability, replacing it with yearnings for self-immersion, for flow, for the free play of oceanic possibilities lying somewhere between the poles of prescription and desire. Within these writings, in other words, we may discover the secret yearnings of a rising middle class.

As they left eastern ports, gold seekers opened their journals and began to write. Their first entries were easy, for they had just experienced a powerful moment of departure. "It was a trying time," wrote one as his ship drifted out of New York Harbor, "at the last moment bidding our Sisters, Brothers, Fathers and Mothers and (some wives) Friends farewell no one knows but he is bidding the last farewell—to some of them!" William Graves of New Hampshire gazed ashore for the first hour or so after sailing, "bidding adue to the land of our Bearth and dropping a Teer in Rememberence." "But adue," he finally added, "to those tyes and adue to those pleasures for the present for it is my intention to keepe a journal of the voyage and therefore I must commence."[6] Another New Yorker, David Demerest, depicted the moment of departure as a blend of hope and fear, high spirits and argonaut tears. "How different were the thoughts and feelings of these 70 men," he wrote; some were "full of hope," some lost in "dreams of gold." "And as the last hills were fading from their view," he added, "a silent tear was dropped to the memory of those left behind—and some even then wished themselves back at home."[7] Still others experienced the departure as a moment of anticipation rather then sadness. "I think whe shal hav good times in California," wrote a departing New Yorker to his sister. Leaving Boston, another adventurer wrote that "as soon as we swung clear of the wharf we had three hearty cheers which were returned by the company, all in good spirits with the exception of two or three."[8]

Once out on the high seas, however, there seemed little to write about and much time to write. The only action, if such it could be called, was the slow roll of the ship, the continuous rise and fall of a liquid horizon. The only event worth noting was seasickness. "The lee-rail is lined with demoralized passengers," wrote one forty-niner, "paying their tribute to Old Neptune. Those who are not able to pay their respects to the deity of the great deep over the rail are casting up their accounts in buckets, wash-basins, and spittoons."[9] With this experience came a feeling among many that they were being emptied out, drained of their shore existence, that they were undergoing some type of transformation, a ritual of death and rebirth. Some resigned themselves with humor and style, adding comic touches to their illnesses after the fact. As Robert Hutchinson, aboard the *Belgrade* out of Cherryfield, Maine, explained it, the "grandeur of the scene now began to excite in some of our stomachs . . . peculiar emotions. Among other things, a sympathy for the . . . tribes of the ocean, prompted us to do what we were most inclined to do, which was to feed them from our intensely naceated stomachs. To come right to the point we were most essentially sea sick."[10] Another wrote that his "dinner and stomach, . . . not wishing to be odd, had struck up a quarrel and made up their minds to part company which they did with a vengeance." He could not avoid recognizing the helplessness that ensued as bodies went limp. "Such woe begone countenances & such supplications and prayers, I will warrant are not often heard. I have heard of dogs eating their own vomit, but here were men wallowing in each other's to say the least."[11]

Seasickness was the "great leveler," recalled Hubert Howe Bancroft, who sailed to California in 1852. It "prostrates pride, purges man of his conceit, makes him humble as a little child; it is especially conducive to repentance and after repentance to resignation." There was nothing like it for bringing on a fear of death, he added, and nothing else "that makes one so ready to die." As their ships rolled in heavy swells and they emptied themselves to the fishes, many gold seekers drew sentimental and morbid pictures, suffering through their own imagined death scenes. "I truly thought," wrote John Beeckman to his wife in New York City, "that the Tuesday night after leaving home was my last in this world." Giving himself up for lost, he added, "I called around me those I held most dear on earth and silently bid them farewell."[12] Garrett Low, an avid reader of Longfellow and Byron, took the time to record these feelings in verse:

Prostrate upon the Cabin floor,
The traveler lies with stomach sore.
And utters many groans pathetic,
    While undergoing his emetic.
His mind is full of fancies drear,

Shipwreck he sees. Death hovering near,
But still by fear he's not oppressed,
He looks on death expecting rest.
And faintly opens his glassy eye,
And prays to God that he may die.[13]

Whatever the metaphor, men as dogs, the spinal column as "flaccid and limpy," manhood oozing "out at finger's ends" as "Ceasar [*sic*] becomes like a sick girl," the main point of reference here seems to have been a conscious awareness of self-reduction, a humiliating sense of impotence as the self of the shore slipped away between retching fits. Even as forty-niners survived this initial trial, what was once heroic may have seemed a process of self-humiliation. Some had second thoughts. One of Bancroft's steamer mates "could not repress his tears as he begged the captain to put him on board the first returning ship." "I will say now if I could have for saw what I have seen," wrote another after a bout with seasickness and storms, "I would never have joined." Reconcilement with fate and helplessness, however, was his only option: "here I am and must make the best of it." "I shall have more to say if I shall be permitted to return home," he added, in the meantime promising to "leave all my concerns in the hands of divine Providence."[14]

As the first great shared experience among forty-niners, this ubiquitous seasickness contained elements of a ritual process. It marked, that is, a moment of transition, a stark boundary between former lives and new existences. The dross of their shorebound lives left behind and thrown overboard, many expressed this transition as a feeling of vertigo, as a sense of dizzy helplessness followed by a letting go of self-control.[15] One week out from Boston, William Graves felt the characteristic dizziness: "for it is the first time that I ever was upon the Salt Water & everything around me seames New and different than I ever experience before." Sensing his helplessness, "serrounded upon all sides by the shurgen [surging] bilows of the mighty Deepe & tosted about by the usages of the Winds and waves," he could only give in and enjoy his helplessness as a form of liberation.[16] Others combined feelings of helplessness with those of vertiginous and sensual delight. Having adjusted to the slow roll of his ship, New Yorker Henry Peters at last opened his gaze to the ocean. Never having been at sea before, he was charmed by the sight: the sun at dawn, solidifying from the liquid horizon; the ocean, a "deep indigo blue," blurred boundaries of sky and sea, unmarked by sail or cloud. "I gazed long and earnestly," he wrote in his journal, "[and] never before thought what atoms we are: here was our vessel, with four hundred persons on board,— separated from all the rest of the world, tossed about like a nutshell; any power we might exert was as nothing when brought to bear against the winds and waves which might, at any moment, conspire and swallow us up to be known no more, and missed but a little time."[17]

The result for Peters as for others was a feeling of liberating helplessness, a sense of alignment with natural forces within and without. Absorbed by the rhythms of "sunshine and clouds, stormy winds and calms, rough sea and smooth, sun-rising & sunsets, moon and stars," one forty-niner wrote that "one finds himself entering imperceptibly into the feelings of poets and others who have written thrilling thoughts and can feel the full force of them."[18] At the same time, trapped as they were on their slow-moving ships, they could for the most part express these feelings only by moving inward, into the sensibilities of the poet, back into recollections of home or the remembered perfection of childhood. One argonaut's metaphor reflected the transition: following a night of rough seas and sickness, "the sun rose upon the calmest sea I have yet witnessed" he wrote as he went on deck, and, "smiling," he felt "as lovely as an infant upon its mothers breast."[19]

These inward transitions were by no means linear processes among all forty-niners. And not all can be measured. Undoubtedly, the ability to dream, and from these dreams to create works of imagination rather than simple records of weather phenomena, depended on their faculties. Some had the ability to express newfound sensibilities. Invoking strong winds and high-rolling seas as his muses, Maine's Robert Hutchinson poetically asked, "who that has ever ventured forth upon the great deep, but will recollect, if he cannot describe, the whirl of contending emotions, with which for the first time he has seen the blue vault of ether resting in an interrupted union upon that glorious mirror where the Almightie's form glasses itself in tempests?"[20] Here we can almost catch Hutchinson's whirl of contending emotions. Others, lacking access to literary style and power over metaphor, had more difficulty expressing their feelings. Sailing with the New Brunswick Mining and Trading Company, William Rowland may have been inspired by shipboard readings from Dana's *Two Years Before the Mast*. Yet he lacked the ability to transform his experience into literature. He tried, recording one morning "the most beautiful sunrise I ever beheld." Another time he attempted a descriptive account of a shark, which had bitten off one of the legs of a pair of pants that a fellow gold seeker was washing over the side of the bark. But for the most part, he limited his entries to weather reports and latitude-longitude readings. His changing moods along with the rhythm of the voyage, from despondency to bursts of optimism and anticipation, were reflected only by drawings of flowers and lavish ornamentations around certain entries.[21]

Still, as Rowland's flowery pictures if not his prose suggest, seagoing forty-niners had a large amount of time for introspective thought. They spent their free time in a variety of ways, writing letters and journal entries, sharing stories, and reading. "I must tell you about the times we have on board," wrote Thomas Forbes to a friend in his hometown of Haddon, Connecticut: "We have religious meetings every Sunday and every week we have a debating society and we [have] dancing . . . and fishing too. We have a great deal of spoart [*sic*] for we have caught a number of fish, . . . we have a newspaper printed on board. It is called the Jornel [*sic*] of the Hartford union mining and trading company."[22] Describing a typical night in his journal, New Englander William Graves wrote that "beeing plesant we all asembel on deck an we was entertain with mussick and singing which past the Eavening [off] plesantly." Looking around, he saw some men "reeding and some writing and some Laughing and talking and some playing fiddle . . . [each] one trying to [amuse] himself to his own Best advantage."[23] Yet as Rowland found, the question of who deserved more praise, "Columbus for discovering America or Washington for defending it," while an interesting issue and one expressly designed by company leaders to kill off as many hours as possible, eventually gave way to long stretches of silent self-reflection.[24] Out of these introspective silences arose creative impulses; and the ship, as an arena apart from normal life, might be just the place for the playing out of resultant dreams and yearnings.

Stuck on their ships with little to do but imagine, many forty-niners gave play to their creative temperaments. They might not be able to spell "poetry" correctly, but now they had time to appreciate art. Just out from Boston, William Graves saw passengers listening to readings from travel narratives. "After which," he proclaimed, "our [steward] read to us for our general entertainment some Poerty which he had been composing for his own mental amusement."[25] Following their own muses, these gold seeker accounts of the voyage reflect a free blending together of fact and fiction. And with plenty of time on their hands, they could make much out of a small creative spark. One spark came with the widely circulated report that the largest of the

California-bound schooners, the *Edward Everett* out of Boston, was carrying two cannons to ward off pirates.[26]

Coupled with the forty-niner imagination, this popular rumor meant that every sail on the horizon might be topped by the skull and cross-bones. Along with his fellow passengers, Charles Ellis, aboard the ship *North Bend* from Maine, sighted distant sails early in his voyage. Like the rest, he leapt to the imaginative conclusion. "There was much speculation," he wrote, "amongst the passengers as to the best mode of proceeding in case she should prove a *pirat*."[27] Thomas Matteson, a young seminary student from Albany, New York, indicated that the pirate's life might even be lived by his fellow passengers aboard the ship *George Washington*. There was, he wrote, "much drinking and shooting," aboard the ship, "sometimes a fight in the forecastle and before that was one in the quarter deck." This wild behavior ceased, however, with the spotting of a sail in the distance. The passengers banded together; here might be play for pistols purchased on depar-ture. With the supposed pirate ship still at a distance, "every man," claimed Matteson, was "armed and on deck." Matteson was caught up in the excitement: the "time will come when it is life or death," he wrote; "God be with us in case we should not survive." Finally, after two days of fear and thrilling anticipation, the passengers identified the "enemy" ship; to some disappointment, it turned out to be a whaling vessel. Matteson's fellow passengers had been brought closer together by what may have been a prank of the ship's crew.[28]

This bonding together of men was not unusual; much of the voyage reflected efforts to bring together diverse individuals within an over-arching culture of masculinity. Certainly, the men aboard the flotilla to California represented a wide diversity of types. "We have," wrote one voyager, "English, Irish, French, Swede, Canadians and every variety of Yankee among us from different parts of our extensive country. Lawyers, Doctors, Tradesman, Mechanics, Farmers, Seamen, Miners, Clerks & Students are found among us in all their varieties."[29] Another saw "men from all parts of the world," aboard his ship and at stopping-off points, men from Wyoming, Batavia, and New York. This diversity, in turn, meant that there was plenty of room for conflict aboard the ships. But differences between Americans from northern and southern states were perhaps most evident and threatening. The shipboard "society of men from all parts," according to Rodney Odall of Roches-ter, New York, "come to points in opinion quite often, especially the North and the South." The southerners, he added, could be derisive of wage earners: "slaves . . . we are termed by pro-slavery men." Odall responded with references to southern morality. "Most of the southerners are gamblers," he wrote, "much to their discredit in my mind." Aboard a steamer to the Isthmus of Panama, another northerner noted that "more than the half of our passengers were from the Southern States nearly all of whom were excessively addicted to swearing and many of them to gambling."[30]

The existence of tensions like these undoubtedly generated the need to bring passengers together, at least during the course of the voyage. One way of doing this was to pit ship against ship rather than man against man. Many companies and trading associations, that is, would envision the voyage as a race to California. This type of friendly competition, while bonding shipmates together, could be dangerous. As the members of the New Brunswick Company aboard the slow-moving *Isabel* found, staying ahead in this game meant taking great risks. Driven far west of normal sailing routes to a short distance off the port of Guam, the New Brunswickers saw sails ahead of them. William Rowland wrote, "we did not like the idea of giving them a chance of seeing San Francisco before us, . . . so we decided . . . to go ahead while we could." They should have stopped. Already out of fresh provisions as a result of packing them in water-logged lower holds, several members contracted scurvy and died shortly after their arrival in California.[31]

A better way of dealing with these inner-ship tensions was to relax, to make the blend of types something enjoyable or to pass it off with a laugh. Undoubtedly, if there was a main characteristic of the Yankee armada to California, or even of the gold rush as whole, it was humor; more often than not, forty-niner creative and competitive impulses took the form of self-reflective jokes. "We have started a Lazy Society aboard," wrote New York City's John Cornelison, adding that the only rules of the club were: "No one must be caught Exerting himself in any way," and no one "must be seen standing when there is any thing near to lean against."[32] Here as elsewhere, the style of these jokes was irony, the comic reversal of social norms. For upwardly mobile men, applied energy might be prescribed and idleness forbidden; but aboard ship, apart from the "real" world, laziness— for the sheer sake of it—could be exposed and embraced as an idiosyncratic alternative to upward striving. Humor of this sort may have worked as a defense, guarding the expression of real desires against objections.[33] Many historians have focused on these jokes to dismiss the rush as an example of hackneyed boyishness or to depict it as a roistering good time. In both lines of analysis, the gold seekers' defenses work; their serious desires remain hidden beneath the perception, conveyed by the forty-niners themselves, that they were "only joking."

Yet forty-niner humor calls for a serious look beyond the opaque screens of foolishness. When it takes the form of ritualistic reversals of order, it suggests desires to play at community, to experiment with alternatives to the pale prescriptions for white middle-class male identity. These communal and experimental tendencies may be especially evident in the shipboard comedy of the dance. Forty-niner journals, diaries, and letters describe these all-male dances, complete with transvestite "ladies," as among the flotilla's most popular, and hilarious, pastimes. On the same day that he joined the "Lazy Society," John Cornelison reported that the "boys had a dance last evening and we were gratified by having some favorite airs played by [a] pretty good musician on the violin."[34] What was most interesting about the dancers was their consciousness as performers. "In the evening," wrote Henry Hyde of Boston in his journal, "the dancers (who had spent many hours in preparing their dress representing the character which they were to act) came out in full costume." To Hyde, these performers really had become "ladies": all together, there were about twenty dancers, he noted, "including 6 or 8 ladies with flowing white drapery."[35]

These shipboard dances blended a thrill of exposure with a conscious sense of doing something out of the ordinary and probably forbidden. Jared Nash, aboard the ship *Belgrade*, from Cherryfield, Maine, joined merrily in the game. "After partaking of a supper," he wrote of the ship's Christmas celebration, "we went on deck and there enjoyed our selves in dancing through the evening, and a merry set of boys we were." Aboard the same ship, Robert Hutchinson described this Christmas dance as a unity of high and low expression: "we called it a Christmas ball," he wrote, "some would call it a sailor's breakdown."[36] New Yorker Griffith Meredith joined in a similar celebration, albeit more self-consciously, adding evasive humor and the thrill of exposure to the ritual. "I wish," he wrote with obvious pleasure, "some of our New York friends could only take apeap [*sic*] on our deck and see the young Gents dancing as '*ladies*' showing off in the different Attitudes. I think if the Miss *G's* could see me dancing as lady and waltsing too they would *laugh heartily*."[37] A month later, Meredith's fellow passengers gathered together for another round of waltzing. This time the dancers, according to Meredith, "fixed them Selves as much as they could like a *Woman*, [which] created quite a laugh among the members and made it interesting to all." One gentleman in particular, according to Meredith, attested to the seriousness with which the passengers took this performance. Perfecting the illusion, this gold seeker "put on a long morning gown and buttend it up all the way to the top then lasted it up in the waist tight then filled it out in the (b——m) like a woman. . . . [Then he] put on a pair of white linen drawers . . . a pair of linen gloves and a fan in his hand and then came on deck which created repeated roars of laughter . . . this woman (gent) was treated like a lady by all members introduced to her."[38]

These are not "normal" expressions. In these accounts, the play is the thing, the play of language and metaphor, the playful oscillation between rigid self-control and idiosyncratic self-expression. Although constituting perhaps the main characteristics of the gold rush, these play elements—the constant and striking reversals of usual patterns of expression and behavior—have rarely been placed in context or taken seriously. Yet they were central to the period. For Horace Bushnell, play was a religious state. It offered an escape from the selfishness of the body into the "perfected freedom and greatness" of the shared soul: "as childhood begins with play," he claimed in an 1848 sermon, "so the last end of man, the pure ideal in which his being is consummated, is the state of play."[39] According to the historian and sociologist Johan Huizinga, play is characterized by a "stepping out" from ordinary life, an entrance into a temporary sphere of activity marked by imagination, stylized competition, rhythm, and harmony.[40] In effect, the goal of play is to open up the possibilities that are denied in the real world; pursued with the self-forgetful, deadly earnestness of the child, it emphasizes process over goal, fluid imagination over hard actualities.[41]

Transvestitism performed with such seriousness might be read in several ways. It may reflect homoerotic yearnings, not unusual in the all-male environments on board ships, but played out in representative heterosocial forms. It can be seen as a conscious effort at containment, a process whereby men bring the identity of an absent female other into themselves, a colonization as it were of identity and experience. Yet the fact that it is in such deadly earnest—and that it is simultaneously so comical to the assembled spectators—indicates that it is representative of ludic—or play—impulses, idiosyncratic desires, half-reasoned but fully felt. These impulses contradict neither homoerotic yearnings nor desires for an expansion of identity, but rather they expose them. These men, in other words, were moving sideways into feminine identity; in part perhaps out of imperial aspiration, in part for the sheer thrill of the movement itself, for the pleasure of being able to provide an exposition of freedom, to float between forbidden pleasures and the prescribed constraints of bourgeois respectability.[42]

Meredith later felt a similar thrill while washing his clothes. The washing, as he recounted, reminded him of laundry day at home, "when I used to see my mother and sisters doing it." Yet it also reminded him that the folks back home were now his spectators. "I presume," he added, "it would without a doubt made some of my acquaintances in N York laugh to see me over a *wash tub*. No doubt it would make some of the young ladies laugh and perhaps *blush* to see how much more handy I can use the wash board than they can."[43] Here Meredith clearly had an assumption of forbidden behavior, or at least nonprescribed male activity. Like the dancing ladies among the forty-niners, he was exposing himself to ridicule. At the same time, while knowing that his audience would "laugh to see me over a wash tub," he took pride in his own laughable role. He was aware that such scenes reflect reversals of gender or behavioral norms. Yet because he was free to make such reversals, to play a widening variety of roles and to shift selves between broken binaries, they were also strangely pleasurable.

Few gold-seeking companies engaged in a wider variety of pleasures than did the Old Harvard Company out of Boston. Most, if not all, of its twenty-five members were students or alumni of the college, its ship, the *Duxbury*, a veritable floating fraternity house. Following the legacies of Dana and Parkman, these young men were going to California expressly for the adventure.[44] Theirs was a pleasure-seeking as well as gold-seeking quest. Along the way they would dance, sing, drink freely, fight, seek prostitutes in South American ports, and in general picture themselves as a group of "b'hoys" on a spree. Their shipboard newspaper, the *Petrel*, published every Monday, reveals attempts to make their entire voyage into a type of poetry. As much as any document of the gold rush, the paper seems the product of desires to play between masculine rigidity and the communal impulses of oceanic dissolution.

Again, with plenty of time on their hands, the Harvardians treated the paper as an outlet for pent-up creative urges. They filled its columns with poetry—from the lowest doggerel to aspiring epics—along with short stories, histories of the voyage, puns, conundrums, and mock rituals invented by the writers. Under a masthead picturing a petrel trailing the banner "Free and Fearless" in its beak, the paper first appeared one month into the voyage. Immediately its writers announced its jocular tone: "We appear before our readers today for the first time, with our weekly budget of fun, fact, and fancy." Fun and fancy would predominate as the editors announced a first issue for shipboard debate by the "I.O. of B'hoys, viz, whether it is right for a temperance man to stir a glass of sweetened water with a shark's tail."[45]

The *Duxbury*, according to an article in the *Petrel*, sailed out of Boston Harbor on 9 February 1849. The ceremony of departure began in sunlight—sparkling on crystal snow and icicles—but following the proper dictates of pathetic fallacy, clouds rolled in, "changing the whole face of nature, . . . dissipating the smiles which had gathered upon many a brow." From here, the Harvardians followed the ritual process of departure, leaving behind the well-lit places of New England for the darkness and deep blue of watery self-dissolution. The ship sailed to the entrance to the harbor, where, according to the writer, "at three o-clock P.M. the pilot gave the order to let her go, the fasts were thrown off, and as her head swung round, she bowed gracefully to the blast that filled her sails, and rising sped onward, like a wild bird, amidst the cheering of the multitude upon the wharf, and the no less hearty cheering of the passengers in return . . . and many a tear drop moistened the cheek of the adventurer, as some white handkerchief was descried waving upon the wharf, as a last token of affection. [Standing out to sea] our good ship [rode] gracefully and easily over the broad blue, swelling waves of the Atlantic."[46] As indicated by this passage, the "farewell" had become ritual, its subjects and objects stylized into poetic forms: a "wild bird" carrying the adventurers away, a "white handkerchief" standing for the women left behind, the ocean a "broad blue, swelling" of unexplored possibilities. Each form reflected an effort to bring countervailing tendencies into harmony, conveying, respectively: helplessness and the disassociation of the individual from responsibility, an imagic shift toward knight-errantry and away from any suffering caused by the forty-niners' departure, and an opening for the display of perceptually subrational but conscious fantasies as past identities faded and dissolved into the deep blue of the Atlantic.

No forty-niner could capture experience in pure form. The passengers aboard the *Duxbury* never even tried. When they became seasick, in turn, they raised the act of vomiting to new heights of play and ritualistic performance. One *Petrel* writer outlined the ritual in an unfinished story called "Jack the Giant or the Haverhill Peg Driver." Jack begins the voyage a "peg driver," or an apprentice shoemaker. The ship entering a storm soon after its departure, he clings to himself below decks. Then as the storm abates but the seas remain high he coughs his old identity overboard. The seas, as the writer described the scene, "continued heaving and swelling, till poor Jack's [stomach] became exceedingly riled, when being unable any longer to contain its load, with protruding eyes he issued forth, rushed to the rail, and clasping it in his devotions, he in the language of the scriptures, cast his bread upon the waters."[47]

All of the Harvardians seem to have shared in this religious experience. And all shared in its following ritual stages: feelings of helplessness, a new awareness of the awesome and sublime power of nature, and finally, a sense of themselves as having stepped out of their former lives. "Toward midnight" a few days out from Boston, as the *Duxbury* entered the Gulf Stream, described another of the *Petrel*'s writers, a "storm raged fearfully, the wind blowing a perfect gale, the waves rising like monsters of the deep, . . . The wheel was carried away [and] we were left at the mercy of the wind and waves . . . As the morning dawned the scene was truly grand, the sea was white with foam, on every side the wind blew the spray, from their tops, in a continual spray that whirled and sparkled, giving forth every colour of the rainbow."[48] With the breakdown of identity in the face of awe-inspiring nature, the world had been revealed in its elemental form; and much like Dana and Parkman before them, a new generation of Harvardians found themselves in a liquid environment of swirling fragments. Here, many seem to have felt that all aspects of their former lives, all limitations and prescriptions, no longer mattered. Or at least they were no longer in the way of their desires. Once a lowly peg-driver, as the story writer continued his series of adventures, Jack would go on to slay the giant. Eventually, he would become the giant, freely surrounding himself with a sumptuous castle, rich feasts, and shimmering piles of golden coins.

In the face of the spray and whirl, some forty-niners felt that they had been freed, at least for the moment. Accordingly, they could re-make themselves as they wanted, as self-consciously authentic men exploring forces within, as "wonderful curiosities" experimenting with new patterns of behavior. "There are some wonderful curiosities on board the Duxbury," claimed one writer, "and no mistake, for instance, the passengers themselves, with their unshaven faces, and uncouth dresses rank among the most conspicuous." The Harvardians' major experiment, as for many other gold seekers and companies, was with collectivity, a blending of individual striving and noncompetitive connectedness into a familial masculine oversoul. They had heard the tales of gold, claimed one of the *Petrel*'s poets; they had severed ties to find new sensibilities at sea; now they had the obligation, or the opportunity, to fuse striving with brotherly love:

> Now as our lot we cannot mend at present,
> Let each one strive to render it more pleasant
> 'Twill cost but very little time or labor
> For each one here to do unto his neighbor
> Those little acts of kindness that endear,
> Men to each other, and which through long years,
> Will dwell within the memory, and impart
> A grateful glow of pleasure to the heart.[49]

Part of this experiment with collectivity involved the refusing—or re-fusing—of class distinctions associated with the rise of the modern marketplace and the breakdown of the household economy. Aboard their ships men played different roles, donning the costume of authentic physical labor, singing sea shanties and pulling songs, blending the refined individual into the collective identity of the common worker or sailor. Perhaps the entire gold rush, with its contingent of well-off artisans, aspiring bourgeois clerks, and merchants dressed in work pants, red shirts, and heavy boots, is reflective of play between the perceived lines of forming classes. Apart from the dictates of the shore, as John Cornelison described it, the identity of the self-styled argonaut might flow into that of the self-styled whaleman. "The boys," he noted one day in his journal, "are raising whales and singing out in all imaginable terms: There she blows—There she flukes—away between the lee scuppers—and the rest gaping upon them thinking they must know something about it."[50]

From whaleman to common sailor, or even to wind-grizzled sea salt, was a short distance; and here was a role that gave forty-niners seemingly endless pleasure. As might be expected, it was sailor's rituals, especially the ritual dunking of those who had not before sailed across the equator, that most interested them. Presiding over this ritual was one man, presumably a crew member or passenger who had crossed the line, and who adopted the guise of "Neptune." He would then divide his fellow passengers into two groups, not according to social or economic status, but into "old salts" and "green sailors," those who had crossed the equator and those who had not. Playing out the rite, the old salts would then shave the latter group—which must have comprised the majority of passengers—coat them with green paint, and dunk them in a vat of seawater.

Thus, in a marked-off arena of fun and play, tensions between passengers, between actual sailors and merchants, between artisans and clerks, could find expiation in a brief, if sometimes violent, over-turning of stylized power relations.[51] The "old salts," whatever their social or economic background, could enjoy a frenzied dunking and humiliation of the pen pushers. Nearing the equator, Charles Ellis, a lumberman from Waterville, Maine, relished the thought: "after we cross we shall consider ourselves real salts as the sailors call it." And, as he added rather ominously and perhaps with an eye toward one or more of his fellow passengers, "some of us are certainly green enough to require salting."[52] Thomas Forbes, describing the ritual to a friend in Connecticut, noted that there "was some on board that was so afraid that they was going to be used so that they went up a loft and stayed in the rigin till sport was over with."[53]

The rough play of this ritual, in other words, might get out of hand, the violence of dunkings and shavings revealing the real tensions just below the surface of the ship's spirit of camaraderie. On other occa-sions, the free movement between the prescriptions of their articles of association and indulgence in physical expression might exacerbate tensions among gold seekers, their ventings of inner forces creating feelings of frustration and instability, giving way to dark fantasies and violent incidents. On Rodney Odall's ship, the *Lucy Allen* out of New York, a Fourth of July celebration and dance started well but turned ugly: "some got drunk, had a fight, finally went to bed at 12 o'clock." Another forty-niner reported that steam might be let off through the abuse of one unlucky passenger. Passengers aboard a small brig, he wrote, "must necessarily find some outlet for amusement; . . . some one among that company, sooner or later, becomes the butt of the wags, while the others look on and enjoy the fun."[54]

For some gold seekers these examples of strained hilarity seemed silly. A lawyer from New York City who sailed around the horn on the *Robert Browne*, John Stone was alternately disturbed and contemptu-ous of his fellow passengers' play. Witnessing one man expressing violent urges, he failed to see any pleasure in his physical exuberance. Instead he saw only a man cracking up under tensions, a man who, "hitherto harmless—suddenly became a raving maniac . . . imagined himself captain of the ship; gave orders to the sailors; drove the men away from the wheel; cut one of the wheel ropes, and attacked one of the passengers." This scene was an example, for Stone, of imagination gone too far. Later he sarcastically dismissed the pretensions of his shipmates. "Some of the passengers," he wrote, "ambitious to be soldiers have formed a company and are taking lessons in military tactics from Mr. Edw. D. Cox, a passenger who has served in the Mexican War. I have no genius for the sport. . . . So let them play 'soger' that like it." A few weeks later, he added an ironic postscript to the performance, writing that "soldiering [was] at a discount. No waving plumes and showy uniforms . . . [it] takes thronged thoroughfares and bright eyes to call out a general muster on a training day. Women are such admirers of Heroes; and when an epaulette makes one, who wouldn't be a Hero? Tis so easy."

Despite his willingness to strip away the pretensions of others, Stone too could give play to violent yearnings, if only in his fantasies. Frustrated at the filthy conditions and poor rations aboard his ship, he directed his anger at its crew and owner. Its captain, he claimed, was "an illiterate, inebriated, demented old imbecile . . . whose greatest delight is to chuckle over the miseries of his passengers." Its owner and the organizer of Stone's association, so-called Sarsaparilla King "Doctor" S. P. Townsend, was a "heartless and most inhuman wretch." Stone fantasized about having the good doctor aboard, beating him, and forcing him to drink a pint from the ship's store of rancid water; "there is no doubt," he concluded with dark humor, "he would gulph down several swallows of his own sarsaparilla."[55]

Similar tensions between collective play and darker impulses existed among the *Duxbury*'s band of Harvardians. An unusually homogenous group, these passengers still had difficulties containing competitive impulses. Certain members of the company seem to have become targets for ritual humiliation, *Petrel* writers giving them derogatory nicknames: the ever-complaining "Sour Kraut," the pompous "Lord Stanley," the pedantic "Philosopher Smith." Each came in for some ribbing in the paper's columns of poetry, not all of which was good-natured. For many of the *Duxbury*'s crew, in fact, their newfound self-conceptions as authentic b'hoys on a spree may have required that someone be constituted as the overcivilized dandy. In the ship's ritual of humiliation upon crossing the equatorial line, several passengers seem to have elevated "Lord Stanley" to a position above the rest. Portraying him as snooty, in his clean white shirt and affected airs, his crewmates shaved, painted, and dunked him with added zeal. "But Philosopher Smith's was the hardest case," claimed one of the *Petrel*'s poets,

> For he hit one of Neptunes' men in the face
> And sighs and groans were mingled with
> The horrible groans of Philosopher Smith
> For they chased him here and they chased him there
> And he doubled and dodged like a frightened hare
> Till at last to the lower cabin he fled
> And with many a sigh and tear he pled.[56]

Thus terrified, Smith kept below decks, hiding until the next day when the initiation rite had run its course. Or did he? Although the issues of the *Petrel* are only dated sporadically, it appears that the poet wrote these lines some time before the *Duxbury* crossed the line. The poem, in effect, may have been an attempt to contain conflict—in this case given a class dimension as "genuine" old salts sought to revenge themselves on the posturing philosopher—through the play of pure artistic invention. It is very likely that this ugly scene never took place, except in the passengers' imaginations.

It would be unwise, however, to assume that what went on in the forty-niner imagination was somehow not real. Real tensions had led to the attack on Philosopher Smith, even if the attack was imagined. For many forty-niners imagination served real purposes: it transformed contradictions into agreements, blending oppositional behaviors, bringing physical authenticity into the gold seeker identity. If, for example, starched men were temperate and real men drank, aboard the California-bound armada temperance and rum could be mutually embraced within a spirit of play. On the *Duxbury*, for example, one unnamed passenger sold a whiskey of his own concoction. The editors of the *Petrel* upbraided him for his efforts, but always in verse. They did not, however, chastise him for selling the brew, only for the fact that he sold it at the outrageous price of a dollar a pint. As long as he responded in verse, the seller could deflect the charge:

> What in thunder is't "tu" you sir
> If I "du" sell liquor: say

Haint you nothing else tu du sir
But to blow me up that way

Sposin I did ask a dollar
For a pint of colored rum
Taint the trade I meant to foller
When I started out from hum[57]

Certainly rum selling was not the trade for a respectable man. But by making an imaginative riposte, the profiteer was able to "one-up" his accusers, hiding behind the license-giving mask of down-home vernacular, inventing a type of "eye dialect" that while having no geographical basis—and no reality—results in our forgetting that many of these men are middle-class in origin and status. In the process, behaviors forbidden by middle-class prescriptive literature—the drinking and selling of alcohol for pleasure and profit—are contained within a mutually accepted field of play that makes their forbidden qualities disappear.

Identifying the contradictions within these examples, exposing them as examples of middle-class hypocrisy, serves little purpose. In effect, the main fact here is not that these men were lying about themselves, but that they were producing culture. This culture would delight in contradictions and strange juxtapositions. Indeed, juxtapositions of nature and civilization, between the homes they left and this new, natural world of "fantastic" shapes and things, were a continuing source of pleasure for many gold seekers. Thomas Williams of Boston's Bunker Hill Mining Company professed this sense of delight as his ship, the *Regulus*, passed a brig out of New York on which a brass band was performing "Hail Columbia." The strange scene, he wrote, "was the most cheering and most reviving of anything I experienced in all my life. I never shall forget the sensation I experienced at the time, the music was not good at all but the idea of having a band of music on the ocean it was delightful."[58] A bit of civilization adrift in *plein nature*, the scene reestablished a sense of balance.

Few characters of the West would be as destructive to the natural environment as the forty-niner, yet few would be as effusive in their portrayals of nature as a source of balance, as something mystical and divine. For some, nature offered possibilities for transcendence; for others it promised adventure and a sense of discovery. "We are now in the same track followed by Columbus," wrote James Tyson, a New York City doctor on the Panama route to California, "when . . . he explored the vasty deep for the discovery of a new world."[59] Certainly the "vasty deep," and the "virgin wilderness," held charms for the gold seekers. Canoeing across the Isthmus of Panama, David Hewes described the scenery as "exceedingly beautiful." Drifting and dreaming, he gazed in wonderment "in passing through the seeming primeval solitudes, scaring the lonely heron from his perch or startling the 'iguana' from his noontime nap, it requires no great stretch of the imagination to fancy oneself a pioneer in the ascent of some hitherto unknown stream."[60] At other times this natural environment appears to have been too mysterious, its charm unbalancing the senses. As Henry Peters of New York described the Panama passage, the self-image of the pioneer might be lost in enchantment. "There were thousands of great trees," he wrote wonderingly, "resembling nothing I had ever seen before, covered with beautiful foliage from bottom to top; others running up tall and slender, and crowned with red and yellow flowers; . . . there were amany sweet singing birds . . . who seemed to spare no pains to make our sail agreeable; we sat in silence, lost in perfect enchantment for hours; it seemed like fairyland, and was certainly more beautiful and intoxicating than ever I imagined the Garden of Eden to be, even when reading Milton's glorious description of it."[61]

Obviously, passages like these cannot be viewed as unvarnished windows onto forty-niner experience. Instead they indicate a taxing of the imagination as an overwhelming natural environment pushed them to the boundaries of aesthetic experience and their own literary skills. Calling on all his talents in a frantic attempt at description, William Graves tried to capture what he saw in language. Beginning well, his attempt quickly became muddled in a whirlpool of failed metaphor and simile. "Here I set," he commenced from the deck of his ship, "till the setting Sun calls my attention as it cast its last ~~rayes~~ golden rayes upon the tranquil watter of the mighty Deep And the gentle zephyers Breese which sprang up which caus our Noble Shipe to glide smothley over thoes tunefull Watters Like a Mighty Vulture with out Spread Wings Lovingly catch the last rais of the departing day."[62] John Cornelison, while trying to describe the transcendent qualities of a ship under full sail, saw his attempt collapse into similar fragments. He looked up at the sails, "filled with wind so completely as to seem almost as if from marble; the rigging glistening in the sun, the mast tapering upward pointing to the clouds as they float in fantastic shapes . . . defined against the deep blue beyond . . . the cry of the sea gull as he dives after the flying fish . . . the water splashing at the bows the occasional breaking of a wave alongside."[63]

These attempts to capture experience in writing are more descriptions of feeling than of the natural environment. In many ways, these accounts are typical of the travel narratives of the time. Euro-Americans had long had difficulties of description and meaning when coming face to face with foreign environments. As a result, according to one historian, they frequently resorted to a language of resistance, making new experiences and objects familiar through comparison and analogy, containing them in a well-marked and narrow field of understanding, draining them of difference and exoticism.[64] Yet in other ways, these writings may have been unusual. For unless we count William Graves's reference to a "mighty vulture" as a quieting analogy, much seagoing gold seeker writing lacks this ability to control difference through language. Instead of transforming the trees of Central America into those of Vermont, they left strange shapes in the realm of the "fantastic." Their analogies seem neither solid nor resistant, their writings reveling in the mysteries of exotic environments. As James Tyson described a sunset, with its "fiery orb" sinking into the sea, its "refluent rays with brilliant and glowing coloring, beautifully traced on the dim and distant horizon," he could find no analogy. "The Spectacle," he could only conclude, "was truly sublime."

Richard Hale had an analogy ready for his own sunset, but it was hardly resonant with geographical familiarity. "As the sun sank behind the ocean horizon," he wrote, "it left the whole western heavens flooded in a blaze of vermillion, thickly dotted with small, deep blue tradewind clouds, bordered by a golden fringe circling the whole flame, while beneath, the ocean shining and varicolored, seemed like numberless highways to fairy grottos."[65] En route across Panama, Tyson happened upon the same image, moving inexorably in his descriptions of isthmus landscapes from the sublime through the "singular, strange, wild, and romantic" to the "truly enchanting." Here he paused, thinking of "the fabled Arcadian groves and bowers, where Pan and his attendant sylphs and satyrs reveled, and of the romantic and improbable stories of the Arabian Nights which had charmed me in early boyhood." Yet none of these metaphors or comparisons quite captured what he saw. Finally he made the last analogous step into the fairy grotto: for "here were scenes and prospects far surpassing any, that the wildest flight of imagination could conceive. It was a perfect fairy land."[66]

Raising internal feelings to a position over external realities, the magic of an animated world of abundance over rational materialism, these are the softest of analogies. But as they dissolved into rapturous treks along these "highways to fairy grottos," at least some forty-niners felt uneasy. The "air was laden with sweets," wrote one on his way across Panama, and the urge to dissolve was disturbing; "the senses," he added, "were almost oppressed by the fragrance emitted from flowers of every hue." "The sunsets, the glorious sunsets" could nearly pull the observer overboard, wrote another while far out in the Pacific Ocean: "oh they are enough to make a man holler for somebody to hold him by the coat tails."[67] Having gone far in their communion with nature, having crossed the boundaries of their former bland and dry existences to enter a fairyland of aesthetic delights, many forty-niners appear to have arrived at Byron's point of self-dissolution. But for them the point raised the question: Where did one go from here?

Dissolving and flowing into the natural environment seems to have carried the concomitant fear of drowning in a sea of beauty. For there seems to be a direct correlation in the gold seekers' writings between the call of the wild and a response of violent destruction. Charles Ellis saw the lure of nature in the form of porpoises swimming in the wake of his ship. They were, he reflected, "a beautiful sight" as they went "shooting through the water like a solid body of fire." Samuel Adams saw the body of fire as well, and he recorded a violent reaction: "several attempts were made to catch them by spearing but without success."[68] The journal of Charles Ellis, who sailed aboard the *North Bend*, resonates with these patterns of engagement with nature. One evening he went soft: "a beautiful clear sky and the full moon shedding her soft light on the broad and trickly ocean lends enchantment to the scene." Three days later a school of porpoises snapped him out of the spell: they were beautiful, but he combined his recognition of their beauty with regret that the ship's harpoons were not ready. In another entry, he directly linked beauty with death. "Those who have never seen the sun rise at sea can have no idea of the splendor of the scene," he wrote, adding, after a pause to note the beauty of the sky reflected on water, "I forgot to mention one of the passengers shot a large bird, in size between a duck and a goose, but he killed him flying and it fell astern."[69]

In spirals of beauty and death, the play continued aboard the *North Bend*. The passengers gazed at flocks of cape pigeons, watching "their graceful motions for a long time with much pleasure." Later they caught Albatrosses with baited hooks and flew them "like kites." They enjoyed the rhythm of sunset and sunrise, dipping pens into metaphor as they watched the "king of Day enthroned in cloudless splendor ready to pour forth a flood of golden light upon the wide stretched ocean beneath." And then they steeled themselves. "We have killed upwards of fifty ducks," wrote Ellis while off Cape Horn, describing it as "the greatest day for sporting that we have yet witnessed." A few days later, he watched as other passengers killed sea lions. According to Ellis, they "found that musket balls had no effect upon them, several being fired in the throat of one animal without stopping him. They were finally dispatched with clubs and axes."[70]

This ultimate association between beauty and death may reveal just how far some forty-niners had traveled in their voyage. At sea they harpooned dolphins, dragging them bleeding to the decks of the ship. Along the isthmus they shot alligators, and the "mud, blood, and water flew up in the air." These were the substances of an elemental reality. For the moment that forty-niners played with these elements, violently but with feeling, through violence and through giving in to their passions, they had made what may have seemed a transcendent connection with authentic forces. Following Byron, they had dissolved into a state of elemental being within the natural and physical world, arriving at a precarious point of balance, closer than ever to a grasp of a higher reality, exhilaratingly aware of their own connectedness to the physical world. As James Tyson discovered, desires might be played out in violence, beauty revealed in the kill. He saw the "beautiful and graceful dolphins" as they "sported around the vessel"; he saw the arousal of desire, the throwing of the harpoons; finally he saw that it was "only in death that the dolphin reveals his brightest and most gorgeous beauty." For a moment, the object of these forty-niners was not progress or gold or even success. For a moment their object was beauty.

So what does all of this say about middle-class culture? To some scholars, certainly, it would say very little. After all, these are idiosyncratic expressions, and the idiosyncrasies of an emerging middle class might seem unimportant if they exist only in specific moments and spaces apart from the more dominant bourgeois realities of repression, firmness of identity, the exploitation of others, and competition. In a sense, who cares if the uptight middle class occasionally dreams of, and even lives in, a world of alternatives to the rigidity of competitive social relations? Its members never appear really to act on these dreams. And if they have them, if they sometimes "step out" of the marketplace and into a transcendent realm of alternatives, into the natural environment, into cordoned-off arenas of harmony, poetry, and play, they always return to begin another round of competitive destruction and exploitation in the name of "progress" and "success." Furthermore, not all of these individuals can be categorized as middle class. Some were headed in this direction, while others probably were not.

And yet, for this moment at least, many if not all of these forty-niners occupied a middle position. The sea voyage was an extended moment between whatever they had been before and what they were about to become in California. All appeared to think that they were about to win the golden lottery and become rich, equally rich, and forever outside the world of competitive social relations that many were busily creating and just as many feared and hated. Within this transcendent moment, they had time to think, to dream, to create, and above all to expose their desires, to express what they really wanted. Much of what they expressed fits almost precisely into a list of activities falling well below a developing middle-class threshold of shame. Yet for a moment, these things had not appeared to be so shameful at all: drinking had been acceptable, so was vomiting, lounging around, playing at sailors' rituals, killing sea lions and dolphins, communing with fairies, and dressing up and dancing as women.

What these men wanted to express, in other words, is not quite what historians have claimed the middle class wanted. It was not, that is, an identity based on exploitation, rigidity, self-control, competition, and social hierarchy. Instead it was one based on flow, harmony, and play—an identity, in fact, with no real basis or fixed qualities at all. Historians might deny this, even members of the middle class might deny it, and both might refer to this voyage as an example of meaningless or idiosyncratic behavior, as yet another case when the forty-niners were "only joking." Still, during these moments of oceanic dissolution and transcendence, when all things had been made possible by anticipations of California's abundance, the possibilities these forty-niners expressed reveal the centrality of utopian alternatives to the marketplace, and alternatives to the rigidity of proper manhood, to the formation of middle-class culture and thought. The main problem, perhaps, was not that these desires were without meaning. The problem for many of these men was that they would never get this close to their desires, or this far from the dictates of a market society, again.

Five

A Great and Perverse Paradise

Theodore Johnson was one of the earliest forty-niners. A would-be newspaperman on the trail of a good story, Johnson booked passage for California almost as soon as the first gold reports reached the eastern seaboard. He made every steamer connection on his way to the gold country; then, after a short stay to absorb the region's local color, he turned around and made every connection on his return east. Accordingly, he managed to write and publish an account of his adventures, *Sights in the Gold Region and Scenes by the Way*, before many of his fellow prospectors had even departed. As the title of his book suggests, Johnson was more interested in the adventure of travel than he was in finding gold. Early in his outward voyage, as his ship sailed into subtropical waters, Johnson and his fellow passengers keenly anticipated the novel sights and scenes of Hispanic America. Approaching the Caribbean, he reported that his shipmates filled "the lovely moonlight evenings with songs . . . till the ship almost danced in chorus." A few nights later the islands of San Domingo and Cuba loomed on the horizon. Johnson's sense of anticipation reached a climax. Along with his crewmates, he rushed to the rails of the ship, "having in sight at the same time," as he put it, "the two greatest and most perverted island paradises of the West Indies."[1]

Johnson's thrill at his first sight of a Latin American environment, his conscious sense that these environments were somehow "perverse," was by no means unusual. Throughout 1849, thousands of gold seekers from the northeastern United States passed through Latin America. Some two-thirds of these emigrants sailed around Cape Horn; another third steamed to the Colombian Isthmus of Panama, crossing the isthmus by foot, mule, and canoe to pick up a sail ship or steamer on the Pacific side. Only a very small percentage traveled overland.[2] Along both major sea routes, gold seekers put in at Latin American ports and Yankee whaling stations. They became stranded in the suddenly burgeoning towns of Chagres and Panama on either side of the isthmus. They stopped off at Rio de Janeiro and the Brazilian island of Santa Catarina. They anchored for supplies at Valparaiso and Talcahuano along the coast of Chile. Many of these forty-niners were well educated and middle class in character, inspired by the chance for new sights as much as gold. They were, in other words, rather complicated individuals, refined but on the lookout for alternatives to refinement, resistant to forbidden behaviors but fired by preconceived ideas of Latin American perversity.

Only rarely have historians paid much attention to these forty-niner contacts with Latin America. On the occasions they have, complexity has not been much of an issue. The forty-niners have been portrayed as advance scouts in the United States' march toward empire, wholly committed to Yankee progress, racial hierarchies, and manifest destiny, completely resistant to cultural difference. For most of these scholars, in other words, these contacts comprise little more than a Yankee takeover of the "black legend" of Spanish conquest, a morality tale pitting one-dimensional colonizers on one side against equally one-dimensional natives on the other.[3] Much of the evidence from forty-niner contacts with Latin America would appear to support this analysis. Yet much does not. And despite the interpretive power of this dynamic, certain questions remain. One of these questions is what to do with statements like Johnson's. Certainly, Johnson's assumption of Latin American perversity contains more than a soupçon of racism, but it contains elements of attraction as well. And undoubtedly, his statement, along with the fact that it was typical of forty-niner reactions to Latin American environments, indicates that these northeasterners had specific values that could be perverted: commitments to progress, Yankee order, and standards of propriety. Yet again, Johnson's thrill at the prospect of perversity indicates that these values were not quite as one-dimensional as many historians have claimed, nor did they necessarily make forty-niners wholly resistant to Latin American culture.

Many of these northeastern forty-niners were like Theodore Johnson. They were, that is, men of a specific time and place. At the moment of their sailing and during their voyages, this time was not the "flush time" of the gold rush and the place was not California. Instead, these were men whose time was a period of market revolution and class formation, whose place was the industrializing Northeast. Beginning in 1827, Charles Finney, the itinerant minister and father of the Second Great Awakening, had swept through this region. He brought with him the fires of Christian revivalism, the guilty bench, and a renewed consciousness of the wages and meanings of sin. The result was a dramatic lowering of the Northeast's threshold of shame. Within a few years, certain activities such as drinking, gambling, and swearing—once normal parts of everyday life—would come under a growing category of sinful and forbidden behaviors. In the following two decades the Yankee Northeast would witness the rise of a set of values that can only be called Victorian. Clothing, particularly for women, had become more constraining, characterized by corsets, bustles, and multiple layers of heavy material. Excess, from excessive sexual display to excessive laughter and shouting and even excessively spiced food, had become a sure mark of low breeding and was increasingly forbidden, at least in public, and at least for members of a growing middle class.

Without the Northeast's commitment to these early Victorian standards, without their eventual spread throughout American society, the California gold rush would have very little meaning. The gold rush, as many forty-niners maintained—and as many later historians have confirmed—was a grand series of comic inversions. As a social experience, what made the rush particularly fascinating at the time—and ever since—was its exposition of forbidden behaviors, its dramatic challenge to proper standards of self-control through constantly repeated anecdotes of gambling, prostitution, and sometimes violent, more often humorous, examples of self-expression.[4] In composing these stories, forty-niners depended on one thing above all: that their readers would be proper enough—or middle class enough—to know the precise meaning of perversity. Gold rush-era California, as one typical forty-niner described it, was characterized by "acts of deathless shame." It was filled, added another, with the "darkest deeds ever recorded."[5] These statements mean nothing without a conscious understanding that shame is a positive attribute, or that respectability, lightness, or *whiteness* is the moral opposite of darkness.

Shameful acts and dark deeds have given the rush much of its mythic energy, its 150-year reign as America's most perverse, and hence enjoyable, historic event. But they have also accomplished something else. For there is evidence that forty-niners meant this darkness literally. They meant, in other words, that these deeds had originated with the dark people of the rush, with Mexican bandits, Chilean gamblers, and Latina prostitutes. An examination of forty-niner contacts with Latin America during their voyage to California reveals the social history of these "dark" deeds. It also reveals the extent to which the social reversals of the gold rush were also, perhaps primarily, racial reversals. They are not usually seen this way. In fact the social reversals of the gold rush are usually understood as examples of California's historical nonconformity. Or they are cited as evidence that the rush was a rollicking good time. Explored as race reversals, they suggest the possibility that the gold rush was *not* a departure from Victorian standards, that the vaunted reversals of norms that characterized the rush may have actually strengthened proper standards of behavior—and racism—by linking "perversity" with ethnic identity.[6]

Shortly after his arrival in Rio de Janeiro in March 1849, another gold seeker gazed in similar wonderment at the surroundings and streets of the city. "Strange it is," he wrote, "that the barbarians have the best corner of the earth." At Latin America's tropical ports, forty-niners discovered abundant landscapes, for each town appeared to be surrounded with hillsides "covered," as one wrote, "with orange trees plantain lemons limes coffee groves and hosts of other fruits." Amid such opulence, another observed, the natives could afford to be "careless of the future." "Nature does everything for them," he added, "they have abundance for life's wants." Throughout Central and South America, nature and culture seemed intertwined: lush vines climbed the walls of giant cathedrals, Spanish castles slowly crumbled into the fertile soil. The strange blend entranced many forty-niners. The natives were "barbarians," according to the travelers, but there was an allure to their brutality; women and children might be nearly naked, but there was glamour in their lack of shame. In all, forty-niners found much that was wanting in Latin American society, but also much that they wanted.[7]

Many of these ambivalent perceptions were a result of contemporary literature. Mid-nineteenth-century literary mappings of the Latin South focused in part on the region's backwardness, in part on its physical charms. At times, these characteristics charted a suspiciously detailed yet negative reflection of Yankee culture. Richard Henry Dana, whose 1840 publication of *Two Years Before the Mast* provided the forty-niners with a literary template for the voyage to California, described the Mexican men he met during his California sojourn as "thriftless, proud, and extravagant," the women as beautiful and immoral. "In fact," averred Dana, "one vice is set over against another; and thus, something like a balance is obtained. The women have but little virtue, but then the jealousy of their husbands is extreme, and their revenge deadly and almost certain." They were, in short, the opposites of the self-controlled Yankee: passionate, sexual, and violent. For Francis Parkman, these perceptions worked to construct racial hierarchies and boundaries. Along the Oregon Trail, he wrote, the "human race" was "separated into three divisions, arranged according to their merits; white men, Indians, and Mexicans; to the latter of whom the honorable title of 'whites' is by no means conceded."[8]

Many forty-niners read the accounts of Dana and Parkman. But they also had access to other readings; and if these narratives too erected boundaries, they might as well picture southern topographies, especially that of "old Mexico," as filled with attractive possibilities. This literature reached as far back as Alexander von Humboldt's 1811 publication, *Study of New Spain*. Its most popular single work, however, was undoubtedly William Prescott's *History of the Conquest of Mexico*. First published in 1843, Prescott's depiction of the rational and manipulative Cortes versus the primitive and fatally indecisive Montezuma was a paradigm for the meeting of cultures, an establishment of the hierarchy of superior and inferior. At the same time, Prescott's eye for the nostalgic and adventuresome, along with his literary debts to Sir Walter Scott, transformed Mexico into a magical field for self-perceived knights-errant.[9] Cortes's success, especially when sketched by the romantic pen of Prescott, would place him in the forty-niner's imaginary pantheon of heroes. Thus, as his California-bound steamer drew near Panama in 1849, Philadelphia newspaper correspondent Bayard Taylor noted the "passengers clustered on the bow, sitting with their feet hanging over the guards, and talking of Ponce de Leon, De Soto, and the early Spanish adventurers. It was unanimously voted that the present days were as wonderful as those, and each individual emigrant entitled to equal credit for daring and enterprise."[10]

If the histories of Prescott and others generated North American interest in the Latin South, the 1846 Mexican War raised this interest to new heights. The correspondence of the United States' first foreign war with the rise of a cheap and sensational daily press made the Mexican War an introduction of South America to a mass public. "Mexico's tropical climate," according to historian Robert Johannsen, "its wild and barren topography and exotic vegetation and wildlife, the unfamiliar ways of its people, the differences in language, customs and heritage all gave the war a romantic appeal that had never before been experienced."[11] Accordingly, he notes, the war spawned a renewed interest in Prescott's history, a rediscovery of older romances portraying the charms of "Old Mexico," and a veritable explosion of new popular romances. The producers of this literature included respectable authors—Timothy Flint, William Gilmore Simms, and Robert Montgomery Bird—as well as more sensational types, dime novelist Ned Buntline and voyeur-sensationalist George Lippard. Together, these writers mapped Latin landscapes with a mixture of old-world charm and primitive exoticism, with the hot-blooded tempers and lurid Catholicism of Spanish dons and sensual friars, and the "flashing dark eyes" and "raven tresses" of passionate vaqueros and señoritas.[12]

To be sure, many forty-niners did what they could to maintain self-control in Latin America; many found much that seemed revolting among these "savages" of the South. "Every thing is at least one hundred years behind the times," wrote John Callbreath to his sister in upstate New York soon after landing at Rio de Janeiro, "you cannot find a white man doing any kind of work and I do believe if it was not for the Yankees and English the race would run out." Boston Brahmin George Payson knew enough to recognize European stock among Brazilians, but still he noted what he perceived as a decline into primitivism. Unlike Anglo-Americans, these Europeans were degenerates of nature. "They have gained nothing of new life and vigour by being transplanted on to this virgin soil," noted Payson, "but seem rather to have lost what little they possessed." "This country has not proved to them the harsh stepmother that New England was to our Puritan ancestors," he added, "but like a foolish grandam, has spoilt them by her foolish indulgence. The result is that they can do nothing for themselves."[13] Stuck in Panama City, Massachusetts-born Henry Peters echoed these sentiments. "The people," he declared, "are a miserable, degraded race with no trade, ambition or anything else desirable; a few of the proud old dons of pure Castillian blood are still left with some lovely specimens of Spanish beauty among the ladies, but these families are very rare." Peters seems to have seen little that was desirable among these people, noting for the most part only their offenses to his sensibilities and senses. Accordingly, he thought it was "no wonder" that cholera was common on the Colombian isthmus, "for such a filthy set of people and such a compound of villainous smells as one's olfactories are regaled with from every shop, is enough to give the most sanguine unbeliever the infection."[14]

At times, these descriptions might reflect little more than racism and imperialist design, an idiom of complete resistance to all that was foreign or exotic. As Callbreath added to his letter: "one thousand troops under Rough & Ready would take the place." As for the Panamanians, Peters said they would soon disappear "before the march of improvement which is already beginning under the auspices of Americans who are about to establish a railroad across the isthmus." Similar dismissive assessments are sprinkled liberally throughout forty-niner journals of the voyage through Central America and points farther south. To Charles Ross Parke, a physician from Illinois and Pennsylvania, Nicaragua was a "god forsaken country of niggers, monkeys, baboons, and lizards, to say nothing about the poisonous reptiles." Brazil's people, according to another observer, were hopelessly backward in their development: "in agriculture, commerce, and invention, indeed in every branch of useful industry, they are, at least, fifty years behind the age."[15]

Still, even the most censorious of descriptions cannot disguise a creeping attraction. Rio de Janeiro revolted New York City lawyer John Stone. It was, he maintained, "a disgusting filthy city. Very many of the negroes who make up the chief population live in a state of nature and nudity . . . their persons and their garments besmeared with grease and smut." While this description reeks of a self-conscious expulsion of the low and the excremental, higher, more pleasing aspects were coming into Stone's line of vision: "But the city has some redeeming features," he added, citing its ornate churches, fine older architecture, and its orange groves.[16] According to the forty-niners, what was most striking about Latin America was its strange contradiction of perceived backwardness and poverty amid exotic abundance.

It was easy for gold seekers to reject the poverty of these scenes. But the abundance of tropical environments remained charming. "The flowers are truly lovely," wrote steamer captain Cleveland Forbes of Rio's gardens. The camellias were plentiful, he noted, along with the moss roses: "Cape Jesmine, & every choice flower of the world grows finely here. The orange, the best in the world, the Banana, the Pine Apple, the coconut, the guava, the Tea, the coffee, Sugar Cane, Lime, Chocolate, or coco . . . and dozens of other fruit too many to name."[17] Discovering opulence amid what they first viewed as corruption, many of these northeasterners stared in wonderment. According to Garrett Low, who joined the gold rush from the northern reaches of upstate New York, the sheer size of its apples, pears, peaches, and grapes undoubtedly made Chile "one of the most productive countries in the world." "It is said," he wrote in a typical bit of gold seeker fancy, "that five or six miles in the country one can travel for miles and step on nothing but strawberries, which are blooming and ripening all seasons of the year." Benjamin Dore from the frosty coast of Maine believed that "every thing" would grow in the lush Brazilian soil: "pine apples oranges lemons . . . peaches figs bananers [*sic*] water melons onions sweet potatoes rice coffee corn cucumbers potatoes Ec." Within this "splendid surplus of vegetable life," according to Bayard Taylor, one's sense of self might be overwhelmed. In this natural paradise, "as on the ocean," he noted, "you have a sense rather than a perception of beauty. . . . You gaze upon the scene before you with a never-sated delight, till your brain aches with the sensation, and you close your eyes, over-whelmed with the thought that all these wonders have been from the beginning—that year after year takes away no leaf of blossom that is not replaced, but the sublime mystery of growth and decay is renewed forever."[18]

Another source of this "sublime mystery" was the equally opulent and pervasive Catholicism of the southern hemisphere. For many forty-niners, twilight silhouettes of gigantic churches seemed to fill the warm air with magic. According to New Yorker Daniel Woods, its cathedral made Santa Maria de los Lagos "the most beautiful city we saw in Mexico . . . more thriving and prosperous than any we had seen." The neighboring town's church, he added, "was even more splendid." For Theodore Johnson, these cathedrals held supernatural secrets: transubstantiation, the promise of granted boons, lurid paintings and icons. "Panama abounds," he wrote, "with ruins of the most diversified and beautiful description. The most perfect of these is the Church of San Domingo." Inspired by these exotic examples, he explored the church, finding plenty of mysteries and secret ciphers "resembling the Arabic or Moorish characters."[19]

Again, it might be easy to assume that North American voyagers to Latin America dismissed Catholicism as another example of the region's backwardness. Many gold seekers did try to be dismissive; not all were wholly successful. Entering a church in Panama City, New York's Asaph Sawyer at first sneered at the Mass. "It will take more time," he wrote in his journal, "than I can spare to describe their mode of worship—suffice it to say such *consummate folly*, *buffoonery* and extreme *ignorance* I never saw before." On the singing of prayers, he wrote that "our back woods Wolves would have sneaked away out of sight at the hearing of such noises." But despite his resistance to these "idolatrous practices," something about the cathedral's architecture and ambiance—which he admitted held a certain magical allure—moved him to flow into prayer: "I here humbly pray to God that I may be so prospered as to be able to return home with a competency."[20]

In a similar manner, Bayard Taylor lamented the "tasteless style of ornament" on the exteriors of many cathedrals, the "glaring paint," "ghastly statues," and "shocking pictures" adorning their interiors. Still, he must have sought out such encounters, he saw as well "numbers of fat and sensual friars." He attended an outdoor Mass in a Mexico City plaza, where "at the tingle of a bell, ten thousand persons dropped on their knees, repeating their *aves* with a light, murmuring sound, that chimed pleasantly with the babbling of the fountain." Countinghouse clerk Samuel Upham recorded many of the same scenes, but with less resistance to their opulence. Visiting Rio's Convent of Saint Benedict, he noted the ubiquitous "jolly fat friars," along with walls "nearly covered with scriptural paintings by the old masters," ceilings "richly gilded and carved," and statues of saints "gorgeously dressed." Resonant with his images of the Middle Ages and the old world, such sights made Mexico, to Taylor, "as motley and picturesque as any of the old cities of Spain." For Upham, meanwhile, the churches of all Catholic countries, their "cowled monks and veiled nuns, . . . brought vividly to mind scenes from the 'Mysteries of Udolpho' and the 'Children of the Abbey.' "[21]

According to many forty-niners, these abundant and opulent environments had one major effect on Latin Americans. They made them lazy. The region's overarching problem was its perceived lack of progress. Unlike the North American observers, Latin Americans had failed to effect a proper mastery over external nature or internal natures. They lacked control over their passions; they were given to violence and overt displays of sexuality. Connected with the lack of progress was the Latin American's apparent total economic irresponsibility: the culture seemed dominated by chance, by an addiction to gambling, and by a too-free use of spices, caffeine, chocolate, tobacco, and alcohol. These behaviors revolted many forty-niners. Yet what is most interesting about these perceived Latin American characteristics is that they describe—with nearly perfect precision—the self-proclaimed actions of forty-niners as they traveled to California, and later as they went roistering about the gold country. Obviously, many would find ways to embrace these apparently quintessential Latin American expressions and behaviors.

One way forty-niners could embrace these behaviors was through envisioning themselves as helpless captives to Latin American pleasures. John Beeckman, a well-born New York lawyer with political aspirations in California, found Rio's "free blending together" of races "disgusting and repugnant in the extreme." At the same time, he enjoyed his stay in the city, remaining there nearly a month while his ship lay by for repairs. He portrayed this period as one of captivity, a typical dinner with one of Rio's leading citizens as a type of martyrdom. If we believe Beeckman's account of this dinner, which is taken from a letter he wrote to his wife, he wanted only to escape. A walk followed the dinner, he wrote, and during this walk he was surrounded. On one side there was "romantic and beautiful scenery as the imagination could conceive." On the other side there was "a Brazilian lady on my arm to whom I could not speak." In the middle was Beeckman, trapped and helpless. Finally, "that too was over," he added, "and I hoped I might be permitted to escape—but no—there was music in the evening and dancing and I was a martyr for three hours longer. I will never again dine with a Brazilian."[22]

Giving in to these sorts of pleasures was one thing; indulgence in what many forty-niners saw as characteristic Latin American brutality was quite another. Yet here too they could envision themselves as captives, as having been "lured" by the natives into their own excesses. One example of this type of experience comes from a missionary, Francis Prevaux, who had been sent by the Baptist Board of Missions to Christianize California. Prevaux had been told that, in his words, "the greatest cut throats in the world" roamed the isthmus. To his surprise, he found these cutthroats to be his fellow northeasterners. Indeed, their abstention had given way to brutality. What he saw, he reported, were bands of Yankees who "shockingly abuse, beat and mangle the poor natives for the most trivial offenses." In explaining this behavior, however, Prevaux placed the blame for these atrocities not on his "fallen brothers," but on the Latin American environment itself. "It is said," he wrote, "that 'man is a creature of circumstances,' that from the character of a man at home we cannot know what he will be in California. How fearfully has this been exemplified in our journey thus far! Young men who at home were temperate, moral and of high promise, I see now with rapid strides in the high road to ruin."[23]

In a similar manner, another missionary, the Reverend Joseph Augustine Benton, noted that along the isthmus formerly respectable men had been "lured to indulgencies and excesses." According to the Reverend Benton, these men had been severed from their former ties, freed from all checks and restraints, surrounded by a "sense of lawlessness." As a result, he declared, they "care not what it is they do, provided it excites and gratifies them."[24] Harsh as such criticism was, it did little to halt this type of behavior. In a sense, the Reverend Benton's criticism fit precisely with forty-niner desires. Certain Latin American behaviors, in other words, might be revolting to respectable white men, but in specific contexts they were seductive and free for the taking. If seduction often led to corruption, it was not from personal moral failure but through extrinsic depravity that they could not—or did not—resist.

In this respect, practically every forty-niner description of Latin American excess may be understood not simply as an example of racism, but also as an attempt to increase their own pleasure. For by seeing Latin Americans as perverted, and then giving in to perversity, gold seekers were able to intertwine revulsion with delight, hatred with love, making fun with having fun. At times, forty-niner accounts of resultant cross-cultural contacts might contain a certain degree of literary albeit sniggering charm. Richard Hale's version of a beggarly and comically inept Peruvian guide, for example, resonates with all the local color of Mark Twain. Leading Hale through the streets of Lima, the guide "pointed out a quaint roofless building, vast in extent, with box doors opening onto a gallery in the open air. This called into play all the dramatic fire of his excitable make up. 'Ah-ah-ver-ver-opera-fine-fine. Ver-ver-opera-presenta real.' "[25] Just as frequently, as George Payson's description of a dinner at Acapulco exemplifies, this type of forty-niner play resonates with a grating and obnoxious ugliness. "Here muchacho!-muchacho! eggs-wavers-mas-wavers—mas chick-een—cafe—mas milk—darn your eyes, don't you know your own language," Payson described one of his traveling companions as bellowing over dinner at an Acapulco hostel. To this verbal onslaught, he had the Mexican server utter a meek "poco tiempo." Thus Payson and his fellow voyagers experienced Latin America as an inverted world. Once there, they were free to take on the perceived characteristics of a barbarous other, free to cut a wide swath of offensive behavior through the countryside. " 'Poker Temper,' " was Payson's account of his companion's rejoinder, " 'I've had poker temper long enough, I tell you, now I want some chicken,' . . . and finishing our dinner with a hearty laugh, we sallied forth into the street."[26]

A threat of violence lies just beneath the surface of this phantasmic conversation. In Payson's account, this element is part of the fun; a hearty laugh with the fellows—especially if it came at the expense of the locals—may have seemed a rather harmless performance of the masculine primitive. Elsewhere, as they locked elbows to swagger through the streets of South American ports and bowl over passers-by, the new spirit of Yankee fun found similar ambivalent expression. From Mexico, Henry Peters wrote that his hosts were "a treacherous . . . cowardly set of ruffians, they hate the yankees, and would, if they dared, shoot every one that comes ashore." Many other forty-niners undoubtedly shared his assessment. At the same time, they delighted in mimicking the Spanish language, in learning exotic-sounding names for things. It is amazing how quickly certain Spanish words—"compadre," "amigo," "fandango," and "tortilla"—entered the forty-niners' day-to-day language. Balancing between engagement with and resistance to these cultural forms, Theodore Johnson wrote of his thrill at learning a few words of Spanish, even while he dismissed them as "jabber."[27]

What we see here is a desire on the part of forty-niners to take on certain elements of Latin American expression, to borrow these elements even as they dismissed them as strange or perverse. Elsewhere, rigid northeastern men could invoke for themselves the somewhat oxymoronic character of the "Yankee dare-devil." This self-image allowed them to join the natives—or their "captors"—in a carnival of expressions that back home would have been expressly forbidden. According to New Yorker John Linville Hall, the Americans on his ship arrived in Rio de Janeiro in an "unnatural state of excitement." There they reveled in a carnival atmosphere, leaving behind, as he put it, "a score of riot, excess and rowdyism . . . which ill beseems the American Character." Throughout the winter and spring of 1849, added another forty-niner, Yankees took over the city. There they "did just as they pleased and the city authorities were powerless to restrain them; but . . . they can well put up with the Yankee dare-devil spirit for the sake of the Yankee gold."[28]

These types of expressions—which were typical of the gold rush as a whole—would make the forty-niners seem far different from the individuals they had been back in the states. Their contacts with Latin America may have had something to do with this apparent transformation, for in this environment even seminary students could become Yankee daredevils. On 15 April 1849, the *George Washington*, a ship from New York, docked at the island port of Santa Catarina off the Brazilian coast. Safely in port, thirty of the ship's passengers, including a young seminary student from Oneida County named Thomas Matteson, went into town to purchase supplies. There, claimed Matteson, a "row began between the Portuguese and the Americans." The result was more riot than row, as Matteson summed it up: "2 Americans killed and 2 Portuguese, 1 American's leg broken, 10 Americans wounded, 14 Portuguese wounded." Matteson was in the middle of the fray. A well-behaved young man at home, he had crossed the southern frontier to find himself first a daredevil, then a ruffian, and still later a prisoner surrounded by 3,000 angry Brazilians.

As much as it is an example of Yankee imperialism, the situation of those aboard the *George Washington* appears to have resulted from an excess of boisterous spirits. But if the scene reflected a playing out of ambivalent longings for physical expression, its final act reveals connections between Yankee ambivalence and Yankee power. For three days Matteson and his mates remained under house arrest. Their ship languished at anchor, surrounded by island boats and unable to move while local authorities investigated complaints and prepared charges. Ultimately, these Yankees had the power to defend their excesses. On April 18, according to Matteson, the captain of the *Washington* warned the locals that he would "resort to arms without they were released immediately." A day later, his ship was again on the high seas, its criminal passengers freed at gunpoint.[29]

Although typically on a smaller scale, similar slippages into brutality marked the passing of gold seekers throughout Latin America. For many, a touch of Latin American violence seems to have offered an exhilarating taste of "real life." This type of contact may have been precisely the intention of Bayard Taylor, who, despite being warned of robbers in the Mexican provinces, decided to take a lone pleasure jaunt into the countryside. As might be expected, it did not take long for Taylor to meet up with a blood-chilling adventure. With a drawing of pistolas and a shout of "La boca a tierra," his yearned-for bandits made their appearance, trussing the travel writer while rifling his saddlebags. Taylor, if his account is to be believed, experienced the moment with a jaunty sense of brutality well met. "I never felt more alive than at this moment," he recalled, "I cannot say that I felt alarmed. My feelings during this preceding were oddly heterogeneous—at one moment burning with rage and shame at having neglected the proper means of defense, and the next, ready to burst into a laugh at the decided novelty of my situation." In fact, immediately following the scene, Taylor recorded a rather curious feeling of refreshment: "It is astonishing how light one feels after being robbed."[30]

Indeed, according to Taylor, there was something quite enjoyable and natural—even healthy—in this type of engagement with Latin American violence. Such adventures with the locals gave gold seekers a sense of freedom. They offered northeastern men a rare chance to throw off the "little arts of dissimilation [practiced] in society."[31] Certainly, the fact that the "little arts" were there in the first place added to the excitement of breaking them in the name of instinct. Sin, in other words, would only remain a source of pleasure as long as it remained sinful. Some northeastern missionaries missed this point. Many forty-niners did not.

Certainly the Harvardians aboard the ship *Duxbury* recognized the fact that sin and pleasure were twined, for they seemed always on the lookout for ways to experience them. Having sailed expressly for the adventure, these self-styled b'hoys sought every opportunity to make contact with the passing examples of Latin American passion. On 20 April 1849, a group of the ship's passengers went ashore at Rio for a night on the town. The next day, the crew charged one member of the group, a certain John Burns, with the crime of soliciting a prostitute. Transcribed in the *Duxbury*'s shipboard newspaper, the case of "Commonwealth vs. Burns" began in seriousness. "Judge Frank," read the charge before an assemblage of passengers forming a "Police Court": "defendant did on the evening of the 20th day of April A.D. in the City of Rio de Janeiro, secretly, maliciously, unceremoniously, with evil intent and malice aforethought . . . seek to have private intercourse with one of the daughters of easy virtue . . . greatly to the injury of the good citizens of said city of Rio—his friends thereby encouraging vice, and greatly endangering his bodily health." One crew member testified that he had heard the defendant complaining of "a burning sensation." Another reported hearing Burns say that "a married man is excusable so far from home," and that "the prices were reasonable in Rio."

John Burns pled not guilty to the charges. But the result of the proceedings may raise the question of why he was tried at all. For in the end, the "trial" was yet another example of the forty-niners' playful oscillation between proper standards of behavior and a tacit acceptance of perceived perversity as a form of manly adventure. According to the report, the next witness "declined answering any questions, as he might incriminate himself." At this point the ironic humor of the situation became obvious. "During the examination," claimed the reporter, "the court ruled several questions inadmissible, it appearing evident that thorough investigation would place his honor in a somewhat delicate position." As it turned out, both the prosecution and the defense were in a similar fix. Neither could raise questions without incriminating themselves. Finally, Judge Frank declared his verdict: Burns was guilty. As punishment he ordered the prisoner "to treat all hands."[32]

On the surface a clear case of the *Duxbury*'s usual fun and games, on a deeper level the trial appears as a more serious exposure of the forty-niners' culture. Clearly the fact that these were married men made the passengers' intercourse with prostitutes something perverse. What is interesting is that the men of the *Duxbury* seemed willing to admit this. Far from glossing over their ethical transgressions they exposed them in ritual, elevating them with the dramatics of a public spectacle. What the trial exposes is the circularity of forty-niner expression and action in Latin America. The abundance of Latin America, that is, its profusion and easy availability of temptation, would cause the forty-niners to give way to indulgence; giving in to forbidden behaviors would be followed by an admission of guilt; punishment would then circle back to a reembrace of forbidden behaviors.

In a sense, the ritual linked the secular pursuit of pleasure with the idiom of the Second Great Awakening. The admission of guilt, so central to the Christian revivalist movements of the mid-nineteenth century, seems here to have become a mode of pleasure enhancement. Back home, of course, ministers such as Charles Finney would have exploded in disgust at such a concept. Yet with its profusion of delights both carnal and aesthetic, and with its distant and exotic apartness, Latin America rolled indulgence and redemption into a perfect circle of Yankee pleasures, even if—especially if—these Yankees had been respectable men back home. Here indeed, the men of the *Duxbury* professed, was a paradise where a self-consciousness of perversity only added to the carnival joy of free expression. As the *Duxbury* prepared to sail from Rio, one of the bards of the company newspaper summed up this perspective in a poem:

O beautiful land
By soft breezes fanned
Where fruits in abundance are growing:
Where cockroaches run
Up our trousers in fun
And where rivers of liquor are flowing
Where each step in the street
Dark damsels we meet,
Tempting us their bananas to buy-o;
We cannot begin
To set forth our chagrin
At leaving thee; City o Rio.[33]

Expressions like these would appear to indicate the forty-niners' free embrace of quintessential Latin American temptations and pleasures, its abundance of exotic fruits, liquor, eroticized women, and even crawling things. But as celebratory as they were of exotic differences between cultures, forty-niner engagements with these subjects rarely proceeded without an undercurrent of condescension and guilt. Nearly always, it seems, what made Latin American cultural expressions interesting to forty-niners was the fact that they came from below, that they were forbidden, and that they were consciously linked to vice. "Many of their dances," as one forty-niner noted, even as he appeared to enjoy watching them, "are got up for the purpose of carrying out their vices."[34]

Theodore Johnson shared this view. One night during his brief stay in Gorgona, he heard a distant rhythm. Always on the lookout for new and exotic experiences, he followed the drums to their source. What he found was a genuine South American "fandango." The dance, he wrote, "consists of a lazy, slow shuffle, until excited by aguardiente, and emboldened as night progresses, the women dance furiously up to their favorites among the men, who are then obligated to follow suit, all joining in a kind of nasal squeal or chant. There is nothing graceful in their mode of dancing, but, on the contrary, their motions are often indecent and disgusting." For Richard Henry Dana the fandango had been a rather "lifeless affair." For gold seekers like Johnson, these dances would become "half barbaric orgies."[35] Clearly, the men who described such scenes were repulsed and attracted at the same time. Johnson was offended, yet he stayed to watch the performance. From his choice of words to describe the dance—his reference to joined bodies, squeals, chants and indecent, rhythmic motions—what he saw, and what seems to have disgusted and attracted him most, was the fandango's embodiment of women.

Even before the gold rush, the Latina's presumed lack of shame was a source of pleasure to male observers, her naked form one of the public legacies of the Mexican War. Stationed along the border at Matamoros, Zachary Taylor's men would watch as local women washed clothing in the river. "Nearly all" of these women, wrote one of these gaping on-lookers, "have well-developed, magnificent figures." These figures, in turn, could be uncovered with imagination: they dressed, the soldier added, "with as little clothing as you can well fancy." "Their bosoms were not compressed in stays," wrote another, "but heaved freely under the healthful influence of the genial sun and balmy air of the sunny South." The gold seekers were similarly attracted. In Chagres, according to one observer, women wore only a "single cotton garment" and children gamboled "in Nature's own clothing." In Panama City, another reported that "many of the Women [wear] nothing but a thin cotton cloth tied around their hips." Some of the younger females, noted still another gold seeker, "were entirely *model artiste*, at least as far as their clothing was concerned."[36]

These obsessions with Latin American nudity reflected nothing new. Early explorers in America had paid similar attention to the nakedness of indigenous peoples. What is interesting about these passages, however, may be their revelation that by the mid-nineteenth century these images reflected not so much what (or who) was being seen, but a way of seeing. In these examples, the forty-niner vision seemed capable of passing right through loose clothing to focus on heaving breasts. As Latin Americanist Frederick Pike has noted, the North American way of seeing the Latina was to link her with na-ture and with "wanton physicality." She was completely sexualized, a source of admiration and disdain filtered through the expectation of "available sex proffered by inferior creatures who ostensibly welcome seduction and subjugation." Yankee perception of Latin American women, claims Pike, was based on a willful form of synecdoche: the prostitute stood for all.[37]

For Pike and other historians, the meaning of such perceptions is singular and clear, their goal simply to reduce the Latin American to in-ferior racial status, to open the way for conquest along with sexual, and later political or economic, exploitation. At the same time, while these perceptions indicate that many forty-niners were racist or imperialist in their thought, they also suggest that the culture of the Yankee Northeast, while committed to proper standards of behavior, was not always based on following them. Perception notwithstanding, there *were* real prostitutes in many forty-niner ports of call. The port of Talcahuano, Chile, for example, contained a particularly large array of brothels and dives. The reason for this thriving business had nothing to do with any natural earthiness of Latin American women. Instead, it stemmed from the fact that long before the argonauts landed, Talcahuano was a favorite port of the American whaling industry. What forty-niners were seeing in these ports was a sexual economy of their own creation: the local prostitutes were manifestations of Yankee culture.[38]

Although prostitution was a flourishing industry in mid-nineteenth-century seaport towns from Maine to Chile, we cannot expect the gold seekers to admit their patronage of these establishments. Despite this sense of propriety, however, they frequently found themselves—somehow—on the bad side of Talcahuano. "As we walked through the filthy narrow streets," wrote George Payson during his visit to the town, "the open doors on each side were full of women, who kept up an incessant cry of 'come in, Californe;' 'Californe, come in;' often adding other allurements of a yet more unmistakable character." Another forty-niner, Joseph Lamson, reported that he tried to avoid these streets, but his straight path seems also to have been pleasured by furtive glances. "As I passed into the cross streets," he wrote, "I saw a great many women seated or standing at their doors . . . Many of them were very filthy, though some were neatly dressed, and were rather pretty. They had dark complexions, fresh, florid cheeks, bright, black eyes, and black glossy hair hanging down their backs. . . . They had a smile and a word for all strangers, but their smiles were those of the siren."[39]

For a man who was just passing by these exotic side streets, Lamson's vision was remarkably detailed. From this level of detail, it is easy to assume a certain amount of repetition in such self-proclaimed victories over temptation. What we see here is an image of straight-laced men walking stiff-necked past allurements and fleshly pleasures, their eyes darting furiously back and forth, passing on in self-congratulatory resistance to sin, then circling around the block and starting again. At the same time, there are indications that visits to Talcahuano might be marked by more than window shopping. "In the city of Talcahuana," wrote one gold seeker to a friend, "there is nothing of special interest or remark but one, and that is its Prostitution." Having been told that "there was not ten virtuous females among a multitude of three thousand," he saw little in the port that would contradict his expectations. Nor did his fellow voyagers. And so, the city "was just the port to suit the tastes and gratify the passions of many of our company among them I regret to say were those who had left confiding companions behind. Very soon after we put to sea, then certain kinds of medicines were in demand and freely administered."[40] Indeed, this account makes it clear that revulsion and attraction might be wed in indulgence.

Undoubtedly, some forty-niners expressed this attraction without a sense of ambivalence, and without the additional thrill that came with a conscious sense of the Latina's position as an ethnic and erotic other. For Frank Buck, the "ladies" of Lima were simply "the most beautiful women I have ever seen." More frequently, the men seemed incapable of separating the Latina's allure from her supposedly intrinsic qualities of immodesty and "darkness." As his ship neared Brazil's main port of call, Samuel Upham reported that its passengers were busily engaged in bathing and shaving; all were desirous, he wrote, "of captivating the dark-eyed *senoritas* on their arrival in Rio." Similarly, Charles Parke noted desires for the "dusky senoritas" of Granada, Nicaragua. In such cases, dusk and dark, whether attached to eyes or bodies, conveyed the Latina's presumed internal passion and lack of shame: "tis only necessary to add," as Parke made sure to mention, "*extreme modesty* is a scarce article in this country."[41]

Unschooled in shame and modesty, the Latina of this vision was a site for the projection of fantasy, a subject of perfect desire and limitless sexuality. Accordingly, forty-niner descriptions of her suggest a lot of wide-eyed gaping. Theodore Johnson's eyes went toward a group of women pounding corn for tortillas: "One of these senoritas," he noted, "was quite pretty, and as she gracefully bent forward in her useful employment, displayed a bust which Saratoga [might] envy." Parke's gaze settled on a part of the female anatomy that while now the subject of "fetishism," was through much of the nineteenth century a more central subject of erotic attraction and mainstream pornography. Like Johnson, he too was transfixed by the sight of women pounding corn, this time with their feet. "I saw the feet when they came out," he exclaimed in his journal, "and I know they were *clean*. Every time after when I ate tortillas, I imagined I could see those beautiful clean feet." Finally, gold seekers imagined that the Latina, like a host of ethnic and erotic beauties from Pocahontas to the Maid of Monterrey, would naturally return their desires. While James Tyson dined with a Mexican family, his eyes rested on the household's eldest daughter. She, at least in his account, returned his interest: "being interrogated whether she preferred Americans or Mexicans, she quickly replied, '*Mexicano Malo, Americano bueno, grande!*' "[42]

Yet again, rarely did these yearnings proceed without a keen sense of guilt. As one of the poems printed aboard the *Duxbury* reveals, these erotic fantasies, however mild they appear on the surface, could delve deeply into forbidden desires. These depths, in turn, might only increase the degree of shame, self-hatred, and ugly projection of destructive tendencies. "She stood there in her beauty," read the first line of the poem to "The Slave Girl at Rio," and through four verses its author expressed his attraction. His eye climbed from her "perfect woman's form" to "her bosom's swelling outlines" to her "dark and lustrous eye"; and then came his penultimate admission: "I should I knew see naught on earth / So beautiful again." Yet the last lines of the poem reflect the ironic antithesis that so frequently characterized the forty-niner's inability to decide between attraction and revulsion:

> But 'twas no use to figger
> In setting up a wail;
> For she's the blackest nigger
> That I saw out of jail.[43]

John Cornelison's description of "Estafania," a vision of Latin American womanhood encountered in Chile and a "specimen of South American beauty," reveals a similar inability to contemplate the attractions of the Latina without a consciousness of depravity. "Cheek bones somewhat high," began Cornelison, "and complexion a shade darker than the brunette; vermilion color'd cheeks, and cherry lips, formed a sweet and expressive countenance at once attractive and romantic." Cornelison's desires are plain in this passage. So are his fears. Estafania's face, he claimed, was perfect "for embellishing a tale of love, murder and suicide. Pity it was that sensuality and depravity enveloped itself in such a lovely mould."[44]

Love, murder, and suicide: together these subjects may have formed the constituent elements of the forty-niners' visions of Latin American womanhood. They may, as well, be elements of a modern pornographic way of dealing with forbidden desires. If, that is, the Latina inspired forty-niners' desires, these very yearnings appear to have raised fears of complete self-dissolution, of a loss of respectability and whiteness. These fears, in turn, might spark violent reactions. Perhaps the best, and thus most disturbing, example is Connecticut-born Charles Palmer's short story about his crossing of Brazil and Argentina. Palmer's story, which he seems to have penned after his arrival in San Francisco, and which he planned to send east for publication, begins with reference to the gold seekers' self-conceptions as daredevil Yankees: "we were all young," he wrote, "hearty, well armed and truly Yankee in our restless love of new scenes and adventures." Its central scene resonates with a pornographic way of seeing and experiencing the peoples and cultures of the southern hemisphere—with, that is, simultaneous longings to embrace and destroy specific elements within these cultures as the source of forbidden pleasures.

Palmer's "A Scene upon the Pampas" involves a meeting with a Spanish don, Señor Muñalta. The key figure, however, is his young daughter: "She is only sixteen," Palmer has one of his characters say, "and it is no wonder that her father is so careful of her, for she is beautiful as the virgin." Having established her virginity and ethnic exoticism, as well as his own position as Yankee adventurer, Palmer appears to be preparing the reader for a tale of seduction, manly rage, and the *duello*. Indeed, he begins in this manner. Señorita Muñalta, as it turns out, has been taken captive by a group of Pampas "Indians." The heroes meet the marauding band and open fire. They manage to kill five of the enemy, but one escapes with the girl. Palmer's main protagonist rides to the rescue; he grapples with the Indian, breaks his arm, and appears to save the virgin. At this point in Palmer's story the stage seems set for passion. Even in imagination, however, he could not bring himself to embrace his subject. Instead of envisioning a romantic consummation he pulls back to a disturbing resistance to miscegenation. His ends his tale in a ritual of destruction, all the more disturbing because it too contains an element of pleasure. Señor Muñalta rides up, and, as he "gazed upon his daughter's upturned face," writes Palmer: "Ha! 'twas only to see the sharp spikes of a war-club crash into her tender brain, and to feel the hot gore of his child sprinkling his face with horrible profusion!"[45]

The fact that Palmer was a graduate of Yale College and a product of an emerging middle-class culture of respectability did not keep him from venturing far into the dark terrain of his fantasies. His narrative, however, appears to reflect a distressing maintenance of respectability and whiteness. Pleasure for men like him appears to have come at a price. The result here is a blend of anger, racism, and misogyny, an attack directed toward both the desire itself and the exotic subject that had called it into being. Thus despite their celebrated penchant for social and cultural inversions, in their meetings with Latin Americans forty-niners generally left prescriptive hierarchies intact. In fact, much like the blackface minstrel performers who dominated the nineteenth-century American stage, these meetings may have strengthened hierarchies by linking reversals of bourgeois norms to the stereotyped expressions of an ethnic opposite. If the gold seekers pictured these alternative behaviors and peoples as enticingly exotic, and if they desired to embrace—at least temporarily—these "low" elements, they still marked them with disgust and shame. Through their perceptions, the peoples of Hispanic and Portuguese America became lazy, intemperate, and sexually charged exemplars of raw passion. Latin America itself became a site for the play of instinctual urges, for momentary but continuously repeated reversals of Victorian morality that seemed to place moral purity in the service of pleasure enhancement.

If these perceptions of Latin Americans suggest a complex interplay between desire and guilt, Latin American responses to the forty-niners appear equally complicated. A few accessible accounts suggest that Latinos had their own attractions to the forty-niners' culture. Chilean Ramon Jil Navarro had nothing against these Yankees, at least before he met them. "I am a Yankee myself," he noted in his diary, "in the sense that I cherish freedom and am in favor of new economic development and improvement." The problem, for Navarro as for others, appears to have stemmed from the way many forty-niners behaved, the way they adopted a "blustering pose" in all their contacts with Latinos both during the voyage and in California. To Vincente Perez Rosales, the passing of the gold seekers seemed "like a masquerade ball of gigantic proportions," with the result that they appeared as mere "animals." For Mary Seacole, a Jamaican who went to Panama around 1850 to help manage her brother's hotel, the more "civilized" forty-niners were, the "more dangerous" they became. As a result, nearly all appeared as "rough, rude men," and nearly all "reveled in disgusting excess of license." The people of "New Grenada," she added, "were strongly prejudiced against the Americans; . . . they feared their quarrelsome, bullying habits."[46]

This fear was not always passive. On the Isthmus of Panama, the interplay of gold seeker perceptions and Latin American response resulted in at least two large-scale riots. The first occurred at Panama City in 1850, when the majority of forty-niners were on their way to California. At this time, the city was a bottleneck for those awaiting steamers that had been impossibly overbooked by eastern ticket sellers; while they waited, highstrung optimism, boredom, impatience, and hot weather combined in a flammable mixture. Finally, during the first week of June 1850, local dissatisfaction with forty-niner excesses ignited; a small quarrel between North Americans and indigenous residents turned into a running battle, leaving several dead on both sides. A second riot erupted in October 1851, as gold seekers passed through Gorgona on the Caribbean side of the isthmus on their return to the Northeast. This time, the spark occurred when two boats, one containing a group of black Panamanians, the other steered by a returning gold seeker, struck each other.

As one forty-niner's account of this second riot suggests, the incident revealed the depth of anger lying just below the surface among the town's inhabitants. Immediately, he wrote, a crowd gathered, "yelling, shouting, threatening the life of every white man, brandishing their weapons." In the following two days locals killed twelve Yankees. Both sides agreed to a truce on October 24, but, claimed the observing gold seeker, "notwithstanding the treaty, there is great hostility in feeling, which occasionally bursts forth, but with no very serious consequences."[47] It is easy to see such hostility as a natural concomitant of manifest destiny. It may be more accurate, however, to view it as at least partly arising from a complex matrix of revulsion and desire. In effect, this type of contact would far outlast the wills of nineteenth-century filibusters and robber barons. Indeed, it appears to reflect a very modern tension: a blend of attraction and revulsion on one side pitted against resistance and reaction to being subjects of pleasure, revulsion, and disgusted embraces on the other.

This tension would frame forty-niner contacts with Latinos in California; to a degree, it would continue to frame cross-hemispheric contacts in the future. Following the forty-niners, North American contact with Latin America would be characterized by dispossession, the building of railroads and canals, and economic exploitation. Yet along the way, the southern frontier would remain a source of delight: "aesthetically stimulating," as William James later referred to it during his 1865 voyage with Professor Louis Agassiz, the "Original Seat of the Garden of Eden."[48] Contact would also be marked by similar examples of self-dissolution, utopian attempts to embrace unresolved yearnings, disturbing and often violent expressions of love and revulsion. Finally, Latin America would remain a place populated with exotic "primitives," "prostitutes," and "passionate children of nature." If historians, scholars, tourists, or even well-meaning activists would later reconfigure these others as victims of imperial design and conquest, this rhetorical move might be considered another turn in a linguistic onslaught, another search for an embrace tinged with revulsion. For whether as primitives, Indians, prostitutes, or victims, as long as they remained situated in a field of play between high aspiration and low impulse, Latin Americans might remain erotically charged subjects of pleasure and desire.

Finally, these kinds of perceptions and experiences would frame the gold rush as a whole. As modern readers know, life during the flush times of California would be characterized by lawlessness and violence, by lynch law, claim jumping, gambling, and prostitution. The forty-niners would blame much of this lawlessness and violence on the Hispanic population of California. The prostitutes were frequently Latinas. The claim jumpers were Mexicans, the gamblers Chileans. The targets of lynch law, those who made lynchings and vigilance committees necessary, were all three. In the end, the forty-niners' greatest and most perverted paradise would not be Latin America but gold rush–era California. And during the gold rush, the meaning of perversity would be clear to the forty-niners and their observers. Perversity was something they could take, or borrow, or bring into themselves, at least in Latin America or California. At the same time, it contained an ethnic dimension: it was Hispanic and dark; it was composed by a set of desires, yearnings, expressions, and behaviors welled up from the "dark side" of a clearly perceived racial boundary; therefore, as great as its charms were, it would remain perverse.

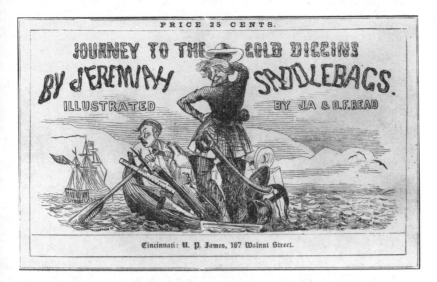

The Fop Goes West. By the 1840s, the overcivilized eastern dandy had become a stock character in literature, minstrel shows, and comic plays. The subject of an 1849 comic strip, Jeremiah Saddlebags was one of these characters. The results of his "Journey to the Gold Diggins" are predictable enough. Burdened with useless mining implements and parlor affectations, unable to perform the physical labor necessary to make a success of gold digging, he is run out of the gold regions. The message is clear: the authentic West was no place for the refined young clerks of the northeastern middle class. Title page, [James A. Read], *Journey to the Gold Diggins* (originally published, New York: Stringer & Townsend, 1849). Courtesy of the American Antiquarian Society.

THE INDEPENDENT GOLD HUNTER ON HIS WAY TO CALIFORNIA

I NEITHER BORROW NOR LEND

The Independent Gold Hunter on His Way to California. At the time of the gold rush, the *New York Herald* referred to the forty-niners as "educated, intelligent, civilized, and elevated men, of the best classes of society." This recognition actually contributed to the charm and humor of the event. For as the character depicted in this illustration demonstrates, the spectacle of respectable men heading for California was both riveting and hilarious. Later, this image would be lost beneath depictions of the forty-niners as authentic westerners and working-class "b'hoys." The change suggests the success with which middle-class gold seekers were able to remake themselves in California and along the way. Lithograph (Hartford, Conn.: Kelloggs & Comstock, ca. 1849). Courtesy of the American Antiquarian Society.

FOR
CALIFORNIA!
Mutual Protection
Trading & Mining Co.

Having purchased the splendid, Coppered and very fast Sailing

Barque EMMA ISIDORA,

Will leave about the 15th of February. This vessel will be fitted in the very best manner and is one of the fastest sailing vessels that goes from this port.

Each member pays 300 dollars and is entitled to an equal proportion of all profits made by the company either at mining or trading, and holds an equal share of all the property belonging to the company. Experienced men well acquainted with the coast and climate are already engaged as officers of the Company. A rare chance is offered to any wishing a safe investment, good home and Large profits.

This Company is limited to 60 and any wishing to improve this opportunity must make immediate application.

An Experienced Physician will go with the company.

For Freight or Passage apply to 23 State Street, corner of Devonshire, where the list of Passengers may be seen.

JAMES H. PRINCE, Agent,
23 State Street, corner of Devonshire St., Boston.

For further Particulars, see the Constitution.

Propeller Power Presses,
142 Washington St., Boston.

For California! During the early days of the gold rush, at least, the most common way for northeasters to get to California was by joining a stock company. The broadside advertisement for this Boston association is typical. Here, the gold rush is not a romantic adventure for independent young rovers, but a serious enterprise for businesslike men looking for the security of "mutual protection," "safe investments," and "large profits." The $300 charge for joining the company represents a year's earnings for the average American in 1849. Broadside (Boston: Propeller Power Press, 1849). Courtesy of the American Antiquarian Society.

HO! FOR CALIFORNIA.

All Classes of Society. This 1849 engraving from the *New York Atlas* pictures the rush to California as a cross-class event. The character at the front of the crowd undoubtedly represents the unaffected Bowery b'hoy. The artist's focus, however, seems to be on the purposeful stride of the young-man-on-the-make, along with a parson type who has abandoned his congregation to the "extensive firm" of "Appolyon, Bezebub, Lucifer & Co." Meanwhile, at least one top-hatted capitalist appears to have discovered an easier method of travel to California. Engraving, *New York Atlas*, 14 January 1849. Courtesy of the American Antiquarian Society.

Experiencing the Rush at a Distance.
Popular in the mid-nineteenth century, rolling panoramas allowed Americans to have a "direct" experience of a host of subjects, from a trip down the Mississippi River to the life of Napoleon Bonaparte. This example, with its 160,000 feet of canvas, and which passed through Worcester, Massachusetts, in 1850, would most likely have been at least three miles in length. For the small price of admission, observers and forty-niner wives could follow along with the gold seekers, sharing their experiences in California and along the way. Broadside (Worcester, Mass.: Tyler and Hamilton Printers, 1851). Courtesy of the American Antiquarian Society.

LITH. & PUB. BY N. CURRIER,   Entered according to Act of Congress

THE WAY THEY W.

"THE STEAMER" AT PANAMA.

The Bottleneck at Panama. The exotic qualities of the Latin South seemed to have a liberating effect on many forty-niners. According to one observer along the Isthmus of Panama, forty-niners there were "lured to indulgencies and excesses. They feel neither checks nor restraints from without. A sense of lawlessness pervades them. For self indulgence some prey on their victims; for killing time many engage in nothing but killing themselves." Lithograph (New York: N. Currier, 1849). Courtesy of the American Antiquarian Society.

The Work Ethic and the Miner. Even during the gold rush era, middle-class emigrants to California did not abandon their cultural values. This lithograph from the 1850s stresses the importance of the work ethic to success in the gold regions. Here, interestingly, the successful forty-niner is portrayed as a virtuous farmer, and thus not a forty-niner at all. Lithograph (San Francisco: Britton and Rey, ca. 1852). Courtesy of the American Antiquarian Society.

The Saloon. If their accounts are any indication, it was a rare forty-niner who did not rush to visit the city's saloons upon arrival in San Francisco or Sacramento. Typically, these accounts followed the eastern genre of immoral reform, excoriating the immoralities within these halls, or "hells," all the while providing readers with as much titillating detail as time and talent allowed. Here, this illustrator has depicted Sacramento's El Dorado as a lavish hall, its crowd a multicultural mix of Mexican bandits, Chinese celestials, Missouri "pikes," New York b'hoys, and eastern gentlemen. Woodcut (Sacramento: Democratic State Journal, ca. 1850s). Courtesy of the American Antiquarian Society.

Enter the Eastern Prude. Social reformer, former matron of female inmates at Sing Sing Prison, phrenologist, and author of several books on female
superiority, Eliza Farnham was a woman of many talents and interests. Few,
however, seemed quite in fitting with gold rush California. Yet when her husband, Thomas Jefferson Farnham, died in California, she leapt at the chance to
take over the running of his farm near Santa Cruz. The debaucheries of the gold
rush, she felt, offered a chance for a revolution against masculine excess, a perfect opportunity to display the superior nature of woman. ©Collection of the
New-York Historical Society.

SHIP ANGELIQUE.
CALIFORNIA ASSOCIATION OF AMERICAN WOMEN.

NEW YORK, FEBRUARY 2D, 1849.

THE death of my husband, THOMAS J. FARNHAM, Esq., at San Francisco, in September last, renders it expedient that I should visit California during the coming season. Having a desire to accomplish some greater good by my journey thither than to give the necessary attention to my private affairs, and believing that the presence of women would be one of the surest checks upon many of the evils that are apprehended there, I desire to ask attention to the following sketch of a plan for organizing a party of such persons to emigrate to that country.

Among the many privations and deteriorating influences to which the thousands who are flocking thither will be subjected, one of the greatest is the absence of woman, with all her kindly cares and powers, so peculiarly conservative to man under such circumstances.

It would exceed the limits of this circular to hint at the benefits that would flow to the growing population of that wonderful region, from the introduction among them of intelligent, virtuous and efficient women. Of such only, it is proposed to make up this company. It is believed that there are hundreds, if not thousands, of such females in our country who are not bound by any tie that would hold them here, who might, by going thither, have the satisfaction of employing themselves greatly to the benefit and advantage of those who are there, and at the same time of serving their own interest more effectually than by following any employment that offers to them here.

It is proposed that the company shall consist of persons not under twenty-five years of age, who shall bring from their clergyman, or some authority of the town where they reside, satisfactory testimonials of education, character, capacity, &c., and who can contribute the sum of two hundred and fifty dollars, to defray the expenses of the voyage, make suitable provision for their accommodation after reaching San Francisco, until they shall be able to enter upon some occupation for their support, and create a fund to be held in reserve for the relief of any who may be ill, or otherwise need aid before they are able to provide for themselves.

It is believed that such an arrangement, with one hundred or one hundred and thirty persons, would enable the company to purchase or charter a vessel, and fit it up with every thing necessary to comfort on the voyage, and that the combination of all for the support of each, would give such security, both as to health, person and character, as would remove all reasonable hesitation from the minds of those who may be disposed and able to join such a mission. It is intended that the party shall include six or eight respectable married men and their families.

Those who desire further information will receive it by calling on the subscriber at

ELIZA W. FARNHAM.

The New-York built Packet Ship ANGELIQUE has been engaged to take out this Association. She is a spacious vessel, fitted up with state rooms throughout and berths of good size, well ventilated and provided in every way to secure a safe, speedy and comfortable voyage. She will be ready to sail from New-York about the 12th or 15th of April.

WE, the undersigned, having been made acquainted with the plan proposed by MRS. FARNHAM, in the above circular, hereby express our approbation of the same, and recommend her to those who may be disposed to unite with her in it, as worthy the trust and confidence necessary to its successful conduct.

HON. J. W. EDMONDS, Judge Superior Court.	W. C. BRYANT, ESQ.
HON. W. T. McCOUN, Late Vice Chancellor.	SHEPHERD KNAPP, ESQ.
HON. B. F. BUTLER, Late U. S. Attorney.	REV. GEORGE POTTS, D. D.
HON. H. GREELEY.	REV. HENRY WARD BEECHER.
ISAAC T. HOPPER, ESQ.	MISS CATHARINE M. SEDGWICK.
FREEMAN HUNT, ESQ.	MRS. C. M. KIRKLAND.
THOMAS C. DOREMUS, ESQ.	

Mission of Redemption. According to this 1849 broadside, Eliza Farnham's mission for the redemption of California called for 130 "intelligent, virtuous, and efficient" women to volunteer as potential wives for the gold seekers. The mission failed. The ship *Angelique* arrived in San Francisco with only three women on board. Even Farnham herself was missing, having been abandoned in Valparaiso by the ship's captain following several confrontations between the two. Yet despite its failure, Farnham's mission helped reestablish class hierarchies in California by suggesting that some men could be made better than others through the redemptive power of respectable, northeastern women. Broadside (New York: George F. Nesbitt, Printer, 1849). California Historical Society, gift of Mrs. George Dunlap Lyman, FN-30858.

The Miner's Ten Commandments. One of the most famous images of the gold rush, this 1853 broadside offers a clear picture of the forty-niner's dual identity. Out West, he appears as the roistering bravo, surrounded by lynchings, claim jumpings, gambling, and drunkenness. Back East, he appears in his true garb, as the respectable bourgeoisie, surrounded by family and parlor, elevated by the redemptive power of his wife. Broadside by James M. Hutchings (Placerville, Calif.: Sun Print, 1853). Courtesy of the American Antiquarian Society.

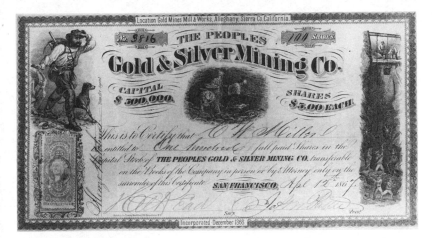

The Enduring Forty-Niner. The image of the lone prospector cannot be debunked. In this 1863 stock certificate from Sierra County, California, the unconnected (except for his dog) forty-niner survives, even in proximity to an opposite image depicting the reality of economies of scale in the mining industry. The enduring power of this myth may reflect its maintenance of another: the even more powerful myth of a hopelessly repressed middle class. Courtesy of the American Antiquarian Society.

Six

California Is a Humbug

As they passed through the "Golden Gate" and entered the harbor of San Francisco, many northeastern forty-niners reached a high point of anticipation. Here at last was their sacred arena, their virgin land that for so long had awaited their embrace. "Fair California!" argonaut turned historian Hubert Howe Bancroft described it, "voluptuous in thy half-tropic bed, . . . redolent with wild flowers, and billowy with undulating parks and smooth corrugated mounds and swelling heights, . . . captivating the mind, and ravishing the senses with thy bewitching charms, . . . thy blushing beauty veiled in misty gauze that rises fresh and glistening from the sun beaten ocean."[1] A landscape of equal parts maternal nurture and erotic charm, this feminized environment would become a stage for the playing out of pent-up exuberance, for exotic cultural exchange and masculine self-enrichment. San Francisco's port was filled with ships "from every quarter of the globe"; its streets teemed with "denizens of every clime," Australians, Mexicans, Kanakas, Peruvians, Chileans, and Europeans. "Money, wines, and liquor flowed like water . . . pistols and revolvers, fired in recklessness or fun sometimes, made the air musical with loud reports." Here was manhood on display: "and verily to coin a suitable word, we were in the Cosmopolis of the world."

Within about a year, longer for some forty-niners, shorter for others, much of this sense of drama, expectation, and carnival enjoyment of heterogeneity would disappear. For within this time, Eldorado's utopias would be debunked, its false promises exposed, and California would become little more than a "humbug." Its landscapes, once soft and voluptuous, would be hardened by competition, its thrilling scenes of "Cosmopolis" displaced by unmarked graves and weeping forty-niners.[2]

For a time after they landed in California, many forty-niners remained "in play." Theodore Johnson continued to invoke Edenic visions of an abundant landscape, noting flowers of all colors, "white, blue, and violet, the orange and lemon fading into the liquid hue of the amber." "Filling our hat bands with these gorgeous plumes," he added, "we looked like fitting followers of Fra Diavolo, and wished that wives, mothers, and sisters were there to see." Massachusetts native Stephen Davis could still at times portray his gold camp as a paradise on earth. It was the "very place my imagination had pictured to me in younger days," he recalled, "the realization of all the airy castles I had built in my romantic spells, where I would live and die, away from the selfish, wicked world."[3]

In California, however, these frolics and "airy castles" would become more rare than they had been during the voyage. Soon after their arrival in the gold country, many forty-niners increasingly found the "selfish, wicked world" of market competition breaking into their sacred arena of male play. As Elisha Crosby described it, the voyage through Panama, if occasionally marked by violence, had proceeded in "good humor." "The scenes and incidents of that voyage," he recalled, "were varied and comical to the extreme." Shortly after landing in San Francisco he adopted a more sober tone: "It was pretty well understood that every fellow must look out for himself as best he could."[4] For gold seekers, as for historians later, this transition would provide the framework for the experience. At the time, many forty-niners would portray it as a movement from "dream to dust," or from "golden dreams to leaden realities." Historians have interpreted this change as a turn from chaos to order, from wild frontier to controlled civilization.[5] The turning point in nearly all of these accounts, both historical and contextual, was the failure of California to live up to its promises, the failure of most forty-niners to strike it rich. Only rarely has this transition been analyzed as a class dynamic. In the few cases that it has, the trajectory seems based on the assumption of a static middle-class respectability. For a quixotic moment, that is, a rowdy and classless mix of dreams, anticipations, and desires characterized the rush. Then came failure, and order; then came the bearers of respectability, white-collar emigrants and women. Meanwhile life in California returned to the mundane rhythms set by the self-controlled bourgeoisie.[6] In the end, the gold rush would be very disappointing.

Thus the failure of the forty-niner's dreams announced the arrival of middle-class realities. Or at the very least, this failure marked a middle-class reassertion of control. For even if many forty-niners were middle class, they would still, according to the standard analysis, be characterized by little more than a one-dimensional and curiously static code of refinement and self-control. It stands to reason that the region's early period of overturned social relations, its free blending of classes and races, would only have made them uncomfortable. They were troubled by California's moral ambiguities, traumatized by its lack of distinctions. In other words, this was not a happy time for the uptight middle class, and its members among the forty-niners would not be content until order was reestablished.[7] What this standard interpretation misses is the possibility that middle-class forty-niners had gone to California to seek alternatives to respectability. For many, the period of social disorder would be represented as "Cosmopolis," as a kind of utopian place of cultural exchange and endless possibility. For most, it was not chaos but the reassertion of order that made California a humbug. The disappointment of the gold rush, in other words, was not, and is not, its social chaos and heterogeneity, but the fact that neither of these supposed characteristics was lasting.

In the early days of the rush at least, forty-niners, even middle-class forty-niners, appear to have gloried in California's diversity. "The population," wrote Samuel Upham soon after his arrival in the mining town of Happy Valley, "is as heterogeneous as their habitations. It seems as though every nation on the face of the earth has sent a representative to this place. Such a medley of languages and jargon of tongues the world has seldom seen. It is a modern babel."[8] The effect of this classless utopia, at least according to Frank Marryat, was a kind of boundless energy, a sense of authentic physicality and happiness. California was a place where "all classes, freed in a great measure from conventional restrictions, appear in their true garbs." Everyone worked. Everyone did hard, physical work; and, as a result "our beards grew, our muscles increased to an alarming extent, our manners were less toned down than was usual, in fact they were *swaggering*, our appetites were very large."[9]

All of this, as forty-niners knew, would look very strange in the East, where large muscles and larger appetites were more frequently associated with a vulgar working class. Yet many reveled in reversals of eastern norms and social orders, particularly in the spectacles these reversals would create for eastern audiences. "I very much wonder what your ideas are . . . in relation to us as a people," wrote John McCracken to one of his friends in New York, "for I assure you we acquire even with a residence of a few months a 'peculiar individuality.' " To Manhattan doctor James Tyson, peculiarities in appearance, behavior, and thought were common in California; what made them interesting was how they would play in the respectable East. Costumed in the properly disheveled habit of his fellows, he noted that the "figure I presented was no uncommon sight in California." Yet it occurred to him "that a ride through one of the great thoroughfares of Baltimore, Philadelphia, or New York in my present guise, would have elicited considerable remark, and been attended with some *eclat*." Another New Yorker, Henry Hunter Peters, delighted in the performances of others, noting stories of fifteen-pound gold nuggets, staring wide-eyed at the spectacle of "black-looking, long-haired Californians who resemble no other class of men that I have ever seen." That these somewhat minstrel characters were playacting only increased his enjoyment: "one might take them for a band of freebooters, at first sight, but he would soon find his mistake, as they are generally an honest, respectable class of men."[10]

Having imagined the Pacific slope and the West through years of reading, many forty-niners took some time on their way to the gold camps to bask in the singular romance of the adventure. If they were like Leonard Kip, a graduate of Trinity College and descendent of New York City's Dutch aristocracy, they found plenty of local color for their memoirs. "What a puzzling place it was to comprehend!" wrote Kip, as he stared at the San Francisco bustle from a street corner, "the comical conjunction of red shirts, gold epaulettes, Spanish panchoes, long queues and coonskin caps gave it almost a carnival aspect." It was a "Tower of Babel," added New Englander Richard Hale, "and every language seems to be spoken, but the babel resolves itself into one great motive 'Gold, Gold!' and still 'Gold!' whatever may be the cost to get it."[11]

In the heady days following the gold seekers' arrival, attempts at literary play, performance, and color still predominated in their depictions of California. Many men, as Kip noted, "affected to imitate the costume displayed by Mexican muleteers"; they would "cultivate the most luxuriant beard and mustache"; some, "whose legs never crossed a mule, stalked along with terrific spurs clattering at [their] heels."[12] Others might engage in play to reconfigure a California more in line with the unpenetrated West of the imagination, transforming a Latinized environment into a pristine wilderness. On his way to the mines,

Doctor Tyson depopulated passing landscapes of all but grizzlies and children of nature. For he noted, "I was passing over a portion of country which probably had never been traversed by any but Indians and wild animals."[13] Similarly, Theodore Johnson pictured himself and his fellows as the first white men to ever tread these shores. On his way into California's inland valley, he could—with perhaps a little effort and a squint of the eyes—forget his Latin and ignore all signs of Mexican or "civilizing" influences. Thus he assured himself that "Sacramento" was an "Indian name." Mexican pastures, meanwhile, were filled not with livestock but with "luxuriant grass and flowers," with "wild" horses and herds of elk, "flowing manes" and "uplifted antlers."[14]

These perceptions of California as pristine slate and carnival stage appear to have allowed many gold seekers to populate its landscapes with the same subjects of pleasure they had met in their passages through Latin America. For a time, self-conscious transgressions of class and ethnic frontiers continued to be a source of delight—with one major difference: here in "Cosmopolis," these exotic peoples had multiplied to include Chinese as well as Mexicans, "real" Native Americans as well as their transformed Latin brethren, "authentic" working-class coyotes as well as red-shirted clerks at play. Here, forty-niners could partake in authentic pleasures associated with lower-class and ethnic others, bonding with them in hearty camaraderie, recovering the passions left behind with the separation of classes. They might labor themselves, complaining manfully about the conditions, all the while reveling in their red shirts, blue work pants, and long beards. And they might speak and write in tones of authentic vernacular speech, of gambling halls and prostitutes, of passionate and violent Mexicans, of "pards" and "Pikes" and "diggins."

California was an extremely heterogeneous society in 1849, and it would remain one throughout its history. Some 10,000 Mexicans would arrive that year, mostly from the northern state of Sonora, along with 5,000 South Americans, and several thousand Europeans. These groups joined a diverse population of Californios, Mexicans, Hawaiians, Indians, and North Americans already in place, and they would be joined by some 35,000 Chinese by 1860. An estimated 80,000 North Americans, or "Yankees," emigrated in 1849, and these too were a diverse group. Often generalized as a mass roughly composed of equal parts eastern and midwestern forty-niners, they would include a large percentage of northeastern clerks, merchants, and "Yankee" types, but also southern slaveholders (some of whom brought their slaves with them), and, perhaps most exotic of all, rustic and hard-handed overland emigrants from Missouri and Kentucky.[15]

This last group would form one of the richest veins in California lore. Throughout the period of the rush, forty-niner literature and letters would be filled with accounts of the genuine and self-expressive qualities of "lower-class" miners from Pike County, Missouri. These were the seasoned forty-niners, many of whom had come overland from rustic locales along the trans-Appalachian frontier; not all were from Pike County, but all seem to have been called "Pikes" by their friends, "Pukes" by their enemies. Their beards were longer, their clothes dirtier, and their behavior earthier. Northeastern clerks and merchants gazed upon them with a mixture of revulsion and awe. For these men were positively of a lower class, yet they were also "brothers." Accordingly, mining camps, at least in the northeastern imagination, would become spaces for homosocial, even homoerotic cross-class and cross-regional bonding, where clerk's hands became "hard and horny," their hearts light, and where they might sit crosslegged by the campfire swapping tales with their temporary social equals: "Kentuck" and "Old Missouri." Such was the vision that one poetic "miner" sent from a camp on the middle fork of the Feather River to the *Knickerbocker*:

> BROTHERS! leave the sluice untended,
>   Shadows darken on the river;
> In the canon day is ended,
>   Far above the red rays quiver:
> Turn the waters out to play,
>   Let the huge wheel crease from creaking;
> Like a slave it toils all day,
>   In its perspiration reeking.
>
> Gather round the cheerful fire,
>   In the deepening darkness gleaming;
> Now the red tongues leaping higher,
>   Seem like banners upward streaming:
> On the swarthy son of labor,
>   How the ruddy fire-light flashes,
> An anon upon his neighbor,
>   Rough and bearded, quickly dashes.

Spread the blankets on the ground,
  Labor needs not couch or feather;
In a circle clustered round,
  We will all lie down together.
Labor brings refreshing sleep
  No luxurious couch can borrow,
And our slumbers sound and deep,
  Give us strength for toil to-morrow.[16]

Oscar Bennett of Rochester, New York, made contact with these subjects as soon as he started for "the *Diggins* as they term it in this part of
the world." Having learned this proper appellation from the authentic
miners, "diggins" it would be, for Bennett and practically every other
forty-niner. Authentic gold camps, in turn, were surrounded by romance and danger; to get to the "diggins," Bennett had to make his
way "not in a road such as you are used to traveling on," as he wrote
his brothers, "but on an *Indian Trail*."[17]

California's native peoples were undoubtedly the primary victims of
the gold rush, particularly the peoples, the Nisenan and the Miwok,
whose lands were in the richest gold-mining areas of the central and
lower Sierra Nevada. Forty-niners overwhelmed these groups, driving
them from their homelands within a few years. As a whole, California's
Native American population declined by some 85 percent between
1848 and 1880. In effect, the rush resulted in a type of genocide, its
causes a mixture of new diseases brought by the immigrants, along
with economic exploitation, forced removal from newly proclaimed
"public lands," and, especially after the mid-1850s, officially sanc-
tioned as well as unofficial massacres of "hostile" populations. As early
as the fall of 1849, forty-niner accounts suggest that Native Americans
were rare in the gold country's foothills; many—to the disappointment
of quite a few—reported having seen none at all. Among historians of
Native American and Anglo relations, the forty-niner has to a large
extent been frozen into place as a monolithic aggressor, an enemy of all
things Indian in California.[18] In actual fact, just as not all forty-niners
were the "single young males" of gold rush lore, not all expressed a
hatred of Indians. Many appear to have held more ambivalent views,
blending romantic visions of noble savages and desires for Native
American characteristics with expressions of racist revulsion and violent dispossession. Targeting blame for this genocide, in other words,

means admitting that even the "good" elements within the gold rush, those who claimed to be attracted to Native Americans as a people, could and did also kill them.

Many forty-niner's accounts do reflect simple racism, and to these observers California's native peoples seemed little more than repugnant and disgusting. For these men the region's Native Americans were "Diggers," a derogatory term derived from their perceived habit of unearthing roots and acorns for their subsistence. As one described them, California's native peoples were worse than others: "filthy and degraded in their habits," without "ennobling traits," "they are ever the most debased of tribes, morally and physically." Another added, "these Digger Indians seem to be the lowest of all God's creation . . . all *wild* Indians are natural thieves and liars." Just as often, however, forty-niner perspectives reveal the same mixture of attraction and revulsion they had expressed in their passages through Latin America. "Some of the young squaws are fairly good-looking . . . with raven black hair and black eyes," noted Charles Parke, "but," he added, again pulling himself back from these desires, "they seem to fade early." Samuel Upham reported that the Native Americans he met near the town of Stockton treated his party with polite "civility," sharing their food with them and presenting gifts at parting. All of this, he noted, was "very acceptable." At the same time, he described them as the "ugliest red-skins I ever beheld." "The Digger eats but very little animal food," he added knowingly, giving himself over fully to revulsion, "like his brother, the gorilla, he is a vegetarian, and subsists principally on wild berries and acorns, occasionally luxuriating on snails and grasshoppers."[19]

Whether they were seen or simply imagined, Native Americans provided forty-niners with many wide-awake evenings around the campfire. As Bennett proclaimed with an emphasis that might chill and excite blood across an entire continent, the way to the diggings necessitated "travel in a wild country among *Wild Indians*." To one miner these people seemed rather quaint, more picturesque than dangerous. "They were always peaceable," he wrote, and "used to come about the cabins some." They generated much interest among miners, who looked, and probably touched, but "could not converse with them." Another recalled that meetings with Native Americans might go against all expectations. Prospecting with his "pards," his group "once came across a tribe of fine looking Indians," in his words, "who to their surprise, instead of robbing and maltreating them, proved very honest and friendly."[20] As their surprise if not the meeting indicates, assumptions of Native Americans as dangerous or repugnant might remain to affect perceptions. Enticed by stories of their exotic customs, one miner leapt at the chance of seeing a genuine Native American funeral. He thrilled at the burning of the body, the ornaments of dancers, the ritual performance of women who, according to his account, proceeded to shave their heads and cover their faces in ashes. In the end, however, he could not conclude his ethnographic tour without a shiver of revulsion. "When I was a boy," he later mused, "I saw pictures of the Devil, and a squaw in mourning ever reminded me of that picture. They are called *tar heads* by the *miners*."[21]

Yet it was as a source of danger that California native peoples could be most imbued with piquant reveries. Although his journal indicates no actual contacts with these imagined forest adversaries, Oscar Bennett seems to have picked up enough campfire information to report knowingly that "they will creep up slyly behind the trees and fire a volley of arrows and then flee—at night they creep slyly up to the camps and steal their camp mules so in traveling through the mountains we have to use a greate [*sic*] deal of precautions."[22] "When they can get a chance to let fly at you they will do it if they think you can't catch them," wrote Rodney Odall, another gold seeker from Rochester. His assertion, however, contained the added power of direct experience: "I had 4 arrows shot at me and one other man in the night while we lay under a tree, but none hit us." For him, these attacks indicated stark contrasts between heroic miners and sneaky savages: "They are," he noted, "complete cowards."[23]

For many others, California native peoples remained figures out of the pages of romantic literature. One of the gold country's most ubiquitous "peculiar characters" was a white man, rumored to have originally come from Illinois sometime prior to the rush, who had sloughed off his past and "gone native." His name, interestingly enough, was "Savage." "Savage as you are aware," wrote Hiram Pierce in a descriptive weaving of legend and grotesquery that he sent to his wife, "is a white man." He was also, Pierce continued, the leader of "several tribes" and "about 2700 Warriors" and the husband of "27 wives." "His Indians are the most wretched & degraded beings I ever saw & appear to make their breakfast from each others heads so far as meat is concerned. . . . I saw them eat & all that they had to eat was lice and clover."[24] The source of much thought, tales of "Savage" and his wild cohort undoubtedly helped pass the time for cabinbound miners during the rainy season. Always, according to John Callbreath, they would tell these stories as eyewitness accounts. One of these stories, a recounting of Savage's involvement in the "Indian War" of 1850, Callbreath thought worthy of including in a letter to his parents. Savage, it seems, along with his friend "Lutario," the chief of the "Mercedes" tribe, was accused by a Mexican miner named Rose of horse thievery. In response to this accusation, wrote Callbreath, "Lutario, who was slightly intoxicated [immediately] sprang from his [horse] and running up to Rose struck him a blow in the face. Rose instantly drew his bowie knife and plunged it in his right breast just below the collar bone and ranging downward in the thick fleshy part of his breast . . . at the same moment Rose was pierced by a number of arrows . . . he sank to the ground in the throes of death." Here indeed was some entertaining violence. And it was only the beginning of a series that might last as long as the storytellers' imaginations. Rose's death, according to Callbreath, would be revenged by the miners. Lutario, finished off by a gunshot from one of Rose's men, would be the rallying cry for Savage as he took over as chief of the Mercedes.[25]

While these stories were heavily imbued with imagination, they are not pure fictions. "Lutario" is most likely a character out of adventure literature; the "Mercedes" tribe is an obvious attempt at exotic invention. But Savage was real. The subject of these tales was James Savage, a would-be merchant who had come to California from Illinois in 1846, and who by 1849 was making his living by working part time as an Indian agent and trader. Savage, it appears, in order to cement his trading relations, had married several women from the various native tribes along his trade route. In 1852, while he was living with a wife among the Yokuts, another white trader by the name of Walter Harvey shot and killed him in a raid on the tribe's trading post.[26] What is most interesting about all of this is what both Savage, and the legends that grew up around him, reveal about early red-white relations in California. Both, that is, suggest a certain level of romance in the idea of riding with the Indians. This romance, in turn, frequently found sexual expression. For James Savage was not unusual in taking a Native American bride. By 1860, census figures reveal that California had one of the highest rates, if not the highest rate, of Indian-Anglo intermarriage in the United States. Historians have professed amazement at these figures, at times attributing them to forced relationships akin to rape, at times labeling them "temporary alliances of convenience." What the numbers suggest, however, particularly in light of the fact that more than one-half of all white partners conferred their last names on Native American spouses and children, is that many forty-niners were genuinely attracted to Native Americans and what they saw as their way of life.

There were other people of color with whom the forty-niners shared the gold country, and from whom they might create gruesome tales and intriguing character traits. Among these, the most exotic, at least in the eyes of many gold seekers appear to have been the Chinese. Although Chinese immigrants began arriving in California in 1849, they remained a rare sight in the gold country until 1852, when over 20,000 arrived, mostly from the province of Guangdong in southern China. Again, the assumption among historians is that they were immediately met with racist perceptions, and that forty-niners were united behind California's infamous anti-Chinese rhetoric and legislation.[27] Many times their perceptions do seem only cruelly condescending and dismissive, witness John Cornelison's comparison of the Chinese walking gait to "frog hopping." Other times, as with Stephen Wing's accounts of Chinese in the gold camps, they might fuse condescension with unself-conscious longings for cultural intercourse. Wing's name, as he was to discover, was a common one in China. And although the young man from Yarmouth, Massachusetts, was not of Asian descent, this seemingly curious circumstance won him many acquaintances among Chinese miners at the camp of Dutch Hill. At Wing's request, one of these friends appended a row of characters to a letter home; the result, as the gold seeker appears to have hoped, would be pure exoticism. "He was in my Cabin this evening and I asked him to write to thee," declared Wing. The message meant, "I am your brother wings good friend, Ah Young!," he explained, adding that "I have numbered the words so thee can read—The original looks like Greek some, dont it? It will to thee no doubt!"[28]

Undoubtedly, forty-niner families found much that was interesting in these tidbits of the mysterious East in the rugged West. Writing to a friend in Connecticut, Thomas Forbes seems to have come to this conclusion. Accordingly, he took the time to witness a Chinese burial, reporting that the "Celestials," after spreading a feast around the grave of a drowned man, engaged in the fascinating ritual of burying "pan cakes" with the corpse. Indicating that he was not alone in his enjoyment of this scene, Forbes also noted that the mourners "then past [*sic*] around . . . brandy to the lookers on." As he traveled the gold camps, Stephen Wing would send his family other exotic souvenirs from his acquaintances: one was an "account book which an unfortunate Celestial *lost*," and which he thought "might be a curiosity to the *children*." Another miner, J. M. Alexander, sent home a lock of a Chinese miner's hair, to which he attached what he may have felt was a properly eerie message: "he sais you Must put it In a Trunk and not lay It on the Ground—he thinks if It is put on the [ground] any where he will not live."[29]

With waves of easterners continuing to arrive in the gold country, these playful descriptions of California's exotic others would continue throughout the gold rush. For individual gold seekers, however, a crisis was coming, and it was only a matter of time before the heady babble and strange sights resolved into the lure of gold. Once the initial thrill of arrival faded, efforts at literary play met the serious demands of prospecting and panning. And, according to the correspondent to the local paper of Morristown, New Jersey, the actualities of gold digging put an end to the hopeful easterner's sense of fun. "Here we worked nearly two weeks," wrote reporter J. A. Hull—who was also the son of the *Jerseyman*'s editor, "but could make nothing at it: it cost us about $2 per day to live, and we did not average more than that washing gold." Accordingly, Hull's description of life in California descended into disappointment: "San Francisco," he added, "is a miserable place to live in: . . . the statements of various writers, making a Paradise of this country, is a very rich joke."[30] The actual work of wading icy streams to pan for gold left forty-niners with little time for the types of literary ritual enjoyed en route. On his way toward the Merced River, Hiram Pierce tried his hand at elevated description. "The senery," he wrote in a letter to his wife, "in Some places was grand & sublime." "At one place as we were ascending the sides of the Mountain on our left far below us lay a beautiful vale," he began, but after this attempt to warm to the task, he brought his effort to an abrupt close. The vale "brought to mind that beautifull Hymn, was the rich vale that proudly shone Etc."[31]

Pierce may have lacked either the time or the skills of his more literary contemporaries. Yet as he extended his stay in the gold country, even Leonard Kip's colorful fabrics of California life began to fray at the edges. Returning to San Francisco one evening, Kip noted the usual carnivalesque scene: there was drinking and gaming, bull baiting, and a circus. "The town," he wrote, "seemed running wild after amusement." But rather than imbuing the scene with charm as was his usual wont, he concluded his account with an uncharacteristic disdain for the vulgar display: "the lower the tastes to which any of them pandered the better it was sustained." Eastern readers may have noticed the decline of elevated language in Kip's landscape sketches; to be sure, he continued to draw "forests of gigantic pines" shrouded in "morning mist," but the effect, once ethereal and sublime, had been shortened to "extremely pleasing."[32]

These changes in tone suggest a shift in the discourse of the gold rush. For George Payson, the swing in mood went from the jolly promise of leisurely accumulation to a return of market sobriety. "There was no laughing in California," he recalled, "everybody was terribly in earnest, and a settled look of more than Puritanic severity was in every face." For Charles Palmer, the transition suggested that California was about to become a utopia; to him, however, the term carried its modern meaning, connoting failed promises and unreality. "The absolute independence which has always given such a zest to mining life," he wrote, "is slowly altering its form. Thousands of discontented miners are compelled to 'hire out' and let a small portion of what they dig pass to them through the hand of another man. The healthy state of absolute, real equality which has been the life of a mining existence is beginning to be attacked by conventionalities and all the warts of civilization."[33] This is not the tone of a man who yearned for order. Arriving with the usual elevated expectations, New Jersey's David Demerest caught the changed tone in a stray comment: "there is another load of victims." Certainly, many forty-niners would remain "in play." Trying to recapture a sense of optimism and promise, they would, according to Bancroft, do "what they could to make themselves boys again." But once in California, they found that the game had changed.[34] Narratives of romantic self-aggrandizement might mean very little without actual wealth. Always aware of being watched, of having created a spectacle, they continued to perform. But without gold there may have been some question concerning the meaning of their play.

As a whole, the forty-niners and the men who followed them did discover and collect an extraordinary amount of gold in the foothills of the Sierras: enough to fund a national recovery from a series of economic recessions preceding the rush, enough to mute eastern critics of the Mexican War and national policies of western expansion. But their sheer number was their undoing. They soon found that despite promises to the contrary there was not enough for all. Dividing the amount of gold produced during the rush by the number of miners and days worked results in a typical forty-niner wage of sixteen dollars per day. While this sum represented a fortnight's wages in Rochester or Hartford, it might fail to cover the inflated costs of a few day's provisions in Hangtown or Dry Creek. As well, the flush times and high wages were seasonal: in most places miners could not work during the rainy season, when streams were high above gold deposits. They had invested great sums of money in getting to California; once there, they envisioned an easy accumulation of wealth, figuring themselves rich men before they had even started. Now, faced with the extremely hard work of mining and the stunningly high prices of goods in the camps, they had to do some drastic refiguring. Most, it seems, felt almost lucky just breaking even.[35]

Such disappointments were hardly unique to the forty-niners. In fact, western resources rushes had worked this way before and would again. Promises would always overrun production. Those wishing to get a jump on the next lead or strike, or hoping to light out before the crowd got wind of it, would nearly always arrive at the next digging—be it in Nevada, Australia, or Alaska—only to find a crowd of competitors already in place. What made the California venture different was the sharp angle of descent from its elevated rhetoric to the depths of realization. Because most participants in the gold rush, including not just those who went to the Pacific but also their observers, had structured the experience according to patterns of romance, failure presented a series of problems. Many, of course, were material, others were problems more of style and appearance. How, in other words, were the gold seekers going to explain the failures of California to live up to its promises, not to mention their own personal failures, to wives, loved ones, and eastern observers?

Having raised their own expectations along with those of their audiences, forty-niner disappointment at conditions in California might at times be great indeed. For many, these expectations were dashed with dizzying rapidity. Upon arrival, Henry Hyde left his ship with a sigh of relief: "we expect great things, for we have a good and well organized company." A mere two days later his company voted to disband: "and," as he noted, "every man's hand is against his fellowman."[36] Hyde's experience was typical, especially among the first waves of argonauts whose expectations were most feverish. With the discovery that finding gold was a competitive business rather than the envisioned pleasure, some of the well-organized northeastern mining companies called meetings and decided that members would operate best in small groups or alone. Most simply fell apart, their members dispersing toward the foothills, their Articles of Association abandoned.

With this disappointment, the rhetoric of male conviviality frequently shifted to fears of intensified competition and overcrowding. "Of all the miseries I ever experienced," wrote Bancroft of his arrival in the gold country, "by far the worst has been the crowd, among whom were always some supremely disgusting persons whose presence one could not escape." Boston's Henry Pierce noted with dismay the ships arriving every day, along with reports that another 30,000 immigrants were coming overland. The "famous South Sea and Mississippi bubbles of England," he angrily warned a friend, "are truly nothing to what we find here." Suddenly, eastern exaggerations of California gold took on elements of conspiracy: the whole thing was an enormous merchants' plot, the forty-niners its innocent victims. Competition for good mining claims, complained John Callbreath, increased with the daily arrival of hundreds of miners. The problem, he added, was that men persisted in believing newspaper exaggerations; "it makes my heart bleed," he concluded, "to see the poor victims wending their way to the gold camps." Oscar Bennett could only warn his friends against *"being deluded into this infernal humbug. Thousands of the avaricious mortals* that left the *land of plenty* to seek their fortunes among the desolate mountains of this country would be glad to seek their homes if they only had the means."[37]

Still the crowds kept arriving. They were "doomed," wrote one despondent observer, "for here they find sickness and death all around them in every direction . . . disappointment stares nearly all in the face." And the forty-niners kept complaining. "What is it that raises such an excitement in the states about California," wrote James Barnes to his family in Massachusetts, "what is the caus of so many hundreds and thousands a coming out here pray rite me a letter and let me know." Yet he seemed to recognize what had brought the crowds. It was the anticipation of "picking up gold by the bushel," the idea that a man would simply "pick up gold as he would chips at home." These men were soon disappointed, he added, and most of the "poor devils" did little more than "scratch about to get enough money to carry them home."[38] Hundreds of disillusioned gold seekers echoed the refrain: "California is a humbug." Wiser but worse for the wisdom, they had "seen the elephant," fallen victim to the most preposterous of tales and confidence games. A few miners, as one admitted to an eastern observer, had been lucky. These were the few the eastern papers focused upon; but for each of these lucky miners, he maintained, there were five thousand others who had failed completely.[39]

Thus did competitive social relations return to the previously perfumed hills of the "New Eldorado." Failing at the mines, tradesmen, clerks, and merchants came down from the foothills to resume their old occupations in Sacramento or San Francisco. Others stayed on in the mining villages and tent camps, hoping that even within a context of competitive mining and large-scale operations they might still salvage something out of the venture or at least earn enough money for the voyage home. If there was a moment of crisis for these gold seekers, this was certainly it. In effect, it was not the early days of cosmopolis that bothered them, nor was it California's free mixing of heterogeneous peoples. These elements of the rush had been enjoyed—self-consciously perhaps, and certainly with an air of condescension and perverse play; still, they had been embraced as thrilling, as providing comic reversals of social norms in the East. What bothered these men, it appears, was not the breakdown of social distinction but the collapse of utopian promises that had allowed the breakdown to happen in the first place. What bothered them was not disorder but the return of a capitalist order, its anxious spirit of gain, its corruption and selfishness, and, above all, its endless competition.

Always it seems this return to order had the same effects. Not long after his arrival in California, for example, one forty-niner wrote his brother that "Chinamen abounded" near his mining camp, adding that "when I return to Ohio I shall take pleasure in showing you a Celestial costume presented me by some of my Chinese friends." Less than a year later these friends had become his competitors and enemies. "In this section of the country," he wrote, "we are overrun with Chinese. I . . . have not formed a very high opinion of them. It would not surprise me if they were driven out of the country by Americans."[40] By the end of 1850, enough forty-niners had realized this transformation to suggest a completed pattern. According to Josiah Royce, 1849 was the "boyish year of California"; 1851 was the year of "lost illusions" and "bitter struggles." In the meantime, California became a state, the forty-niners passed a "Foreign Miner's Tax," they attempted more than one removal of Mexican competitors from the southern mines, they formed vigilance committees and advocated for lynch law. By this time, foreigners, particularly "foreign capitalists" and mining cooperatives, had become the cause of all their troubles, and "any mysterious outrage," as Royce put it, "was attributed to Mexicans."

Order, in other words, had returned, but it was certainly not the order that many forty-niners wanted.[41]

All of this may have reflected the end of a quixotic period of class-lessness, ethnic mixing, and frontier democracy and the return of market realities. At the same time, of course, these "realities" had already been there in the first place. For as forty-niner accounts reveal, California had never "really" been lacking in class and ethnic distinctions. Rather, it was the thought that these distinctions might be broken down, the idea that the region's plenitude might allow a return to a golden age of classlessness and family harmony, that appeared to inspire their imaginations in the early days of the rush. Nor for that matter had the mining camps ever been lacking in capitalism and competitive social relations. A look at the earliest claims books from the camps reveals that economies of scale and small group operations existed side by side in the mining industry from 1849. As for the much vaunted democratic principles of "Miners' Law," their supposed basis in social equality and protection of independent miners, these codes reveal a far more common proclivity for litigation between competing forty-niners. One finds little evidence, in fact, that they were designed to protect lone prospectors from unscrupulous business operations.[42] Indeed, these elements of the rush only appear to have become "real" as individuals found they were not actually there, the reality of the present confirming the dream-reality of a lost golden past of freedom and harmony.

This falling of scales from forty-niner eyes, their perceptions of California as a failed utopia, their sudden realization of its return to capitalist relations, cannot be situated on a time line. It happened on an individual basis, again and again as new immigrants arrived. Indeed, long after most arrived in the gold country only to "stare disappointment in the face," eastern papers continued to be filled with outrageous claims of fortune: stories of stream beds, beaches, and mountains composed entirely of gold, the "boob's luck" of the miner whose pick, thrown in frustration, had unearthed a single nugget the size of a large melon. Many of these stories were sent east by the forty-niners themselves. Still, their complaints raise a question: What do we make of such sturm und drang amid the welter of publicized representations of lucky strikes and roistering good times? An answer to this question requires the recognition of a certain doubling of voice in gold seeker writings from California. They could, that is, depict the rush as both a raucous adventure and a living hell of male suffering. These contradictory accounts in turn may have reflected different assumed audiences. In recording adventures they were writing for a male audience—including themselves—that expected adventure stories. In their list of complaints they were more often than not, either directly or by implication, addressing women.

In analyzing these inherent inconsistencies in accounts of forty-niner experience, the temptation has been to separate romanticism from suffering. The latter should debunk the former, disillusionment, raw violence, and pain becoming the "truth" beneath the exaggerated rhetoric of male play and golden dreams. Private correspondence between men and women, that is, rooted in the concept and idiom of romantic love, provided an outlet for the expression of one's "true self." And forty-niners, as we might assume, could express the truth about California—along with their fears and emotions—to wives and female loved ones more easily than they could to other men.[43] As the letters of Samuel Adams to his wife in Maine suggest, communications between husbands and wives did reflect a more intimate and conversational style. Samuel likened his missives to Philomela as a conversation; letter writing was for him a "delightful task," more like speaking than writing: "I must talk a few minutes with my loving partner before retiring for the night." Accordingly, these letters home might reflect the intimacy of private communication. But intimacy itself was a literary style, and the same letters were often written with an imaginative pen and an eye for sentimental imagery. At home in Peacham, Vermont, Chastina Rix, for example, imagined her husband's experiences through his letters. At the same time, she recorded in her diary that "I am & have been reading Bayard Taylor's letters from 'New York to Mineveh.'" Thus, as she indicated, nineteenth-century letters could be read as literature: noting that Taylor wrote intimately of "little things" but that he brought them to life through artistry and powerful description, she added that "I never read any letters so interesting."[44]

Eastern women would read many interesting letters from California during the gold rush. These letters, in turn, while they resonate with elements of intimate confessions, and while they express certain private "truths," are also literary products. Above all, they challenge the assumption that women writers or observers "sentimentalized" the gold rush, the idea, as one historian claimed, that "religious fervor, sentimental glorification of home and family life, and hatred of vice" were female literary domains.[45] Quite the contrary, forty-niner letters from California resonate with precisely these sentiments. Frequently encoded in a discourse of romantic love, these letters were rife with sentimental suffering, with calls for pity and understanding. Along with adventure stories and news from the gold regions, they carried the implicit idea that love could resolve what gold—or the lack of gold—could not.

Always one for a direct prognosis, New York physician James Tyson captured the condition of his fellow forty-niners in one sentence. "In a far distant land," he noted, "away from friends and home, and among many who are unprincipled, their cases are truly pitiable."[46] It was at the moment of this realization that gender, class, and the importance of distinctions returned to a central place in forty-niner experience. Above all, it seems, they had to make one distinction clear to the women back home: they had not failed in California, California had failed them. Women needed to know that this world was far different from the way it had been imagined, and even more different from the world of the home. Here, failure did not mean they were failures; and even if they had failed, they should be pitied rather than blamed.

Again, nineteenth-century gender relations cannot be limited to contact between husbands and wives. Charles Dulany relied on the love of his sister Elizabeth to salvage his experience. He called for her to send "one of those kind & affectionate letters that you were wont to write in days of yore, one of those, that came from the heart & went to the heart." He went on to portray himself as a sentimental knight-errant, as a banished wanderer: "Ah!" he wrote, "how long I have wished in travelling over the scorching desert, the bleak & towering mountain, and tosling in the sultry mines of California, to hear *one* single accent of her, who loves me dearly & loves me true."[47] Unmarried miners, too, could turn their thoughts to those at home. Twenty-year-old New Yorker Isaac Halsey was a wanderer whose "chief delight" was to "sing my songs of home." And he too would imbue his experience with sentiment, capturing his suffering in verses sent home from the gold camp of Mokelumne Hill:

By the frosts of old age when the blood of life is chilled,
And the pulses of passion (once restless) are stilled,
When the roses of beauty are wilted by frost,
And the fervour of youthful affection is lost,
   Then why should we dread,
   To ly [*sic*] down with the dead,
When the pleasures we count are withered and fled.[48]

In letter after letter, forty-niners confessed similar sentiments to their wives and loved ones. Yet these conversations were not, as might be assumed, wholly private. These forty-niners may have held to conceptions that the "truth" rested in the private and intimate sphere of gender relations. But they also expressed their emotions in public performance. Thus we have the seemingly strange and practically ubiquitous image of men articulating their California experiences through a veil of tears, failed gold seekers solidifying a masculine world with the softest of sentiments. Heartfelt emotion, because it was the most intimate and truthful form of expression among men, and because it was not their usual mode of expression, was actual "proof" that forty-niner suffering was real and heroic, or at least so they hoped it would seem.[49] California was a living hell, according to Bancroft. As evidence he offered the vision of the weeping miner: "as he reads that letter, written by a tender loving wife . . . you may mark the twitching of the muscles in his face, the tears trickling down his cheeks, and the bosom swelling with emotion."[50] Male bosoms did not often swell with emotion. When they did, implied Bancroft, something truly grievous, perhaps even heroic, was happening.

In private and public confessions of emotion, forty-niners filled the landscape of the gold country with weeping men. Their eyes became admittedly misty when they thought of home. As Asaph Sawyer wrote: "many is the time when home and all that is dear to me . . . comes into my mind, the tears will fill my eyes in spite of all I can do to prevent them." They wept at the head of the trail. The beginning of his journey, wrote Henry Billington Packer to Mary Judkins, "called forth the unbidden tear, and prevented me from writing several minutes. I saw the arid plains, the sandy desert spread out before me; then the months, perhaps years of toil and lonely musings before we can meet again." And they wept at trail's end, especially as they opened their first letters from the East. Herman Le Roy was "not ashamed" of his tears while opening letters from his family in New Rochelle. When Packer received his first letter from his fiancée, the tears "came deep and full, like the flowing of a gentle stream, not subject to constant ebbs and flows like the troubled waters unconnected with the mighty ocean." The ocean of tears flowed as well when they wrote letters: "and now Julia good bye," wrote Harrison Allen at the close of a letter to his wife in New Bedford, "god bless you I am all done at present & I believe I shall have to cry a little."[51]

Through these tears, forty-niners announced the return of market competition and strife to the gold rush. If this reflected a return to reality, and if the real world came crashing down on them, it did so as a sentimental burden. With failure, the need for order had returned to California. If forty-niners had to rebuild this order, and if they had to re-create distinctions between classes, races, and genders in order to explain their failures, they did not welcome its return. All the while they continued weeping, and when they wept, they wept publicly. They paid two dollars for letters from home, then cried while reading them in front of their fellows assembled for mail. Worse, they might receive no letters at all. Having failed in their heroic quests, a lack of news from home might raise the possibility that they had been forgotten. "And," wrote Massachusetts native Stephen Davis, "as they look upon their fellow miners (who are more fortunate)," they would cry harder still: "frequently a tear comes unbidden to the eye, while the heart grieves at being thus forgotten by loved ones at home."[52]

California had become a hard place, a violent world where competition, loneliness, and the lack of "female influences" often gave way to a type of male hysteria, where even the smallest reminder of home could result in a communal crying jag. When, for example, the "Alverson girls" performed a piano concert in Stockton, they drew "scores of men in the street as far as the eye could see, and some were sobbing."[53] In this world, desires for male camaraderie and transcendence might remain, but always in conjunction with lamentations over unmarked graves, as hosts of scribbling males penned odes to their departed fellows. Transforming sentiment into experience, these poetic expressions worked to displace gold as the symbol of the rush and to replace it with another: the lonely dying forty-niner. Part fantasy, part fear, this morbid trope was wholly an obsession. To "die so young, . . . to die of neglected cold," wrote Augustus Taylor of the New Brunswick Company, was "terrible to anticipate at any time." But some deaths were worse and hence more sentimental than others: "to lay gradually waiting for his approach away from the soothing cares of females and friends, from home and kindred. To have the last sad offices performed by strangers in a strange land. Oh! God, that I may never experience their terrible awful calamity!"[54]

As a literary vehicle, the dying forty-niner—his inevitable death unmourned and unmarked by a gravestone—provided direct evidence of the vicissitudes of frontier life. Accordingly, corpses began appearing everywhere in forty-niner writing: dying of cholera, scurvy, gunshot wounds, or just broken hearts, imagined bodies stacked up in desert plains, river banks, and isolated camps like cordwood. "Many a poor fellow," recalled Benjamin Martin of the California "scirvey," "has been found dead upon the banks of those streams, who have fell victims, and died, with the latter dreadful disease, made more so, from the fact of dying without a fellow mortal to render him any assistance, and with no kind affectionate hand, to administer to his relief."[55] He would die unnoticed in his tent, held Leonard Kip of this figure, indisputable proof that "one of the great characteristics of the mines is a dreadful, heartless selfishness, which seems to attach itself to the souls of all." Merely entering this world was enough to counter failures at the mines, and failing to survive it was the ultimate form of imagined success. Heroically ending the argonaut's quest, an unmarked mound was nearly equal to making a pile of gold. "O what tears of anguish will flow from that fond Wife and those helpless orphans," wrote Asaph Sawyer. And as he imagined the effect of a shipmate's death back in the East, he lost himself in his own sentimental weavings: "I must leave further reflections . . . for my eyes are already giving vent to my feelings."[56]

While there is real pain in such accounts, and while these emotions cannot be dismissed as mere exaggerations, there was something romantic in gold seeker suffering. These morbid and tearful musings played well "back home." The spectacle of lonely, dying forty-niners dotting the prairies also dotted the columns of eastern publications. In the April 1851 edition of the *Knickerbocker*, for example, the magazine's editors gave its readers some "feeling stanzas" suggested by the last words of a married man who died on his way to the gold region. Affirming duty and love through the power of intimate morbidity, the poem offered a vision of self-justifying heroism: "O my children! Heaven bless them!" began its second verse,

> They were all my life to me;
> Would I could once more caress them,
>   Ere I sink beneath the sea!
> 'T was for them I crossed the ocean;
>   What my hopes were I'll not tell,
> But I have gained an orphan's portion,
>   Yet He doeth all things well.

Similar poems would follow in the pages of the *Knickerbocker*. These included J. Clement's "The Graves of the Goldseekers," wherein the "vales" of the Sacramento were bedecked with soon-forgotten mounds, with the bodies of men who had "found a premature and lone repose,"

> Where grief its tribute tears may rarely pay,
> Or Friendship rear the slab that sobbing memory owes.

Still later there appeared the anonymously penned "The Dying Californian," in which the forty-niner could actually die "while a smile played o'er his features." For here, as the poem's conclusion attests, was an ennobling and thus rather happy death indeed:

> In Nevada's mountain gorges, in every golden glen
> In Sacramento's valley, repose New England men:
> Along each gliding rivulet, with music in its flow,
> Full many a hopeful dreamer is sleeping lone and low.

> California hath her treasures, whose value is untold,
> But her soil holds treasure . . . more priceless far than gold:
> For many noble spirits in her bosom are at rest,
> And the gold sands of her valleys shroud many a manly breast.[57]

Constituting the gold rush as a sentimental experience, these literary efforts—whether penned by the gold seekers or their observers—could accomplish precisely what many men accused mid-nineteenth-century female writers of doing. They could, that is, make emotion the primary measure of reality. What the forty-niners may have discovered was that sentiment and romantic love might salvage both the adventure and their sense of manhood, resolving failure into a type of ultrarealistic heroism. "Some would say it was weakness for a man to shed a tear," claimed Benjamin Martin at a lecture upon his return from the gold country to Chelsea, Massachusetts, or that it "was womanish, but I say it was manly, and many a man has shed a tear in Cal. and is not afraid to own it, as I said before, man was stripped of all outside covering, his feelings were allowed to take their natural course, and the manly tear showed it. Nature was not swallowed up, as is too often the case for fear of being called weak, or unmanly."[58] Through the manly tear and an ardent sentimentalization of experience the gold seekers could articulate a male world so tough, so filled with pain and suffering, that merely entering it was heroism enough.[59] It was just this process, this return of invidious distinctions between male and female tears, that elevated gender discourse to a central place in the production and exposure of culture during the gold rush.

The writings of the men in California suggest that they worked hard to make these distinctions. If they suffered, they rarely suffered in silence. Instead they wept. And when they were done weeping, they wrote, penning long and detailed screeds equating their suffering with manly effort, making their experiences real through the power of language and exaggeration. "The prospects here are very good, . . . so far as *Plenty* of *Gold* is concerned," wrote Alonzo Hill to his family in Worcester, Massachusetts, soon after arriving in San Francisco, but success required heroic effort: "he who gets it must endure great suffering & hardship, must have an iron constitution, . . . and have the firm determination to run all risks, & sacrifice all comfort & decent society." Later, after he discovered that even these efforts might not be enough, he could only refashion the experience as one of pain and tragedy. "O' Lord," he used a letter to his sister to exclaim, "how the panic for Gold did rage in the Western states—Men sprung up from the deathbed of old age and hobbled off over the plains. Children in the swaddling clothes of infancy smote their cradles and bawled most lustily, and could not be pacified until its parents picked up their duds and set off for the renowned 'California,' . . . there will [be] 5 times as many die in this accursed land as will get any gold."[60]

In letters to wives and loved ones in the East, other forty-niners took parallel linguistic turns. "What I suffered through those dreadful days I can never tell you," wrote Frederick Tracy to his wife on his trip through Panama. But as Emily Tracy read on, she found that he *would* tell her: "In those long weary, sick days and nights," she read, "as I lay panting on the ship's deck, with no one to bathe my burning brow, or even give me a glass of cold water, how much I missed your kindly care." There was no such thing as comfort in California, he added, and "such a thing as *home* is out of the question."[61] Other gold seekers told their wives similar stories, juxtaposing positions of home and California, the comforts of one magnifying the torments of the other. Starvation stalked the men of the gold camps, read one wife, her husband noting that he had seen "men begging for a handful of parched corn, they [said] they had had nothing but frogs for 4 days." Philomela Adams read of Samuel's failures, but also that his pain had taken on elements of wealth: he was richer than his fellows, if only in the coin of suffering. "When any tell of tedious passages," he wrote, "I tell them to stop till they hear from me & none come into competition. Here we are struggling alone as it were, our helpmeets, partners, sympathizers & dear ones who lighten the cares of life are afar off."[62]

These representations of home and California might lend an air of nobility to the forty-niner's venture, even if it was a failure. Again they might play, blending the role of Byron's outcast hero with that of the dutiful husband. Although he showed no interest in mining for gold, even the long-married steamer captain Cleveland Forbes depicted himself as a wanderer, his home and wife as a haven of repose. "Welcome Sweet Dawn, 'oer Ocean's Crest," he began, in a poem marking his wife's birthday,

> Thy golden light inspires this breast
> With gladness, love & strife.
>
> I am not happy & know she cannot be so while
> separated and I pray that God may restore my health
> & permit me once more to press to my lonely heart
> my beloved wife & dearest children.

Similarly exiled from his "native land," Jared Nash portrayed himself as the outcast, forced "to wander to unknown lands where misery and dangers are liable to overtake him." But, as he added, because his wandering had been induced by "anxiety for my family that they might [prosper] for time to come," he counted "it an honor and credit to myself." When his sufferings raised doubts about his chances, Asaph Sawyer thought of home, and, "I say to myself you have embarked in an unknown honest enterprise." Samuel Adams thought often of how "pleasant" would be his return to Maine. "When shall I be ready to go home again," he mused, "how sweet the name to a wanderer like myself. What comforts, pleasures, happiness, & peace associated with it."[63]

In portraying California as a humbug, the male world as a place of competition and strife and the feminized home as one of repose and peace, many of these forty-niners may have been conscious of a singular difficulty. Most had left wives or family members in difficult positions. Many had asked them to take responsibility for home *and* business until they could send bank drafts. When these individuals then failed to find enough gold to send these drafts, they may have run into an unavoidable fact: wives and families were suffering equal hardships of toil and competition. Worse still for married miners, women's work at home seemed to reflect actual accomplishment: their care for families could be measured, whereas unfound gold could not. The construction of the home as a refuge from the market, in other words, might necessitate a reconstruction of lines partly erased in negotiated departures. It would require a substitution of male experience for what had begun as a partnership of shared responsibilities. Above all, this reworking of the central meaning of the rush might require a certain degree of competition across region and gender, an agonistic play between male and female experience to answer the question "whose suffering was more real?" Indeed, competition had returned to California, and it would have its ugly and lasting effects: lynchings, xenophobia, lasting legacies of environmental destruction, and extreme racism. But with this question of suffering competition began to extend east, across gender; and here it might have the most lasting effect of all.

Seven

Widows and Helpmates

Harriet Dunnel envisioned her situation as much like that of the forty-niners. Forced because of expenses to move from Manhattan to the countryside around Athens, New York, she was, as she put it, a "stranger in a strange land." Her husband missed his home, she missed hers: "the country," she exclaimed, "looks very dull and dreary to me who is accustomed to City life." The house she was to occupy in his absence was even drearier. "I had never looked into such a dismal place," she thought at the time, later writing that "if my husband was here to take a look with me he would pity me." And yet, as she had promised, she would keep up a brave front, only exposing her true feelings to him: "according to your request," she wrote, "I have endeavored to make myself as happy as possible, and have so far succeeded as to make many in this place think I bear your absence very well, it only shows my dear John how little they know of this heart of mine."[1] Indeed, her brave facade seemed to be working. "Don't get uneasy about your family," wrote one of the Dunnel family members to John, "you are taking better care of them in California than you could here." All was well, added another, "Harriet has *purty* good spunk, . . . she has kept up uncommon and [is] as busy as a little bee—from all I hear they think a great deal of her in Athens."

Assumed bonds of intimacy allowed Harriet to express a different story to her husband. Despite word to the contrary, she was suffering: "had I been told," she wrote him, "for a certainty, you would not return in two years, I do not believe I would have lived through the [confinement], . . . it is very unpleasant in this place in the winter." As for the good people of Athens, they too were a source of strife: "there is a great degree of selfishness in this place," she added, "and it impresses me with the perfect inactivity and want of energy of most of the inhabitants."[2] For John Dunnel, meanwhile, the very word *home* raised "a throng of delightful appreciations." None appeared quite in fitting with his wife's reports. Instead there was "the cheerful fireside, my dear little wife—the sunny faces of my own dear children—the pleasant rooms."[3] If Harriet was suffering, John did not see it, nor did he appear to believe her letters; after all, she was at home while he was in the competitive world of California.

Much of the written communication between husbands and wives involved in the gold rush is concerned with suffering. Men complained about being lonely, the hardships of the frontier life, its lack of emotional support, and the difficulty of gold digging. Women too complained about being lonely, and about the difficulties of caring for families and businesses. Both had reasons to complain. But when historians analyze suffering across gender, many seem to adhere to a rather curious double standard. Men complained, or so the assumption goes, because they were striving in the competitive sphere of business; women complained because they objected to being dislocated from the domestic sphere. Male suffering, according to this logic, is intrinsic to masculine self-assertion. Female suffering, especially if it is vocalized, is an indication of feminine softness and a desire to return to the safety of the home. Women, to be truly heroic, must make suffering an act of self-negation. Certainly, the picture of the forty-niner wife has been heroic in this manner. Always "patient and devoted," she might be seen "waiting and watching for the husband's return, toiling early and late for the support of her children, ever faithful, ever having him in her thoughts, and so passing her life away, until hope became charred and black."[4]

A closer look at these "women-in-waiting" reveals a more complicated and self-assertive reality. Forty-niner wives were patient. They did suffer. But in neither capacity were they silent. Nor can their willingness to express complaints be read as a desire to return to the safety of the domestic sphere; for an analysis of their writings and of their activities apart from men reveals that no such option existed.[5] Above all, a focus on forty-niner wives widens the lens to include the meanings of becoming middle class. The gold rush, with its extreme separation between the home and the locus of male aspiration, brilliantly reveals that for women, this dreamed-of or realized elevation of status meant spending an inordinate amount of time on their own. It also reveals that they might have had to work more than ever, that the evolving middle-class home was not, at least for them, a refuge from the marketplace. At the same time, such a focus breaks down the distance between these husbands and wives, indicating that every act of status-seeking men must be viewed within the context of the family. Seen in this context, examples of forty-niner risk and heroism might actually appear perverse and irresponsible. Thus it may be only through the gold seekers' own imaginative and literary twists of focus that male risk-taking could be transformed into self-evident truths about independent heroism.

Even at the time, women might contest this turn of the lens with their own literary perceptions of the adventure. Few events invited ordinary nineteenth-century women to convey their every thought and experience as did the California gold rush. Gold-seeking husbands relied heavily on letters from home to assuage their loneliness. At the same time, they wanted to keep these communications private. Having left their wives the job of seeking credit, they feared that reports of successes or failures at the mines would bring either more competitors to the gold regions or, worse, a bushel of notes suddenly due. Thus they urged patience, wariness against the prying of neighbors, and if not complete silence, at least *public* silence. "If you & my creditors will wate with paitience," wrote one, "untill I can get enough to pay my debts and a little more I will be back again never to leave you more." And while asking his wife to write, he also asked her to be circumspect in public: "I don't want every one to Know how poor or how well I am doing."[6]

Implored by their men to write, to freely express their most mundane feelings, but also warned against giving any information to prying eyes, many of these women turned inward for the subject matter of their letters. Reporting that she would keep her trials to herself, Ellen Apple wrote her gold-hunting fiancé that she would try to "appear cheerful and indifferent" in public, but added that her anxiety was "beyond description."[7] The solitude of these arrangements left plenty of time for self-questioning. Still disturbed by the idea that their husbands were running away rather than pursuing family security, some women blamed themselves for the separation. "The day you went away," wrote Julia Allen, of Freetown, Massachusetts, to her husband, "I went down to the Orchard to reflect on your leaving home and the past and it seemed to me as though I had done many things wrong since I was united to you but I hope you will forgive me for them all."[8]

As they turned inward to the private world of their doubts and fears, many women found that the home could be a confining and desperately lonely place. Within these confines, patience was not easy. Still, they worked to pay bills, to feed their families, and to seek the credit necessary to survive. As Julia added in her same letter, she was able to get "along nicely" since her husband went away. But compared with even the most complex business dealings, being alone was a heavier burden by far: always, she wrote, "there is something whispers in my heart I am alone."[9] In Youngstown, New York, Sabrina Swain faced similar doubts and arrived at the same conclusions. Shortly after William Swain's departure, she wrote him of her intentions to be more appreciative of his "worth and society," and hoped that she would be "better qualified to fill the place of a wife." Sabrina may have been beginning to understand that her own mental anguish could match her husband's physical trials. Left alone with private misgivings, she was ready to question the entire undertaking. "Oh! my dear William," she added to her letter, "when I contemplate my loneliness and your absence I am ready to exclaim 'would to God you had never left me,' for what is gold in comparison to the constant anxieties of one's mind?"[10]

Trying to stay busy, but still lonely, women like Julia Allen and Sabrina Swain may have questioned their own positions in the gold rush, wondering what they had done to deserve such a fate. Self-criticism, however, cannot be seen as a first step toward self-effacement. For once they began questioning motivations, it was but a short distance to criticizing the gold seekers themselves. Sabrina Swain cached her criticisms by saying that they represented "women's weakness." But at the same time she could tell William that she wished he "had been contented to have staid at home." She could, at times, even question his professed sense of duty. In the same letter, she informed him that "most people tell me that I am a fool for letting you go away and that no man that thought anything of his family would do so. They say that I need not indulge a hope of seeing you again."[11]

As Sabrina's reference to "other people" indicates, despite being warned against sharing information, these wives were not completely alone in their anxieties. They sought companionship from other women-in-waiting. Although it might be a stretch to argue that the sexual separations inherent in the gold rush contributed to the development of a "woman's culture," a sense of shared crisis and camaraderie could easily develop among California widows. In most small eastern communities and in some large city neighborhoods, the rush brought women together; in the home of one forty-niner wife, many shared their troubles, their winter provisions, and even their husbands' letters.[12] This need for sharing, combined with husbands' requests to reveal nothing about how they were doing at the mines, may have indeed forced them to bond together, for there might be no one else they could trust with their misgivings. Chastina Rix spent her time in Peacham, Vermont, after her husband's departure trying to stay busy. She was often alone, sewing, making dresses and candles. In her diary, however, she also recorded the sharing of articles from the *Knickerbocker* with Mrs. Isaac Watts and Mrs. Harriman, two other forty-niner wives.

The news shared by these women did little to calm their worst fears. Public reports in the newspapers, frequently to the effect that the gold rush was a roistering good time, only added to their worries. Some, like Pamelia Fergus of Little Falls, Minnesota, received reports that their husbands were "a spreeing in the mountains."[13] More common for eastern wives were reports that ships had been lost at sea, that husbands had been washed overboard or abandoned on the trail to die of cholera. True or not, enough forty-niners did die en route to make the rumors entirely believable. "When I hear of the woes & sufferings of those bound to the gold regions," wrote Chastina to herself, "I am sick & wish that *my friends* were at home."[14]

Chastina's need for the support of neighboring women may have increased in proportion to the number and creativity of these shared and published reports. While Alfred was on the way to California via the Isthmus of Panama, she heard news that his steamer had burned at sea. Aware that such items were commonly false alarms and refusing to give the news full credence, she could not help wondering, "But if it should be true!! What misery and anguish of heart it would cause among the families of those left behind." Again, such dark thoughts when shared with women equally bereft of any direct communication may have exacerbated feelings of solitude and frustration. Later, Chastina's confidantes appear to have conjured forth the "rumor that the ship had her captain in irons & was on her way home." Alone at night, with only a flickering candle and the wind for company, and with plenty of time to dwell on the subject, to forty-niner wives even the gloomiest of these possibilities seemed real. As Chastina explained it: "How anxious we are to know the worst. The agony of suspense is almost unbearable. What can the matter be? Why this delay to return? are things which have taken a thousand different forms in my mind. I have fancied all sorts of misfortunes which they are undergoing and more. Can it be that the first report is true?"[15] Having imagined these misfortunes a thousand different ways, women could only wait for the mail to confirm or deny their worst fears. For Chastina the overdue letter finally arrived in early November. This seems to have been something of a pure moment, and in her diary entry for that day she tried to capture it exactly as it happened. At seven in the morning, the mail finally came: "& O! good good, a letter . . . they are at the Isthmus. Have had a storm & rather a hard time. But I am thankful to hear that they are alive & so well."[16]

The receipt of such information, while it could calm the worst of women's fears for their husbands, might be little consolation to their growing feelings of frustration. In most cases, they did the best they could to veil these feelings. Middle-class emotional norms dictated that they should be careful not to express anger. Left to take care of the home, they were supposed to be in a haven of comfort; it was their husbands, after all, who were assumed to be actively suffering. Still, these norms were difficult to maintain. Chastina Rix tried to be patient, writing that she seemed "to have everything to comfort me, or more properly to be comfortable." But she could not avoid the frustrating fact that "the one object, which is necessary to my happiness, is away far away."[17] Equally lonely and faced with a similar lack of information, Sabrina Swain feared for her husband's physical and moral well being during the voyage. She wrote that her "nervous constitution could not endure" the thought "that while I am writing these lines to you your body may be mouldering back to its mother's dust from whence it came."[18]

With the reception of reports of California lawlessness and violence, Sabrina turned to religion to assuage her growing frustration. Although she filled many of her letters with what may appear, to some historians, as meandering sermons against moral slippage, this device may have served to convey other messages. If, that is, William was in the devil's playground, she would remind him of his moral obligations. "Concerning the subject of religion," she wrote her husband, "there is no enjoyment for one that has sinned against so much light." Certainly this statement, which she applied to herself, could also apply to William. And even as she clarified the reference, the message could still get across. When she thought, she continued, of those who had "once professed to love God and rejoiced in his presence and then turned so far aside I am ready to exclaim can God forgive such a one?" The answer was yes, but barely, and it was a forgiveness that applied only to herself: "may God forgive my past conduct and may I strive by his help to live nearer to him and enjoy his presence more."[19] As for William's forgiveness, Sabrina remained silent; for having gone to California for the root of evil, he had larger problems.

Historian J. S. Holliday, who in his journal and letter-bag narrative of the Swain family's "true experience" of the rush paints Sabrina with the brush of heroic patience, cut this passage from his transcriptions of her letters.[20] But it reveals some real, if not altogether heroic, examples of one woman's impatience. As well, it reveals her ability to find a community—in this case the church—and a rhetoric that would allow her to express reservations about William's participation in what by many accounts and to many appearances already seemed a rather silly undertaking. Such a passage belies the notion that forty-niner wives were patient, powerless to attempt to exert control over their husbands, or silent in their sufferings.

Emotional norms should not be mistaken for emotions; forty-niner wives, while constrained in expressing their anger by the prescribed virtue of womanly patience and sacrifice, could be angry.[21] It does not take much reading between the lines to reveal their emotions, nor could they hide their willingness to trespass on their husbands' self-proclaimed status as the greater sufferer. Because forty-niners typically wrote far more than their wives, much of the pain that women felt is difficult to measure. But if patience can be assumed from women's silence, so can anger and frustration. Emily Griswold left no available account of what she suffered in New York. But as her husband's letters indicate, she must have suffered indeed. Soon after he left she faced the death of their two children, along with her own serious illness. Josiah Griswold looked forward to hearing reports of her health with, he wrote, "fearful anxiety." Receiving no word from his wife, he seems to have felt her frustration at a distance; and if she remained silent, he was willing to chastise himself. He admitted that his wife's burdens outweighed his own. Referring to his children, he wrote a family member that he "should have been there to relieve if possible their sufferings and to bless them ere they died, tis this My Brother that has grieved me, and caused me to regret that I left my humble but happy happy home."[22]

Cornelius La Tourette received news of a parallel disaster on his arrival in California. Upon opening the first letter from his wife in Bound Brook, New Jersey, he learned that his two sons, Frederick and Charles, had died of cholera. Cornelius had gone to California in part to earn money to buy a farm, in part to do his duty as a father, promising that if he did well he would send the children to a better school. Yet to Margaret La Tourette, the death of their children canceled both reasons, making any further efforts in California pointless. And she did leave a record of her anger and frustration. Unable to contain her emotions, she wrote her husband that "no human being can ever [know] the anguish I suffered when those precious children were torn from me." The problem, she claimed, was that Cornelius was not around to help in a time of need. "Next," she added, "no tidings came from you, every prospect seemed blasted, every hope crushed. I loathed every thing around me, and thought only of those from whom I was, for the present separated." Perhaps hoping that the news would speed her husband back to the East, Margaret tried to temper her frustration with sympathy. Writing of her sorrow "when I think of the sad heart rending news that you so soon must hear," she urged him to "turn your thoughts from these scenes, think of Christ blessing little children and . . . think what a world of sorrow and toil they have escaped."[23] Cornelius followed her advice, although perhaps not in the way that Margaret envisioned. He turned not toward home, but toward the foothills of the Sierra Nevada.

This unexpected response freed Margaret from much of her restraint. From this point on she repeatedly urged her husband to give up the venture: "it is useless for you to struggle longer against the decrees of fortune." Writing that she was tired of answering the question of when he was coming home, she added that she hoped "by this time you are either engaged in something profitable or have made up your mind to return."[24] Perhaps aware that her calls for her husband's return might go unheeded, Margaret channeled much of her frustration into other avenues, into requests for letters and money, and into morbid accounts of the burdens women bore during the forty-niners' long absence. She complained that she had not heard from Cornelius often enough, writing that he "might have written a volume in those *four months.*" Fatigued at being asked to borrow for her living, she reminded him that "I am anxiously expecting the return of the money I sent you at Panama." Finally her letters carried regular reminders of the sufferings she had to face alone. They took on the characteristic of death counts, recording the demise not only of their two sons, but of at least nine other acquaintances.[25]

Several among the dead were forty-niners. This fact, along with the tone of Margaret's letters, suggests the possibility that she consciously designed this information: her morbidity, she may have felt, would remind Cornelius of the pain caused by his stubborn efforts to make something out of a doomed venture. Remarking on the death of Voorhees Fisher, a member of the New Brunswick Company whose family lived near Bound Brook, she raised the question of her husband's responsibility. She did not precisely blame him for anything, but wondered why he had left Fisher during the illness that preceded his death. She reported telling the unfortunate Fisher's parents that "you could not have thought him dangerous or you would not have left him." Of course, these very statements carried some critical questions. Had Cornelius abandoned his friend? And did he know that Fisher's parents were "disconsolate?" Finally, Margaret reminded him that these scenes did not simply reflect the sufferings of the miners, but they had dramatic consequences for families in the East. "Perhaps he left a message for his parents," she added, "or expressed to a friend his feelings in view of death. Anything from him will be interesting to them."[26]

For Margaret La Tourette as for many other forty-niner wives and widows, what had once been a business venture would become increasingly linked with a sense of loss. She continued to remind Cornelius of her pain, in one letter reporting a trip to New Brunswick to purchase headstones for the children, in another that "some of our kindly disposed people have reported that you are dead."[27] By this point, he may have finally deciphered the implied message in her letters. That is, if he stayed in California she was mentally prepared to trade the California widow's patience for actual widow's weeds. Margaret's message may have repeated that of another wife, but she transformed the statement: if you stay, she seemed to be telling her husband, I will look upon you as dead.

Historians of women and historians of attitudes toward death have made connections between the two: especially in the nineteenth century, they claim, women channeled much of their artistic and rhetorical energies into obsessions with morbidity. In the gold rush, such a connection does seem apparent. At the same time, there were reasons for these women to equate male risk with family disaster that went beyond death as a vehicle for "feminine" sentimentalism on the subjects of grief, heaven, and heroic martyrdom.[28] For one thing, death really was all around them. One of the most often overlooked facts of the gold rush—and one that undoubtedly contributed much to the frustrations of women and wives in the East—is that the forty-niners chose to go to California during one of the worst cholera epidemics in American history. For another, equations of male risk with destruction and death contained as much anger as sentiment. Containing more than a hint of criticism toward male-based adventure narratives, this equation concluded the self-aggrandizing narrative of the gold seeker with a female voice. For female writers and average women alike, ending the gold rush with the death of the forty-niner was an emphatic "I told you so."

Mary Louisa Hulbert adopted this motif in depicting her husband's decision to join the rush as a "fatal mistake." At the time of the gold rush, Mary's letters to Eri Hulbert were constrained by the language of wifely duty. While she did not approve of his going, she kept her doubts to herself: "we must make the best of our lot and try and not sin against God by repining or murmuring." After her husband's death in Panama, she transformed the experience into a critique of adventuring impulses. The transformation was not difficult, nor was it a case of adding "feminine" sentiment to her husband's own tragic tale. From the outset of his voyage, Eri's letters had resonated with a characteristic tone of forty-niner sentimental regret. His regret deepened in Panama, for like other forty-niners his arrival on the isthmus corresponded with yet another expansion of the cholera epidemic. Repentant, pathetic, and dying, admittedly trapped by his own male impulses, he signed his last letters "your unworthy husband" or "your distressed and weeping husband."[29] In a letter to her son written a dozen years after the event, Mary Louise refocused the narrative on her efforts to talk her spouse out of his plans. Eri, she claimed, refused to listen. His exercise of arbitrary power might have its way, but only at a disastrously high cost. He left for Panama and California. Mary reluctantly gave her support. From this moment the manly adventuring impulse could have only one result: "So the die was cast," she wrote, "and our family destroyed."[30]

Actually, Mary's family was not quite destroyed. Left with just seven dollars and the income from boarders, she managed to raise her children. In fact, her narrative of Eri's death was more directed toward the function of her family than it was sentimental. Quite likely, it also reflected a return of repressed bitterness at being forced to comply with a dangerous male scheme. First, her account made her the real source of authority and reason during the gold rush; Eri's plans, in her telling, became little more than a case of the fantods. Second, having reworked the narrative, she was able to make her real point to her son:

"Do you wonder at my anxiety about my children's associates?"[31] Her recollection of the rush, and of her husband's obstinacy, contained a shift in perspective from the image of the forty-niner as acting alone, to the reality of the forty-niner as tied to families. This shift exposed the fact that the risk elements of the gold rush had a price. If, that is, gold seekers were viewed as acting alone, death on the quest may have appeared heroic. But if they were tied to families, it became an example of male irresponsibility.

Certainly the experience of another wife and husband team, Margaret Gardiner Beeckman and John Beeckman of Virginia and New York, reveals that this shift in focus might make women's criticisms of forty-niner heroism understandable. Margaret Beeckman's part in the California venture was that of a true partner. Her husband had political and business aspirations, but she had the connections as sister-in-law to former president John Tyler. After her husband left for the gold fields in 1849, she spent her time commuting between New York City and the capital. In New York she kept track of departing gold seekers, communicating to John the needs they would have on arrival. He would make the proper investments. She would also send some of the more remunerative products by freight.

As she prepared to send these goods, her letters indicated that she could take the lead in their business affairs. "It is a wide field for me to speculate upon," she wrote her husband in reference to the wild price fluctuations for staples in California, "and I must again urge you to be more minute in your details." She was also in a position to take the lead in John's political affairs. From the Tyler estate in Virginia, she was able to gauge the changing political currents. Having left with the idea of involving himself in California's foundation as a state, John depended on Margaret for the timing of his political moves. These moves would have to be made carefully. There were complex and dangerous issues at work, as she reminded him: one was the question of whether California would enter into the Union as a slave or free state; another was whether the growing sectional crisis would allow it to enter in at all. If the former happened, John had to be prepared to come down on either side of the fence. If the crisis worsened and California remained outside the Union, then she felt that war would soon follow: "and the territories of the Pacific will receive a new impetus and become the great [markets] of commerce and prosperity." Either way, she indicated, the coming sectional hostilities might be turned, with the proper timing that only she could give him, to their advantage.[32]

All of these plans came to nothing when John Beeckman accidentally shot himself to death while boating down the Sacramento River. A typical anecdote of forty-niner excess, his death contains the usual tragicomic elements of men at play. Inspired by visions of California lawlessness, Beeckman traveled with his gun loaded. Like other neophyte frontiersmen, he did not know enough to carry it with the barrel turned away from his chest. According to a witness, while traveling in this fashion, he tried to change positions in the boat: "the trigger of one of the barrels caught upon the bottom of the seat and instantly the contents of the barrel were discharged into the upper part of the right lung severing the large arteries . . . and lodging against the spinal column." He was, in effect, another victim of his own dreamy puerilism, his last words a fitting epitaph for the adventurous male: "My God I am shot."[33]

If for some observers John Beeckman's death revealed a heroic play with risk and adventure, for Margaret it was a costly tragedy. The costs may have been primarily emotional. She was, according to a relative who kept watch over her after she received the news, "cast in the deepest affliction." "In the first paroxysms of grief, she seemed inconsolable," wrote her brother-in-law from her home in New York, adding that she did not sleep for days, and only then after being "finally exhausted by the violence of her emotions."[34] She was not, however, allowed to retire behind the widow's veil. For if John's death left heartache, it also brought financial burdens. About a year after her husband's death, she received a letter from J. A. Lowerey, a merchant in New York, informing her that she would "find inclosed statements of account due for goods sold Mr. Beekman [sic] when he first went out to California & for which we have been promised pay & long since." Lowerey made sure to explain the note's delay: "Out of delicacy we have not pursued the claim as wrought."[35] This notice only added to Margaret's burden, for soon after John's death a California merchant who was not so "delicate" had sued her for repayment of her husband's outstanding debts in Sacramento. He also claimed, dishonestly as Margaret's brother believed, that all of Beeckman's property in California had been destroyed by fire or claimed by squatters.[36]

For John Beeckman, the California risk ended badly; but Margaret Beeckman had to live with the consequences: the death of her husband, the end of their grand plans, and the additional burden of having to pay his outstanding debts. Many women seemed to recognize this problem at the time, and many women writers, accordingly, worked to bind forty-niners to home and family, at least as far as eastern readers were concerned. The grave of the lone forty-niner, they seem to have felt, would appear much less romantic if viewed as a symbol of the burdens placed on women. For some historians, this literature might be categorized as sentimental. On closer inspection it seems to have been written in a debunking mode: exposing the reality of the gold rush as not a golden plenty but a wild dream followed by failure, its meaning not individualism or democracy but death and loss. "Cousin Alice," the author of *All's Not Gold That Glitters*, was typical in depicting the forty-niners as hopeless dreamers. "Lumps of gold were to be picked up for the stooping," she wrote scornfully of their early visions and public accounts, adding that every "remarkable piece of good fortune was exaggerated, and the sufferings and privations, even of the successful barely touched upon." None of these dreams were charming to Cousin Alice; their results more often than not were disastrous.

Like other writers, Cousin Alice saved her most cutting criticism for the obstinate husband and father who dared to go to California and die. "I've about made up my mind to go to California—there—and that's the end on it," declares this character, in a bit of foreshadowing, striking his fist on the kitchen table "so that every dish rattled." And so he goes to the gold country, taking his son with him, but leaving his wife behind. Once there, of course, he dies. The son provides one moral, thinking to himself "how much better it would have been for them all if his father had been as good and contented as their mother was." Cousin Alice provided another: "*What shall it profit a man, if he gains the whole world, and loses his own soul?*" In a similar manner, an 1851 article from the *Ladies Repository* carried the implication that the gold seeker's grave, while a sad sight, was a deserved fate for men who had severed their connections with family and friends: "how will the rallying senses of the dying wanderer recall the bright scenes of youth and home that once cheered him[?] . . . How will the loneliness, the fearfulness of the solemn hour, weigh down his soul! . . . For gold he sought these distant shores; for gold he has given up his life.

> Slave of the dark and dirty mine,
> What vanity hath brought thee here?"[37]

A sentimental epitaph perhaps, but not one without a certain degree of anger. Looking beneath the veil of the California widow, behind the self-effacing image of stoic patience, reveals a parallel experience of the gold rush. While from the outset of the rush, at least, women's experience reflected shared ideas of companionate duty, their experiences and the ways they thought about them also seemed to challenge equations of risk with heroism. Elements of risk may have added to the adventuresome spirit of the rush. But if women had to pay the real consequences of this spirit, it became something childish and irresponsible, more puerile than heroic, and women's impatience and morbidity may have reminded men of these consequences. Perhaps for this reason women had to be wrapped in veils of silence, limited to the role of patient helpmate. Yet here too there might be perceptual problems. For even the woman who fit into the role of helpmate might be *too* supportive, *too* felicitously heroic in her handling of burdens. Her work at home, that is, might undermine perceptions of forty-niners as fully independent individuals.

A look at the gold rush from the perspective of women in the East immediately reveals an apparent contradiction of cultural assumptions. Women did a lot of work in support of their husbands. Much of this work required a large measure of independence. Men, to the contrary, were extremely dependent. As the historian Jeanne Boydston has argued, male risk-taking in the competitive marketplace of the nineteenth century was only made possible by women's work. Their unpaid labor "provided the needed 'safety net,' enabling middle-class families to maintain some degree of both material stability and health in a volatile economic environment."[38] As an economic venture, the gold rush was more risky than most male business activities. It required such a degree of women's work, including the maintenance of home and business, kinship and economic networks, that it threatened to bring the woman as helpmate out from the shadows and toward the center of the experience. In effect, it threatened to make the helpmate a subversive figure, one that might challenge both ideals of a sexual segregation of labor and male perceptions of independence and self-reliance.

As they developed in the mid-nineteenth century, ideologies of labor and gender reflected the needs of middle-class manhood. Increasingly based on white-collar employment, the bourgeois man's work became better paid but less physically demanding, cleaner but almost entirely lacking in heroic qualities. In fact, much of this work required few essentially masculine traits at all, for who could not push a pen or add figures? Middle-class ideologies of domesticity and the sexual segregation of labor were attempts to solve this problem. Here, the point seemed to be that proper women would do no labor at all. Relegated to the private sphere by these proscriptions, women might have status as mothers, but aside from reproductive functions they were nonproductive members of society. Not just unpaid and unseen but also perceptually nonexistent; whatever work they did simply could not be counted as real without trespassing on the developing ideal of the lone male provider. Thus even as men counted on their wives' labor to ensure their success, because women's work was not perceptually real, measures of masculinity could be imbued with an increasing stress on independence. Their wives relegated to the home, men were free to succeed or fail entirely on their own merits. They were, at last, fully free and alone in the battle for success.[39]

Precarious at best, this ideology was undermined at its very foundation. As men freed themselves from former patriarchal lines of dependency, and as the lines between public and private life became more thickly drawn, economic activity became increasingly risky. Thus, even while a gender system that made women's work disappear was becoming a "cherished truism," women's work—their maintenance of a safety net and a mooring place for the family—was becoming more, not less, important.[40] The internal contradictions of mid-nineteenth-century gender ideology might be especially apparent in the West or during folk migrations. On the westward trail, where risk and fragmenting forces of geographic dislocation were constant, women's roles in holding communities together could not be ignored.

Even during western migrations, however, women's work might be screened by gender expectations. These migrations, as many historians have pointed out, were composed of families, not lone frontiersmen. At most times and places, pioneers were men, women, and children. If the frontier was a place of gendered rather than wholly male experience, migrations still proceeded under ideological assumptions that masked the reality of women's work. During these migrations, women soon discovered that their work was as important to success as that of their husbands. Many found that there was no sexual segregation of labor on the trail, and that in fact not only was their work of equal importance to men's, it involved practically the same tasks. Instead of being freed by these necessary transgressions of ideological constraints, these women, according to many analyses, experienced a threatening dislocation from security. So even on the trail, the gender system remained intact. As historians of western women have concluded, westering women resisted frontier liberation; they feared the "breakdown of the sexual division of labor as a dissolution of their autonomous 'sphere.'"[41]

Again, this conclusion seems to rest on the idea that if women complained—as men frequently did—it was because they wanted to return to the security of the home. Certainly out on the trail, where security seemed hard to come by, the home might be layered by nostalgia. To women collecting buffalo dung for campfires, the domestic sphere may have actually looked like a receding oasis. If this conclusion has some basis in fact, and if it is combined with studies of women working under the same gender system in the East, it suggests an interesting point: in terms of women's actions and how they were perceived, the West differed very little, if at all, from the East. In both regions, women regularly crossed the boundaries of the sexual division of labor; in neither could these crossings proceed without producing internal and external tensions. Even if actual experiences differed according to region, in both the East and the West gender was a structuring agent, defining men's and women's everyday lives.

The California gold rush, however, took place in both regions. Or, perhaps more to the point, as an event negotiated in dialogues between home and California, it took place in neither. Men went west, women stayed east, and this separation partially lifted the screen of gender expectations. For a brief period of time, the maintenance of a sexual division of labor was impossible, and the record of what women did without men becomes clear. With men gone from the home, we may see plainly that women in the East could not be outside of the market. It becomes apparent that commodities, types of money and units of trade, and production and consumption all flowed through the home. The fact that women directed this flow may suggest that the sexual division of labor cannot simply be causally linked with the rise of modern capitalism or the market revolution, as it was also highly dependent on the presence of men.[42] Few of the economic activities expected of California widows were wholly new. Yet the fact that these women performed them alone may have had repercussions for the future. For many men, being middle class meant working away from home. For women the same status meant working between the home and the market. Operating increasingly alone in a world of consumption, cash, and credit exchange, women had to develop talents and skills independent of husbands. These capabilities, required as they were by a sexual segregation of labor, might also be the ones that would enable women to break the ideology of separate spheres.

As they left for the gold country, many married forty-niners placed their businesses in the charge of their wives. They did not, however, envision the possibility that their wives would act alone. If these women were to be business agents, their husbands still planned to issue orders at a distance. Thus these departing businessmen left careful letters of instruction, informing their wives of how to maneuver in the competitive world, giving them directions on everything from how the children should be clothed to ways of stalling creditors. Try as they might to maintain these connections and power relations, however, such control from ever-increasing distances was impossible. It took neither men nor women long to realize that the rhythms of business would far outstrip the pace of an overextended mail service. Within a short time of their husbands' departures, eastern women-in-waiting were no longer merely waiting; they were making business decisions without advice. By this time, the advice might have become uselessly vague anyway. "You must not deprive yourself of the comforts of life," read one wife, while others, reading husbands' apologies for not sending money, were simply urged to fend for themselves and the family as best they could.[43]

In their engaging study of gold rush wives in Minnesota, Linda Peavy and Ursula Smith claim that while women were used to doing work in their men's absence, they did not welcome this work as a test of independence. Of one typical wife they conclude: "Her term as head of household was, then, something to be endured, not relished." These authors provide a summation of activities that, although they describe the work of rural or midwestern farming wives, are similar in quantity if not always in type to the tasks of eastern women in more urbanized locales. The list of tasks is long, and it would have left little time for women to enjoy their accomplishments; it would include the usual tasks of cleaning, cooking, and sewing, along with the keeping up of kinship ties, and the supervision of children, their health, education, manners, and discipline. But it would also include chores outside the household, the planting and harvesting of crops, the feeding of animals, and the killing, preservation, and preparation of cows, hogs, and chickens.[44] Women in the eastern states performed many of the same tasks, including the regular domestic work of caring for children, making meals, and maintaining kinship connections. If they did not find themselves milking or slaughtering cows and hogs, they did frequently have to oversee husbands' employees, rent abandoned shops to other tradesmen, collect on debts, receive credit while stalling creditors, and trade goods and services for food and wood and coal.

Few of these tasks might be particularly relishing in themselves. The constant need to avoid creditors, even while having to seek out new sources of credit to maintain home and family, could be particularly humiliating. Keeping up kinship ties was a social and economic activity, a labor of primary importance in the exchange of commodities that would ensure family survival. Yet it might frequently have been the hardest work of all.[45] Despite all the talk among historians about the decline of kinship relations with the market revolution and the rise of the middle class, for women it seems this decline never occurred. Perhaps what these historians mean is that maintaining kinship ties became women's work, and thus no longer worthy of study. For many forty-niner wives, these ties were all-important. And certainly, they were numerous and complicated. Sara Davenport, a young girl from New Canaan, Connecticut, reported the regular comings and goings of four "Aunts," five "Uncles," and thirteen "Cousins," along with friends, wives and children of cousins, ministers, and hired girls during her gold-seeking father's two-year absence from home. The timing of these visits, along with the feeding and care of these kin, had to be organized and overseen by Sara's mother. Margaret La Tourette's work in this capacity brought her in contact with her family and that of her husband. At the family homestead in Bound Brook, she had to maintain friendly relations with a relative, James Bayles, whose intemperance made him, as she said, "a fine specimen of the Bayles family." She made it clear to her husband that such work was barely supportable, writing that she did not think she could stand it much longer: "Interests clash too much," she added, "and I must forever associate with those who feel no interest in me."[46]

If the work that gold rush wives did in their husbands' absence was to be endured, not relished, they did not shirk in their performance of tasks. Welcomed or not, the work conveyed a sense of independence and accomplishment. They might have no real desires to become "businesswomen," yet to themselves and their husbands this work led to an unavoidable realization: they could, under these conditions, perform all the tasks necessary for their family's well-being. That this work transgressed the boundaries of a sexual division of labor, that it was difficult or something to be endured, did not preclude these women from taking pride in their efforts. A close look at two women in the East, Charlotte Prince and Sara Jane Pierce, both from New York State, reveals just how much was expected of forty-niner wives. At the same time, it reveals what they expected of themselves, their willingness to step into the world of business and competition, and their sense of pride in accomplishment. This sense was not something that could be easily defined away or covered over, not by the ideology of a paternalistic gender system, and perhaps not even by the return of their husbands.

The record of the activities of Charlotte and William Prince during the gold rush does not include what Charlotte had to say about the event. All the surviving letters are from William Prince. Still, if these letters do not give Charlotte a voice, they do give her agency, and they provide a clear record of what she did in her husband's absence. They also suggest her husband's growing, if grudging, respect for her business sense and ability to prosper. Charlotte's husband was the owner of one of the four most successful nurseries on Long Island. When he departed from Flushing for California in the spring of 1849, he did not close his famous "Linnaen Botanic Garden and Nurseries" but left it, along with his gardeners and groundskeepers, under Charlotte's charge. As he departed, William seemed to realize the extent of the work he had left with his wife. Despite his misgivings that he had "by my troubles caused you great sorrows," he expressed his confidence: "I have always," he reminded Charlotte, "found you true."[47]

If William's confidence was merited, and it appears that it was, Charlotte Prince had to be an extremely hardworking woman. The Princes had three children, a daughter named after Charlotte, and two sons, Willie and Le Baron. They were merchant offspring, not farm children. Charlotte would have to do more than just assure their survival while her husband was away. As William's letters reveal, he had aspirations for their success; they needed to be well fed, well clothed, and well educated. To accomplish all of this, the Prince nursery would have to continue running at its usual brisk pace. Charlotte, in turn, would have to balance motherhood with overseeing the business. If this expectation contradicted many nineteenth-century gender prescriptions, it was nevertheless a direct reflection of the middle-class aspirations of the Prince family. As a woman, Charlotte's status evolved from her role as a nurturing mother; as a middle-class woman, she had broader responsibilities. Within the privatized family unit, Charlotte was her husband's closest confidante; she had his trust, whereas his employees did not. William's attitude toward his workers at the nursery—they were to be watched with suspicion—indicates that he never considered the possibility of placing the business in their hands. Charlotte had to move in both worlds, that of the home and that of competitive business, not in spite of middle-class prescriptions, but *because* she was a middle-class woman.

Charlotte found a transgression of the sexual division of labor unavoidable. In fact she was expected, especially in keeping with her position, to cross this line. Prior to William's departure, she received power of attorney over his property. Although she also received his letters of instruction, she had complete control over putting these instructions into effect.[48] These instructions left plenty of room for her to develop a business style. William even encouraged her to do so: as a "deputy husband" she would also have to be deputized as a full business partner. He prompted her to read treatises on horticulture, to go through his old account books and use them as models in drawing up her own. He gave her advice on collecting and paying bills. Above all, he urged her to be wary: "you will," he warned her, "learn about every man's [accounts] & business." She should not, he told her, depend on the workers to act without orders. She would have to tell them when to plant and what to plant, keeping in mind the proper growing-rhythms of the apple, cherry, and plum trees. The hired hands were not to be trusted, he added, and she might have to deal with them harshly. Referring to one worker, he informed her that if he did not show up for work on time, he was to be fired immediately. In this case she should raise the wages of one of the younger "boys" and hire another.[49]

William's letters indicate that Charlotte performed all these tasks with great skill. While her letters do not survive, she seems to have written regularly. He received and commented approvingly on news of her regular engagement in large cash transactions. She ran the nursery efficiently, making only one adjustment to his absence by cutting back on the number of its "experimental" plants. These, as she said, and he admitted, did not often pay well anyway. Business at the nursery ran so smoothly under Charlotte's care that William was surprised when he heard the news—which Charlotte kept from him in order not to cause worries—that she had in the course of overseeing some planting broken her ankle. By the time of William's arrival in California, she wrote that the ankle had healed. Rather than allow the injury to slow her activities, she looked to increase them by reviving the experimental section of the nursery. Inspired by her husband's descriptions of flora during his voyage, and perhaps by a chance to do business while the fire was hot, she urged him to send home seeds and bulbs, South American and California "exotics" for the consumption of eastern gardeners.[50]

By the fall of 1849, only a short time after William's arrival in California, the Princes may have become aware of a remarkable conclusion: Charlotte was doing a lot better at running the nursery than William was at finding gold. William's disappointment was increasingly obvious. He had tried prospecting; he had turned his hand at selling goods, all without result. "I cannot by any turn," he wrote, "realize any certainty of doing well here."[51] His letters continued to arrive with regularity, but although they still carried detailed instructions on the running of the nursery, he increasingly wrote them in response to her business dealings as faits accomplis. Meanwhile, no longer expecting William to send home bank drafts, Charlotte began selling off small lots that the couple owned on Long Island. Despite her husband's misgivings that unscrupulous buyers might take advantage of her situation, she reported profits. William could only approve; she had made the deals without his aid and, better yet, without commissions to lawyers. Finally, while William's letters continued to be filled with advice, it was obvious that he looked on her as a partner and not as a business neophyte. Directing her to collect on outstanding claims against other merchants, he left the specifics up to her: "I authorize you to receive all [amounts] whatever."[52] By this time, he was already thinking about giving up and coming home. Although there is no record of William's homecoming, it seems likely that his return could not undo the fact of his dependence on Charlotte. Nor could he forget her achievements in the public world of business. Even his letters carried the implied admission: in the gold rush it was Charlotte, not William, who had the greater success.

Although not as prosperous as the Princes, Sara Jane and Hiram Pierce of Troy, New York, experienced the gold rush as a similar overturning of the assumed patterns of female dependency and male self-reliance. Like the Princes, the Pierces were among the leading families of their community. Again, their arrangements for coping with exigencies of the rush reflected developing patterns and tensions within middle-class attitudes toward home and work. Sara Jane (Wiswall) Pierce's husband left for California at the age of thirty-eight. Their family, while only a little larger than the mid-nineteenth-century average, was still large: Sara would be in charge of seven children. Confident that he would find gold while regaining his declining health caused by an eye affliction, Hiram instructed Sara to get by as best she could and wait for his bank drafts. Sara did more than wait patiently; Hiram did far less than strike it rich. Their correspondence reveals his failures and her successes.

Like many women, Sara Pierce did not welcome the increased responsibilities generated by her husband's absence. She doubted her abilities, writing Hiram soon after his departure that "when I think of the responsible place I occupy my heart allmost failes me—and I feel my utter inability to fill that place." Seven children and no income was a desperate equation; as Sara added, she could only hope for guidance: "my daily prayer to God is that he will give me grace strength and wisdom to discharge my duty."[53] Her desperation, however, was blended with aspirations. As an aspiring middle-class wife, she could easily dream of the status that gold would bring and knew the value of keeping up appearances. She also loved her husband and professed to him that if he could do his duty, she would persevere in her own. "You know," she wrote Hiram, "if our friends see me low sperited they will blame you and that I cannot bare. I some times think they will think we did not love each other very much but they cannot see our hearts, the fact is I think our motives are good and God will approve and you may depend a little of the Calafornia gold will come acceptable at this time, if I could get hold of some of the money doe you think I could make good use of it[?]"[54]

Admittedly lonely and fearful that her abilities would not be enough to meet the crisis, Sara still felt that she could endure the separation, at least until her husband began sending back the promised money. In this hope, however, she was soon disappointed. During the fall after Hiram's departure, just as the family's winter needs became pressing, she received word of his failure at the mines. "I feel most deeply to regret," she read in his missive, "that the season has so far passed away & I have earned nothing to enable me to make any remitance." "You see from this how grossley things have been misrepresented," he wrote, adding that "if I could get decently home I will bid good by to Cal with all its humbugary." Sara must have received this news with dismay. Despite his disappointment, Hiram could not come home; he could only tell her to "depend on Mr Boutwell [a neighbor] this winter." And he could only add regretfully: "I am Sorry I cannot fix things up as usual or better for you."[55]

Sara Pierce managed to make it through the winter. Engaging in the work of kinship, she sought help from neighbors for her supply of coal. "Mr. Boutwell" did indeed furnish her with flour for bread. But it appears that she depended above all on her own initiative. Although the family's potato supply, collected before Hiram's departure, was "not very good" and "rather inclined to rot," she made it last the winter. For money, she sublet her husband's blacksmith shop. The rental of the shop, in turn, provided the first test of her business abilities. The renter, she suspected, was stealing and misusing Hiram's tools. Her suspicions were later confirmed, and, as she wrote her husband, "I called a meeting [with him] and myself took an inventory of the tools and turned him out without any ifs or ands." Having rented the shop to a more trustworthy tradesman, she could not conceal her pride at the way she had handled the crisis. "I guess you will begin to think I am getting to be quite a buisness *caracter*," she wrote Hiram. Her attempt to maintain the rhetoric of a sexual separation of labor only added what seems to be a conscious touch of irony: "I think you would laugh," she concluded, "if [you] could see me fly about some times, I get along very well concidering what [a] weak vessel I am."[56]

By the spring of 1849, Sara had settled into a busy schedule of business and social activities. The money from the rental of the blacksmith shop allowed her to keep the family fed and housed. She did her husband's work and her own, lifting the stove, "corging" the bedsteads, and still finding time to go door-to-door collecting for a church fundraising. She may have been especially good at this task, for she received practice enough in maintaining her networks of kin and credit. At the outset of 1850, she reported that she had collected a "little more than half the notes and bills" brought against neighbors. To this income, she shrewdly balanced her own repayments of debt, recording that she was "[o]weing about two hundred dolars." Thus within a year of her husband's departure she had become a self-proclaimed expert in the competitive arena of credit exchange and debt collection. "Mr Groat has not paid a cent," she wrote her husband, "I have repetedly dunned Smith, and finally got a note payable on demand, I mean to tease it out of him yet, Mr Hale has paid $5 Mr Waller $60 Mr Hows $6.50 Mr Langdon not one cent, he has moved to Shenectdy [*sic*], the rest have paid all."[57]

By this time Sara appears to have felt confident in her own abilities. Still Hiram had done almost nothing in California. He had sent her only a small morsel of gold and a daguerreotype. She wrote back that she thought "a great deal about that gold," and she urged him to be patient. Be faithful, she told him, "we can not expect to prosper if our hearts are not right with God." Hiram was far from prospering. Admitting defeat at the gold diggings, he was on the way back to San Francisco to work for wages. Still under the impression that Sara was in the care of the ever reliable Mr. Boutwell, he could only repeat his "regret that I have ben able to make no remitance."[58] Hiram's despair and disappointment, coupled with his inability to recognize Sara's work for the family, may be seen as half call for sympathy, half effort to lessen the importance of her business successes. If so, she was willing to give him one but not the other. Her letters indicate that she loved her husband and was sympathetic to his plight, but at the same time, she was understandably proud of her achievements. She would give him solace, but he should know that her success was not by the grace of Boutwell or anyone else.

Sara was ready to calm Hiram's fears of failure with expressions of endearments and need. "If I could get you back," she claimed, "I should be willing to live on very small fare." Success or failure, "gold or no gold," she continued, "your presence here is better far than gold, all there is there would not tempt me to endure half the anxiety of the past yere." At the same time, she made it clear that Hiram would have to accept and recognize her successes. In a letter postmarked late in the summer of 1850, she made a point of detailing her activities. The children kept her constantly busy. She was also caring for "Aunt Nancy," who was staying at the Pierce home while recovering from smallpox. To this schedule, she added her wide-ranging business dealings. Hiram's blacksmith shop, she wrote, was again vacant; she was engaged in renting it again—for the fourth or fifth time. She had repeatedly dunned Mr. Waters, and he had finally paid his note. She had worked out a deal with the recalcitrant Mr. Groat; he would pay off his five-dollar debt in milk. As for Mr. Smith and his debt of twenty dollars, she was involved in similar negotiations. She needed the cash, she wrote Hiram, since a toothache had turned into a potential dental bill of thirty dollars, but she was willing to accept an extension of credit at Smith's dry goods store. Indicating that no detail was too small for her accounting, she reported repayment on a fifty-cent debt from Mr. "Searces." Extracting the debt, as she put it, "by littles," she accepted one time a quart of currents, another time five-cents worth of potatoes.[59]

It would appear that Hiram finally got the point, or at least part of it.

He increasingly recognized Sara's work on behalf of his venture. He could not, however, easily grasp the idea that she might be enjoying herself. It may have taken him a while to shake loose from the well-ensconced images of the patiently suffering California widow, the home as a refuge from travail. Admitting that his wife was taking on extensive business obligations, he assumed she was enduring, not relishing her activities: "I fear [the work] will weare you out," he wrote. A month later he asked her to "let the girls do most of the work" and to "let others take care of the public business for a spell."[60] Sara did not slow her activities. If her letters are an indication, she may indeed have been relishing the experience. "You would laugh," she wrote Hiram, "to see me at work. I am my own tinker have set nine fruit trees kleened house with Maria's help mend fence set glass mend my own stove grate in the oven, moved the front room stove out alone, in fact I am kept very busy here."[61]

Without underestimating the pain of her admitted loneliness, it appears that Sara Pierce enjoyed her role in the gold rush. Her obvious sense of pride in her accomplishments illuminates the possibility that for women, as well as men, the gold rush might offer a widening of social and emotional space. Certainly, her letters evince a growing felicity of style and self-expression. She too could engage in a play of language. At times such play might be in response to Hiram's need for news of the family. Describing their son for his pleasure, she experimented with adjectives, writing "I wish you would see his bright eyes and rosy cheaks." Coloring her own sights, making real her own experiences, she asked him to "look in upon us: You must fancy you see all but our little Himer, on our way to church, first Elvira & Laura then Alfred and George, then myself with Frances & Mary one at the right and the other on the left and I am happy to say they are both strieving to enter in at the strait gate."[62] At other times, she could articulate her own embodiment, teasing her husband with newly envisioned romantic possibilities. "You must come soon," she later wrote in a strange tapestry of love, adultery, and death, "or you will be entirely behind the times. You know there is no use of being out of fashion, however I will not be so follish as to follow the example of a couple at the American [Hotel]. It seems she left her Husband and ran away with another man. [T]hey stopped at the American and call'd for a room they took poison which did not take effect and then cut their throats with a raisor and were found the next day in each others arms."[63]

Fashions, along with Sara's space and vision, were obviously changing. Thus the spirit of play dominant in the gold rush could extend east; it could be shared between husbands and wives. Certainly Sara felt that it could. If her husband played with her, she played with him, blending the imagery of patience with the physicality of sexual need. "Oh if we could kiss," she wrote him, "but alas it will be a long time before we shall be permitted to embrace one another, but in my dreams you may depend I have fine times, in one of my night visions I thought you had come home but you cant think what a time we had." She continued to tease Hiram, her longing ardently physical: "oh how I wish you were here," she wrote, adding that while she saw more men than he saw women, "if I could get you where I could see you it would make but little difference."[64] He responded in kind, suggesting that she invest in her needed dental repairs, "but," he teasingly added, "not so as to bite me when I get home." Finally, as he earned the wages for his return, Hiram seems to have realized that Sara had changed. She had seized some opportunity, the presence of which he had been unaware. Yet he liked the result. "I perceive by your last that you are getting quite prosey & some what racy in your wrighting," he noted, "& i conclude you must be growing younger again. If you think it will renew your youth by my beeing away, perhaps I had better stay another year."[65]

Despite his jocular postscript, Hiram did not stay in California another year. Like nearly all eastern seaboard forty-niners, he returned home after only a season at the gold diggings. Sara, suddenly youthful and undoubtedly proud of her ability to move in the world of business, may have demanded a period of adjustment. Returning to wives who had developed increasing senses of self-worth and pride in accomplishment, many forty-niners discovered new tensions within their families. Women like Sara Jane Pierce and Charlotte Prince, as Peavy and Smith suggest, must have had difficulty returning to their old role "of acquiescent, unquestioning wife, readily deferring to her husband's judgment in matters outside her sphere."[66] At the same time, the idea that such women would automatically return to these roles may be somewhat anachronistic in light of the changes in family life corresponding with the mid-nineteenth-century rise of a new middle class. The California gold rush, as a cross-gender event, reflected and exposed these changes. It revealed that the new middle class would not be limited to an ethos of respectability; further, it indicated that neither aspiring bourgeois women nor men would be relegated to private worlds.

With the departure of their husbands, many eastern women of the gold rush seem to have become conscious of something that had long been before their eyes: the home was not outside of the world at large. In the market for some time, they discovered the market as a place in which they could belong and thrive. Undoubtedly, this realization generated tensions. It would not, perhaps, visibly alter women's status for some time. Yet the change might have lasting effects. Men, in going to California, had done a lot more than blaze a path for their own liberation. As Peavy and Smith say of their Minnesota couples, husbands and wives had become used to being apart; both had found large measures of physical independence. "Now," the authors claim, "forced to meet on common ground, they found themselves unable to decide where to give in, how to live and let live."[67]

Few gold seekers would have predicted that an increase in women's autonomy would be the result of their efforts. At the same time, they might have to live with this result. In the gold rush, both men and women had discovered a sense of their physical selves; both could now see themselves as a part of the market culture they were creating. Between these selves and spaces, male and female, public and private, there would be tensions, of course. It seems doubtful that husbands and wives could simply relearn or return to the old rules for domestic harmony. Such efforts could only end in frustration. More likely, they might have to constitute wholly new patterns for living together. For some men, and many women, this process, fraught as it was with tension, might be welcomed rather than lamented. At the same time, the results of these renegotiations of power appear to have been more social than ideological, more reflective of the changing realities of home and family life than of changes in the culture at large. For in the end, the work that these women did in their husbands' absence, along with the suffering they endured, would be relegated to the perceptual margins and shadows of the gold rush. In terms of actual accomplishment, many of these women were more successful than their husbands. Their experience of the gold rush, in turn, was just as rich, even richer. But as it turned out, the place for the "real" women in the gold rush would be out West, in California.

Eight

A Wild, Free, Disorderly, Grotesque Society

There was something unreal about California, noted George Payson after his return to Boston. A lot of men had sailed from eastern ports in 1849, that much was sure. But as for the existence of California, while there had been a lot of promises and talk, few of these promises had been delivered, and much of the recent talk had been about humbugs and elephants. Payson decided to address this problem in an introductory comment to his recollections, writing as "Francis Fogie, Sen., Esq." "To be sure," wrote the skeptical Old Fogie, "any number of men and ships have set sail for California, but that's no sign that they ever got there. They say so of course, for no one likes to be humbugged, but for all we know, they might just as well have gone to India, or China, or Japan. I have noticed . . . they say very little about the gold they have brought home, though that after all is the only real proof; and they go into a huff if any one asks them how much they made. So you see that, reasoning *a priori*, the balance of probability is decidedly opposed to the existence of any such country."[1] Indeed, for many eastern observers the entire gold rush seemed like something out of the *Arabian Nights*. It contained, that is, quite a number of fascinating and gruesome tales, and much literary style, but it lacked substance. The United States Mint was reporting major shipments of gold, and so was the Pacific Mail Service. But for wives and loved ones, the reports were nearly always the same. Their forty-niners were failing at the mines. Many had sent home daguerreotypes of themselves dressed in authentic miner garb. Others had sent a morsel of yellow metal, presumably gold, enough to make a cufflink or a small ring. But they sent little else, apart from tear-stained letters of complaint; and they never seemed to strike it rich. In fact, if anything was accomplished during these men's absence it was by their wives, running businesses, taking care of children, stalling creditors. The forty-niners, by any real measure, had apparently disappeared.

Within a few years of Payson's skeptical introduction, few men would be more real than the forty-niner. They were *men*, as Mark Twain would have it, "stalwart, muscular, dauntless young braves . . . the very pick and choice of the world's glorious ones." They had settled a region, founded a state, lynched countless numbers of claim jumpers, and cleared the territory of Indians. Together they composed a "splendid population" of pioneers. The gold rush had assembled "a driving, vigorous, restless population," a "*curious*" population—one could not call it a society—characterized by a host of manly excesses, fighting, whoring, gambling, dueling, and lynching. There were no dandies in this crowd, no "simpering, dainty, kid-gloved weaklings," no "slow, sleepy, sluggish-brained sloths." Those types generally stayed at home, or if they came to the gold country, they quickly left. "For these people hated aristocrats," claimed Twain, "and if a man wanted a fight on his hands, without any annoying delay, all he had to do was to appear in public in a white shirt or a stovepipe hat, and he would be accommodated." As for the place of women in the gold rush, why they simply had no place. In fact there were no women at all, anywhere, only "swarming hosts" of men as far as the eye could see, "none but erect, bright-eyed, quick-moving, strong handed young giants."[2]

Somehow, between Old Fogie's remarks and Twain's depiction of California's "flush times," the gold rush had become not just real but extraordinarily real. Women, meanwhile, had disappeared from the gold regions, nearly vanishing from the narrative itself. How did this happen? A clue for the unraveling of this great transformation may be found in one gold seeker's diary. John Cornelison was a simpering and dainty weakling. A New York City clerk, he was dying of tuberculosis before he left for California in 1849. And, despite the fact that he had read Dana's *Two Years Before the Mast* and hoped his journey west would effect a cure, he was even closer to death when he arrived. Too weak to go ashore he passed his time in a ship's hold, writing tales of adventures that he would never have. As he put it: "I write until dinner time. After dinner I write or sit and think until tea is ready." This was Cornelison's gold rush. He sat, thought, and drank medicinal tea; in the meantime he traveled, in his mind's eye, outside the confining hold of his ship. "Out there" he had adventures and saw new sights—

adventures and sights, as he made sure to note in his journal, that were completely unvarnished by romance or invention.

One of these sights concerned a shipmate by the name of "Mantalini." Mantalini, as Cornelison described him, was a young dandy from New Jersey who, although he had no discernible connection with a newspaper, fancied himself a reporter. He was also a shirker, a weakling who preferred to stay below decks, always writing, always inventing stories, while his crewmates did their daily labors above. One day, according to Cornelison, the ship's captain discovered the scribbling dreamer, writing as usual, hiding out while the rest of the crew and passengers prepared the ship for a long anchorage. Cornelison was there, capturing all that happened in an eyewitness account. "What the h—l have you been doing here," shouted the captain, "while I've been to work, do you suppose I'll do your work while you sit here writing your d—d trash. I'll give you something to write about. I'd just as soon punch your eye out." The young man simpered a reply to this outburst: "speaking through his nose," according to Cornelison, lamely declaring that he had done his share of work but that neither the captain nor the crew had seen him. "D—m, you cursed shirk," the captain bellowed in response, "You're a liar, d—m you you're a liar, (shaking his fist in his face and touching his nose) say two words back and I'll give you as good a trouncing as you ever had." As might be expected, Mantalini did not say two words. Instead he went "shrinking away," his feminine "trembling hand and blanched cheek" bespeaking his humiliation in this frontier world of hard work and violent self-assertion.[3]

Given the context of Cornelison's illness, his admitted feelings of failure and frustration at his inability to prove himself on shore or at the diggings, it seems almost certain that he made up this scene. "Mantalini," in other words, with his penchant for writing and dreaming while others worked, is far too close to an exact replica of Cornelison to be anything but an invention, a somewhat pathetic projection of the consumptive writer's identity. At the same time, in its themes of violence, brutality, and suffering, this story resonates with other forty-niner eyewitness narratives, with, that is, the "unadorned" primary experience of a wild West. The West, in other words, became real through the power of invention.

Generations of historians have treated similar gold rush–era accounts of violence and excess as evidence for the essential qualities of the American frontier. For Frederick Jackson Turner this violent frontier offered free space for the overabundant energies of a burgeoning American democracy. By the early twentieth century, it became seen as responsible for producing an American "type": anti-intellectual, committed to material things, hostile to the life of the mind. For these critics and historians, the frontier experience had wrought only damage to the American character; they would look elsewhere (to Europe, for the most part) for "higher" or more refined cultural traditions. A generation later, cultural historians returned to the frontier, revising analyses of its "myths" as rationalizations for actual violence toward indigenous peoples, wildlife, and the environment. Continually dwindling yet still clinging to life, this cohort has most recently been displaced in popularity by a "New Western History," by studies of frontier life with all of its harsh realities—including and at times especially its violence—and without its rationalizing mythologies.[4]

These layers of revisions, if they have successively celebrated the frontier, turned away from it, exposed its myths, or left them out in search of unadorned reality, have by and large maintained the West's harshness and violence as unquestioned facts based on primary experience. Few scholars have interrogated the ideological work done by such accounts. Fewer still have explored how they subsume class differences in gendered logic: men, no matter their class status, congregate in a material world in which trouble and temptation lurk; women occupy an "ideal" world of affective ties in which nothing of much importance happens. And although debunking the past is perhaps the favorite approach of those who are paid to study it, practically none have debunked the "nature" of frontier violence. Instead, the myth of the violent frontier is the basis for a "go-getting" American character, an individual whose reaction to the patterns of overcivilization and bureaucracy is two-fisted direct action. In "reality," the frontier—here posed as the real space of the West—is pretty much the same. It is a space characterized by vigilante justice and the code of "lynch law," a code marked by the immediate execution of moral trespassers, without trial, without sentiment, and without red tape. It remains a seed bed for a pervasive "culture of violence" existing at any given historical moment, a free space in which violence naturally occurs for the simple reason that affectation, pretense, and "literature" are absent.[5] In effect, the frontier, as a place of primary or firsthand experience, is violent and excessive; violence is another name for freedom and reality. These ideals would do much to make the California gold rush. They would also contribute much to the emergence of a dominant middle-class culture, making men of this class real, erasing women from the sphere of experiential reality.

The forty-niners, of course, did not create the idea of an essential linkage between male experience, freedom, and violent self-expression. In the literature of the frontier and elsewhere, the connection had existed long enough to raise expectations that life in California would produce a host of frightful stories. To many eastern observers, however, there was a curious lack of violence in the early days of the rush. "As soon as the gold mines in California were discovered," read easterners in the *New York Herald*, "it was feared—and naturally, too—that the absence of all government there would produce a most disastrous state of society—that the worst passions of man's nature would be loosed— . . . that murder would be committed in open day—that the weak would be the victims of the strong—that the revolver and the bowie knife would be the sole arbiters between man and man." Yet, as the writer rejoiced, "such is not the case." Borrowed almost directly from Parkman's *The Oregon Trail*, the language of this article raises several points about experience in California.[6] Its elevated rhetoric of violence and its reference to nature contains a sense of disappointment, the intrinsic idea that the forty-niners were not living up to the proper plot of masculine frontier drama. Above all, it suggests that while violence may have been an expectation, the gold country may not have been as "naturally" violent as has been assumed.

If gold seekers suffered many hardships in the early days of the gold rush, they also reported much friendliness and male conviviality. The country was "peaceable," wrote one, and there was virtually no fear of crime. "Here you can leave every thing you have out in the middle of the road for a month," claimed Herman Le Roy, adding that nothing would be touched, and that "the idea of robbery and murder is all humbug." Despite their obsession with the "root of all evil," wrote Benjamin Martin to his wife and the Chelsea *Pioneer*, his fellows were respectable: "there is better order here than in the city of Boston." Always on the lookout for signs of sinfulness, Protestant missionary David Hewes was a bit disappointed by the prevailing peace and quiet surrounding him; he noted some gambling, but added that the miners were regular churchgoers, and there was "but little" drunkenness. At the same time, the spectacle of some gambling and a little drunkenness seems hardly to have upset the overall sense of law and order. In Troy, New York, Sara Pierce learned that the occasional revels of her husband's comrades seemed more charming than threatening. "Although the men in this place drink some & gamble much," she read in one of Hiram's letters, "yet it is perfectly peaceable & quiet & friendly."[7]

With the failure of increasing numbers of forty-niners, these references to friendliness and peace began to disappear. It is precisely at this moment that historians of the rush have seen a turn toward "stark reality." That this reality was marked by excess and scenes of male depravity stands to reason: failure would lead to frustration, and frustration—among men—would lead naturally and directly to violence. Certainly, such analyses appear to be entirely consistent with their source materials. Depicting the gold rush as a downward spiral from anticipation to frustration to violence, these accounts follow, with care and precision, practically every forty-niner narrative, every eyewitness account of what actually happened. But to accept gold seeker narratives of western violence and depravity as evidence for what happened is to miss the way they also *explained* failure.

By October 1849, Hiram Pierce was ready to admit his failure at the mines. He had spent more than seven months away from home, and, as he guiltily wrote Sara, "I have felt very uneasy at . . . yet having done nothing for my self worth naming." Like many miners, his uneasiness inspired a need to explain. The cost of provisions was too high; "formerly the climate was good—now it's bad." He had been taken with chills; his back was lame. A few months later he added another reason to this list. All was no longer peaceable, quiet, or friendly. "I am surrounded," he reported, "by a very profane wicked Company. Their whole conversation is about their Jurney through Mexico or horses & vile & filthy & obsene conversations half & half with Oaths & curses." Having moved in search of better prospects to the largely Mexican-populated southern mines, he could only try "to hold a faultless example" before his fellows; success amid such depravity, he implied, was out of the question.[8] At the same time, as George Payson pointed out, faultless examples were extremely rare in the gold regions. When the respectable eastern youth, surrounded by the licentious masculine mass, "proud of his first beard" and hoping to fit in, was urged to drink, claimed Payson, he frequently or almost always did so: "partly to show he is not afraid, and partly from an indescribable, often unconscious pleasure of doing what he would hardly have dared to even think about at home. He thinks of his mother and sisters and Aunt Mary, and wonders what they would say, if they saw him in such company and drinking brandy, at a bar! and in a gambling house besides!! The idea of their horror and incredulous wonder is rather pleasing to his selfish vanity; one is apt to be very vain of such loving tender pity."[9]

In both of these accounts, California's wickedness served conscious purposes. Pierce's self-image as a virtuous soul adrift in a sea of depravity contains an element of success, a type of immaterial accomplishment that while smaller than gold was still measurable as a moral victory. Payson's image, although not his own and distanced by irony, portrays moral turpitude as unavoidable in all male environments, and for this reason, a source of pleasure in that it was all the more pitiable. Pierce imbues the reality of forty-niner depravity with explanatory power; Payson suggests that these accounts reflected self-conscious and vain gold seeker performance. Most important perhaps, both accounts assume the existence of an eastern, and female, audience.

Scenes of California's depravities only really made sense in this context: for what were depravities without constant references to their opposites? Again, what is so striking about the gold rush, particularly after the forty-niners reached California, is the extent to which its narratives constructed not just the West, but also the East. Because immorality could not exist without a moral reference to frame it, the "wild" West could not exist without increasingly mild versions of the East. And because they had the strongest points of reference, middle-class forty-niners were in the best position to recognize, or even create, examples of the region's innate depravity. "What a contrast there is between the cities of our quiet home and the cities of California!" exclaimed Garrett Low, "at home, each one is guarded and influenced by society, the palings of which he dares not break over, even were it his natural disposition to do so. There on every Sabbath we hear the distant chimes of the well known church bells calling us together lest our feet should wander in some forbidden path." Framed by this reference, Sunday in California was a very different picture. On this day, claimed Low, there was "more noise, gambling, auctioneering, [and] horse racing" than on any other. It was a day of drunken revels, its hours marked not by distant chimes but by the "report of firearms" along with "hallooing, shouting and singing" of men as they worshipped "at the alter of their Bacchanalian God."[10]

Clearly, as these firsthand experiences declared, California was a place of raw democracy, unrepressed and essential competitive drives, the very opposite of the refined East. And thus, as many historians might assume, it was no place for refined young men on their way to middle-class status. Indeed, a number of respectable men seem to have felt this way. "I regret to state," wrote Alonzo Hill to his sister after giving up at the mines, "that the society of California is not so good as it was when I wrote some letters previous. Blood & crime and such acts of Deathless Shame are common." In fact, life in California had become so violent and depraved, and he had become so cut off from all moral influences, he declared that he would have been better off committing "suicide at home." Eventually Hill did commit suicide, as did many lonely young men during the gold rush. For others, however, California was a place where rough anonymity allowed for expressions of "natural" depravity. Cut off from home influences, according to Theodore Johnson, it was far more common for respectable men to picture themselves as "roystering mountain blades," and "reckless characters." Embracing the chaos of the gold regions as a bracing experience, they went "wild with intoxication," expressing freedom in brandished knives, gunshots, and fistfights, by filling the air with "profanity of the vilest description, oaths such as we never conceived could be uttered by human lips."[11]

Again, such examples of disorder should have been a problem for middle-class forty-niners. After all, they were used to self-control. As reformers, many were accustomed to imposing control on others, on laborers, children, and what they considered overly self-expressive ethnicities. Here, according to most historians who have identified a middle-class element in the rush, is where these men faced a critical decision. They could either hang on to their bourgeois backgrounds, placing themselves in a frustrated position above this sea of authentic self-expression, or they could join in the fun, becoming "mutineers" to their class. The standard view, it seems, is that they chose the latter, abandoning their "cultural baggage" in the gold regions or even along the trail, and that, accordingly, California was a classless society no matter the previous background of individual forty-niners.[12] Against this view, historian Susan Johnson has offered an intriguing alternative, claiming that rather than fully joining the era's vaunted reversals of social order, middle-class men oscillated between Protestant codes and the seeking of pleasures. In this sense, she claims, the gold rush provoked a "crisis of representation" among these men; trapped between internal moral codes and external pleasures, unable to come down on one side or the other, they did not quite know what to make of their position, or their surroundings.[13]

Far from reflecting a crisis, this middling position may have been what middle-class men had been looking for all along. Furthermore, they did have a method for representing themselves even within these surroundings. In fact, they could refer to the most popular literary genre of the day. This was the period's genre of reform, a literature of sensation and violence, of crime, murder, and urban miseries all written in the name of exposing atrocities to the withering light of day, all (or nearly all) read in a spirit of pleasure and excitement. Indeed, many of the genre's writers were not merely reformers but immoral reformers. Faced with depravities committed by others, the infamous "foul moral sewers" of the period's temperance tracts, crime pamphlets, and city mysteries, their point and goal was not simply to move their readers to self-righteous indignation but also to entertain them, to titillate them with anecdotes from the dark regions of society. This required careful and precise descriptions of immoralities; the writer had to delve into them as deeply as possible, even to the point of engaging in them.[14] Through this literature, immoral reformers provided readers with exploitative and sensational tours of "secret" dens of iniquity and venal behaviors; they nearly always covered the same subjects: drunkenness, prostitution, and the unrestrained sexuality and violence of laboring-class or ethnic cultures.

That forty-niners invoked this mode of representation seems obvious: their narratives would focus on precisely the same subjects in almost precisely the same manner. Certainly, this was the case with many gold seekers when faced with San Francisco's gambling halls. Practically every forty-niner, no matter how eager to get to the mines or to get back home, seems to have taken the time to wade into these sewers. "A volume could not describe their splendor or their fatal attractions," wrote Daniel Woods of these enormous saloons. If every forty-niner description of their interiors and activities were gathered together, they would certainly fill more than one volume. Some easterners, such as Thomas Matteson and John Callbreath, rushed to explore these sights as soon as they arrived in San Francisco. From their descriptions, they appear to have rushed through the halls themselves. His choice of halls was a regular "gambling hell," wrote Callbreath to his family, adding only that "rum is of course doing its dirty work." Matteson reported seeing "a man dead" in his saloon, again pausing just long enough to note that the men around the stiffening body continued "drinking and gambling the same."[15]

Others took more time to describe the halls' notorious splendor. They may have rushed to San Francisco's "Plaza," or "Portsmouth Square," as this central district was alternately called, but once there, these forty-niners engaged in leisurely explorations of its various temptations: the "Parker House," the "El Dorado," the "Empire," and the "Bella Union." "On entering one of these saloons," wrote Frank Marryat, "the eye is dazzled almost by the brilliancy of chandeliers and mirrors." What most attracted these men, it seems, was the sheer opulence and abundance; after all the promises about California, after all the feverish visions that had enticed them to join the rush in the first place, here at last were places where gold piled up in giant and shimmering mounds. The gaming tables within these halls were "literally covered" with bags of gold dust, according to one observer; "pyramids of golden nuggets" were everywhere, wrote another, "aggregating in value thousands of dollars . . . displayed on the gaming-tables to excite the avarice and cupidity of the unwary."[16] Filled with opulent decorations, piles of gold, and noisy music, these saloons were enticing places. They were also subversive. For within this atmosphere luxury had again taken on elements of excess and sin, and the gold piles, for all their high-stacked plenitude, seemed to have little or no value. If one image dominates these accounts, it is that of the stoic gambler, usually Mexican, almost always foreign, who would bet an enormous pile of gold or stack of dust bags on a single throw of the dice, lose, and then walk away from the table "without batting an eye."

These images, obvious reversals of normal and accepted behavior as well as subversions of eastern values, including the value of money and gold, may have appalled the forty-niners and the eastern readers of their accounts. At the same time, the very numbers of detailed accounts indicate that both also found them fascinating. "There is a good deal of sin [and] wickedness going on here," wrote one gold seeker in a letter home, making sure to fill in the details: "Stealing, lying, Swearing, Drinking, Gambling, murdering. There is a great deal of gambling carried on here. Almost every public House is a place for Gambling, this appears to be the greatest evil that prevails here. Men make lose thousands in a night, frequently small boys will go up bet $5 or 10—if they lose all, go the next day dig more." Another noted that "monte" was the favorite card game of Mexicans, adding that often "bags of gold dust would be staked on the turning of a card with apparent indifference as to the result."[17] Equally subversive was the indifference with which the denizens of gambling houses treated examples of violent self-expression. From time to time, yawned Marryat, two or three pistol shots would ring out above the din of the crowd and the music. For a few moments, at most, there would be a "general row," but this would quickly subside as games were resumed. Murder, he added, was common as well: sometimes a monte dealer would shoot a player, sometimes one "gentleman" would shoot another. Either murder might be lost in the clamor, and one would only learn the details of who killed whom in the next day's paper: "if the former it will be headed '*Murderous Affray*,' if the latter, '*Unfortunate Difficulty*.'"[18]

Many forty-niners attributed these subversive and violent behaviors to California's "lower order" gold seekers, or as Marryat did, to an abstract population of "Irish bricklayers" and "western people, small farmers from Missouri." Others, perhaps the majority, attributed them to the gold country's ethnic others, Mexicans and Chileans for the most part. Still others simply admitted their own participation in their charms. Writing from Sacramento in 1850, Frank Buck freely admitted his attraction to the city's new saloons. "Our city has improved very much since last month," he wrote. As proof he cited the construction and opening of two new gambling houses. One of these saloons, See's Exchange, contained "splendid" chandeliers, "fine" paintings, a good orchestra, and several gaming tables and would "rival anything in New York."[19]

Yet no matter who patronized the saloons or behaved in this manner, the most subversive fact could not be ignored: the forty-niner had to be there to describe their excesses; he had to wallow in these sewers to expose their fascinating examples of licentiousness and desire. Within the context of immoral reform, sometimes the less the forty-niner said the better. Faced with the lewd pictures decorating these halls, one gold seeker simply refused to describe them: they were just too shocking. Here, of course, readers would be tempted to imagine themselves in similar positions, free to fill in the outraged gap with their own pornographic images. At other times, forty-niners might fill in these gaps for their readers. "The walls are hung with French paintings of great merit, but of which female nudity forms alone the subject," noted Marryat. Here, the allure of the subject—which while now more detailed still offered much food for thought—is confirmed by the outrage of the writer who has experienced it.[20]

Depicting these dens in similar terms, another forty-niner reported that gambling was a "universal vice." He attributed the ubiquity of such slippage to an expression of nature: it was "as if man's moral sense and rule of morality were wholly fixed and formed by the customs of the community into which any accident might cast them." In this account, we again hear the strains of the captivity narrative; cast ashore in the marketplace of desires, the individual is free to identify temptations, freed by his outrage and their ubiquity to explore them in such meticulous detail that giving in to them could only be assumed. Constituting their surroundings accordingly, respectable men noted the "showy style" of gambling halls, their "handsome chandeliers," the rows of "fancy-ladies" dealing cards and liquor, their walls hung with irresistible paintings "in the French style." The Reverend Joseph Augustine Benton of New England may have called for respectable resistance to these alluring "hells," yet his admonitions also contained a similar exploration of market pleasures. "Here," he noted, "were gilded bottles, colored drinks, . . . painted women, in flaunting and costly attire . . . bold looks, honied words, blandishing attentions, and enticing smiles, . . . music, and voluptuous dancing."[21]

These accounts, many forty-niners claimed, were "leaden realities." They were also the expressed pleasures and temptations of respectable men. "The prostitutes," according to one miner, "began to come into the mines in 1850, from the east." Along with them came a new host of forbidden yet expressed depravities. For prostitutes were valuable coin, lending gambling halls an extra allure, forty-niner accounts an extra frisson; in both cases they suggested the rise of the market's capacity for the production of forbidden commodities. Accounts of these commodities are predictable enough: very "modern" in their resonance with current sex industries, they are not altogether the tame and quaint examples of pornography from a bygone Victorian age. Saloonkeepers set up platforms on both sides of their halls, or so say the stories, and "on them placed, totally nude and assuming indecent poses, these exemplifications of California modesty and decency." Elsewhere, Yankee traders auctioned off these women as soon as they arrived at the city docks, taking the "shameless creature" by the hand, "praising her figure, her youth, and beauty," and then dispatching her for a night with the highest bidder. Always, it seems, the bidders were numerous and the "bidding began at once."[22]

"For the first twelve months," added one observer, "that style of women were wholly supported by married men, and the young men were the only moral ones in the community." Yet again, married men may have had more reason to reveal this demimonde, particularly to their wives and loved ones. For again, depictions of this wicked world might rationalize all their failures, and their experience of its harsh realities all they had to show for themselves. Certainly, Henry Packer offered a detailed glimpse of this world to Mary Judkins. "Look a back door stands ajar," he wrote his fiancée, inviting her to "take a peep in—papered walls, a table on which a fire globe lamp stands,—seats around,—ah, hold, a form approaches—a [fairy] form—by heaven a woman stands at the door. She is richly dressed. In her ears and on her fingers are massive gold rings displayed around her neck a chain of the same. Glossy curls play over her full neck and shoulders. On her countenance plays a smile that would bewitch if not beguile a minister—Hist she speaks, 'Come in you fellow with the mud on your hat, I like a miner.' And the *hombre* minor or major is very apt to walk in accordingly." Here is Packer's depiction of an experiential reality; it is not written, however, without an anticipation of Mary's reaction. "Do you blame him?" he asked her, knowing she would, admitting contritely that he "did go in just once—only once, and then but for a few minutes."[23]

Packer's question was to the point of such accounts: faced with these enticements, *could* forty-niners be blamed for submitting to worldly pleasures? Even the Reverend Benton seemed caught up in the allure, or at least so it was for his favorite sermon character, the "California Pilgrim." Benton's pilgrim was good at resisting temptations, but only barely, and only after they had been explored in detail. In one of these sermons, the Reverend Benton had his protagonist led blindly by a beautiful woman down into the moral depths of Portsmouth Square. The Pilgrim was dazzled by the saloons, nearly overwhelmed by the fragrant temptations at every door. "Perfumes were wafted through them," intoned Benton, "and the soft light that fell from astral walls gave the whole scene an air of enchantment." Within these halls were "gay women, in splendid attire," and, as he added knowingly, for "a moment they might have seemed the abodes of innocence and beauty." Only at the last possible instant does the Pilgrim pull back, recognizing that this "strange woman" is leading him along "the way to hell." "None that go down unto her return again," Benton cried to his sweating audience, for "many strong had been slain" by these painted women, cast down into "the chambers of death."[24]

By this time the Reverend Benton's listeners were undoubtedly paying close attention, readied by desires for a moral lesson and a call for repentance. And if in the end they resisted this downward path, they too mapped it with voyeuristic precision. Elisha Crosby recounted the "high-class" parties of "The Countess," noting that the ladies of the "demimonde" were always invited, "making quite a display of female beauty." Many of the best men of society were there, he added, and "when the hour of leave-taking arrived those who saw proper would depart. To the best of my belief there were a number who remained for private enjoyment of a different character." Another gold seeker noted the "remarkable" fact that many married and even "religiously inclined" men kept houses of prostitution. "The younger men," he claimed, "conducted themselves better than the older ones."[25]

From these flashy anecdotes the California gold rush emerges as something perhaps unique at the time but entirely indicative of future market pathways. What we see here is an economy based on the constant trade in expressly forbidden desires, their "forbidden" qualities relegating them not merely to the private realm of the repressed but to the public spaces of the market, and, above all, adding to their value enormously. And here, too, may be where the visceral West becomes a stylized articulation of the market East. For both marketplaces were filled with devils. The difference was that the western version was not restrained by the dictates of polite culture or the Golden Rule. It was merely a fact, perhaps the major fact of the gold rush, for it had replaced gold as the central symbol of the event. As John Callbreath described it: "Gambling, Duelling, Murdering, Lectioneering and Digging are the principle topics of the day." Indeed, this order may have reflected a priority of interests; certainly his placement of "digging" at the bottom of his list of topics may indicate that gold was disappearing from gold seeker anecdotal nuggets. "I could," he added, "fill a page with the names of men who have been murdered and a volume in the narration of the darkest deeds ever recorded."[26] Although Callbreath could only come up with two names, the volume of "dark deeds" would be sketched in by others. "Duels are very common here," wrote Henry Peters to a friend in Boston. To support this claim he provided an account of fatal play in which an archetypal western gunman with the unlikely name of "Mr Denver" had gunned down a prominent newspaper editor. Such were the types, he implied, who populated San Francisco streets: men who would first hurl insults, who "being excellent shots," would immediately choose weapons, open fire at forty feet, and leave behind a trail of blood.

Along with the blood there was vigor, a sense of giddy push and energy, and always laughter. Some forty-niners seemed positively invigorated by the climate of violence, adopting new guises—at least in their letters home—as steely-eyed western gunmen. "I found a squatter on a small piece of land that I bought and paid for," wrote Oscar

Bennett to his family in Rochester. "I ordered him off [and] if he had not gone I would have put a cold chunk of lead through him." Others, such as the former New York City lawyer Elisha Crosby, infused these anecdotes of dark deeds and masculine energy with humor. A woman was crossing the street in Santa Cruz, began his tale, when a rampaging steer charged her. A "mexican vaquerro" managed to run his horse between her and the bull, saving her but knocking her to the ground. "The woman it seems was *enceinte*," added Crosby. And if his sense of Victorian delicacy forbade him from using the term "pregnant," it did not keep him from completing what turns out to have been a naughty joke. The excitement caused the woman to miscarry. Her husband charged the Mexican with reckless horsemanship. And the local judge provided the punch line: "after considering the case very solemnly," concluded a delighted Crosby, he sided for the plaintiff, ruling "that the vaquero should put the woman in the same condition as he found her."[27]

Fired by such performances, Francis Prevaux may have remained a respectable Christian missionary, but as he implied in a letter to his parents, among men—even among Christian men—a certain degree of toughness was necessary. "You may wonder," he wrote, "that I should go in for Lynch law. But there is no such thing as justice in our courts. . . . The time has now arrived when no man is safe after dark on the streets."[28] At the same time, even the serious subjects of vigilance committees and lynch law, while reflective of a move toward order, might be turned into comic reversals of order. One of the most frequently repeated stories concerns a group of rough vigilante forty-niners who hold a Mexican outlaw prisoner while his case is submitted to court. Sometimes cited as a typical atrocity, sometimes as an example of raw frontier justice, sometimes merely as a good joke, the tale includes all the life-affirming elements of the liberated frontier. According to one account, the ruffians mill around outside the court-house while one enters to ask the jury for a verdict. "Not guilty," answers the foreman, and the rest is predictable: "With a volley of oaths, and ominous laying of hands on pistol hilts, the boys slammed the door, with 'You'll have to do better than that!' In half an hour the advocate gently opened the door again. 'Your opinion gentlemen?' 'Guilty!' 'Correct! you can come out. We hung him an hour ago.' "[29]

Of course, not all examples of gold rush–era excess were merely the products of exaggeration, and not all were humorous. There was real violence in California. In the 1850s, vigilante groups attacked Chileans in San Francisco and Mexicans in the southern mining region near the town of Sonora. In the 1850 "Clear Lake Massacre," a volunteer military company killed some seventy-five Indians. Another company killed some 150 Indians encamped along Northern California's Trinity River in 1852. As a state, California's "Indian Policy" itself was an example of violence. According to an infamous 1851 statement from Governor Peter Burnett, much of the policy was predicated on a "war of extermination," which would "continue to be waged between the races until the Indian race becomes extinct." Indeed as early as 1860 this system, whereby all Indians living outside of white homes (a little more than half the population) would be forced onto small "rancherias," seemed to be heading the state's "hostile" Indians in this direction. What is interesting, however, is how rarely forty-niners actually mentioned these examples. When they did, it was always to attribute these "atrocities" to some other part of the population: to Mexicans, to runaway soldiers, or to the rabble from Missouri or Kentucky.[30]

These others, according to many accounts, were exotic peoples, and they gave much life to the gold rush through their authentic behaviors. But they were also sources of danger and depravity. Thus the exotic other, from the vulgar Missourian to the passionate Mexican, was also an unredeemable other, a being who transformed the male world into a perverse paradise that could just as easily be portrayed as a living hell. They populated the gambling halls, they committed the robberies, and they perpetrated the majority of the broad daylight or dead-of-night killings and beatings. The better sort of forty-niners, meanwhile, were merely standing around and taking notes. "Chinese, Chileans, and Mexicans" formed the racial makeup of California sinners, according to one miner. "You read in the papers of murders & robberies," wrote another to his wife, adding that these "crimes are committed chiefly by Mexicans." From these Mexicans, claimed a later source, had "arisen more of robbery, rapine, and deeds of blood, than from any other class of our population." At the same time, these unredeemable others were elements of the real world, and it was their excesses, according to the miners, that lured fellow gold seekers into their own crimes and acts of selfishness.[31]

As the dominant idiom of expression in this world, violence flowed naturally into forty-niner experience. The perceived formula was clear: Mexicans, Chileans, and Chinese would commit crimes, vigilante groups composed of motley Missouri "pukes" would respond, always in kind. With this formula, violence was a given: "last night," wrote one forty-niner with bare simplicity, "a man got stabbed . . . while on a drunken spree." "Now and then," wrote another, "someone gets murdered, robbed; stealing is quite common." Because these accounts had been framed by eastern expectations, they required no garnishing and very little explanation. In fact, by this time, violent self-expression had become the California code. According to this code, said Frank Buck, "if one man strikes another without provocation he has the perfect right to shoot him down. Everyone goes armed and at the least quarrel at a gambling saloon out come the revolvers. Someone sings out, 'Don't shoot,' the crowd surges back, and they blaze away. A man's life is but little thought of. Sunday these two persons were killed; yesterday buried; and today almost forgotten."[32] Without ornamentation or varnish, accounts like these do indeed resonate with the quality of unadorned reality. As Alfred Barstow, of Lowell, Massachusetts, described it, the spectacle was everywhere. Having little to do one day, he went with his fellows to Downieville, to see the hanging of "Juanita." Historians would later make much of the hanging of this young Mexican woman as a rare case of frontier brutality and racism taken to extremes. Barstow recalled it as a typical scene, as if killing, fighting, and lynch law were the understood reference points of his daily life: "The woman had killed a prizefighter and was hung the same afternoon by a vigilante court."[33]

A mere thirty-five years after the gold rush, Josiah Royce would refer to these accounts as "undoubted absurdities." Certainly, he admitted, there was much violence and excess during these years, but there was also much peace and quiet. "The dissipation was, of course, always showy," he would write, as were the forty-niners' continuous boasts of the "phenomenal wickedness of their fellows in the early days." And yet, he added, both were more dream than substance: for "no such thing ever took place." The problem with these accounts was that they excluded all that was not violent or excessive. Their goal, meanwhile, was to leave an impression: and, as Royce concluded, one thing the forty-niners knew was that "violence leaves a deeper impression than peace." This assessment is undoubtedly true. But violent impressions had their effects as well. In the first place, by turning their focus only on certain examples of violence and excessive behavior, they masked the existence of others. While there was much gambling, prostitution, and rowdiness in these accounts of lawlessness, in other words, there was very little on attacks against Mexicans or Chileans, less still on Indian removal. Second, these accounts would substantiate

California as a place of liberation from constraints, even while beginning the process of rebuilding gender and class distinctions.

"Scattered all through the mountains," claims folklorist Constance Rourke, "the miners were nothing less than a huge variety troupe." Certainly, their self-consciousness as performers, along with the plethora of actual forty-niner-produced plays, would seem to support her claim. According to the majority of their expressions we might expect them to perform variations on the theme of idealized home and wifely patience. At times, says Rourke on the subject of gold rush–era theater, gold seekers did perform this drama. Through 1850, for example, the Eagle Theater Company of Sacramento staged a play titled *The Wife*, a "tale of the constancy of a woman," and one that "seldom failed to bring tears to the eyes of a company of argonauts in spite of the stilted confusion of its action and its battered blank verse." More often, forty-niner performances were marked by realism, by "scenes of mountain life, not in utopian form, but in close, rough view." They performed, in other words, their own actual experiences: the roaring gold camps, gambling houses, and violent claim jumpings. They re-enacted themselves—their long beards, rude cabins, and frustrated mood swings.

Yet in describing the stage setting of these dramas, Rourke herself belies this split between utopian visions of home and performances of actual reality. Home and Eldorado, as she indicates, existed in proximate relation, one always defining the other. To watch forty-niner performance is to see a playing out of the male world, to witness competition, excess, and violence as a dramatic exposition of freedom and stark reality. To understand it, one must see it as they did. The spectators of these dramas were watching themselves on stage, their plays giant mirrors framed by images of home and womanhood. The actual audience of this drama seems to have been built into the stage itself. While stage drapes opened onto a view of male reality, the curtains themselves were frequently decorated with the miner's dream: the paradisiacal home, the forty-niner recumbent, the wife floating in the air.[34] If the dramas on these stages expressed realities, they also implied that this juxtaposition was what the masculine world was like, that respectable men could—or had to—occupy this center stage and that women would occupy the margins.

Practically all of these accounts, in other words, were written with an audience in mind. Sometimes this envisioned audience was the general public of the East. Nineteen-year-old William Lorton of Peekskill, New York, structured his accounts in this manner. "Gold! Gold! is the only thing that predominates in the mind of the avaricious gold seeker," he wrote in a journal sent on to the *New York Sun*, "on they go dodging in between dead cattle, amid the crys of half starved children, & fainting women, amid the groans of the sick and forsaken, who have been left because of weakness & in ability to go any further . . . the [motto] is 'strength is right' and the weak is overcome . . . the gold canibal now devours the most noble work of God's design. The weak, the helpless & the innocent are sacrificed on the alter of 'Hecate' thus they live in a grave yard, till the [plains] are whitened with human bones."[35] More frequently, they were addressed, either directly or by implication, to women, to those who would, and should in light of these depravities, show their men a great deal of charity. For these accounts of general wickedness made California, along with the forty-niner's experience, into something real. And, as Stephen Wing readily admitted to his family back in Yarmouth, Massachusetts, this cruel world explained everything, particularly failure. "Another reason of unsuccess," declared Wing, "is the fascinating power which the liquor and the Gambling Saloons have over [the gold seekers]—those that err therein have not generally sufficient charity shown them by their friends at home—I speak as I *think* persons that have never been much from home and consequently have seen but little of the world *cannot* have an idea of the state of things in this country."[36]

The point of these accounts was too explicit to be misunderstood by eastern audiences. Every description of masculine depravity, every competitive impulse turned ugly, every whiskey-charged shooting and lynching, would give further evidence of the weight and solidity of west-ering male experience. Each, in turn, further floated the eastern home upward to the realm of comfort and immeasurable spirituality. Un-doubtedly, some of these accounts were true. And certainly, mining was difficult work, the mining camps and newly erected towns of the gold country rather raw environments for clerks and merchants. At the same time, the stridency with which gold seekers contrasted their experi-ences with those of wives contained a degree of defensive assertiveness.

In some of these accounts, it is quite clear that their goal was a forcible imposition of one type of experience over another. In main-taining their home on Houston Street in New York City, Rachel Powell may have had experiences and sufferings to match those of her hus-band. Yet a combination of love, sentiment, and firsthand experience imbued with power as evidence made Albert's claim difficult to challenge: "you of coarse are very lonesome but you have the children and friends about you then only think of me here alone to cook my own victuals wash my clothes and live in a house [all] alone."[37] When writing home, William Swain saved postage by sending letters to Sabrina and his brother George in the same envelope. His letters to George were complaining, but he saved his most painful accounts of misadventure for his wife. In comparing his situation to hers, he could not resist a dismissive tone. "While you and George," he wrote, "were comfortably seated in the family circle on Sabbath, . . . enjoying the comforts of home in a civilized land, the hand of fortune was dealing rudely with me—dealing out the bitterest pills of the journey." From here he went on to describe his difficult crossing of the Sierra Nevada. Written with meticulous detail and considerable literary skill, his letter may have captured his experience, but in the process it also positioned Sabrina—certainly in opposition to her experience and likely against her will—firmly in a cozy family circle.[38]

William Swain had left for the gold country with professions of his duty. Having failed to live up to these promises he may have been pressed to explain why, to somehow proclaim a sense of duty not in his accomplishment but in the heroism of a doomed but noble effort. Like other miners, however, he may have felt his nobility would be compromised by a recognition of his wife's suffering. James Fergus's dismissal of his wife Pamelia's pain went directly to this point. "You speak of sometimes being lonely," he wrote her with some anger, "now I tell you, if you was shut up in these mountains among the snow, half clad and half fed, working day and night except when asleep or eating, no acquaintances, few newspapers, and the prospects gloomy ahead, then there would be some chance of feeling lonesome and having the blues."[39]

Sabrina Swain and Pamelia Fergus appear to have sensed their husbands' defensiveness. Sabrina was doubtlessly disappointed by William's failures to send money. She could not, however, question his experience. Nor, apparently, could she raise the subject of her own tribulations without treading on his pride. Accordingly, throughout her husband's journey, and even within the language of romantic intimacy, she remained careful. "I want very much to describe my feelings as near I can," she wrote her husband soon after his departure, "but in doing so I hope not to crusify [sic] yours." Pamelia, for her part, responded with the apology that James's letter seemed to demand.

"You speak of my saying I am lonely," she wrote, "I do not mean to complain or whine or plague you for I am aware you have all you can bear."[40]

Finally, these accounts of California were calls for salvation. If, that is, they pronounced the gold rush West as a place of liberation from social constraints, they also announced that some constraints, at least, were necessary. "No one but those who have witnessed it," wrote one miner to the *New York Herald*, "can form the least idea of the perils and temptations that surround all, . . . they have no home or social circle . . . but the bar room, the gambling table is the resort for excitement and amusement." Again, within this environment, the forty-niner could hardly be blamed for giving in to the allure of vice, nor could he be blamed for failing. As another gold seeker put it: "If the good old saintly people of the States could only look in on these gambling dens for a moment or two, I know they would feel like calling home all foreign missionaries and turning them loose on this God-forsaken people."[41]

Faced with these statements, women might have no choice but to respond. "My dear," wrote Sabrina Swain to her husband, "how often— O! how often I think of various temptations you are surrounded with and how many men of good morals at home—yes and professed Christians too—that have been led into all kinds of vice."[42] Thus if William Swain had been led "into all kinds of vice" he might remain a good Christian, and he might remain a good man at home. At least as long as his wife was willing to grant him grace. But to do so, she would have to give something up. She would, that is, have to give up her experience to recognize his; she would have to admit that gold or no gold, proof or not, the California experience was the harshest form of reality, and that the gold seeker, in turn, was the most real of men.

According to a large number of eyewitness accounts, California during the gold rush was a place of raw frontier violence, irresistible temptation, and great suffering. But as some western historians have pointed out, it is likely that these elements of frontier life were exaggerated. The point of these anecdotes, as these scholars have maintained, was not merely to expose western realities but also to "legitimate" the six-gun justice and self-reliance of a culture of violence.[43] The idea of a violent frontier, in other words, was not so much a perspective on what was, but of what seemed desirable. This assumption explains a lot; yet it leaves certain questions unanswered or even unasked. If, that is, the cultural construction of a violent frontier served specific purposes, then whose purposes did it serve? Who had these desires? And why did they feel a need for their legitimization?

It is perhaps only by raising these questions that the connections between a nascent middle class and a culture of violence become clear. As one critic of adventure literature has said, depictions of frontier vicissitudes in fiction referred to a specific class of men. They were, he claims, privileged men and frequently members of an eastern elite; but out there on the plains they would answer the question, were they "strong enough, American enough, to rule in America?"[44] It is precisely this question, it appears, that many gold seekers sought to answer in their accounts of California experiences from 1849 into the 1850s. The response to this question—a resounding "yes"—appears to have been predicated upon a reconfiguring of differences into opposites. The home, according to so many of these accounts, was a place of repose, the frontier a field of violent self-assertion, the East a place of self-control, the West one of freedom. And certainly, if they were tough enough to survive the frontier, these forty-niners could see themselves as strong enough to rule at home.

In effect, these forty-niner experiences appear to constitute a type of gendered reality. They reflect a mapping of the realm of freedom as a space of violence, mobility, action, and, above all, as a place dominated by men, by "swarming masses" of men. Such conceptions were powerful and lasting. Later generations of western writers, including Mark Twain, Jack London, Frank Norris, and Hamlin Garland, would reject the romanticism of the mid-nineteenth century for violent depictions of the "real life"—because only violence was real. For current thinkers, such conceptions inform the idea that a "real" experience should be unvarnished by convention, uncluttered by eastern values or female refinement. In effect, the violence that constitutes the historical reality of the West constitutes the meaning of reality for a nation. These realities teach important ideological lessons. They establish gendered subject positions: battlefield codes for manhood, domestic codes for womanhood.[45] These gender ideals may be exposed as myths, as founded in exaggeration. Just as important, however, may be a recognition of the ways they bar women from possibilities inherent in a transition to middle-class social and economic dynamics. Many forty-niner wives had grasped these possibilities; their husbands' experiences in California, if taken as examples of unvarnished "reality," might proclaim that none of these women's accomplishments in the marketplace mattered.

At the same time, there are some crucial differences between writers of literature and the forty-niners. The forty-niners were real, and however they may have exaggerated them, their experiences were real. Many may have been middle class in origin, or headed in this direction. Many were well-read men, with access to literary modes of production that allowed them to create experience, and that allowed them to structure these experiments as paradigmatic human events and masculine activities. But they cannot be called mere writers of fiction, and they cannot be called an eastern elite. Perhaps the best term to describe what they were doing in these accounts of western wickedness has a very modern resonance. In effect, these forty-niners were slumming.

Slumming is more than just a fiction (although it can exist in this context). Instead it requires a real movement, a movement out, away from ordinary life, away from the social restraints of the home, along with a movement down, down the social scale, down into the real depths and spaces occupied by lower classes and ethnic others. The forty-niners had followed this characteristic path, and few places in history would be lower than gold rush–era California. Here, there were plenty of lower classes, despite the frequency with which historians of the rush laud its classless nature; here too were plenty of ethnic others, even though a focus on forty-niner enjoyment of their "lower" characteristics has frequently masked their presence.

At the same time, the thrill of slumming comes from the fact that it is only temporary. The slumming individual, like the immoral reformers of the mid-nineteenth century, does not really belong in these depths; if he is thrilled by the "darkness" within them, it is because he knows that he is above this crowd.[46] He has abandoned his status-enhancing codes of resistance to immerse himself in their behaviors for a night, to stand back and describe them, maybe even join them when the time is right. But he will return to his elevated position in the morning. Slumming, in other words, requires a high side as well as a low, a clean, well-lighted place to which the individual can return, a source of redemption from this temporary darkness. In the end, there were no women to be seen in California, only "swarming hosts of stalwart braves." Yet for middle-class forty-niners, this high side, this well-lighted place, and this source of redemption, would be "woman."

Nine

The Prude Fails

Toward the end of 1848, Eliza Woodson Farnham, the well-known administrator of female inmates at Sing Sing Prison and a prominent New York social reformer, learned of her husband's death in California. If the news was cause for grief, it also offered an opportunity. Long enamored of the free spaces in the West, the author of several writings with obvious affinities for the transcendental qualities of nature, Farnham welcomed the chance to go to California and take over the running of her husband's farm near Santa Cruz. As she prepared for her voyage, her plans quickly broadened. For soon enough, she discovered that events in California offered her a much wider field of action. Reports from the gold camps indicated that the region's bachelor culture was slipping into complete ethical dissolution. A controversial and frequently militant proponent of domestic feminism if not women's rights, Farnham began envisioning the possibility of putting her beliefs into action. Her trip to California, she seems to have hoped, would provide an exposure and critique of the self-destructive speculations of competitive masculinity. In doing so, it would give irrefutable proof of the redemptive power and superior nature of woman.[1]

Farnham's story has usually been depicted as little more than a footnote to the gold rush, a comic tale about the fate of the prude in the Wild West. Indeed, her activities, while central to the ideology of the rush, can be characterized as marginal in terms of what actually happened in California between 1849 and 1852. If we measure her actions according to "what happened," according to how many sun-bonneted "gentle tamers" followed her across the frontier, or how many masculine souls she saved, her public efforts to locate a woman's place in the gold rush seem futile, even desperate. Still, her well-publicized writings and experiences were significant to the development of middle-class culture. Nobody likes a gloomy gus, and everybody hates a prude. At the same time, these figures would be absolutely necessary to the gold rush and the West, and they have remained crucial to American culture as a whole. For without them there would be no standards of respectability to despise, no social restraints to throw off in the name of "liberation," no moral codes to identify and warn against "forbidden" appetites, elevating them into the world of commodified pleasures that would come to characterize the modern marketplace. Entire careers have been built on the basis of "shocking" the prude. Certainly, this would be true of the long historical career of the forty-niner.

Eliza Farnham was this prude. She even looked the part. She was not only a woman, she constantly reminded any man who would listen that she was a woman, and that, accordingly, she was better than they were. Everything about her seemed a bit harsh: her hair was rather short, often pulled back tightly, her dress prim, as the times dictated, her jaw set behind a tight and high collar. She often wore harsh wire-frame glasses on her harsh and hawkish nose. Behind these glasses, her strong brows were frequently furrowed, her eyes sharp and disapproving as she surveyed some scene of male brutality and excess. She was no believer in women's rights; in fact, she seemed to be no believer in "rights" at all. All this talk of rights, she believed, was only justification for brutish behavior and vulgar self-expression. She seems to have inspired hatred, even violent hatred, from practically everyone she met or came in contact with for any length of time. She was particularly good at inspiring hatred from men. And, for the most part, she was good at hating them back.

Still, in late 1849, Farnham set out to save the gold seekers from themselves. In doing so, she would target the same problem that had led so many men to join the rush: the problem of competition, and the tension between the necessity of status and the drive for success, the moral problem posed by a marketplace based on the constant trade in desires, on the mundane dailiness of dirty deals, lying, and cheating. Yet she would approach this issue from a different direction. Unlike the forty-niners, who attempted to solve it by looking for and embracing alternatives to both the market and the crippling requirements of respectability, she would push for respectability alone as the best alternative to competitive and brutal social relations. She attempted, in other words, to take standards of behavior that historians have overwhelmingly associated *with* the middle class, and impose these standards *on* the middle class. For this, she would find herself hated, outcast, ostracized, humiliated, and very nearly alone. Her mission would save respectability—as a despised bourgeois necessity. And it would save the gold rush—for men, and from women. In the end, Eliza Farnham's failures would overshadow all the successes of forty-niner wives: the prude, always necessary, always hated, would become the most visible woman of the California gold rush.[2]

At several points during the flush times, California seemed fairly begging for prudes. "A great field for the Missionary is here opened," wrote one San Francisco observer near the end of the 1849 immigration. And as the region's moral structures continued in perceptual decline, similar calls, especially from ministers on the Atlantic Coast, increased in frequency. There were from the outset of the rush, however, a number of clergymen already in the foothills. One of the most popular was the Reverend Joseph Augustine Benton.[3] Between 1849 and 1852, Benton toured the gold camps. From a variety of rough pulpits, surrounded by scarred hillsides, swaying pine trees, and weeping miners, he preached in the New Englander's time-worn jeremiad style, borrowing his sermons directly from John Bunyan's *Pilgrim's Progress*. As a "California Pilgrim," he had come on shore with his Massachusetts company. Together, they arrived "with rules of good living" in their pockets, carrying their Articles of Association before them like crosses, along with their "packages of Bibles and Testaments." The pilgrim's fellows soon strayed from this proper path.

As he looked over his audience, Benton could only compare his listeners to a host of Bunyanesque characters. One was "Dr. Moneymakes," a formerly respectable man whose new motto was "circumstances alter cases." A typical case of the argonaut turned confidence man, this character explained his entrance in the liquor trade with a flippant "we're here to make money." Another was the Reverend "Artful Smooth." Having given up on the miners' redemption, the clergyman had changed his name and become a professional gambler. "As to the community," Benton had the Reverend Smooth thunder in a denunciation of lapsed faith and shifty manhood, "this community sir, isn't worth a ——; all are knaves, thieves, swindlers, and hypocrites! I don't intend to stay long among such infernal scoundrels as this country is full of. . . . I did not come to California sir, to be either a preacher or a Christian. I am only an adventurer, sir. I shall make my pile, go home, and be a gentleman."[4] Filled with these types, every California town from "San Fastopolis" to the state capital of "Bustledom" was a Vanity Fair.

Certainly, Benton's adaptation of the jeremiad seemed to fit the California experience. The problem for the Reverend Benton, however, was the doubleness of his listeners' moral slippage. Respectable men in California, that is, had not simply moved downward, they had moved laterally into temptation. Thus while he might still look upward to the heavens for redemption, just as frequently Benton looked to the East. There, he claimed in an aside, the "gendered influences" of a "well regulated social state" had been "thrown around men to repress their worst instincts." In California, man's nature was "free to develop." Its development, in turn, had brought down "the educated and refined to wallow in filth with brutes."

Benton's reference to the "gendered influences" of the East reflects perhaps the major emplotment of experience in California. It was also a tacit admission that the gold rush had ended in failure. The cure that gold fever offered to the uneasiness of social segregation now seemed a new sickness; in effect, by reaching to embrace their former housemates in the new working classes, the forty-niners had apparently become them. As a result, the old problem of class distinctions had returned: the region's utopian promises had evaporated, and not all forty-niners were about to become equal. Some would remain better than others, in fact they *had* to be without the leveling influence of plentiful gold: and yet how would anyone distinguish between the refined and the brutes if all insisted on behaving in the same manner? Trapped between their desires for elevated distance from market passions and for low participation in its pleasures, willing to give up neither the aspiration to privilege nor the freedom of brutality, many gold seekers began to address this question during the summer of 1849. As a result, the overall level of rush ideology fell from democratic utopianism to gendered rationalizations, into ongoing dialogues between instinctually perverse masculinity and redemptive femininity. All men, in other words, *would* be brutes, but some would be better than others, elevated by the refining graces of woman.

If this idea represented a fallback position from the democratic utopianism of the rush's early days, it was tenuous at best. For as the Reverend Benton noted, women too might give in to the allurements of the gold country. In his meetings with "Miss Wiseacre," "Mrs. Breath," and "Mrs. Screech," the pilgrim saw only a love of amusements and the high life. The forty-niners, he concluded from these meetings, "were looking to the advent of woman, to reclaim and re-generate California; but how could she do it when she herself . . . gave countenance to some of the very vices and indulgences that were ruining the country?" Accordingly, through his travels the pilgrim has only a glimpse of redemption. It rests with the "Makebest Family," specifically with "Theodosia Makebest," the one woman he meets who recognizes "her duty to be with her chosen companion, . . . to act nobly a woman's part," and that "in duty was happiness." One glimpse is enough, however, to convince him that redemption is possible. California, Benton has the pilgrim conclude, is a Promised Land: "in due time . . . it would so appear to all. It only needed better moral influences."[5]

The Reverend Benton's sermons reflect a telling imbrication of New England traditions with those of the frontier, a crucial nexus of Calvin-ism and Californiana. In Bunyan's older jeremiad tradition, God's Heavenly City implied a devil's playground, but his allegorical Vanity Fair, sinful as its material charms were meant to be, remained for the most part an abstract threat. The newer style mapped its glittering temptations and excesses onto a real geography, pitting the respectable East against an exuberant West of ethical dissolution. Sin and salva-tion, heaven and hell, had moved from allegory to the plane of lived experience. The difference in style rested with their different sources of salvation: from God, this responsibility had been shifted to woman. The temptation may be to view all of this as a process of secularization. Undoubtedly it was; yet there appears to have been something of the old-time Calvinism in the language of domesticity as it reached across the frontier. If, that is, the idiom of salvation had descended from heaven to earth, it had become neither wholly liberating nor emptied of tensions: it remained rooted in a battle between good and evil.

If there is one concept that dominates modern understandings of the frontier, it is the equation of masculinity with sin. Certainly, the California frontier was an evil place, at least according to forty-niner accounts. And it was an overwhelmingly male space, at least from an ethnocentric standpoint that often refused to see women who were not eastern, proper, or white. At the high point of the migration to the Pacific, a United States Army census at Fort Laramie, Wyoming, re-ported the overland passing of 39,560 men to only 2,421 women. Through the summer and fall of 1849 the harbormaster at San Fran-cisco counted 22,086 passengers arriving by sea, of which only 309 were women. As California's 1850 census would reveal, the population of the new state was over 92 percent male. In many mining camps it was 97 percent male or even higher.[6] While such disparities between the sexes may have held for brief periods during resource rushes, they hardly typified the family migrations that commonly marked westward movements. That they do, however, characterize perceptions of the frontier as a whole may indicate lasting impulses—spiritual yearnings as it were—to conceptually elevate the years 1849–52 above all others.

In both contextual and historical accounts of the rush, the assumed absence of women implies a lack of grace and salvation. It remains, in turn, the primary explanation for the frontier as a place of masculine excess and violent competition. For Hubert Howe Bancroft, women played a large part in the gold rush, their contribution "abnormal as much by reason of its absence as its presence." Their absence "had a strange effect" on the gold seekers: "like a void in nature, something dropped out of their existence." For J. S. Holliday, forty-niner "gambling, drinking, and lawlessness" should not be taken as evidence of their "dissolute character," but rather as a concomitant of "disillusionment, loneliness and despair." This sense of despair, he goes on to argue, was a direct result of women's absence, a point that harkens back to Bancroft's conclusion regarding relations between women and men: "with her men are fools; without her devils."[7] Apart from the personal pronouns, few old-time Calvinists would have said it differently.

At the same time, there is evidence to suggest that the region's vaunted dearth of women may have referred to a specific type of female influence. California's lack of women, that is, was very much subject to specific perceptions about womanhood, about what constituted this category and who fit into it. As one popular bit of gold rush doggerel went:

> The miners came in forty-nine,
> The whores in fifty-one;
> When they got together,
> They produced the native son.[8]

Certainly, the "whores" were there in fifty-one—earlier, if gold seeker accounts are to be believed—but they were not "real" women. "We have but few females in this country," claimed one forlorn forty-niner in a letter home; in fact there were none, he noted, within miles of his camp. "The Cities are however filled up with prostitutes," he added,

"I almost dread to have you walk their polluted streets."[9] So prostitutes did not count as women.

Nor, apparently, did the Mexicans and Native Americans who had been in California from the time of the first gold discoveries. On the subject of Mexican women, Hinton Helper could only note that "their pumpkin hues and slovenly deportment could never awaken any admiration in me, even in California." According to such perceptions, when forty-niners thought of women, and when they calculated sex ratios, they envisioned respectable eastern women, ciphers of hearthside comforts. As for these women, added Helper in a bit of poetic abstraction: "They are the books, the arts, the academies / That show, contain, and nourish the world."[10] What these men imagined was an absent femininity, a rarified image that because it was so rare was likely to remain absent—at least in *this* world. The pure woman was an obsession in California. Yet she seemed nowhere to be found. As a direct result, one observer reminisced: "we had no place to go at night except the gambling houses." The very vicissitudes of California life made her presence improbable. If these kinds of eastern women did come to the gold country, their purity was in eminent danger of being polluted by the pervasive atmosphere of sin and maleness. For as rare commodities in the West, women who came risked being commodified as male pleasures. As one forty-niner recalled: "when our vessel came into harbor, we were boarded by half a dozen or more boats, and they all inquired if there were any women on board; they would give them two or three hundred dollars a month to sit behind a gambling table or fill some similar position."[11]

As a result of this risk, forty-niner needs for female redemption appear conflicted. They desperately needed proper women, but they were not so sure these women should actually come to California. Sailing with the poorly provisioned New Brunswick, New Jersey, company, Augustus Fitz Randolph Taylor, for example, arrived in the gold country suffering from scurvy and dysentery, too weak to mine and in desperate need, as he put it, of female refinement and support. "I have not seen the face of a female since I left New York," he wrote in his travel journal, "and this for me, who has had daily intercourse with females all my life . . . is one of the privations of a newly settled country." On further reflection, however, Taylor "thanked his stars" that "no female that I am interested in, will ever be placed in any such situation, and I think death among her friends at home would be preferable, and no female with any refinement could exist for one month in such a society or want of it."[12] Another gold seeker found that while he had learned to cook, sew, and do his own washing, he still needed a type of support that he felt only women could provide. "I *thought* I could do without a wife," he wrote to his sister, "but when I think of my loved, but distant home, the smiles of women there—the tears of *sisterly* affection— . . . all, all, banish such, unholy thoughts." Conversely, while the thought of life without the refinement of women was unholy, and while he longed for redemption, he did not wish to see the purity of his sister soiled by the frontier of masculine desire. Life in California remained filled with examples of male excess. There was no "female society" in sight. Thus he reasoned, "I should be very unhappy if either of my Sisters were in California at present, however much I may want to see them."[13]

Despite these internal conflicts, or perhaps because of them, gold seeker homesickness developed in direct proportion to their failures at the mines and disillusionment with California's false promises. Married or not, many recorded a growing appreciation for the value if not always the actual presence of a wife or a proper woman. Lamenting that he was "cut off from all female society," Oscar Bennet wrote his brother in upstate New York to tell him that "if you were separated from *those dear little creatures* as I am, you would know how to appreciate their value . . . you would get *married immediately*." Jokingly affirming this value—"a woman, a woman, my Kingdom for a *woman*"—he added his desire to settle down: "tell the *girls* to be ready—for married I must be as soon as I arrive."[14] According to one married gold seeker, a man who was "doing well" and "living comfortably" and who "takes the notion to leave his family & come to California" should be "indicted forthwith as *non compos mentis* and incapable of taking care of himself." Noting that about one-third of the men he had met had done just this, and had left families in the East, he added that "most complain feelingly of the separation and the long uncertainty between the receipts of letters."[15]

With these nearly constant references to the refining qualities and saving graces of women, many forty-niners made a belated discovery. In a social sphere of shiftiness and flowing identity, one in which a respectable eastern preacher could simply change his name and become a professional gambler, some differences were essential, particularly differences in status engendered by proper women. "It was only after leaving home," noted Hinton Helper, "and removing to a sphere where she had a better opportunity of displaying her power, that I could estimate her real worth."[16] Indeed, her real worth would be further confirmed by the self-proclaimed "first book published west of the Mississippi," Felix Wierzbicki's *California As It Is & As It May Be; or, A Guide to the Gold Region*. Calling for women to come to California and thus commence the "process of crystallization," Wierzbicki likened eastern womanhood to the cement in a stone building. Here was a comforting and familiar image: she would be the rock upon which ethical structures might stand. "The society here," he proclaimed, "has no such cement; its elements float to and fro on the excited, turbulent, hurried life of California immigrants."[17]

These statements heralded the return of dialogues pitting the market against ethical standards, the transference of the weight of upholding these standards to women. Having discovered that some differences were essential even in California, forty-niners had to return to the very unromantic project of essentializing difference. According to Wierzbicki, omnipotent visions of abundant wealth for all had been replaced by a desire to "make a respectable competency." Even this lowered expectation was impossible without feminine moral influences. There were many among the forty-niners, he continued, "who would like to be married and settled in life, as honest and sensible men should do; but for want of the fair ones, they think only of getting away from here as soon as possible." In providing it with an ethical foundation, women would be agents in bringing order to the perceptually turbulent, classless, and flowing environment of California. The arrival of proper women would reestablish the boundary lines dissolved in the heady days of the rush. They would redraw distinctions between the saved and the damned, between a middle class and a host of unredeemable others, including unattached laborers, Hispanics, Chinese, and Native Americans.

Far from representing separate categories for the making of distinctions, in other words, gender, class, and race would be inextricably linked in dialogues surrounding the redemption of California. Mexican women, according to many forty-niners, were too passionate, too given to their own vices to offer redemption. The problem with the Chinese, in turn, was that they so frequently left their women behind, and those who did come appeared to be prostitutes. The Chinese, according to one later California publication, "have sent hither swarms of their females, a large part of whom are a depraved class." As for the lower-class forty-niners, what set them apart from their betters seems to have been their sexual attraction to California's Native American women. In the vast majority of personal and official accounts, forty-niners who married Indian women, along with those who committed sexual crimes against them—particularly rape and kidnapping, but also murder— were all immigrants of the lower sort. "In all the frontier settlements," wrote one observer, "there are many men from Missouri, Oregon, Texas &c., who value the life of an Indian just as they do that of a *cayota*, or a wolf, and embrace every occasion to shoot [one] down." "Squaw Men," the derogatory term given Anglos who married or lived with Indian women, were "poor white trash" from Missouri and Arkansas.[18] Thus class distinctions, obvious class distinctions, that is, had returned to California with a vengeance. Yet they had returned through gender discourses: the point of these perceptions was that the better sort of forty-niner would never do such things. For he had a wife or a female loved one in the East. And she would save him.

Without a doubt, forty-niner calls for salvation contained an undercurrent of irony, an ill-concealed imposition of mundane patriarchal privilege. Refined eastern women, according to Wierzbicki, could best effect redemption through their daily tasks, by providing the miners with clean clothing and undergarments, for the "greatest privation" of bachelors, he held, was "not having clean linen."[19] At the same time these calls carried an undeniable force. For references to female redemption worked well alongside accounts of gold country wickedness. Faced with both, one mother could only write: "I feel so anxious about you . . . and hear so much about that part of the world where you are if you dont die a natural death I am a fraid you will be killed." Finally, these appeals cannot be seen as part of a simple plot to silence women or protect an imagined patriarchy. As the dialogues surrounding redemption indicate, middle-class ethicality would be constituted as a gendered system of thought. Any challenge to its logic was a challenge to the social fabric as a whole. The unrecognized problem with this logic was that it seemed to demand that women, in order to uphold the social fabric, constantly and repeatedly wage war on men. Far from effecting a gender ideology of female submissiveness, and far from wholly denying female access to a male sphere of violence and conceptually brutal social and economic relationships, if its calls for salvation were taken seriously, this gendered logic was a blueprint for women's militant action. Eliza Farnham took these appeals for salvation seriously. And late in 1849, she went into action.

Farnham's mission of redemption to California has remained one of the most popular anecdotes of the gold rush. Conceived and articulated in a language of high aspiration and moral reform, her well-publicized intention was to bring 130 virtuous females to California. There they would serve as wives for the uplift of formerly respectable forty-niners. Her mission ended in abject failure. Its failure, it appears, contained an important lesson: it provided experiential evidence of a woman's role and place in the West. For Farnham, women's role was to be central, their place a position of importance in a California society that, having already confirmed women's value, should have been ready to welcome their presence, prepared to reorganize its social structures along feminine, even feminist, lines. In the experience, however, Farnham's mission established the female as a symbol of absent and marginal refinement. Conceived as a feminist strategy but played out in a tactical field of male power, her mission and its result would offer a vision of the prudish female, central and separate, necessary but ridiculed. This vision would serve as the foundation for middle-class market ethics.

Born 17 November 1815, in Rensselaerville, New York, Eliza Woodson Burhans had a childhood marked by yearnings for place and home. She was the fourth of five children born to Cornelius Burhans and Mary (Wood) Burhans, and she was apparently much closer to her Quaker mother than to her busy and often absent father. When her mother died in 1820, her father sent her to live with an aunt and uncle living in further upstate Maple Springs, New York. As she later recalled, this was the formative period of her life, a time of familial loss and introspection. From 1820 to 1831 she lived in Maple Springs. "In this somewhat backwards section," wrote a dictionary biographer who must have read Farnham's reminiscences, "she found little kindness; her aunt was jealous and nagging, her uncle addicted to whiskey, and Eliza became obsessed with the desire to alleviate misery in the world."[20]

During her years in Maple Springs, it appears that Farnham received no institutional schooling. Holding that "nature" was the best teacher, she later claimed to have been almost entirely self-educated. She did, however, manage to sneak into her aunt's "atheistic" library, where she read the works of Paine, Volney, and Voltaire, a "whole school of infidel writers." In the mid-1830s, she returned to eastern New York, where she finally enrolled in a ladies seminary in Albany. There she appears to have begun a lifelong interest in social reform, phrenology, and biological sciences. However formative it was to her later ideas, this period of schooling must have been brief; for in the fall of 1835 or spring of 1836, Eliza went to live with her sister Mary, who was farming with her husband on the Illinois frontier. She arrived on the prairie with a mind formed "not only in a natural but moral wilderness, away from society, away from schools, away from everything but the tyranny of a selfish, passionate woman, and . . . that woman an Atheist." In a word, she was different. Her sister, as she recalled with pride, was shocked at her independence of mind; for Mary as for practically all others who met her, Eliza's character and behavior reflected "more than a woman's boldness of thought and speech."[21]

Later in 1836, she met Thomas Jefferson Farnham, a surveyor and land speculator. Their courtship appears to have been a rather hurried affair, and before the end of the year they were married. They lived together in Illinois for some two years, during which time Eliza suffered in close succession the death of her sister and of her first child. In 1840, following Thomas's yearlong trip to Oregon, the Farnhams returned to New York, settling near Poughkeepsie. They spent another two years together. Thomas wrote an account of his expedition, *Travels in the Great Western Prairies* (1841), which garnered him some renown as an expert on the West; Eliza began work first as a volunteer and then as a professional social reformer. By 1844, theirs was a marriage of divergent professions, separated by a continent. Thomas had returned to the West to try farming in California; Eliza had become the matron of female inmates at Sing Sing Prison.[22] Still, her mind if not her body frequently joined her husband. She maintained a longing for the utopian spaces of her western childhood as a proving ground for women's spiritual action.

From the mid-1840s to her death, Eliza Farnham became increasingly well known as a social worker and proponent of domestic feminism and female superiority. Her 1846 preface and notes to Marmaduke Sampson's *Rationale of Crime and Its Appropriate Treatment*, along with her publication of *Life in Prairie Land* in the same year—one stressing nurture over punishment for female prisoners, the other the value of nature in Farnham's own intellectual development—established her as a leading member of New York's reformist intelligentsia.[23] By 1849, she could include among her acquaintances and friends Bronson Alcott, Margaret Fuller, Ralph Waldo Emerson, Orestes Brownson, and Caroline Kirkland. Although never an advocate of women's equal rights, her closest confidante was Georgianna Bruce (later Kirby), an English-born feminist, who, fresh from her participation in the transcendental socialist utopia at Brook Farm, Farnham had hired as an assistant at Sing Sing.[24] She was also close with William Cullen Bryant. A few months after learning of her husband's death in California, she sent the poet a note from her Fourth Avenue home: "When I saw you this morning," read Bryant from the hand-carried missive, "I forgot to ask if you would feel any objection to have your name used with those of other gentlemen on the circular I read to you. Please answer by the bearer."[25]

Quite likely, this circular was the announcement of her mission of redemption to the California mines. If so, Bryant responded in the affirmative. On 2 February 1849, Farnham's handbill made its appearance on New York streets and in eastern papers. It was undersigned by the poet, along with Horace Greeley, Henry Ward Beecher, Catherine Maria Sedgwick, and several leading local reformers and politicians. According to the broadside, Farnham would combine the settlement of her husband's estate with "a desire to accomplish some greater good," with her belief that "the presence of women" in California "would be one of the surest checks upon many of the evils that are apprehended there." She would, it followed, reserve space on her voyage for some 130 "intelligent, virtuous and efficient" women, "persons not under twenty-five years of age" who would uplift the forty-niners through marriage. The cost of the voyage would be only $250. Lest anyone think this was a cheap way to get to the gold country, the mission's criteria were strict. Applicants to Farnham's address would require "satisfactory testimonials of education, character, capacity, Etc.," from clergymen or local town authorities. The *Angelique*, a ship chartered for the mission, was scheduled to sail the second week of April 1849.[26]

Aside from the rather obvious goal of providing the forty-niners with wives, what did Eliza Farnham have in mind for her mission? Certainly, her stated intentions and actions, combined with her behavior, defy attempts to come to an unambiguous understanding of her motivations. She has been depicted as a conservative force, urging women to maintain their domestic duties even in the liberated atmosphere of California. In the folklore of the gold rush, she has been celebrated as a harbinger of California's liberal tradition toward women's rights, portrayed as one of the region's early suffragists, which seems doubtful, and as a "truly liberated woman," which seems accurate enough as applied to her behavior if not her beliefs.[27] While such perceptions, disparate as they are, hint at Farnham's complexities, the best way to interrogate her contributions to the rush, and the thought behind her mission, may be through an examination of her writings. For, perhaps as a result of her self-education, perhaps out of a failure of imagination or a desperate need to rationalize her life's accomplishments, nearly every word she wrote was about herself.

Farnham's published works fit squarely within the nineteenth-century literature of domesticity, her prescriptions for woman's place within the confines of "domestic feminism." As one historian has described them, the prescriptions of these literary domestics, who included Catharine Beecher, Harriet Beecher Stowe, Lydia Maria Child, and E.D.E.N. Southworth, revolved around the themes of love, duty, selflessness, and sacrifice. Above all, their works reflected a search for a valued position for women: "they expressed and professed woman's need to feel useful, to believe that she could shape a life of significance and live a life of demonstrated accomplishments."[28] At the same time, and as the term "literary domestic" suggests, these writers offered few direct challenges to the ideology of domesticity. Their adopted and professed method of effecting the goal of usefulness was not to move women out of the home, but to stress women's superiority. They would posit the higher moral standards of the domestic sphere as an organizing principle for social relations in the world at large. Such a position, as many historians have pointed out, contains an explicit critique of a male-dominated society, in particular of the self-assertive, shifty, and morally suspect qualities perceived in the mid-nineteenth-century transition to industrial capitalism and its emphasis on destructive regional or individual competition. Yet this stance left women in precisely the quandary suggested by the oxymoronic sound of the term "domestic feminism." For while the idea of women's superiority gave them the all-important role of redeeming society from market excess, their acceptance of home as their proper sphere meant that they were unseen, devalued as persons. In effect their own ideology both called for and denied the propriety of extending feminist designs beyond the confines of the hearth.[29]

Perhaps because she did not fully understand the selfless implications of domesticity, perhaps because she understood its other implications all too well, Farnham's career and writings revealed the militant elements within this thought. Like other literary domestics, she seems to have been frustrated by the boundaries of her stated womanly virtues; her actions were far more independent and assertive than would seemingly be countenanced by an ideology of self-effacement. Yet as with other self-taught thinkers, she was willing to blend disparate intellectual currents. What set her apart was her combination of womanly virtue with a type of nature worship and transcendentalism. Much of this synthesis in thought, or so she would later claim, stemmed from her upbringing in the backwoods of New York or out on the prairies. This background, as she made clear in *Life in Prairie Land*, had left her a child of two worlds: one east, one west, one of abandonment and one of belonging. To her, life in upstate New York had been surrounded by friendly and nurturing woods, and the great western prairie had been a "strong and generous parent," its trees "elder brothers." Practically everything and everywhere else had been characterized by artifice, competition, and the destructive presence of men. Nature, particularly the unspoiled nature of the West, was a place in which she could make up for the family she felt she had lost as a young girl. In it, she had discovered both a sense of familial or female bonding and the freedom to exercise superior talents. It is perhaps this transcendental vision of home and family that gives much of Farnham's writing a radical edge. Perhaps more than any female writer in the mid-nineteenth century, her writings affirmed the belief that out West the fusion of family and nature, home and external world, was entirely possible. Unlinked from the home and dispersed into the environment, an alternative and essentially feminine value system strongly critical of competitive market striving was not only real, but its victory was eminent.[30]

If Farnham's brand of domestic feminism offered a means to direct action, and if it was accordingly more radical than most, it also reveals an almost precise fit with the utopian elements in forty-niner fantasies of the gold rush. In her hopes for a female redemption of California, in other words, she would target many of the same dualisms, the same crippling boundaries between society and nature, refinement and authenticity, that middle-class men—for a moment at least—had publicly transgressed on the way to the gold country. "Living near to nature," she wrote in *Life in Prairie Land*, "artificial distinctions lose much of their force." Years later, she penned perhaps her clearest expression of the motives behind her mission to California. As she explained in a series of articles that served as the basis for the later publication of her most radical statement of female superiority, *Woman and Her Era*, California had clearly revealed the ugliness and artifice of male competition. The region's excesses had provided women with an opportunity, not for equality, but for an assertion of difference, for an exposition of a feminist alternative. She was no advocate of women's equality, holding that women "fail in so far as they enter the masculine world of motives, and are penetrated by its selfish, striving spirit." Instead, she preferred an overturning of male-dominated society, its "diabolic spirit" of competition between men, and between women for men's affections. Her goal seems to have been the redemption of market society itself, a system of social relations and consumed refinements that made men prey to their own brutality and trapped women in a "ridiculous imitation of foreign fashions," in "obedience to the fashion plates of Godey and Harper."[31]

But if she objected to the refinements of the marketplace, Farnham was certainly no enemy of refinement as a whole. In fact, what probably made her seem so unusual was her defense of natural refinement as a form of liberation. For her, nature was a woman, and like a woman, the primary characteristic of nature was self-sacrifice. Self-sacrifice, in turn, had many of the same characteristics as polite culture. It was obviously hostile to competitive social relations and the scheming of the marketplace. It was also hostile, or seemed so at least, to free expression, particularly the loud noise of masculine amusements. Farnham wanted no part of a freedom defined as liberation from social constraint. Her most annoying quality was her proclivity for referring to *all* examples of this kind of liberation—no matter how harmless, no matter how "fun" or enjoyable—as little more than "brutality." In this respect, she appears as the strangest of characters: for her, fun was brutality, liberation from social restraint was slavery to the market-place. In their "natural" expressions, she believed, both would take far different forms from the violent self-expression, forced hilarity, and strained *bonhomie* of the gold regions. She often spoke of these ideal forms as abstractions, as "spiritual realms" of freedom awaiting the rejection of masculine models before they could be mapped. But when she spoke of them in more detail, in terms of the activities she actually enjoyed as liberating, we see something stranger still. For Farnham enjoyed two pursuits above all others: gardening and reading. To her, both were fun and liberating. Just about all else was "brutality of a low, coarse nature."[32]

To be sure, these beliefs contained conservative elements. Farnham admonished her readers against women's rights, or the right of women to enter the marketplace, holding that the "law indeed of women's nature forbids her becoming a competitor." She warned them against becoming "coarsened" by the public sphere, against becoming "mannish" in action and behavior. Yet her thoughts evince radicalism as well. Positioning herself squarely within the idiom of domesticity and submissiveness, she had no problem also moving beyond its boundaries to defend such "mannish" and radical women as George Sand, Margaret Fuller, and Frances Wright. "*These* women," she proclaimed, would eventually triumph in their goals, even if scoffed at "in the days of her action as 'strong minded,' 'unsexed,' 'forgetful of her sphere,' 'masculine,' and so on." If Farnham was not an advocate of women's equal rights, she refused to criticize the means of women who were. For above all she saw herself as a revolutionary. Whether as a thinker, artist, reformer, or worker, she maintained, "every woman is a revolutionist. She leaves a broad, inviting path behind her, in which others of her sex will infallibly follow [to] the COMING ERA, the ERA of spiritual rule . . . that world of purer action and diviner motion which lies above the material one of intellectual struggle and selfish purpose, wherein man has held and exercised his long sovereignty."[33]

In the early months of 1849, with fresh reports of the latest excesses resulting from masculine speculation littering her Fourth Avenue home, Eliza Farnham felt that a revolutionary moment was at hand. Her handbill began appearing in New York streets and eastern papers on 2 February 1849. A short time later came a response from California: the editors of the San Francisco *Alta California* would, they announced, applaud any effort "to bring a few spare ribs to this market." This jocular tone appears to have caught on with many eastern reporters. "Despite the Rally Day tone of her invitation," as one historian has noted, "and the overpowering respectability of her sponsors, Mrs. Farnham in the weeks that followed found herself more or less accused of being a procuress for sex-starved maiden ladies."[34] It is difficult to ascertain the effect these criticisms had on her. That they did have an effect may be surmised from the fact that soon after her mission's broadside hit the city streets, she fell ill and temporarily postponed her plans. Still, as she later recalled, she continued to see the situation in California as an opportunity for action: "The present is a war," she wrote, "not between parties or persons, but between the principles of good and evil."[35]

This last announcement may have been one of the clearest declarations of a "gender war" in the nineteenth century. Listening carefully to the reports of gambling, violence, drunkenness, and especially the overall spirit of excessive "speculation," Farnham reached the usual conclusion: men, without the refining qualities of women, were undoubtedly brutes. Only the presence of women, she maintained, would effect an "efficient remedy for those great evils." At the same time, strong as her rhetoric was, her actual battle plan held to an apparently less radical position. For in these pronouncements she had maintained self-sacrifice at the core of her agenda, all the while turning it into a type of militant action. A gymnastic rhetorical gambit, this turn of thought had its problems. What she said, in effect, was that women would have to sacrifice accomplishments made in men's absence in order to make a revolution in dominant male values. They would have to take several steps back into wifely duty to prepare for the great revolutionary leap forward. "The woman who presided virtuously over a home in the earlier periods of the gold emigration," she wrote, "is entitled . . . to look back from the remainder of her life, upon a good work well done." But now, she added, in an argument that seemingly denied both the value of women entering the marketplace and the actions of many California widows, redemption required a woman's sacrifice. Her "place" now, she declared, "is not the seat of luxury by the fireside of an eastern home—not the resorts of the gay." Instead, it was beside men, beside the forty-niners, "sympathizing with their successes, soothing their disappointments, lightening their burdens, . . . by all those little acts which the housewife has at her control, and which, in her higher character as a woman, she is prompted to exercise for the well-being and happiness of those she loves."[36]

The idea that such "little acts" might make a revolution probably occurred to few of Farnham's readers. At the same time, the ardent domesticity of her tone seems to have turned the eastern press to a support of her mission. And according to early reports at least, it appealed to women. By early spring 1849, the local papers claimed that some 200 applicants had expressed a willingness to join her "Association of California Women." She had just returned from a successful trip to interview likely candidates in New England and was receiving a large number of inquiries at her new address at 63 Barclay Street in New York. By the end of June, word had reached San Francisco that her "Women's Association" was "now busily engaged in making final preparations for the departure of her expedition on the ship *Angelique.*" According to the *New York Herald,* she had recovered from her mysterious illness. Her mission was a "good one," claimed one of its writers: "Mrs. F deserves success [and] evinces much moral courage. Her reward will be found in the blessings which her countrymen will invoke for her when the vessel in which the association is to sail shall have arrived in California with her precious cargo. May favoring gales attend the good ship Angelique."[37]

In the third week of July 1849, the *Angelique* finally set sail from New York Harbor. By this time, Farnham's mission had caught the imagination of many forty-niners. One wrote that "home influence is unknown in San Francisco"; thus, he added, the "all important and most interesting subject here, is the arrival of the ladies."[38] Beneath the excitement and anticipation, however, there were disturbing reports. Even before the ship sailed, the *Alta California* made the claim that "this enterprising lady, after all her efforts, . . . has had to leave for California with a very small number of ladies accompanying her." With the *Angelique* still somewhere in the Atlantic, an article in the Sacramento *Placer Times* "regretfully" noted that the "enterprise has turned out to be a sad failure." Membership in Farnham's association, went these rumors, was limited to only three women, including Farnham herself.[39] Although men in California's newly established cities and mining camps continued to hope, these reports turned out to be true enough. The *Angelique* entered the Golden Gate in December. Its passenger list did indeed include only three women; all were friends of Farnham, none was of the publicized likely age for marriage, and only one was unmarried anyway. Stranger still, Eliza Farnham herself was not on board.

Something had gone very wrong. Farnham's account of the voyage, comprising the first chapter of *California, Indoors and Out* and which she claims to have revised from her journal, is virtually silent on the question of what happened to the more than 200 applicants for the mission. The likeliest explanation may be that they never existed in the first place, that very few women were attracted to what appeared to be a conception of domestic servitude as a way of redeeming the world. When she did address this discrepancy between supposed applicants and actual passengers, it was according to prevailing conceptions of nature and California society: though liberating for her, for other women the natural environment of the Pacific threatened complete moral degeneration. "The guarantees required in this plan," she explained, "would have sufficed for almost any other country in Christendom; but the moral life in California is to the character what the seven-times heated furnace is to the ore of the metallurgist—only purity itself can come unwasted through it." Her standards, in other words, which had to be high, were *too* high: searching for "purity itself," she claimed to have taken only 3 of the more than 200 women who communicated with her.[40]

There were problems as well during the voyage itself. Farnham described it as fraught with "mental anguish," "racking anxieties," and "numberless humiliations." Indeed, as it turned out, her trek around Cape Horn was typical of her relations with the world, and it followed a typical pattern of her life. In her writings, Farnham portrayed herself as the very soul of feminine refinement and self-sacrifice. In her actions, she was in constant battle as a militant activist. On the surface, this discrepancy appears to indicate a distance between ideology and action, an admission, with certain hypocritical undertones, that she could not live by her own philosophy. On a deeper level, however, her militancy fit with her views. Soon after her association's departure from New York Harbor, she found that the ship's captain was an unmitigated brute. Faced with such a man, she did not shyly retire to her cabin; nor, apparently, did she follow her own ideology of female submissiveness. Her self-professed role as a woman was to rid the world of brutality. And so, faced with a brute, she went into battle, fighting the captain's authority every mile of the journey.

Tensions between Farnham and the captain of the *Angelique* began early in the voyage. Still stinging from the "vulgar slanders that heralded my emigration," and likely anticipating the disappointment and criticisms that would undoubtedly herald the arrival of her three-member organization, she may have been in no mood to accept the captain's assertions of shipboard authority. As captain of the ship, neither was he willing to follow the will of the ship's charter, especially if this charter was a woman.[41] Their confrontations were undoubtedly frequent, but they centered on two issues. One was Farnham's leadership in complaints about the "dreadful quality" of the ship's water supply. By the time the ship reached Saint Catherine's Island, a traditional stop for the refreshment of water barrels off the coast of Brazil, this seemingly mundane complaint had ripened into a test of wills. Quite possibly looking for any means to assert his authority, the captain refused to put in at the port. Farnham drafted and circulated a petition among the passengers demanding that new water be taken on board. At last the captain relented, but from this point on he was the avowed enemy of the "Women's Association," of most of the male passengers booked to help defray the cost of the charter, and of Farnham in particular. "He took especial pains to make the position of his lady passengers as uncomfortable as it well could be," she recalled, "and . . . he never named women but to depreciate them in the coarsest terms." Even in his best temper, she claimed, adding that these were rare moments anyway, he was "destitute of that respect for [women] which argues somewhat of refinement in the rudest, and of nobility in the meanest, so in his ill-humor, he was restrained by no scruple."[42]

Such enmity may have greatly exacerbated their second issue of contention, but it evolved more to the captain's advantage. Farnham's personal maid—one of the five women who started the voyage—had been spending increasing amounts of her time with the crew of the *Angelique*. Although hired to take care of Farnham's two children, she seemed to prefer waiting on the officers' table. At length Farnham discovered the reason for this strange preference. Her maid had fallen in love with the ship's steward. Furthermore, she found that the steward, in her words "a lazy, lying, worthless creature—a mulatto," had proposed marriage. What most irked her was that the captain, likely seeing a chance for vengeance after the water affair, actively encouraged the union. Her anger swelled by her racist distaste for the girl's suitor and the captain's obvious pleasure at her outrage, she brooded over the issue in the months the *Angelique* sailed around Cape Horn and into the Pacific. Finally, all agreed that the two should be married in Valparaiso. The captain embraced the idea with no small measure of glee; Farnham, despairing at her former girl's "dark lover," was "sickened at heart of the whole disgusting affair." Once in port at Valparaiso, she left the *Angelique* looking to hire a Chilean girl as a replacement.

Then, as she described it, came the captain's ultimate revenge. Farnham found a likely maid and returned to the ship. The captain refused to board the girl without a passport. Again Farnham had herself rowed to port, only to receive word from the Chilean consulate that the papers were unnecessary, that the captain, in other words, was playing a cruel joke at her expense. Returning a final time to the docks, perhaps ready for a final confrontation with the brute who would play such a game, she met a shocking sight. Far away on the horizon she saw the receding outlines of the *Angelique*. Having tricked his nemesis ashore, the captain had quickly trimmed the ship's sails and set course for California. He left her, "destitute, in a city of strangers." Worse still, he had taken her two children.

"He hated me," recalled Farnham of the captain; certainly she had evidence for this hatred on that day in Valparaiso.[43] It is interesting, though, that it was precisely this hatred, this "brutality of a coarse, low nature," that allowed her to mesh her beliefs with her assertive behavior. Because she was an exemplar of refined and self-sacrificing womanhood, and because of her domestic ideology, she needed the presence of such a brute to call her forth to militant action—as a Christian soldier. But if the captain's behavior had freed her assertive energy for a good fight, it was one battle that Farnham lost. The prude, in other words, had failed in her mission. Her failure would not be forgotten. If she had listened very closely as she stood abandoned, miserable, and humiliated on Valparaiso's docks, she might have realized this: for she might have heard the sound of distant laughter, far off but growing louder, ever more hilarious and scornful through time.

Ten

The End of the Flush Times

According to gold rush lore, the failure of Eliza Farnham's mission devastated the forty-niners. Two years later a writer in the San Francisco *Alta California* recalled that word of the *Angelique*'s voyage had been met as a "cheering intelligence." While his comrade miners thought its "precious cargo" was a full one, "joy sat upon many a bachelor's countenance that had been weathered in sorrow at the thought that his days were to end in this country, with no wife, no dear loved one to pass through the weary world with him." But soon came word that the "speculation" had "busted up." Then "came the old sorrow again," as he added, "and from that time to this, no attempt has been made to introduce amongst us in any number, respectable and virtuous young women who should become helpmates to those who have made this God-blessed land their permanent home." With the "old sorrow" came the usual result. As another San Franciscan remembered: "there was more drunkenness, more gambling, more fighting, and more of everything that was bad that night than ever before."[1] In effect, the failure of Farnham's mission of redemption unleashed another round of the forty-niner bacchanal. And yet, if indeed this was her mission's result, it may not have been a failure at all, or at least not a failure in terms of naturalizing the gender dynamics of an emerging middle class.

The public drama of Farnham's mission seemed to confirm what many forty-niners had professed since shortly after their arrival in California. Women were necessary to a respectable society. At the same time, the rough world of the gold country was simply too dirty for their presence. With this equation, women would be central to the gold rush yet absent from its daily life, Farnham both a heroine for confirming woman's role as redeemer and a source of ridicule for believing women could do anything else. From its utopian beginnings, the male space of the gold rush had become real with violence and excess. While the ultimate goal of this real world may have been spiritual salvation at the hands of wives, sweethearts, or sisters, when it came to action it would brook no womanly utopias. Thus Farnham became a type of running joke for rugged Californians. New York's Samuel Adams heard about the captain's trick on the former prison matron when he met one of the few female passengers of the *Angelique*. While he noted the laughter attending the story, still he felt that the "Captain will have to smart for it, for justice is quick here & the transgressor quick knows his doom."[2]

To the contrary, according to Farnham, nothing happened to the captain of the *Angelique*. Discovering little more than laughter upon her eventual entry through the Golden Gate, she found few supporters for the damages she hoped to bring against her tormentor. She spent two months in San Francisco, "in the foolish hope of obtaining some semblance of justice for the outrage and wrong I had suffered." During this time she endured, as she described it, "a variety of annoyances and trials sufficient to make the place forever disgusting and wearisome to me."[3] Thus ridiculed, she faded from public attention—at least so far as most gold seekers were concerned. For the next few years, she would farm, garden, and read near Santa Cruz, gaining some marginal notoriety as a member of the town's bohemian community of transplanted eastern artists and intellectuals.[4] But if Farnham herself was scoffed out of town, her ideals remained central to most gold seekers. As the sympathetic Adams mused after hearing her tale of woe, it was her plan, not its outcome, that mattered. "The plan of Mrs' Farnhams was a benevolent & brilliant one and deserved success," he wrote in his journal, "however she may be ridiculed about it. I see what would have been the result had she succeeded. Men without female influence would go back to almost barbarism in their habits."[5]

The local press had already come to the same conclusion. Farnham's ideals were "laudable," surmised a writer for the *Alta California*, notwithstanding that her mission had "proved so futile." "The will is always taken for the deed, and bachelors will unquestioningly cherish the liveliest feelings of regard for the lady who so warmly exerted herself to bring a few spare-ribs to the market."[6] Such a melange of tribute and condescension reveals a certain power in fortyniner ambivalence toward women. By this process, women might be necessary and marginal at the same time, central to the development of a respectable male character and absent from the arenas of manly action. The formula was clear: alone, men might descend into abject barbarism, but the abstracted love of women would lend a certain air of refinement to their rough exterior—taming them for an instant, yet always passing on to nothingness and silence, leaving them free to resume their violent self-assertions. The problem with Farnham was that she could never simply pass by a scene of brutality without making some scornful remark about the brute. If other women could just remain silent and womanly, they might still offer redemption.

One eastern publication encoded this formula for redemption in an anecdote that offered an "important lesson." Men, the magazine implied, might be brutes, in fact reality dictated that they would be; but they could still be respectable at heart—because women were angels. The key to this image seems to have been that women would appear only for an instant. The story began with a typical miner on his way back from California, "the *very* hardest-looking of customers." From here its author proceeded naturally to the inevitable savage moment of violent male assertion: the "hard customer" confronts an overcharging baggage carrier, draws his revolver, and in self-conscious eastern authentic style exclaims, "I am a man of few words; but if in ten minutes that mule ain't ready packed, there will be one dead nigger about these diggings." Yet here too violent self-assertion becomes a means to effect its opposite. "At that instant," readers learned, the woman-as-angel appeared, flitting through just long enough to sprinkle the dust of refinement on the gun-wielding protagonist:

> At that instant a lady upon a mule, and two beautiful girls, on their way to California, were trying to pass the blocked up thoroughfare. His eyes met the appealing gaze of the mother. In an instant his whole countenance was changed. He doffed his hat to the lady . . . and with a sweep of his arm, called the attention of his comrades: "Back, boys," said he, "make way for the lady!" The way was cleared and the lady passed. Our stalwart friend stood gazing after them for a minute or two, and as he turned round, we could perceive his face suffused with tears: on wiping them, he perceived we were regarding him closely: "I have been away from home sir, Sir," said he in a faltering voice, "for two years; that woman, and the faces of the little children, remembered me of my family. GOD bless my girls and their mother!"[7]

Appealing gaze, not scornful tongue, had revealed this miner's respectable nature. Constantly repeated both in California and the East, even by this time the anecdote was a gold rush trope. Its gender and class positions provided the basis for a seemingly endless string of plays, poems, yellow-backed books, and pamphlets: Alonzo Delano's *A Live Woman in the Mines*, Albert Brewster's *The Devoted Wife*, John Ballou's *The Lady of the West*, Brett Harte's "The Luck of Roaring Camp." In all of these statements, the forty-niner was exposed as a respectable and decent creature at heart, thanks to the presence of usually silent women. (In Harte's tale the "woman" is a newborn baby, and thus actually incapable of talking.) More than mere frontier anecdotes, these tales offered an ethical system resonant with the necessities of the modern marketplace. If, that is, the "real life" contingencies of the world beyond the home demanded a certain engagement with perversity and vulgar behavior, and if these engagements made respectable men into brutes, the presence of proper women, at least at certain moments, might still salvage class distinctions. To achieve these distinctions, perverse manhood had to coexist in an oscillating unity with redemptive femininity. Still, there might be tensions within this ideal. For as the title and text of C. W. Kenworthy's 1850 novel, *Amelia Sherwood; or, Bloody Scenes at the California Mines*, makes clear, the ideal of the angelic woman, while leaving the West open for some "bloody scenes," might be seen as also opening it to women's agency.[8] Amelia Sherwood, while a woman, and while refined and respectable, was also quite active. No shrinking violet, her role in the novel was to repeatedly step into the path of danger, between gun-toting men hell-bent on killing each other.

Together, these gender ideals might form a bourgeois whole: a male-gendered market self made respectable through redemptive feminine virtues, above the bestial fray in which these virtues were lacking, yet still capable of making headway in a visceral world of physical allurements. According to Francis Prevaux, such was the value of a wife who would come to California. "Lydia now sits on the sofa beside me," he wrote his parents soon after arrival, "she is all that a wife *should* or *could* be, *faithful* affectionate and kind and will, I doubt not, continue so." To this Lydia Prevaux added a postscript that articulates how the necessity of a redemptive wife amid a society of dissolute strangers really could effect a closer and more equitable partnership. "We often talk of home," she wrote, "and when we think how far we are from it, among strangers, we are united to each other more closely than we could otherwise be."[9]

But if there was partnership in this perceptual bridging of the chasm between home and world, male and female, there were also elements of risk and danger. For one thing, as Eliza Farnham discovered, men hated a prude; also, women had to be careful not to step between male combatants too early, not before they moved from the usual rhythms of male combativeness and liberation from moral restraint to more threatening examples of real violence. Redemptive womanhood was not to spoil the sport of market social relations as a whole. For another, this redemptive position for women, while it did promise them a useful role in social relations, might seem to them as doing little more than legitimating, or at least rationalizing, the public sphere and the West as spaces of male brutality.

Like the other women in her vicinity, Mary Ballou found that her role as a redeemer was central to gold camp society. "I am trying," she wrote her family in the East, "to relieve all the suffering and trying to do all the good that I can." Masculine excess thus offered her a way toward agency and self-assertion. At the same time and unlike Lydia Prevaux, when it came to putting her will to effect she found that conceptual partnership could quickly transform itself into actual frustration. When an argument broke out between rough types at the camp store, and when one of the disputants left the scene only to return with a pistol, she performed her womanly duty, even if this duty required publicly asserting herself in the male world. "I ran into the store and Beged and Plead with him not to kill him . . . for the sake of his wife and three little children."

Saving souls in this manner may have allowed for agency and a degree of pride; but it was ugly work. Running away, Ballou wrote that she could only bury her face in her pillow and cry: "Oh . . . if I had wings how quick I would fly to the states." Amid these scenes of raw frontier equality, burdened by the weight of cultural statements that seemed to raise the importance of women to new heights while making them the sole sources of salvation, Mary could only echo the sentiments of neighboring wives: "Clark Simmons wife says if she was safe in the States she would not care if she had not one cent. She came in here last night and said, 'Oh dear I am so homesick that I must die,' and then again my other associate came in with tears in her eyes and said that she had cried all day."[10]

Mary Ballou, along with the neighboring women of her gold camp, seems to have sensed a major ambivalence of mining society culture. Again, a large number of forty-niners, as promoters of both western progress and their own class position above the common mass, saw women as essential to California. At the same time, the nature of the gold camps, the unrestrained "human nature" of the gold region's burgeoning towns and cities, raised the question of whether women would, or *should*, be allowed to participate in such a squalid world at all.[11] This nature of mining camp society was, of course, its violence, its daily scenes of manly excess and competition, its overall context of dirtiness and hard work. What is interesting about this nature is its precise fit with middle-class gender ideologies as they would be developed for the marketplace as a whole. For there too a competitive version of "human nature" would win out, and its victory would question women's participation in the public and competitive sphere of cutthroat and visceral business activity. The gold rush exposes the history of this cultural proposition. The nature of mining camp society had to be worked out through experience, through the encoding of experience into writing in order to give it meaning. And as the experiences, letters, and writings of Louise Amelia Clappe reveal, women also had a hand in making this cultural proposition a "fact of nature."

Few documents have done more than Clappe's famous *Shirley Letters from the California Mines* to make middle-class yearnings in the gold rush appear natural and authentic. For this, Clappe—or "Dame Shirley," as she is called from the pen name she adopted when she published her letters in a single volume—has become perhaps the favorite woman of the gold rush. Her letters, according to one admirer, reveal a "naive honesty," a "womanly wit," and, in their "close observation, . . . a real woman's enthusiasm" for the liberating qualities of gold rush life. They are "marvelously skilful," claimed Josiah Royce, and "undoubtedly truthful," providing an "infinitely more helpful account of mining camp life than the 'perverse romanticism' of a Brett Harte or an Alonzo Delano."[12] Clappe, it seems, was similar enough to Eliza Farnham to be useful, but different enough to be embraced. Like Farnham, she was a refined eastern woman, originally from New Jersey but raised as an orphan by well-to-do relatives in New England. Also like Farnham, she was no advocate of women's rights or equality. Yet she was not a prude. When her husband, Fayette Clappe (a medical doctor who like many in his profession went to the mining camps to mine the miners), asked her to join him, she willingly made the voyage into a new and rugged life. For Clappe, scenes of male self-expression were not examples of brutality, not always at least; some were even charming. Unlike Farnham, she neither inspired hatred nor was she a good hater. If she was frustrated at the conditions of men, and for women, in California, her frustrations were probably not noticed by forty-niners; they have certainly not been noticed by historians who have celebrated her vision of the gold rush.

Clappe's vision of the gold rush comes about as close to utopia as was possible without a leveling abundance of gold. Her letters reveal a bourgeois utopia, a space in which respectability and the elevation of carnal desires necessary to run market capitalism blended perfectly together. What they exposed was that middle-class ethics might contain a healthy degree of worldly perversity and self-expression, but that both would be mediated by the presence of women. They also include a large dose of romanticism along with much enjoyment of ethnic and class-based others as subjects of pleasure. Finally, this system of ethics, in that it allowed for a natural male brutality by locating salvation with women, might also legitimate women's actions as Christian soldiers. At the same time, her letters again indicate the limits of this type of female agency, its creation of a field of action in which women, as often as their graces were invoked, might just as easily vanish, or suffer at the hands of men whose souls cried so violently for salvation.

Gold, to Clappe, was the "root of all evil." Yet it was an evil available to all men, including respectable men like her husband. California's mining camps, in turn, represented a world dominated by an earthy, back-to-nature form of harsh masculinity. Acquaintances, she indicated, warned her against entering this world. One declared that she was "undoubtedly mad to think of such a thing," and that she "ought to be put into a strait jacket"; another said "it was indelicate, to think of living in such a large population of men." Apparently, these warnings only increased her sense of adventure. In response, she adopted the voice of the intrepid argonaut: "I laughed merrily at their mournful prognostications," she wrote, "and started gaily for Marysville."[13]

Written in this adventurous spirit, it is not surprising that Clappe's letters from the mining camp of Indian Bar would evince much local color. In populating her gold country, she rounded up the usual exotic characters, a multiethnic blend of people from whom came a "melody of Spanish, piquant polish of French, silver clearness of Italian, harsh [gargle] of German, the limpid sweetness of Kanaka, languid East Indian, and guttural native Indian."[14] In her descriptions of these subjects, she would resort to the usual intertwining of revulsion and attraction, imbuing them with exotic power and charm even as she drew proper distinctions. "It is said," she remarked on the subject of *not* seeing any Indians on her way to a camp, "they would have killed us for our mules and clothes." She imagined the possibilities of this threat with a certain wistful longing: "They generally take women captive and who knows how narrowly I escaped becoming an Indian Chieftainess, and feeding for the rest of my life upon roasted grasshoppers[.]" Later, when she actually did pass a Native American woman on the trail, her description suggests a familiarity with the standard tropes of the period's frontier literature. The woman was, predictably enough, an "Indian Princess," although her face was that of a "Macbethian Witch." "I was perfectly enraptured with this wild-wood Cleopatra," she reported, "and bored F. almost beyond endurance with exclamations about her starry eyes, her chiselled limbs, and her beautiful nut-brown cheecks."[15]

Such would be the subjects of pleasure of Clappe's map, the ethnic and class-based others populating both the physical geography of the gold camps and the internal geography of a well-read middle-class imagination. Among these subjects were prostitutes, described by Clappe as "those unfortunates, who make a trade . . . of the holiest passion, when sanctified by *love*, that ever thrills the wayward heart of poor humanity." Signs of the male world of physical gratification and excess, these "unfortunates" would sound a tocsin for militant and redemptive action. After her arrival, accordingly, she reported that the men at the camp spurned their charms, looking "only with contempt or pity upon these, oh, so earnestly to be compassionated creatures." Thus empowered by her active role as redeemer, Clappe's letters frequently invoked the liberating qualities of her pastoral surroundings. On all sides, she wrote, there were the "majestic solitudes" of a personified nature, a "solemnly beautiful wilderness" lending itself to transcendent visions, "tableaus" of "stately deer . . . framed by embowering leaves," "radiant distances" that called forth the mind to plunge into "the evergreen depths of those glorious old woods."[16] This natural environment may have freed men to pursue desires; but these desires, in turn, had increased Louise Amelia's sense of importance.

At the center of this imagined and experienced wilderness stood the figure of the forty-niner. According to Clappe, these men had their share of refinement; their canvas-and-wood-framed "cabin" libraries consisting of "bible and prayer-book, Shakespeare, Spenser, Coleridge, Shelley, Keats, [and] Lowell's Fable for Critics." They were romantic sorts, blending these samples of elevated literature with readings and thoughts of a more physical nature. Retiring to their bunks with Ned Buntline's novels, they dashed off—"in fits of melancholy," according to Clappe—"thrilling accounts" of their "dreadful" adventures at the diggings.[17] Moving freely between Shakespeare and dime novels, libraries and lynchings, inkwells and gun play, Clappe's miners occupied a middle ground between refinement and the masculine real life. Fresh from passages of Coleridge or Keats, they were free to gather at the feet of African American trailblazer James Beckwourth, an exotic figure who, Clappe added, "chills the blood of the green young miner, . . . by the cold blooded manner in which he relates the Indian fights that he has engaged in."[18] Later, these same individuals took the time—after dog-earing a page of Spenserian couplets, no doubt—to lynch a man for stealing. Many of the camp's men, she recalled, laughed and shouted at this "piece of cruel butchery, . . . as if it were a spectacle got up for their particular amusement." Elsewhere in her letters, they proceeded from Shakespeare to shooting grizzly bears for fun, to setting afire large stands of trees, enjoying "the flames leaping and curling amid the dark green foliage, like a golden snake, fiercely beautiful."[19]

Clappe's position amid these scenes of refined cruelty appears to have been central as a redeemer and narrativist, limited as an active participant. Certainly, she denied any desire to equitably partake of such masculine pleasures. "How can women," she wrote her sister, ". . . spoil their pretty mouths and ruin their beautiful complexions, by demanding with Xantippean *fervor*, in the presence, often, of a vulgar, irreverent mob, what the gentle creatures, are pleased to call their 'rights'?"[20] More narrator than actor, she seemed content for a while at least to describe the forty-niner, to note his charming qualities and his excesses with the hope that she could better tame him. Accordingly, for her gold camp life reflected oscillations between masculine democracy and a "bacchanal madness." The wildest swings in behavior within this oscillation began with a midwinter "saturnalia," an explosion of cooped-up male energies during the dreary season of cold and cabin-confining rain. "The revel was kept up for three days," Clappe complained, and it seemed to her to grow wilder by the hour. "On the fourth day," she added, "they got past dancing, and, lying in drunken heaps about the bar-room, commenced a most unearthly howling;— some barking like dogs, some roared like bulls, and others hissed like serpents and geese. Many were too far gone to imitate anything but their own animalized selves."[21]

During the summer, Clappe balanced this vulgar scene of men turned beasts with a more charming vision of male play. The high point of the year to her came with a Fourth of July celebration. Here, her miners announced the ritual event with a song of welcome and perceptual inclusion:

> Ye are welcome, merry miners!
>   in your blue and red shirts all!
> Ye are welcome, 'mid these golden hills,
>   to your Nation's Festival;
> Though ye've not shaved your savage lips,
>   nor cut your barbarous hair
> Ye are welcome, merry miners! all bearded as ye are
>
> Ho! Sun-kissed brother from the South,
>   where radiant skies are glowing;
> Ho! toiler from the stormy North,
>   where snowy winds are blowing;
> Ho! Buckeye, Hoosier, from the West,
>   sons of the river great—
> Come shout Columbia's birthday song,
>   in the new Golden State.[22]

As Clappe described them, these festivities resonated with Whitmanesque visions of utopian democracy. Masculine energies might sometimes descend into puerile madness, but they also might be elevated with professions of duty and cross-class or cross-regional expressions of camaraderie. Consciously or unconsciously, however, her narrative could not avoid a tension regarding her role in this balanced vision. To be sure, her role was central to the society at Indian Bar. After all, she was the camp's narrator. She represented its primary female presence, passing judgments, lending refinements, offering salvation. At the same time, her own marginality to these scenes may have been increasingly apparent. For the oscillation was between brutes and brothers, and neither saturnalia nor song contained a woman's voice or part. This inherent tension in Clappe's depiction of gold rush life erupted to the surface in a long letter describing the camp's descent into chaos.

Her longest letter from the mines and her most conscious literary effort, Clappe's description of the riot that destroyed the camp of Indian Bar is quite likely a product of equal parts experience and invention. Within its elements of romance, however, we may see that the nexus of class and gender articulated in the rush was a rather unstable foundation for bourgeois ethicality. She began this account with an idyllic description of nature, an exposition of the harmonies existing between the soft streams flowing through a feminized landscape and the masculine energy of long toms imposing the will of men on their flowing waters. Suddenly, this gendered balance between man and nature is shattered by shouts and shots. From here, her true subject is the fine line that existed between the "real life" of the mines and chaos, the crossing of that line from romantic exoticism to total degeneracy. One romantic figure, an authentic laboring miner—a man "said always to have been a dangerous person when in liquor"—had been stabbed and killed by another—a Mexican of "dark antecedents," a "most reckless character, mad with wine, rage and revenge."

As might be garnered from these descriptions, Clappe takes a certain pleasure at these exotic combatants. The victim of this conflict, a "young Irishman," is a pure embodiment of laboring-class exuberance, a manifestation of physical self-expression through liquor and fists. She portrayed the Mexican, in turn, as an exemplar of hot-blooded exoticism. He was a "tall, majestic-looking Spaniard, a perfect type of the novelistic bandit of old Spain." When the Irishman strikes, he responds with a knife. Again, her narrative reveals that for women as well as men, these figures might be subjects of romantic yearnings. But it reveals something else as well. The conflict, according to her letter, developed into a full-scale race riot. The camp's white miners demanded revenge, its Mexican miners vowed to defend themselves. And here, Clappe—along with the two other eastern women at the camp—made an alarming discovery: at the precise moment when her presence should have been most needed, at least according to gold rush conceptions of redemptive womanhood, she was shunted aside. Intent on violence, the men of the camp had their riot. "We three women," wrote Clappe, "left entirely alone, seated ourselves upon a log, overlooking the strange scene below." From a hillside above the bar, they could do nothing more than helplessly watch as the "sea of heads, bristling with guns, rifles and clubs" clashed together in an ugly scene of manly chaos.

For the most part, Clappe's riot consisted of noise and loud threats. Its results, as Royce claimed later, were practically negligible in this rough environment: two Anglo forty-niners were wounded, two Mexicans received the blame and were flogged the next day.²³ Yet for Clappe, the scene and its aftereffects—which included the setting up of a vigilance committee—may have revealed the limitations within a code of redemptive femininity. Despite her presence, that is, and despite the pervasive rhetoric celebrating redemptive female influences, the gold camps remained no places for women. The Committee of Vigilance, she indicated, merely served to shore up the implication. Its members, rather than controlling violence, appeared to make it an institution. They paraded "the streets all night, howling, shouting, breaking into houses, taking wearied miners out of their beds and throwing them into the river."²⁴

Undoubtedly, Clappe's account of these scenes contained a share of exaggeration. Her conclusion of this letter bespeaks her objective: "There, my dear," she wrote her sister, "have I not fulfilled my promise of giving you a dish of horrors?" If, however, her accounts drew upon the imagination to fulfill promises to her eastern readers, they may have also served purposes that are easy for historians to miss. Because it is interwoven with her evident enjoyment of mining camp romance, it has remained difficult for historians to see Clappe's criticism of the gold rush, her dissatisfaction at the playing out of this male utopia. It is there, however, in a warning to her sister: "this coarse, barbarous life would suit you, even less than it does your sister." It is there in her description of the abandonment of Indian Bar a few months after the riot, a description implying that the democratic promise and masculine thrust of the gold rush had become so much litter, that nature's obliteration of the camp might only effect an improvement. "The whole Bar," she remembered upon leaving, was covered with "empty bottles, oyster cans, sardine boxes, and brandied fruit jars, the harsher outlines of which are softened off by the thinnest possible coating of radiant snow. The river, freed from its wooden flume prison, rolls gradually by. The green and purple beauty of these majestic, old mountains, looks lovelier than ever, . . . like an immense concave of pure sapphire, . . . the wonderful and never-enough-to-be-talked-about sky of California, drops down upon the whole, its fathomless splendor."²⁵

Finally, her dissatisfaction may be evident in the fact that not long after these experiences she left her husband, later divorcing him and returning to New England. Certainly, within that "fathomless splendor" that was California's sky, Clappe beheld a promise. For many historians, it seems, it has been far easier to depict her wonder at that promise than her frustration at its never having been delivered. It is easier to see her letters as unvarnished depictions of a "natural" male exuberance, as another example of an American character that was respectable and physical, without distinctions of class or privilege. And it is also easy to celebrate Clappe—as generations of California historians and antiquarians have done—as an exemplar of the pioneering helpmate, a woman who stuck by the miners despite their insistence that brutal excess was a necessary element of manhood. She was, after all, a woman who witnessed the equation that "men will be boys," and lending it an unvarnished romance, she helped make it a fact of nature.

For many, the arrival of women like Eliza Farnham and Louise Amelia Clappe in California's male preserve announced the end of the gold rush. As early as 1850, according to some observers, gambling and prostitution were doomed to go into decline or disappear entirely. In that year, Sara Royce, along with a small host of respectable women, led a confrontation against one of San Francisco's leading businessmen when he showed up at a benevolent society meeting accompanied by his mistress, Irene McCready, the madam of the El Dorado Saloon. The mere fact that there were "benevolent societies" in the city, along with women like Royce, may have signaled an end to the flush times. As many knew from western literature, when these women came to confront prostitutes, to gaze disapprovingly on the drunken forty-niner, to hang flowerpots from windowsills and paintings from rifle hooks, the story was at a decided end. But in other ways women's stories, particularly Farnham's story, indicated that the rush would never end: for this male world would never abide a prude. One of the first "histories" of the gold rush stated that California during its flush time needed the moral influences of women, that it was a place where "reason tottered and passion ran riot," but, its authors added lest women get the wrong message, "let none wonder that the time was the best ever made."[26]

If some women insisted on getting in the way of manly self-assertion, if they insisted on spoiling these "best of times," they might find themselves out of the picture entirely. Their role was to make proper distinctions between forty-niners, to aid in the territory's transition to statehood, and to lend a veneer of respectability to the region's rising economy. Elsewhere, Josiah Royce's mother provided a good example of this role. By the mid-1850s, she claimed, the "majority" of forty-niners were "accustomed to life in an orderly community, where morality and religion bore sway." Mingled with these better sorts of men, as she made sure to add, were others of an opposite stripe, a "motley assembly" of Indians, Mexicans, and Chinese, along with forty-niners "of a different class." These, she claimed, were "roughly-reared frontier-men almost as ignorant of civilized life as savages. Reckless bravados, carrying their characters on their faces and demeanor, even when under the restraints imposed by policy."[27] Thus could the respectable and middle-class forty-niner enter this world of nonconformity and lack of social restraint, and still remain above the common stew.

For some forty-niners as well as for many observers, even this veneer of respectability was too much; with it, the rush lost much of its attraction. To most, it seems, perceptions of the era's passing were idiosyncratic, marked not by a particular time or date but by a personal feeling: having experienced enough of the world, they could finally go home. New York City's Charles Palmer began coming to this realization in the spring of 1850. He had discovered even by this early date that California was changed, that its frontier possibilities were already disappearing. Society and civilization had come to the region. The territory had become a state. Economies of scale had shouldered aside the pick and pan of the lone forty-niner. The result, for Palmer, was a feeling of nostalgia and loss. "It is only when ranging free over the mountains which [others] have [not] yet penetrated," he concluded, "that I can find the California I knew a few months ago."[28]

It is likely that his efforts to recapture the California he knew delayed Palmer's decision to return to the East. Finally he came to the conclusion that his adventures were at an end; the experience had worked its transformation. "You will find that California has left me capable of domestic happiness," he wrote, this time to his grandmother; "the rest of my life," he added, "will pass quietly with my books and pen. I do not care to die rich in anything but memories. . . . In short you will find me very different from the Enthusiastic boy who left home nearly five years before, to taste the mysteries of a new life, and who has never yet regretted that step."[29] Having tasted the "mysteries" of life in the corner of America where they came at their rawest, Palmer was ready at last for the quieter rhythms of middle-class respectability.

After a season or two in California, married forty-niners may have been readier still for the quiet life. William Swain booked passage on a

New York–bound steamer after a summer in the mines. Writing his family soon before departure, he lamented that he would return with no more than 800 dollars. Yet in what for him was a rare bit of poetry, he averred his contentment at returning:

Were so ere I roam
There is one land beloved
of Heaven above the rest;
One spot above all others blessed.
That land is *My Country*
And that *spot* is *My home*[30]

Doctor Augustus Fitz Randolph Taylor's stay in the gold country was shorter still. Having landed in California too sick to work, he steamed home at the earliest opportunity. He returned to New Brunswick, New Jersey, where by the end of February 1850 he could report that his wife and mother were "glad to see me of course." When Taylor arrived, according to Margaret La Tourrette—whose husband remained another year on the Pacific Coast—he could "scarcely walk." Indeed, as indicated by his diary, the former town mayor would require some six months of bed rest before resuming his medical practice.[31] Hiram Pierce returned to Sara Jane in Troy, New York, at the end of 1850. He regretted, he said, "to go home with nothing," and perhaps realizing that he had failed to find gold when Sara had succeeded in running the family business, he worried over how she would feel. "I hope that you will not be disappointed," read Sara in his last letter from California, "[but] I will not longer Sacrifice all that is dear on earth or worth living for, for the hope of gain." His steamer arrived at New York Harbor on 5 January 1851, and the next day he closed his journal: "Joined my family with rejoicing Still weak & feeble with the Chargres fever."[32]

As to his own readiness for the quiet life, Richard Hale was not so sure. By 1854, five years since his departure from Newburyport, Massachusetts, he was ready to admit that the search for gold had been a "fiasco." Although he would "have liked to return with well-filled pockets," if only to prove himself to "those more cautious," he had amassed enough of a different type of currency: "I could still say that it had all been a most valuable experience." At the same time, having discovered within himself a sense of authentic manhood, and having developed this sense in a rugged environment, this self-conceived frontiersman looked homeward with ambivalence. "After an absence of nearly five years," he wrote as his returning steamer entered the northern waters of the Atlantic, "I am facing home. Mingled emotions stir me! What changes would the course of the years disclose? What had this bearded man, myself, lined and bronzed by exposure, in common with the stripling who had gone in quest of the 'pot of gold at the foot of the rainbow' years before? . . . Would my mother and father warm to this rugged man, as they had to the vanished boy?"[33] Still, like many individuals who had experienced California as a transition from naive boyhood to rugged manhood, Hale came home to "civilization."

Transitions made during extended absences were not limited to the returning argonauts. Undoubtedly, the experience had wrought great changes within many forty-niners, but so could it change family members who stayed in the East. For married men in particular, coming home might mean reacquainting themselves with wives who had developed measures of independence during the separation. This fact, coupled with the forty-niners' feelings of frustration at having failed to live up to their own professed duties and promises, undoubtedly resulted in some tensions among reunited couples or families. Few men or women, however, were likely to voice these tensions in written records. Their adventures at an end, returned gold seekers put away their diaries and journals. Their separation from husbands or loved ones over, women no longer needed to express their every feeling in letters.

Still, there are a few hints that eastern wives might have retained a sense of disappointment over the venture. Margaret La Tourrette was undoubtedly glad to welcome Cornelius home. She could even play on a few left-over romantic elements of the rush: "Don't stop in N.Y. to fix up," she teasingly told him, "but let us see you in your long beard and miner's costume." Just beneath this good-humored welcome, however, there may have remained some frustration at lost opportunity. Indeed, her reference to her husband's authentic miner's garb as a "costume" may have carried the implication that she was still not fully convinced the rush had been quite real or substantial. As well, she could not resist reminding Cornelius that by delaying his return—and by leaving in the first place—he had given up a situation in a New York bank, at $600 per year. And finally, she reminded him that his adventures had done nothing to accomplish their goal of moving off the oppressive family homestead: "Oh!," she concluded in her last letter before his arrival, "I do so much want a quiet home, some place I can call my own."[34] William Swain's family offered a parallel warm welcome to its returning argonaut. In a postscript to Swain's final letter on the adventure, one family member indicated that this welcome could be tinged with doubts about the rush's value. "He never regretted the adventure," read the scribbled addendum; yet its writer added that despite Swain's returning with some $1,000, the near two-year quest had resulted in "less than he would have made on his beautiful farm."[35] Returning home in a similar position, William Prentiss found that along with his welcome, he would have to eat some crow. "I am rejoiced that you . . . found your family well & happy to receive you," wrote a neighbor soon after his arrival. But, as he made sure to remind William, "has all your enjoyments put together equaled the happiness you experienced in once more realizing the embraces, comforts & kisses of your wife? I don't believe you will ever be cross to her again—do you? . . . I think your . . . wife proves a blessing to you in the end, but wasn't you disgusted with yourself?"[36]

Many forty-niners planned to resettle in California, and many among them never returned to the East. For New York's Joseph Chaffee, however, the idea of being cut off from his family was difficult to contemplate. "As much as I love this country," he wrote his parents, "I cannot remain here when it is your wish for me to Return, . . . and if it is your wish for me to come home immediately I would do so with pleasure."[37] Married forty-niners faced more difficult decisions and dialogues in proposing resettlement. Having found a degree of success at the mines, William Elder appears to have pondered this option at length. Only on further thought did he rule out the idea, writing his wife that "the moral influence to which the children would be exposed would I fear prove to their injury."[38]

Other married men were less willing to give up on this possibility. Mary Ann Meredith welcomed her husband, Griffith, home only to see him immediately begin planning for the family's permanent removal to the golden state. Together with Griffith and their two children she made the steamer passage through Panama—by this time reduced to a one-month voyage—and arrived in California in March 1859. From Peacham, Vermont, Chastina Rix also eventually acquiesced to her husband's intention of resettling the family. Her decision, however, was made all the more formidable by Alfred's refusal to return to the stultifying atmosphere of his Vermont village, even if only to help organize the move to California. "Were I only there," wrote Chastina on receipt of Alfred's letter inviting her to make the trip with the children; "but how," she asked herself, "can I ever think of going there without Alfred. I was scarcely ever out of my own town & how can I go so far when there is so much to go through."[39]

If Alfred's decision to stay in California was difficult, once made, its physical and emotional burdens would be transferred to Chastina. She would have to make what was then still a taxing steamer voyage. Furthermore, in debating the idea with herself and with Alfred, she spent much of her time worrying for the safety of her two children on the voyage. In the fall of 1852, a few months after learning of his intentions, she still wrestled with the issue. She had "almost," as she put it, "made up my mind to go California." A month later she had apparently come to a resolution, promising the family diary that she would make the trip "as soon as I can go." Yet only two days later her doubts had returned: "Oh!," she wrote in some frustration, "how much I would give if Alfred was only here to help and encourage me about going."[40] Finally, in the spring of 1853, Chastina along with her children boarded the steamer *Ohio* bound for Panama. From there it was on to California, where by the 10th of May Alfred could make his first entry in the family diary in some two years: "Again we open our old Journal & proceed as before with our daily reckoning." As their lives took on a more mundane rhythm, however, the couple's additions to the diary became more sporadic. Life after the gold rush, it seems, could not match the creative pangs of anticipation and separation.

Despite the difficulty of such decisions, many eastern women would eventually overcome their reservations about relocating to the Pacific. Most, it appears, were like Mary Ann Meredith, who moved with her husband to California after the forty-niners returned. Some, like Chastina Rix, made the trip alone or with children. Yet in these two cases, perhaps these women were right in their reservations and doubts. Chastina Rix died, probably in childbirth, in February 1857, four years after her arrival. Mary Ann Meredith died while giving birth in 1861, one and a half years after entering the Golden Gate.[41]

These fatal outcomes may have actually been rare among the families that relocated permanently in California following the gold rush. At the same time, they could mesh well with perceptions, with visions of the society on the Pacific as rife with dangers and lacking in civilized amenities. For gold seekers who had generated these visions in letters home or sent east for publication, convincing wives to join them in California proved a difficult task. Still, if they were like Albert Powell of upstate New York, they were willing to make the effort. Many men with wives and children, Powell reported, "come to see me and eat melons and appear so happy and all that I can tell them is that I will soon have my Wife and Babys here too." By this time, however, Rachel Powell had heard far different stories, both from Albert himself and from other returned gold seekers. Writing about a mutual friend who, embittered by the experience, had rationalized his failures by filling Rachel with tales of gold country horrors, Albert could only try to explain: "he was one of the home sick children and of course he will not praise the country very much. But this is the country for me above all others or any poor man. There is pleanty of Gold, the Mines are inexhaustible or they are thought to be so here."[42]

Albert's attempt to return Rachel's perceptions of California to a point of high anticipation and easily available wealth came a bit late in the overall eastern narrative of the rush. After all, for some time, forty-niners had been regularly writing that California was a humbug. Even Albert seemed to recognize this, and he could not resurrect the image of inexhaustible mines without adding that it reflected what some people "thought" rather than what they knew was real. Accordingly, his plea fell on deaf ears. "I want you to understand there is no gass [*sic*] in what I write to you," he complained later, "but I am well aware it looks rather like it to you." Indeed, having heard much to the contrary, Rachel may have seen too much that was vaporous in her husband's visions of melon-parties and domestic happiness. She refused to join him. He, in turn, finally gave up and prepared to come home. He did not admit defeat, however, without a degree of frustration and anger. "When I go amongst the familys that are here," he wrote soon before his return voyage, "they laugh at me because I have got a Wife that has not got spunk enough to come[.] Mr Milne [an] old acquaintance of mine in New York who is in business in the City received a letter from his wife that if he staid in Calafornia she was a comeing to. So he wrote for her to come and the very next Steamer brought her and the little ones out." Having made sacrifices enough in support of her husband's venture, Rachel did have spunk enough to resist this last request for wifely duty. And, as he prepared for his return steamer passage, Albert could only bluster helplessly: "you must lookout for Squalls when I come home."[43]

Although he experienced a similar sense of futility, Enos Christman also went to great lengths to convince Ellen Apple to leave West Chester, Pennsylvania. He built her a house. He promised that the profits from his budding newspaper serving the gold camps around Sonoma would provide financial security. He even contracted acquaintances to write testimonials to his hesitant future bride, confirming his ability to provide a safe domestic hearth. Still she resisted his pleas. "I am afraid," he wrote, hoping to dissuade her from reservations about gold country violence, "that you make the picture of life in California a little darker than what it really is. And I believe if men had their sweethearts, wives and children out here, we should have as good order and as much protection to life and property as in any new country."[44] Ellen was impressed with her suitor's business energy, house, and testimonials. She remained unconvinced, however, that California was ready for her presence. Her "dark picture" of gold rush life, after all, had not been of her own creation. Rather, her visions of Grizzly fights, Indian ambushes, Mexican violence at the southern mines, her pictures of drunken brawls settled with revolvers and bowie knives, could all be directly traced to the imaginative pen of Enos himself. "Do not, dear Enos," she merely wrote in answer to his pleas, "put off coming home later than next spring." Finally she dashed his hopes entirely. "That part of your letter which speaks of California being made as good as any new country, if men had their families there," she proclaimed, "I think is a mistake. Enough of the right kind of men will never go there to conquer the bad part of the community."[45] Faced with the solidity of such perceptions, forced to argue against the very visions that they themselves had partly constructed in their writings, Albert Powell, Enos Christman, and many other forty-niners in similar circumstances would have to give up their intentions and come home.

In March 1852, two groups of adventurers met on the banks beside the Chagres River on the Isthmus of Panama. One of the groups was on its way to California, the other returning from the gold country. As the Pacific-bound men climbed out of the small boat that would take their homeward-bound fellows to the Caribbean, nineteen-year-old Hubert Howe Bancroft witnessed the striking differences in their appearances. The fresh emigrants, he later recalled, had the confident air of high expectations. They swaggered ashore, "rude and unaccommodating in their grumbling selfishness, stupid in their perverse independence and surly in their unreasonable opposition to order and regulations." The returning forty-niners, in contrast, were humbled men. Having failed in their individual ventures they were heading back to the safe confines of their wives and families. According to Bancroft, they had "been licked into some degree of form and congruity by their rough experiences." Having once shared the illusions of the departing miners, they were now quieter and more subdued; California had shredded their illusions and exposed their foolish dreams. They waited patiently for the boat to empty, wanting only to go home.[46]

This meeting, as the young man who would later become California's leading historian described it, resonates with two of the main themes of mid-nineteenth-century American history. Historians have often depicted this history according to two divergent and bipolar paths: one leading outward, fired by rising expectations, ideas of manifest destiny, and male fantasies, to the frontier; the other turning inward toward the home and the construction of an established middle-class family. At the same time, these simultaneous movements appear to have been imbued with a class and gender dynamic. The frontier is understood and interpreted as a place of visceral male adventure. It is a public and male sphere, a visible space for the playing out of low impulses. Free and fraught with temptations, it is a conceptual space occupied by an authentic working-class or ethnic other. The home is a female sphere, a haven for the respectable refinements of an emerging middle class. An enclosed and perceptually claustrophobic private space, increasingly feminized by a developing cult of domesticity, it is embraced as the central anchoring point of middle-class formation.

As articulated in dialogues between men and women, the experience of the gold rush, both in the East and in the West, did much to strengthen this ideology of separate spheres. As well, these dialogues applied this ideology to new purposes, using it to legitimate a bourgeois identity in which moral status and the amoral pursuit of success might be twined. Gold rush dialogues rooted these ideals in actual space, providing through the evidence of primary experience concrete "proof" that home and world were physically separate, and that this continued separation was necessary to the maintenance of the marketplace. Bancroft's moment of meeting both captures these cultural dynamics of the rush and reveals something about these conceptual spaces. It reveals that the rugged forty-niner, his face "burnt black as an Indian's," and the clerk, his hands ink-stained and soft from counting money, were two sides of the same coin. The frontier, in other words, if it was a place for the low, was also a space for the denial and atomization of middle-class identity. Out there, middle-class men did not have to act middle class; nor would they be crippled in doing business by a bourgeois standard of respectability.

These gold rush images suggest that a social geography of gender and class would help constitute the moral basis for an apparently classless and liberal American marketplace. The gendered spaces of home and market were separate but absolutely necessary to each other; bound together in an oscillating unity of homebound virtues and worldly sin, they could simultaneously create, explain, and effectively mask the existence of hierarchies of power. The cross-regional and cross-gender dialogues of the gold rush reveal that the middle-class character would not be hypocritical. Instead, this character would be Janus-faced, characterized by respectability, a daily mutiny against respectability in the name of doing business, and a nightly reembrace of respectability for the sake of higher status. Passionate masculinity, with its competitive engagement in worldly pursuits, its component necessities of false claims, dirty dealings, and daily perversities, would be balanced by redemptive femininity. Such a blend need not be seen as a product of functionalist rationalizations for excess or social control. If it indicates the successful construction of a single, transcendent, and male individual, it is only through a romantic marriage of opposites, men with women, status with success, East with West.[47]

In effect, the outward thrust of the frontier world of individualism and excess and the inward pull of the respectable home were not separate or competing impulses. Rather, they were parts of a whole, intrinsic elements of a forming middle-class character that would be balanced between respectability and physicality. Accordingly, middle-class forty-niners would return home only to return, again and again, to the frontier. "In the east the Yankee was walled about by forms, creeds and conventions," Richard Hale said upon his return; the East, he thus implied, was not the place for authentic masculinity. At the same time, his experiences had effected a cure. "It is an easy matter to make a Yankee into a Californian," he added, "but no easy matter to change him back again."[48]

Like many of his fellow argonauts, Hale would remain a Californian, with one foot in the respectable East, one in the visceral world of authentic experience. He had returned to civilization a "wanderer." His old friends would gather around, asking a few questions about the gold that had once been the West's major promise and source of salvation, but many more about his experiences, about his own personal charting of the realm of liberation. At last, he recalled, "I realized that my experiences had been as valuable to me as the bag of gold I had come home without." "The gold might easily vanish," he noted, but his experiences "could never be taken away." Many of Hale's fellow forty-niners would have agreed. Accordingly, they sought publishers for their diaries and listeners for their lectures, marketing their memories as valuable coin, themselves as self-made men. On these recollective stages, the unities of middle-class character might be easily apparent. Benjamin Martin's career as a gold rush lecturer began with his return to Chelsea, Massachusetts. Feted by the local citizens, he sat at the head of a table, upon which "the most conspicuous object was a large ham, on the exterior of which . . . appeared the magic words—'There's no place like home!' " The scene having been tempered by this morsel of respectability, he proceeded with his tales of adventure, chilling the blood of his listeners.[49]

Thus could refinement temper the gold rush, the gold rush spice respectability with a dash of the "real life." And, as Bancroft pointed out, it was a rare argonaut who missed the market importance of this experience in the realm of visceral social relations. The "returned Californian," concluded Bancroft, "was proud of himself for having gone there, proud of the old clothes and shaggy beard and gold dust which he had brought back, proud that his eyes had been opened so as to take in a view of the world. He regarded with pity his old comrades who still plodded along at the rate of a dollar or two a day." Dirt, violence, and excess had become the signs of authenticity, California "the only place where men filled the ideal of manhood."[50] Consequently, if the experience lent itself to a sense of a middle-class "real life," these genuine qualities, as New England's Stephen Wing maintained in his own lectures, were bankable as sources of future profit. "And now comes the question," he exclaimed at the end of a talk filled with entertaining sallies, jokes, and violence, "was this long absence from home of any profit?" The answer was no, he averred, but only in a "pecuniary sense." For as he made sure to point out: "I have never for a *moment* regretted the time I spent there. Although my purse was no heavier, I had in another direction profited greatly by the *experience* gained. During this time, I had been thrown altogether upon my own resources, and I think Every young man who has been for years in California, will testify, that those who were not ruined by the associations which *always* exist in a new country, received lessons of self reliance which will ever be remembered with *profit.*"[51]

If Wing's version of the gold rush, like that of many other aspiring middle-class forty-niners, provided a model of respectable authenticity, it also contained an undercurrent of tension. Certainly, the lesson of the event was self-reliance, the idea that middle-class men could be rugged individualists, that if the competitive world of business required a heavy touch of the savage within, they could play this game. Toughened up by authentic experience, they could now venture forth from domestic havens, readied for the realm of unrepressed desires characterizing the modern marketplace. The problem with this logic was that the whole equation rested on gender. Here we find the absent but central subject within Wing's lecture and the narratives of so many gold seekers. If forty-niner experience had readied them for the marketplace—if, that is, the "associations" prevailing in a visceral male space had not "ruined" them—it was only due to the redeeming support of women.

This narrative resolution of the tensions between respectability and the necessities of doing business might combine engagements in competitive desires with class hierarchies based on self-control and ethicality. It would contain both family duty and manly desire, fifty years of respectable service and sneaking off to the club for highballs and ribald jokes, stolid respectability and occasional slumming forays into the fleshier pleasures located in an exotic but always lower-class or ethnic other. But as the foundation for a bourgeois identity that remained classless in action *and* ethically above the brutal fray, it was shaky at best.

At the edge of Philadelphia's Pine Street wharves, a returned Enos Christman gazed longingly at a California-bound ship, his mind's eye returning to that moment of oceanic dissolution, "to the day that I turned my face towards a land of promise." But even while dreaming, he was conscious that he remained above the fray. He had been elevated by Ellen Apple, "the dear burthen on my arm," his new bride and constant reminder that "my hopes have been gratified and I have realized a fortune."[52] Men like Enos Christman may have known that the ethical basis of this fortune depended on a homebound female subject. What they could not forget was that having mapped the regions where fortune lay, so had they once dreamed of alternatives to their own bland existences. Furthermore, once they found that these suspiciously socialist alternatives would not come to fruition, they had extended invitations for women to enter this world, to save it from its own characteristic dirtiness, to save them from their own brutality. This invitation would have its lasting effects, not just in the West but also in the American Northeast. For there, as influential an observer as Thomas Wentworth Higginson would note in 1853 that there "was wisdom in that hearty recognition given by a party of rough California miners to some brave New England women who were crossing the

Isthmus, in the rainy season, to join their husbands. 'Three cheers (said they) for the ladies who *have come to make us better!*' "[53]

Ellen Apple refused this invitation. Eliza Farnham accepted it. Ellen refused because the darkness of the male sphere was filled with violence and brutality, Eliza accepted because this darkness was merely a covering for "something else—some '*spec*'—from which great results are hoped; some scheme, or schemes, that will scarce bear examination by daylight."[54] Here were two positions for women within a system of gendered ethics. Ellen had tamed her forty-niner, and accordingly, he was free to enter the untamed world of the marketplace. Eliza remained a hated prude and a militant, always in proximate relation to male brutality, always trying to make men better and never lending masculine competition the legitimacy it so desperately needed. Indeed, as her friend Georgianna Kirby found, Farnham seemed to be mysteriously attracted to brutish men. To help run her farm near Santa Cruz, Kirby recalled, she had hired "an Irishman without self-respect . . . and with no idea of straight forwardness or speaking the truth." When her farm began to fail, she hired "a half fool, half knave . . . who did no better." Then, according to Kirby, "she married the greatest blackguard in the country who strikes her and otherwise ill treats her."[55] These relations, disturbing as they are, may have been entirely consistent with the logic of domesticity, with bourgeois or liberal ideals of gender and class. In adopting brutality as the meaning of freedom and competition as a way of life, privileged men might deny their own status and expand the sphere of respectable action. In living with these men, women might be free for militant action as Christian soldiers.

Eliza Farnham would continue as a proponent of womanly virtue and Christian militancy, the epitome of self-assertion within an ideology of self-sacrifice. But if she remained in battle, so might this position have forced a realization: a revolution in values had proceeded without her; suddenly there were more brutes than ever, and brutal self-assertion had become a positive attribute. Thus, it had been no revolution at all. Certainly, in proposing her mission to California she had recognized that a revolutionary moment was at hand, that a transcendent realm offering the oceanic dissolution of old boundaries and the possibility of new social relations had opened up with the gold rush. Her mission's successes and failures, however, may have indicated that these utopian possibilities had been denied, at least to women. If, that is, the liberated spaces of the West had been mapped, the result was the same old "spec," the same old examples of brutality—lying, scheming, cheating, fighting—all now enacted by the bourgeois male in the name of liberation from bourgeois restraints. No one, particularly among these brutes, was about to call gardening and reading liberating. To Farnham, having spent her life around the brutality of men, the failure of California's possibilities indicated that her ultimate victory over these types would still be a long time in coming. She was not, despite Kirby's perceptions, altogether content with this situation. When her closest friend returned to the East and when, shortly thereafter, her daughter died, she wrote her publisher that "I am so cut off from communication with the Eastern world and so frozen up in this Polar Sea of humanity that I am very wretched most of the time, sometimes almost desperate. I do not know if I shall ever find my full measure of life again in the Mortal state. My only rejoicing is in the tho't of that which awaits me beyond."[56]

Still, Farnham would continue her fight. She left the brutality of California and her new husband in the late 1850s. When she died, it was as a direct result of her lifelong battle against male excess, her willingness to join the fray. She succumbed to an illness contracted as a nurse at the Battle of Gettysburg. But during the years she spent with Georgianna Kirby on the Pacific Coast, Eliza still found a full measure of life amid her disappointments. Surrounded by the sounds of a revolution gone redundant and sour, together the two would go strawberrying along the cliffs above Santa Cruz. There they would revive the revolution in talk, Georgianna urging her friend to speak at the upcoming woman's rights convention, Eliza agreeing but maintaining that what mattered was a victory of difference over equality. Occasionally she would feel the "delicious breeze" coming up from the Pacific. She would glance toward "the great surf rolling in"; having looked, she said, one "could not fail there to understand the anguish of that exquisite song,"

> Where is the sea, I languish here!
>   Where is my own blue sea,
> With all its barks in fleet career,
>   And flags and breezes free?[57]

Conclusion

Horatio Alger found the California gold rush irresistible. Indeed, for him it seemed a perfect vehicle for another in his line of rags-to-riches stories, another example of the democratic possibilities inherent in the American marketplace. In 1891, not surprisingly, he published *Digging for Gold: A Story of California.* The typical stuff of Algeresque dreams, his narrative begins, of course, with a young man. His name is not important. What is important is that he is a go-getter, a decent fellow whose reasons for joining the rush would place him somewhere above the common stew of "pukes" and prospectors. His motives for going west, in other words, had to be eminently respectable. And so he goes to California not out of greed or any lower motive, but to make a liberating competency: to free himself from an evil and scheming step-father, to free his long-suffering and patient mother from an unhappy marriage. Through luck and pluck he prevails. Good fortune smiles upon him in the form of Alger's stock characters, what today would be suspiciously friendly older men; one gives him a pair of new under-shorts, another a gold mine. He has the backbone to stay at the diggings until he has unearthed and washed $10,000 in dust and nuggets. With this sum, he returns to save his mother, expose the machinations of his stepfather, and to have the remains of his treasure made into the ultimate symbol of bourgeois attainment and status: a shiny gold pocket watch.[1]

By the 1890s this little trophy represented a happy ending. Yet few writers or thinkers in antebellum America would have missed some rather disturbing contradictions in what Alger's young protagonist flashes as a single and unified sign of success.

Gold, after all, was the "root of evil." As an element it was mired in the muck of an occult past. Welling up from the very "bowels" of the earth, where according to traditions it was protected by sprites and devils, it had long been linked with low motives and passionate drives. Its mystical and base properties made it the enemy of virtuous moderation and Yankee common sense, inspiring men to madness, adventurers to the ends of the earth, witching rods, seventh-sons, and visionary cultists to uncontrolled quiverings and visions of magical abundance.[2]

The timepiece would come to represent the stabilization of this occult and backward past. It would be the foundation of a modern Protestant work ethic, the basis for the de-skilling process and the acceleration of the assembly line, a primary tool of eastern capitalists and corporate managers as they worked to transform treasure-seeking dreamers into factory workers.[3] Well on the way to becoming a dominant symbol of America's liberal culture, not to mention a reward for fifty years of loyal company service, Alger's gold watch is an alchemic blend of disparate elements: it is a melding of romance and realism, vernacular past and managerial future, exuberant West and respectable East.

For historians who claim the existence of an American "liberal consensus," Horatio Alger is the prophet of the bourgeoisie, his heroes the models of a middle-class identity.[4] For many historians of the California gold rush, the event represented every quality the middle-class could never have: self-expression, violent physicality, a free embrace of uncontrolled passions and forbidden behaviors, drunkenness, debauchery, and unfettered avarice. What is so interesting about Alger's narrative of the rush, however, is its almost precise fit with the written experiences of many men and women who actually took part in the California exodus from 1849 to 1852. Like many of theirs, Alger's narrative exposes a free individual, an archetypal ambitious young man, one who is able to move between, or combine, polarities of respectability and the pursuit of success in a highly competitive and sometimes perverse world of men. The ethical nature of Alger's protagonist is established by his mother, as that of many gold seekers was established by an abstract pole of refined womanhood and higher duty. Once established and then shunted to the margins of physical experience, this ideal of redemptive femininity allowed them to blend Christian virtue with the pursuits of material success, manhood, and adventure. For Alger as for many forty-niners, the pursuit of wealth tended westward, toward a frontier of abundance and opportunity, away from the moral restraints of the home, away from the competitive constraints of the market.

Although it took place right in the middle of America's market revolution, for the most part, the California gold rush remains resistant to serious analysis, occupying a place rarely visited by sober-minded historians. In many ways, these scholars are barred from the event by their colleagues, many of whom will greet the person who risks such a presumably hackneyed topic with open smirking, with sotto voce versions of "Darlin' Clementine" or "Paint Your Wagon." At the same time, the rush remains central to American culture. Along with the forty-niner, it remains a symbol of freedom, perhaps the last and best case for the West as a place of liberation from bourgeois restraints and middle-class respectability. The image of the lone, independent, and unconnected forty-niner is a myth. Yet it is a myth that resists debunking, supported because it upholds several others. One is the myth of the self-made man. Another is the ideal of the violent outsider. According to this ideal, the man who settles scores with shooting sprees, who destroys the environment and kills ethnic others, is always an outsider, a lone figure or group of loners, distanced from respectable society—never one of us. Still another is the myth of a universal model of liberation, a model based on the presumed existence of a one-dimensional and prudish middle class.

There is little doubt that the gold rush was liberating, at least for some individuals. It was not liberating for William Joseph. A Nisenan Indian who survived the gold rush, Joseph saw little to celebrate in the vaunted freedoms of the forty-niners. "The Indians were very much afraid of the whites in the early days," he recalled later, adding that "the whites were bad in the old days, those who prospected for gold. Those who came next were good whites, married people."[5] What signified liberation for many forty-niners, their avowed freedom from eastern prudery and puritanical codes, their avowals of free opportunity and free land, frequently meant rape to Native Americans, and it nearly always meant dispossession and loss. Not that Joseph's perspective would have bothered the forty-niners; most would probably have agreed with his distinction between bad whites and good whites. In a sense, Joseph's critique of white liberation, of "bad whites," is precisely the kind of perception that allowed the "good whites" of the gold rush-era and later to simultaneously kill Native Americans and express outrage toward atrocities committed against their "red brothers."

Nor was the gold rush particularly liberating for Maria Amparo Ruiz de Burton. A member of the Californio aristocracy, the land-owning elite who dominated California up to the rush, Ruiz de Burton wrote her own account of the era and its effects in an 1885 book, *The Squatter and the Don*. The book is a bizarre set of reverse perceptions, bizarre because they are virtually unique in their accuracy, and because they are so "beyond the pale" of standard American thought as to be practically unintelligible to American scholars. Here, the aristocrat becomes the victim. The forty-niner, meanwhile, is little more than a squatter, a character entirely lacking in charm or romance. To Ruiz de Burton, the gold rush was a series of losses, a bourgeois revolution followed by the rise of a corporatist dictatorship. In her book, the members of the Californio aristocracy, as patrician and civilized landed altruists, really are better than the common rabble. The forty-niner, in turn, is portrayed as the Anglo-invader, which is common enough, but also as a vulgar, money-grubbing squatter, a bourgeois gentleman using the gold rush as an excuse to make a land grab from his natural superiors. Finally, both displaced aristocrat and displacing bourgeois are overthrown by a kind of socialist revolution, as a small number of government-sponsored, impersonal, and anonymous corporations take over California's inland valleys. Perhaps only a true conservative could afford such an accurate account of the rush and its effects. To Ruiz de Burton the gold rush contained the entire dialectic of Marxian class conflict. And of course, as a member of California's pre–gold rush aristocracy, none of this dialectic was particularly liberating for her.[6]

The main beneficiaries of the flush time's vaunted freedoms would be members of the middle class. For this reason, perhaps, memories and celebrations of the event most frequently take the form of reenactments. These reenactments, in turn, contain a host of dominant yet conflicted yearnings: to find softer alternatives to competition and capitalist social relations, to liberate the market and the individual from moral codes and government bureaucracy, to silence opposition against the violent dispossession of ethnic and subaltern peoples, to bond with these people in hearty camaraderie. According to the dominant ideals of these celebrations, no one told the forty-niners what to do, or how to live, or when to come in at night. They made their own rules, forming a kind of masculine brotherhood around the tenets of miner's law, a system of few codes apart from the code of individual property and the right to defend it. They did hard physical labor, bonding with working-class men, wading icy streams, washing tons of gravel, overturning massive boulders. Their hair grew long, their beards unkempt, and no one told them to shave. Their bodies and clothing became encrusted with dust, mud, and sweat, and no one could make them bathe. By day they were free to ravage the landscape, dredging rivers, washing away entire mountains of soil, and leaving behind mounds of trash. By night they gathered around campfires, singing minstrel tunes with "Old Kentuck," exchanging tales of lucky strikes and the day's findings. And through all of this they heard no squeamish words of caution. There were no "big government" bu-reaucrats getting in the way of their right to exploit, accumulate, and expand. There were no prudish voices questioning the world's largest and greatest camp-out.

These celebrations reflect a type of cultural alchemy, appealing to people who can appreciate the event's reversals, people who have privilege and security enough to shrug off their status-giving white codes of behavior for a bit of play on the "darker side." Accordingly, reenactments of the rush, while they contain much of the language of multiculturalism and many references to the event as responsible for California's great ethnic diversity, have an air of "whites-only" min-strelsy about them. In a sense, they appear to celebrate multicultural-ism and diversity much as the forty-niners themselves did in the early days of the rush. Diversity is most often depicted as exoticism, ethnic peoples as fixed and earthy subjects of white pleasure and desire. Thus if Mexicans or Native Americans appear in these celebrations, it is nearly always as "folklore performers," as minstrel characters forced into "brownface" or "redface" performances of songs and dances for white onlookers who perhaps imbibe a bit of *aguardiente*, or who perhaps go a bit "primitive" to the rhythms of drum and fandango. Then, having consumed their opposites, and therefore contained them, they return to their gated communities.

Among the most interesting aspects of these reenactments is their cultural accuracy. Indeed, in watching the celebrations and celebrants with a critical eye, one sees not only the way the gold rush is remem-bered but the gold rush itself. For here one finds all the elements of the rush: respectable men dressed as roistering forty-niners, redemptive women lending a measure of dignity to the occasion along with a few "Calamity Jane" types announcing their own liberation from the femi-nized "prudes" of the east. And here as well are dancing Mexicans, generic Indians, painted prostitutes, and countless references to gone-but-not-forgotten gambling halls, whiskey dens, and vigilante lynch mobs. On the margins of these events one is likely to find a group of

Miwok and Nisenan protesters, still around despite numerous stories of "vanishing" Native Americans and "last Indians," still protesting despite the event's rhetoric of multicultural inclusion and the fact that its organizers have trucked in a handful of specimens from New Mexico to perform a dance or two. No celebration of the gold rush, no reenactment of the flush times, would be complete or accurate without an Indian protest.[7] For these protests provide a constant reminder that they too were in California during its flush times, that the gold country was once their land, and that the celebrated freedoms of the rush came at a heavy human price. At the same time, many gold rush reenactors have missed this point, trying repeatedly to bring real California Native Americans into the celebrant fold. Yet the protesters remain adamant in their refusals, their protests not against the inaccuracy of the reenactment, but against celebrations of the gold rush itself.

All in all, the fact that gold rush celebrations so frequently take the form of reenactments, along with their "whites-only" minstrel imagery, is a testament to the event's importance in the making of the American middle class. In a sense, by reenacting the gold rush, today's middle-class celebrants are reenacting themselves. For like the middle-class forty-niners, they are respectable, but not too respectable to make their way in a world of visceral competition. Like the forty-niners of this study, they are refined, polite, and moral, but not to the extent that they cannot on occasion roll up their sleeves, kick up their heels, and "get down" with a frequently ethnic common folk. And like the forty-niner, today's middle class seems liberated without being liberal, capable of committing mutiny against itself on a daily basis without losing class status. In effect, during the gold rush as now, the most powerful characteristic of the middle class would be self-denial. Yet this would not be the sort of self-denial that many historians talk about in reference to the middle class. Rather than reflecting a denial of the self's access to appetites, passions, and pleasures, it would involve a real denial of one's self, a constant assertion of class privilege, an equally constant assertion that one does not occupy this position.

In effect, the primary characteristic of the American middle class may be its members' ability to create a definition for themselves and then deny that they belong in the definition. Thus their greatest privilege, and their greatest source of power, is an ability to declare freedom from themselves. From the period of the gold rush to the present, two great myths have gone into the making of this characteristic middle-class privilege. One is the myth of the lone forty-niner, the independent man without a past, declaring his freedom from eastern codes of respectability. The other is the myth of a middle class that is fixed by repression, incapable of having fun. Both of these subjects are based in myth; neither is likely to be debunked. For a time, it seems, Americans struggled with the image of the forty-niner. In 1849, northeastern observers regarded the forty-niners as "educated, intelligent, civilized, and elevated men, of the best classes of society." Some twenty years later, Mark Twain would refer to them as exemplars of antiaristocratic democracy, as a band of roistering bravos thumbing their noses at the stuffed shirts of the east. In 1886, Josiah Royce would again raise the subject of their respectability; in 1920, Frederick Jackson Turner would call them "types of that line of scum that the waves of advancing civilization bore before them."[8]

The confusion is understandable, for the forty-niners would occupy both positions, containing them within a character in constant oscillation between polarities of repression and expression, refinement and brutality. This oscillation was apparent at the time of the event. In fact, in James Hutchings's 1853 broadside, "The Miner's Ten Commandments," it would be portrayed as the forty-niner's primary characteristic. Hutchings's broadside is a famous document, often reprinted and sold in California tourist shops. Indeed, its fame is deserved: it is one of the best examples of the rush as a charming expression of social reversal. It is, in other words, an expression of liberation entirely dependent on the existence of a repressed middle class. Here, in a series of engravings that frame a text of frontier moral scriptures, the forty-niner is depicted in all his various guises. In one he "sees the elephant." In two others he confers with his "pard," while in the background a claim jumper swings from a hangman's tree and a miner falls victim to frontier gunplay. In at least two he is depicted in the saloon, drinking with Pike County types in one, playing cards beneath a painting "in the French style" in the other. And finally, in two others he is portrayed as the middle-class gentleman, surrounded by hearth and family in a well-appointed parlor, meeting his redemptive wife in a sentimental homecoming.[9]

Yet if these contemporary illustrations picture the hard-handed miner and the counting-house clerk as one and the same, most current historians have returned to an image of the forty-niner as a working-class hero, a ruthless and isolated stampeder. In doing so they have separated this binary figure, cutting him in half like sideshow magicians. These historians are working with formulas for class analysis that are clear and seemingly inviolable: vulgarity and fun mark the working class, and respectability and repression mark the middle; masculinity and unfettered freedom mark the common folk, while feminization and prudery mark the bourgeois elite. The working class is the liberated forty-niner; the middle class is Bartleby.

Given the fact that this has become a standard formula for class analysis, the metaphor of the magician may be more apt than it first appears. For perhaps this analytical formula represents a conscious misdirection, a sleight-of-hand effort on the part of the middle class to uphold repression for the sake of rebellion, another example of middle-class power, its members' ability, so to speak, to be *and* not to be. Certainly, just as the forty-niner will endure as a symbol of anti-bourgeois self-expression, Bartleby will endure as a representative of the repressed middle class. The forty-niners of this study knew better. They knew that holding on to their status required a Janus-faced character, a constant shifting back and forth between the roles of respectable father and street-smart businessman who could deal with the devil and win his way to success. The result of their knowledge would be a series of mutinies without an overturning of power, an elevation of women without feminization, a repeating cult of freedom and liberation without liberalism. The result, in other words, would be modern middle-class culture.

Notes

INTRODUCTION

1. Herman Melville, *Billy Budd, Sailor & Other Stories* (New York: Penguin Books/Viking Press, 1967), 57–99.

2. On Bartleby as a symbol for fears of isolation, see Michael T. Gilmore, *American Romanticism and the Marketplace* (Chicago: University of Chicago Press, 1985), 133–39.

3. James A. Read, *Journey to the Gold Diggins, by Jeremiah Saddlebags*, illustrated by J. A. and D. F. Read (New York: Stringer & Townsend, 1849).

4. H. L. Mencken, *The Vintage Mencken* (New York: Vintage, 1955), 76, 92. See, for example, C. Wright Mills, *White Collar: The American Middle Classes* (New York: Oxford University Press, 1951); Walter E. Houghton, *The Victorian Frame of Mind, 1830–1870* (New Haven: Yale University Press, 1957), 54–89; John F. Kasson, *Rudeness and Civility: Manners in Nineteenth-Century Urban America* (New York: Hill and Wang, 1990); Norbert Elias, *The History of Manners: Volumes I–II* (New York: Pantheon, 1978 [1939]); C. Dallett Hemphill, "Middle Class Rising, 1750–1820: The Evidence from Manners" Paper delivered at the meeting of the Organization of American Historians, April, 1995; Daniel T. Rogers, *The Work Ethic in Industrial America* (Chicago: University of Chicago Press, 1978), 18–19; Richard Bushman, *The Refinement of America: Persons, Houses, Cities* (New York: Alfred A. Knopf, 1992); and Stuart M. Blumin, "The

Hypothesis of Middle Class Formation in Nineteenth-Century America: A Critique and Some Proposals," *American Historical Review* 90 (April 1985): 299–338.

5. See, for example, Roger D. McGrath, *Gunfighters, Highwaymen & Vigilantes: Violence on the Frontier* (Berkeley: University of California Press, 1984); and R. E. Mather and F. E. Boswell, *Gold Camp Desperadoes: A Study of Violence, Crime and Punishment on the Mining Frontier* (San Jose: History West, 1990).

6. Mark Twain, *Roughing It* (New York: Signet, 1980 [1871]), 309–10.

7. On forty-niner "vulgarity" as an expression of the working class, see Eric Lott, *Love and Theft: Blackface Minstrelsy and the American Working Class* (New York: Oxford University Press, 1993), 169–210; Richard Stott, *Workers in the Metropolis: Class, Ethnicity, and Youth in Antebellum New York City* (Ithaca: Cornell University Press, 1990); and David Roediger, *The Wages of Whiteness: Race and the Making of the American Working Class* (New York: Verso, 1991), 116–20. Singing seems to be a hallmark of the working class, an example of middle-class historians envisioning poverty as something enjoyable; see E. P. Thompson, *The Making of the English Working Class* (New York: Vintage/Random House, 1966); and Sean Wilentz, *Chants Democratic: New York City and the Rise of the American Working Class, 1788–1850* (New York: Oxford University Press, 1984).

8. Peter Arnold to William Prentiss, 17 February 1850, Prentiss Collection, Bancroft.

9. Allan Nevins, ed., *The Diary of George Templeton Strong*, vol. 1, *Young Man in New York* (New York: Macmillan, 1952), 345; "The New Eldorado," *Godey's Lady's Book* 47 (July 1853): 406.

10. Caspar Hopkins, MS "Autobiography," Bancroft; Benjamin Thompson Martin to the *Chelsea Pioneer*, 17 August 1849, Hopkins Collection, CSL; Stephen Wing, diary, entry for 27 April 1852, Wing Collection, Bancroft.

11. See, for example, Hubert Howe Bancroft, *California Inter Pocula* (San Francisco: The History Company, 1888); J. S. Holliday, "The Influence of the Family on the California Gold Rush," *Proceedings of the Third Annual Meeting of the Conference of California Historical Societies*, June 20–22 (1957), 157–69; on the ideologies behind this traditional conception of the West, see Madelon Heatherington, "Romance Without Women: The Sterile Fiction of the American West," in Barbara Howard Meldrum, ed., *Under the Sun: Myth and Realism in Western American Literature* (New York: Whitson, 1985), 74–89; Nina Baym, "Melodramas of Beset Manhood: How Theories of American Fiction Exclude Women Authors," *American Quarterly* 33 [2] (Summer 1981): 123–39.

12. See, for example, Jo Ann Levy, *They Saw the Elephant: Women in the California Gold Rush* (Norman: University of Oklahoma Press, 1992); Julie Roy Jeffrey, *Frontier Women: The Trans-Mississippi West, 1840–1880* (New York: Hill and Wang, 1979); Silvia Anne Sheafer, *Women of the West* (Reading, Mass.: Addison Wesley, 1980); Mary Jane Megquier, *Apron Full of Gold: The Letters of Mary Jane Megquier from San Francisco 1849–1856* (Albuquerque: University of New Mexico Press, 1984); Ida Pfeiffer, *A Lady's Visit to California* (Oakland: Biobooks, 1950); Sarah Bayliss Royce, *A Frontier Lady: Recollections of the Gold Rush and Early California* (Lincoln: University of Nebraska Press, 1977).

13. On the importance of female networks of kinship and their decline in the

nineteenth century, see Laurel Thatcher Ulrich, *A Midwife's Tale: The Life of Martha Ballard, Based on Her Diary, 1785–1812* (New York: Vintage Books/Random House, 1990).

14. These "eyewitness" accounts range from the "Crocketesque," such as Joseph G. Baldwin's *The Flush Times of California* (Athens: University of Georgia Press, rpt. 1966); to the rather obvious fakes, such as Chauncy Canfield's *The Diary of a Forty-Niner* (New York: Houghton Mifflin, 1920); to the scholarly synthetic, such as J. S. Holliday's *The World Rushed In: The California Gold Rush Experience* (New York: Simon and Schuster, 1981); as a result of this emphasis on "experiential realities," the rush appears closed to cultural analysis, a quixotic upwelling of desires and sensations having little meaning aside from the experience itself. On the gold rush's fall from favor as a subject for serious historical analysis, see David Goodman, *Gold Seeking: Victoria and California in the 1850s* (Palo Alto: Stanford University Press, 1994), ix–x.

15. Here, much of this analysis is informed by Joan Scott, "The Evidence of Experience," *Critical Inquiry* 17 (Summer 1991): 773–97; Jane Tompkins, *Sensational Designs: The Cultural Work of American Fiction 1790–1860* (New York: Oxford University Press, 1985); Johan Huizinga, *Homo Ludens: A Study of the Play Element in Culture* (New York: Harper and Row, rpt. 1970); Peter Stallybrass and Allon White, *The Politics and Poetics of Transgression* (Ithaca: Cornell University Press, 1986); Raymond Williams, *Culture and Society, 1780–1950* (New York: Columbia University Press, 1958). Overall, this shift in approach responds to Foucault's call for scholars to analyze social discourses—like that of middle-class respectability—not merely for what they say, or for their repressive functions, but also for the types of expressions and ideals they produce; see Michel Foucault, *Power/Knowledge* (New York: Pantheon, 1980); idem, *The History of Sexuality*, vol. 1, *An Introduction* (New York: Vintage Books, 1980); idem, *Discipline and Punish: The Birth of the Prison* (New York: Vintage, 1979).

16. The classic account of the gold rush as an exposition of a distinctly American "national character" is Josiah Royce's *California: From the Conquest in 1846 to the Second Vigilance Committee in San Francisco* (Boston: Houghton Mifflin, 1886). Beginning soon after the gold rush and continuing into the mid-twentieth century, historical accounts of the rush frequently portrayed it as a democratic epic, an example of America's commitment to free opportunity; the best examples of this literature are Edward E. Dunbar's *The Romance of the Age, or, The Discovery of Gold in California* (New York: D. Appleton, 1867); and Hubert Howe Bancroft's *California Inter Pocula* (San Francisco: The History Company, 1888). These themes have occasionally been revived in works stressing the event's spirit of camaraderie, its anecdotes of roisterous good times and examples of male play: Joseph Henry Jackson's *Anybody's Gold: The Story of California's Mining Towns* (New York: Appleton-Century, 1941); Owen Cochran Coy's *In the Diggings in 'Forty Nine* (Los Angeles: California State Historical Association Press, 1948); Donald Dale Jackson's *Gold Dust* (New York: Alfred A. Knopf, 1980). These themes have played well with history buffs, as exemplified in Time Life Books' publication *The Forty Niners* (New York: Time Life Old West Series, 1974). Sober-minded or serious efforts to analyze the rush remain surprisingly rare; the best are John Walton Caughy's *Gold Is the Cornerstone* (Berkeley: University of California Press, 1948); idem, *The California Gold Rush*

(Berkeley: University of California Press, 1948); Rodman Paul's *California Gold: The Beginning of Mining in the Far West* (Lincoln: University of Nebraska Press, 1947); and Charles Howard Shinn's study of "miners' law" (a return—without tragicomic or epic overtones—to an emphasis on ties between the frontier and democracy), *Mining Camps: A Study of American Frontier Government* (New York: Harper and Row, 1965).

17. Peter R. Decker, *Fortunes and Failures: White-Collar Mobility in Nineteenth-Century San Francisco* (Cambridge: Harvard University Press, 1978); Ralph Mann, *After the Gold Rush: Society in Grass Valley and Nevada City, California, 1849–1870* (Stanford: Stanford University Press, 1982); Rodman Paul, "After the Gold Rush: San Francisco and Portland," *Pacific Historical Review* 50 [1] (February 1981): 1–21.

18. Paula Mitchell Marks, *Precious Dust: The American Gold Rush Era: 1848–1900* (New York: William Morrow, 1994), 22–23 and passim; Malcolm Rohrbough, *Days of Gold: The California Gold Rush and the American Nation* (Berkeley: University of California Press, 1997), 12 and passim.

19. Goodman, *Gold Seeking*; Susan Lee Johnson, "Bulls, Bears, and Dancing Boys: Race, Gender, and Leisure in the California Gold Rush," *Radical History Review* 60 (1994): 4–37.

20. On these developments, see George Rogers Taylor, *The Transportation Revolution, 1815–1860* (New York: Rinehart, 1951); Alfred D. Chandler Jr., *The Visible Hand: The Managerial Revolution in American Business* (Cambridge: Harvard University Press, 1977), 81–121; Charles Sellers, *The Market Revolution: Jacksonian America, 1815–1846* (New York: Oxford University Press, 1991); Burton J. Bledstein, *The Culture of Professionalism: The Middle Class and the Development of Higher Education in America* (New York: W. W. Norton, 1978); Stuart M. Blumin, *The Emergence of the Middle Class: Social Experience in the American City, 1760–1900* (Cambridge: Harvard University Press, 1989); David J. Rothman, *The Discovery of the Asylum: Social Order and Disorder in the New Republic* (Boston: Little, Brown, 1971); Paul S. Boyer, *Urban Masses and Moral Order in America, 1820–1920* (Cambridge: Harvard University Press, 1978); Paul E. Johnson, *A Shopkeeper's Millennium: Society and Revivals in Rochester, New York, 1815–1837* (New York: Hill and Wang, 1978); Mary Ryan, *Cradle of the Middle Class: The Family in Oneida County, New York, 1790–1865* (New York: Cambridge University Press, 1981).

21. For a classic on middle-class lack of doubt, see Louis Hartz, *The Liberal Tradition in America: An Interpretation of American Political Thought Since the Revolution* (New York: Harvest / Harcourt Brace Jovanovich, 1991 [1955]); some historians have focused on tensions between middle-class respectability and the market revolution; see, for example, Karen Haltunnen, *Confidence Men and Painted Women: A Study of Middle Class Culture in America, 1830–1870* (New Haven: Yale University Press, 1982); Daniel Walker Howe, "Victorian Culture in America," in Howe, ed., *Victorian America* (Philadelphia: University of Pennsylvania Press, 1976), 3–28; Amy Dru Stanley, "Home Life and the Morality of the Market," in Melvyn Stokes and Stephen Conway, eds., *The Market Revolution in America: Social, Political, and Religious Expressions, 1800–1880* (Charlottesville: University Press of Virginia, 1996), 74–98.

1. Edward Neufville Tailer, diary entries for 18 December 1848, 23 December 1848, and 7 November 1849, vols. 1, 7, Tailer Collection, NYHS.

2. Tailer, that is, fits into the "respectability" or "repression" thesis of middle-class identity. For examples of this thesis, the reader may turn to practically any work dealing with class or class formation. Specific examples include Max Weber, *The Protestant Ethic and the Spirit of Capitalism* (London: Unwin Hyman, 1930); C. Wright Mills, *White Collar: The American Middle Classes* (New York: Oxford University Press, 1951); David Rothman, *The Discovery of the Asylum: Social Order and Disorder in the New Republic* (Boston: Little, Brown, 1971); Daniel T. Rogers, *The Work Ethic in Industrial America* (Chicago: University of Chicago Press, 1978); Herbert Gutman, *Work, Culture and Society in Industrializing America* (New York: Random House, 1966); Karen Haltunnen, *Confidence Men and Painted Women: A Study of Middle Class Culture in America, 1830–1870* (New Haven: Yale University Press, 1982); Stuart Blumin, "The Hypothesis of Middle Class Formation in Nineteenth-Century America: A Critique and Some Proposals," *American Historical Review* 90 (April 1985): 299–338. This is a very short list, containing only a few of the best examples from this enormous body of literature.

3. Examples of the comic or "folk" literature produced by these earlier rushes include Joseph Baldwin's *Flush Times* series on the "flush times" of Alabama and Georgia, Johnson Jones Hooper's *Adventures of Captain Simon Suggs*, and C. W. Harris's *Sut Lovinggood*; on early California attitudes toward gold, see Walton Bean and James J. Rawls, *California: An Interpretive History* (New York: McGraw Hill, 1983).

4. Marshall's discovery, the "remarkable coincidence" thesis, and the Barnum story appear in Donald Dale Jackson, *Gold Dust* (New York: Alfred A. Knopf, 1980), 12, 22, 90–91.

5. Cited in Ralph P. Beiber, "California Gold Mania," *Mississippi Valley Historical Review* 35 (June 1948): 3–28 (quote, 17).

6. Samuel C. Upham, *Notes of a Voyage to California Via Cape Horn, Together with Scenes in El Dorado* (Philadelphia: n.p., 1878), ix.

7. Beiber, "California Gold Mania," 20–21.

8. Cited in Rodman W. Paul, ed., *The California Gold Discovery: Sources, Documents, Accounts and Memoirs Relating to the Discovery of Gold at Sutter's Mill* (Georgetown, Calif.: Talisman Press, 1967), 71, 73.

9. Paul, *California Gold Discovery*, 74.

10. *[Hunt's] Merchant's Magazine and Commercial Review* 20 (January–June 1849): 55–56.

11. "Gold! Gold!" (advertisement), *Jerseyman* (Morristown, N.J.), 15 November 1849.

12. Advertisement for Potter and Smith Dry Goods, *Jerseyman*, 22 November 1849.

13. "For California," *Newark Daily Advertiser*, 10 January 1849; Henry Louis King, "Statement," Bancroft; For a short list, and brief look, at certain mining companies, see R. W. G. Vail, "Bibliographical Notes on Certain Eastern Mining

Companies of the California Gold Rush, 1849–1850," *Papers of the Bibliographical Society of America* 43 (third quarter, 1949): 247–78.

14. Bernard DeVoto, *The Year of Decision 1846* (Boston: Little, Brown, 1943), 144.

15. Ella Rodman, "Going to California," *Peterson's Magazine* 15 (January–June 1849): 168–72, 202–4, 170.

16. Ibid., 202–4.

17. Carolyn L. Karcher, "Lydia Maria Child and the *Juvenile Miscellany*: The Creation of an American Children's Literature," in Kenneth M. Price and Susan Belasco Smith, eds., *Periodical Literature in Nineteenth-Century America* (Charlottesville: University Press of Virginia, 1995), 90–114 (quote, 99).

18. See Charles Sellers, *The Market Revolution: Jacksonian America, 1815–1846* (New York: Oxford University Press, 1991); George Rogers Taylor, *The Transportation Revolution, 1815–1860* (New York: Rinehart, 1951); Alfred D. Chandler Jr., *The Visible Hand: The Managerial Revolution in American Business* (Cambridge: Harvard University Press, 1977), 81–121.

19. These settings and changes are outlined in Jack Larkin, *The Reshaping of Everyday Life, 1790–1840* (New York: Harper and Row, 1988); Mary Ryan, *Cradle of the Middle Class: The Family in Oneida County, New York, 1790–1865* (New York: Cambridge University Press, 1981); Paul Johnson, *A Shopkeeper's Millennium: Society and Revivals in Rochester, New York, 1815–1837* (New York: Hill and Wang, 1978), see especially 25–31; Anthony F. C. Wallace, *Rockdale: The Growth of an American Village in the Early Industrial Revolution* (New York: W. W. Norton, 1972); Thomas Dublin, *Women at Work: The Transformation of Work and Community in Lowell, Massachusetts, 1826–1860* (New York: Columbia University Press, 1979); Mary H. Blewett, *Men, Women, and Work: Class, Gender, and Protest in the New England Shoe Industry, 1780–1910* (Urbana: University of Illinois, 1988); Christopher Lasch, *Haven in a Heartless World: The Family Besieged* (New York: Basic Books, 1977). On the dynamics of kinship and the transition to industrialization, see also Christopher Clark, "The Household Economy, Market Exchange and the Rise of Capitalism in the Connecticut Valley, 1800–1816," *Journal of Social History* 13 (Winter 1979): 160–90; Janet Suskind, "Kinship and Mode of Production," *American Anthropologist* 80 (1978): 860–72.

20. Johnson, *A Shopkeeper's Millennium*, 106; Blumin, "Middle Class Formation."

21. These images of the city appeared frequently in publications like the *National Police Gazette* as well as in the sensationalist literature of the time; see, for example, George Thompson, *City Crimes; or, Life in New York and Boston* (New York: William Berry and Co., 1849); and George Foster, *New York by Gas-Light* (Berkeley: University of California Press, 1990 [1850]); for the way the middle-class interpreted these images, see Richard Stott, *Workers in the Metropolis: Class, Ethnicity, and Youth in Antebellum New York City* (Ithaca: Cornell University Press, 1990).

22. Frank Buck to his sister [Mary Sewell], 24 November 1846–16 February 1848, in Franklin A. Buck, *A Yankee Trader in the Gold Rush: The Letters of Franklin A. Buck* (Boston: Houghton Mifflin, 1930), 1–13.

23. John F. Kasson, *Rudeness and Civility: Manners in Nineteenth-Century Urban America* (New York: Hill and Wang, 1990), 4, 11–15, 53.

24. See ibid., 11–37; Norbert Elias, *The History of Manners: Volumes I–II* (New York: Pantheon, 1978 [1939]); C. Dallett Hemphill, "Middle Class Rising, 1750–1820: The Evidence from Manners," Paper delivered at the meeting of the Organization of American Historians, April, 1995; Richard Bushman, *The Refinement of America: Persons, Houses, Cities* (New York: Alfred A. Knopf, 1992).

25. Daniel Walker Howe, "The Market Revolution and the Shaping of Identity in Whig-Jacksonian America," in Melvyn Stokes and Stephen Conway, eds., *The Market Revolution in America: Social, Political, and Religious Expressions, 1800–1880* (Charlottesville: University Press of Virginia, 1996), 259–81; Thomas Haskell, "Capitalism and the Origins of the Humanitarian Sensibility," *American Historical Review* 90–91 (April, June 1985): 339–61, 547–66; Karen Halttunen, "Humanitarianism and the Pornography of Pain in Anglo-American Culture," *American Historical Review* 100 [2] (April 1995): 303–34.

26. *A Manual of Politeness, Comprising the Principles of Etiquette, and Rules of Behavior in Genteel Society: For Persons of Both Sexes* (Philadelphia: J. B. Lippincott, 1856 [1837]), 8, 41–42.

27. See, for example, *The Young Man's Own Book: A Manual of Politeness, Intellectual Improvement, and Moral Deportment Calculated to Form the Character on a Solid Basis, and to Insure Respectability and Success in Life* (Philadelphia: Mielke & Biddle, 1832), 132–35. *The Canons of Good Breeding; or, The Handbook of the Man of Fashion* (Philadelphia: Lea and Blanchard, 1839), 3, 4, 51–53.

28. On the centrality of the Golden Rule to middle-class culture, see Kasson, *Rudeness and Civility*, 116–17. References to the "Golden Rule" taken from, in order, *The American Chesterfield: or, Way to Wealth, Honour and Distinction: Being Selections from the Letters of Lord Chesterfield to His Son; and Extracts from Other Eminent Authors, on the Subject of Politeness* (Philadelphia: John Grigg, 1828), 226–28; *Canons of Good Breeding*, 33; Lydia Maria Child, *The Girls Own Book* (New York: Clark and Austin, 1833), 284–86; see also L. E. Craig, *True Politeness; or Etiquette for Ladies and Gentlemen, Containing the Rules and Usages of Polite Society, Along with Directions for the Toilet* (Philadelphia: L. E. Craig, 1847), 5.

29. Frank Buck to Mary Buck Sewell, New York, 16 February 1848, *A Yankee Trader*, 13.

30. Frank Buck to Mary Buck Sewell, New York, 2 December 1848, 17 December 1848, *A Yankee Trader*, 24–25, 27.

31. "Emigration to California," *New York Herald*, 11 January 1849.

32. "The Character of the California Emigrants," *New York Herald*, 17 January 1849.

33. The sources for the membership rolls of six eastern mining companies are: for *Ark* (sailed out of Newburyport, Mass., 31 October 1849), log of the brig *Ark*, AAS; for the Bunker Hill Company (the *Regulus*), journal of Thomas Williams and diary of Benjamin Osgood, Bancroft; for the *Emma Isadora* out of Boston, diary / log of Henry A. Stevens, CSL; for the Fremont Company (the *Selma*), log of the bark *Selma*, Bancroft; for the Salem Mechanic Trading and Mining Company (the *Crescent*), diary/papers of William Graves, Bancroft. Passenger lists for

the brig *North Bend*, out of Boston, and the steamer *Robert Brown*, out of New York, are from John E. Pomfret, ed., *California Gold Rush Voyages, 1848–1849* (San Marino, Calif.: Huntington Library Press, 1954), 95–96, 172–76.

34. Henry Hovey Hyde, [typescript] diary, "A Voyage from Boston to California via Cape Horn," CSL.

35. "Emigration to California"; Irving S. Kull, "The New Brunswick Adventurers of '49," reprinted in *Proceedings of the New Jersey Historical Society*, n.s., 10 [2] (January 1925): 3.

36. Report from a meeting held 3 February 1849, papers of the New Brunswick and California Mining and Trading Company / James V. Spader papers, Alex; the company's finances are also reported in John P. Wall, *The Chronicles of New Brunswick, New Jersey, 1667–1931* (New Brunswick: Thatcher-Anderson, 1931), 330–31.

37. See Blumin, *The Emergence of the Middle Class*; Ira Katznelson and Aristide R. Zolberg, eds., *Working Class Formation: Nineteenth-Century Patterns in Western Europe and the United States* (Princeton: Princeton University Press, 1986), 3–41.

38. Helen L. Winslow, "Nantucket Forty-Niners," *Historic Nantucket Quarterly* 4 [3] (January 1956): 6–28; on the decline of the Nantucket whaling industry, see Alexander Starbuck, *History of the American Whale Fishery* (Secaucus, N.J.: Castle Books, 1989 [1877]).

39. Mary Ann Tucker to David Hewes, Deerfield, Mass., 10 June 1835, David Hewes Collection, Bancroft.

40. David Hewes to his mother [Ruth Swain], Yale College, 3 October 1847, David Hewes Collection, Bancroft.

41. This information comes from several letters and papers: John H. Beeckman to Margaret Gardiner Beeckman, "At Sea," 13 February 1849; Rio de Janeiro, 27 March 1849; San Francisco, 7–31 August 1849; box 27, John H. Beeckman Collection, CSL.

42. Sarah Staats Bayles [Margaret's mother], diary, La Tourette Collection, Alex.

43. Background on Hulbert is from a biography file; Eri Hulbert to Ambrose Hulbert [in Burlington Flatts, N.Y.], Chicago, 5 December 1851, Eri Baker Hulbert Collection, CSL.

44. Samuel Adams, diary, undated entry, CHS.

45. "Correspondence of the Newark Daily Advertiser / Michigan Railroads," *Newark Daily Advertiser*, 12 December 1848; "From California," *Newark Daily Advertiser*, 19 December 1848.

46. Cousin Alice [Alice Bradley Haven] *"All's not Gold that Glitters"; or, The Young Californian* (New York: Appleton and Company, 1853), 5; "Emigration to California" and "The Wonderful News from California—A Revolution in the Civilized World," *New York Herald*, 11 January 1849.

47. Josiah Royce, *California, From the Conquest in 1846 to the Second Vigilance Committee in San Francisco* (Boston: Houghton Mifflin, 1886), 276, 392.

48. J. Howard Wainwright, "Wed Not For Gold," *Knickerbocker* 37 [6] (January 1851): 506–7.

49. H. L. Tuckerman, "The Gold Fever," *Godey's Lady's Book* 38 (March 1849): 205, 207–8.

50. R. J. De Cordova, "A Dreamy Hour in the Gold Regions," *Godey's Lady's Book* 41 (December 1850), 366–73; Charles Dickens's *A Christmas Carol* appeared in 1843.

51. *Manual of Self-Education: A Magazine for the Young* (August 1842), excerpted in David Brion Davis, ed., *Antebellum American Culture: An Interpretive Anthology* (Lexington: D. C. Heath, 1979), 72; these ministers' warnings are cited in Malcom Rohrbough, *Days of Gold* (Berkeley: University of California Press, 1997), 38, 50; Ralph Waldo Emerson, "Uses of Great Men," from *Representative Men: Seven Lectures* [1850], in Joel Porte, ed., *Essays and Lectures of Ralph Waldo Emerson* (New York: Library of America, 1983), 615.

52. Herman Melville, *Mardi, and A Voyage Thither* (New York: Albert and Charles Boni, 1925 [1849]), 452–55.

53. James P. Delgado, *To California by Sea: A Maritime History of the Gold Rush* (Columbia: University of South Carolina Press, 1990), 7, 18–21; Frances Alida Hoxie, "Connecticut's Forty-Niners," *Western Historical Quarterly* 5 [1] (January 1974): 17–28; "Commerce With California," *[Hunt's] Merchant's Magazine and Commercial Review* 22 [1] (January 1850): 208.

54. Garrett W. Low, *Gold Rush by Sea* (Philadelphia: University of Pennsylvania Press, 1941), 155; Charles Ross Parke, *Dreams to Dust: A Diary of the California Gold Rush, 1849–1850* (Lincoln: University of Nebraska Press, 1989), 83; John Beeckman to Margaret Gardiner Beeckman, At Sea, 13 February 1849, CSL.

55. Edward Neufville Tailer, diary, entry for 8 September 1853, Tailer Collection, NYHS.

CHAPTER TWO

1. Caspar Thomas Hopkins, MS "Autobiography," Bancroft.

2. See Samuel Richardson, *Pamela, or, Virtue Rewarded* (New York: W. W. Norton, 1958 [1740]).

3. "California Gold and European Revolution," *Southern Quarterly Review* 17 (July 1850): 281–83, 298.

4. "Integrity of Business Men," *[Hunt's] Merchant's Magazine and Commercial Review* 20 [6] (June 1849): 682–83.

5. Henry Ward Beecher, *Lectures to Young Men* (Boston: J. P. Jewett, 1846); and Henry Bellows, "The Influence of the Trading Spirit Upon the Social and Moral Life of America," *American Review* (January 1845); both excerpted in David Brion Davis, ed., *Antebellum American Culture: An Interpretive Anthology* (Lexington: D. C. Heath, 1979), 72, 111.

6. One of the best analyses of antebellum optimism remains Perry Miller's *The Life of the Mind in America* (New York: Harcourt, Brace and World, 1965); see also John Higham, *From Boundlessness to Consolidation: The Transformation of American Culture 1848–1860* (Ann Arbor: University of Michigan, 1969); Frederick Merk, *Manifest Destiny and Mission in American History: A Reinterpretation* (New York: Vintage Books/Random House, 1963).

7. See Mary Ryan, *Cradle of the Middle Class: The Family in Oneida County, New York, 1815–1837* (New York: Cambridge University Press, 1981); Paul E. Johnson, *A Shopkeeper's Millennium: Society and Revivals in Rochester, New York, 1815–1837* (New York: Hill and Wang, 1978); Whitney Cross, *The Burned-*

Over District: The Social and Intellectual History of Enthusiastic Religion in Western New York (Ithaca, N.Y.: Cornell University Press, 1950); Nathan O. Hatch, *The Democratization of American Christianity* (New Haven: Yale University Press, 1989).

8. Mrs. A. J. Graves, *Women in America: Being an Examination into the Moral and Intellectual Condition of American Female Society* (New York: Harper and Brothers, 1843), excerpted in Davis, ed., *Antebellum American Culture*, 19; H. T. Tuckerman, "The Gold Fever," *Godey's Lady's Book* 38 (March 1849): 207.

9. John Humphrey Noyes, *History of American Socialisms* (New York: Dover, 1966 [1870]), 24; for the popularity of these experiments, see the essays in Donald E. Pitzer, ed., *America's Communal Utopias* (Chapel Hill: University of North Carolina Press, 1997).

10. "Integrity of Businessmen," 683.

11. Elisha Oscar Crosby, *Memoirs: Reminiscences of California and Guatemala from 1849 to 1864*, edited by Charles Albro Barker (San Marino, Calif.: Huntington Library Press, 1945), introduction, 4.

12. Isaac Sherwood Halsey, [typescript] diary, the poem is the entry for 15 August 1850, "Home of My Childhood." Bancroft.

13. Alonzo Hill to his sister [Alvira], 18 July 1849, Alonzo A. Hill Papers, Yale.

14. Sara Wiswall Meyer, *A Forty Niner Speaks: A Chronological Record of the Observations and Experiences of a New Yorker and his Adventures in Various Mining Localities in California* (West Sacramento, Calif.: Sacramento Corral of the Westerners, 1978), introduction, 53.

15. Augustus Fitz Randolph Taylor, diary, entry for 3 March 1838, Taylor Collection, Alex; Rutgers Biography File, A. F. R. Taylor (1832).

16. James Barnes to his parents, Blooming Grove, N.Y., 21 October 1849, James Barnes Collection, Bancroft.

17. Stephen Fender, *Plotting the Golden West: American Literature and the Rhetoric of the California Trail* (London: Cambridge University Press, 1981), 12.

18. Jack Larkin, *The Reshaping of Everyday Life, 1790–1840* (New York: Harper and Row, 1988); Kenneth M. Price and Susan Belasco Smith, eds., *Periodical Literature in Nineteenth-Century America* (Charlottesville: University Press of Virginia, 1995), introduction, 4–5; Frank Luther Mott, *Golden Multitudes: The Story of Best Sellers in the United States* (New York: R. R. Bowker, 1947), 76–79.

19. Franklin A. Buck to Mary Buck Sewell, 3 January 1849, 17 January 1849, in *A Yankee Trader in the Gold Rush: The Letters of Franklin A. Buck* (Boston: Houghton Mifflin, 1930), 29–30; Frank Marryat, *Mountains and Molehills, or Recollections of a Burnt Journal* (London: Longman, Brown, Green and Longmans, 1855), 128, 170, 178–79.

20. For an overview of *Crusoe*'s popularity as both literary work and foundation for a genre, see Martin Green, *The Robinson Crusoe Story* (University Park: Pennsylvania State University Press, 1990): the quote is from p. 2.

21. John Sekora, *Luxury: The Concept in Western Thought: Eden to Smollett* (Baltimore: Johns Hopkins University Press, 1977), 111; as Sekora adds, in the second half of the century defenses of luxury and appetite would become far more necessary, culminating in the cosmopolitanism of Oliver Goldsmith and the free market philosophy of Adam Smith (112–27).

22. John J. Richetti, *"Robinson Crusoe*: The Self as Master," *Modern Essays on Eighteenth Century Literature* (1983): 209–16; Daniel Defoe, *"Robinson Crusoe": A Norton Critical Edition* (New York: W. W. Norton, 1975), 47–63, 86.

23. For historians who have recognized *Crusoe* as the gold rush's inspiring myth, see Oscar Lewis, *Sea Routes to the Gold Fields: The Migration by Water to California in 1849–1852* (New York: Alfred A. Knopf, 1949), 114; John Walton Caughey, *Gold Is the Cornerstone* (Berkeley: University of California Press, 1948), 90; Quote on Crusoe taken from George Payson, *Golden Dreams and Leaden Realities* (Upper Saddle River, N.J.: Literature House/Gregg Press, 1970), 21.

24. Richard Lunt Hale, *The Log of a Forty-Niner* (Boston: B. J. Brimmer, 1923), foreword.

25. Hale, *Log of a Forty-Niner*, 47–48, 50; John C. Callbreath to "Parents" [in Sullivan County, N.Y.], New London, 29 January 1849, Callbreath Collection, Bancroft; John N. Stone, diary, entry for 17 June 1849, in John E. Pomfret, ed., *California Gold Rush Voyages, 1848–49* (San Marino, Calif.: Huntington Library, 1954), 132; E. I. Barra, cited in Oscar Lewis, "South American Ports of Call," *Pacific Historical Review* 18 [1] (February 1849): 57–66 (quote, 65); Robert Hutchinson, diary [typescript], entry for 23 March 1850, NYPL; On *Crusoe* as an inspiration for bourgeois play, see Green, *The Robinson Crusoe Story*.

26. For an examination of this modern aesthetic, along with its antimodern underpinnings, see T. J. Jackson Lears, *No Place of Grace: Antimodernism and the Transformation of American Culture, 1880–1920* (New York: Pantheon, 1981); idem, *Fables of Abundance*, 346–58. For the seed of the idea that the aesthetic is transhistorical, and extends from at least the rise of a modern bourgeois sensibility, see Sigmund Freud, *Civilization and Its Discontents* (New York: W. W. Norton, 1961), 11–13, 36–37, 49.

27. [George Gordon] Lord Byron, *Childe Harold's Pilgrimage*, from Thomas Moore, ed., *The Poetical Works of Lord Byron* (New York: Johnson, Fry, and Company, 1867), 62.

28. See Northrop Frye, "Lord Byron," in Harold Bloom, ed., *George Gordon, Lord Byron* (New York: Chelsea House, 1986), 55–56; Paul G. Trueblood, *Lord Byron* (New York: Twayne, 1969); Harriet Beecher Stowe, *Lady Byron Vindicated: A History of the Byron Controversy, From Its Beginning in 1816 to the Present Time* (New York: Haskell House, 1970 [1870]); Thomas Moore, "Biography of Lord Byron," in *The Poetical Works of Lord Byron*, i–xxii (quote, ii).

29. Ralph Waldo Emerson, "Self Reliance," in *Essays by Ralph Waldo Emerson* (New York: Harper and Row—Perennial Library Edition, 1951), 36.

30. See David S. Reynolds, *Beneath the American Renaissance: The Subversive Imagination in the Age of Emerson and Melville* (New York: Harvard University Press, 1988), 54–91; George Foster, *New York by Gas-Light* (Berkeley: University of California Press, 1990 [1850]), 73, 107, 167, 208–9; George Lippard, *The Quaker City, or, The Monks of Monk Hall* (New York: Odyssey Press, 1970 [1844]), 5.

31. Foster, *New York by Gas-Light*, 169–77 (quote, 151).

32. "Farther West, or Rough Notes of the Dragoon Campaign to the Rocky Mountains in 1845," *Spirit of the Times*, 7 March 1846.

33. See David Leverenz, "Hard, Isolate, Ruthless, and Patrician: Dana and Parkman," chapter 7 of *Manhood and the American Renaissance* (Ithaca: Cornell

University Press, 1989), 205–26. These yearnings for escape from respectability and doubts about the gospel of progress have long been ignored in studies of New England Brahmin values; see, for example, Paul Goodman, "Ethics and Enterprise: The Values of a Boston Elite, 1800–1860," *American Quarterly* 18 [3] (Fall 1966): 437–51; Goodman's point is that "the elite shared a common set of values which defined proper behavior, transmitted goals to the young and provided a measure by which to judge and punish deviance" (437); the actions and writings of Dana and Parkman suggest otherwise, that one might be both deviant and Brahmin, *à la fois*.

34. Richard Henry Dana Jr., *Two Years Before the Mast: A Personal Narrative of Life at Sea* (New York: Penguin Classics, 1986), introduction by Thomas Philbrook, 7–10.

35. Wilber R. Jacobs, "Francis Parkman—Naturalist—Environmental Savant," *Pacific Historical Review* 61 [3] (August 1992): 341–56; Roderick Nash, *Wilderness and the American Mind* (New Haven: Yale University Press, 1967), 98–99.

36. Dana, *Two Years Before the Mast*, 458.

37. Francis Parkman Jr., *The Oregon Trail* (New York: Random House/ Modern Library Edition, 1949), 31–32; on Parkman's illness as an example of early neurasthenia, see Bernard De Voto, *The Year of Decision: 1846* (Boston: Little, Brown, 1943), 297. As for Parkman's indebtedness to Byron for his style, oceanic longings, and internal tensions, on one occasion he returns to his tent to read after finding that he is too sick to ride. The literary material at his disposal consists of Shakespeare, the Old Testament, and Byron. "I chose the worst of the three," he admits, "and for the greater part of that day I lay on the buffalo-robes, fairly revelling in the creations of that resplendent genius which has no more signal triumph than that of half beguiling us to forget the unmanly character of its possessor." (Parkman, *Oregon Trail*, 263).

38. This quote is taken from DeVoto, *The Year of Decision, 1846*, 256; Parkman, *Oregon Trail*, 109.

39. Josiah Royce, *California, From the Conquest in 1846 to the Second Vigilance Committee in San Francisco* (Boston: Houghton Mifflin, 1886), 232; Donald Dale Jackson, *Gold Dust* (New York: Alfred A. Knopf, 1980), 72.

40. Royce, *California*, 233.

41. Henry I. Simpson [George Foster], *Three Weeks in the Gold Mines, or, Adventures With the Gold Diggers of California In August, 1848* (New York: Joyce and Company, 1848), 14–15, 18, 20–22, 25, 37; the pamphlet also went under the title *The Emigrant's Guide to the Gold Mines*.

42. H. T. Tuckerman, "The Gold Fever," *Godey's Lady's Book* 38 (March 1849): 207; for later examples of this logic, see "The New El Dorado," *Godey's Lady's Book* 47 (July 1853): 101, 406; "Gold Digging Mania," *Littell's Living Age* 36 (1853): 599.

43. "Method of Washing Gold Dust in California," *[Hunt's] Merchant's Magazine and Commercial Review* 20 (January–June 1849): 232.

44. George Payson, *Golden Dreams and Leaden Realities* (Upper Saddle River, N.J.: Literature House / Gregg Press, 1970), 21, 62.

45. "The Gold Mines of California," *[Hunt's] Merchant's Magazine and Commercial Review* 23 [1] (July 1850): 19–27; "The Gold Regions of California,"

[Hunt's] Merchant's Magazine and Commercial Review 20 (January–June 1849): 55–64.

46. "The Gold Regions of California," 60–61; statements on the breakdown of distinctions are cited in Malcolm J. Rohrbough, *Days of Gold: The California Gold Rush and the American Nation* (Berkeley: University of California Press, 1997), 17, 19.

47. Gunn's story is cited in Lewis Perry, *Childhood, Marriage, and Reform: Henry Clarke Wright, 1790–1870* (Chicago: University of Chicago Press, 1980), 179.

48. "California Gold Discovered by Signor D'Alvear's Goldometer," *Newark Daily Advertiser*, 8 January 1849; "Gold Grease" advertisement cited in Jackson, *Gold Dust*, 71.

49. Cited in Georgia Willis Read and Ruth Gaines, eds., *Gold Rush: The Journals, Drawings, and Other Papers of J. Goldsborough Bruff*, vol. 1 (New York: Columbia University Press, 1944), xxix.

50. Isaac Sherwood Halsey, MS "Journal of events while on a voyage around Cape Horn from New York," first entry, undated, Bancroft.

51. James L. Tyson, M.D., *Diary of a Physician in California* (Oakland: Biobooks, 1955), 7–8; cited in James E. Davis's "introduction" to Charles R. Parke, *Dreams to Dust* (Lincoln: University of Nebraska Press, 1989), xix; Elisha Oscar Crosby, *Memoirs: Reminiscences of California and Guatemala from 1849 to 1864* (San Marino, Calif.: Huntington Library Press, 1945), 4.

52. Franklin A. Buck to Mary Buck Sewell, 17 December 1848, *A Yankee Trader*, 27–28.

53. Garrett W. Low, *Gold Rush by Sea* (Philadelphia: University of Pennsylvania Press, 1941), 59.

54. Taylor's "complimentary supper" was reported in "Local Matters," *Newark Daily Advertiser*, 25 January 1849; Isaac Halsey, "Day of Sailing," diary entry for 12 March 1849, Halsey Collection, Bancroft; Buck to his sister, 17 January 1849, *A Yankee Trader*, 31.

55. Lewis, *Sea Routes to the Gold Fields*, 3; Joseph Chaffee to his parents, New York, 13 March 1850, Joseph Bennet Chaffee Collection, from original in California State Division of Beaches and Parks, Interpretive Services Collection, typescript in NYHS.

56. Reverend Samuel Worcester, *California: Address Before the Naumkeag Mutual Trading and Mining Company, Given at the Tabernacle Church in Salem, on Sabbath Evening, January 14, 1849*, pamphlet, Bancroft.

CHAPTER THREE

1. Harriet Dunnel to John Dunnel, 82 Sixth Street, New York City, 4 February 1849, John Henry Dunnel Collection, Bancroft.

2. [Typescript] "The Diary and Letters of Jared C. Nash To the Goldfields Around the Horn from Maine to California in the Schooner *Belgrade*," compiled and edited by Grace Nash Smith and Renee Nash Hamilton, copyright 1956, Nash Collection, CSL.

3. This is not to say that the study of women in California during the gold rush is anywhere near completed. There appears to be plenty of room for more work

here, especially on nonwhite women. See Jo Ann Levy, *They Saw the Elephant: Women in the California Gold Rush* (Norman: University of Oklahoma Press, 1992); Silvia Anne Sheafer, *Women of the West* (Reading, Mass.: Addison Wesley, 1980); Mary Jane Megquier, *Apron Full of Gold: The Letters of Mary Jane Megquier from San Francisco 1849–1856* (Albuquerque: University of New Mexico Press, 1984); Ida Pfeiffer, *A Lady's Visit to California* (Oakland: Biobooks, 1950); Sarah Bayliss Royce, *A Frontier Lady: Recollections of the Gold Rush and Early California* (Lincoln: University of Nebraska Press, 1977).

4. Joan M. Jenson and Darlis A. Miller, "The Gentle Tamers Revisited: New Approaches to the History of Women in the American West," *Pacific Historical Review* 49 (1985): 173–213; Peggy Pascoe, "Western Women at the Cultural Crossroads," in Patricia Nelson Limerick et al., eds., *Trails Toward a New Western History* (Lawrence: University Press of Kansas, 1991), 40–58.

5. "California Song," *Newark Daily Advertiser*, 29 January 1849.

6. Nancy Coffey Heffernan and Ann Page Stecker, *Sisters of Fortune: Being the true story of how three motherless sisters saved their home in New England and raised their younger brother while their father went fortune hunting in the California Gold Rush* (Hanover, N.H.: University Press of New England, 1993), 46, 71.

7. Barbara Welter, "The Cult of True Womanhood, 1820–1860," *American Quarterly* 16 (1966): 151–74; Nancy Cott, *The Bonds of Womanhood: "Women's Sphere" in New England, 1780–1835* (New Haven: Yale University Press, 1977), 60–67, passim. The stress here again is on separate spheres ideology, not actual separation; see Linda Kerber, "Separate Spheres, Female Worlds, Woman's Place: The Rhetoric of Women's History," *Journal of American History* 75 (1988): 9–39.

8. Julie Roy Jeffrey, *Frontier Women: The Trans-Mississippi West 1840–1880* (New York: Hill and Wang, 1979), 32. 107.

9. Mary Jane Hayden, *Pioneer Days* (San Jose, Calif.: Murgothens Press, 1915), 7–8.

10. Cited from the *Hartford Daily Courant*, 29 January 1849, in Frances Alida Hoxie, "Connecticut's Forty-Niners," *Western Historical Quarterly* 5 [1] (January 1974): 19–20.

11. D. K. Shoemaker to Andrew Cochran, 14 March 1849, Andrew Cochran Papers, Bancroft.

12. C. M. Mancourt to Andrew Cochran, 24 March 1849, Andrew Cochran Papers, Bancroft.

13. For contemporary and influential views of the American West as a place of lawlessness or backwardness, see Charles Dickens, *American Notes and Pictures from Italy* (London: Oxford University Press, 1974); Theodore Dwight, *The Northern Traveller* (New York: John P. Haven, 1841); and Harriet Martineau, *Society in America* (New York: Saunders and Otley, 1837).

14. Articles of Association of the Mutual Protection Trading and Mining Company, recorded in Henry A. Stevens, diary/log, CSL; Articles of the Bunker Hill Trading and Mining Association, recorded in Thomas Williams, diary, Bancroft; Contract—Indenture for the brig *Ark*, AAS; Articles of Agreement for the Perseverance Mining Company, cited in Samuel C. Upham, *Notes of a Voyage to California* (Philadelphia: n.p., 1878), 105. For the idea that these articles

reflected socialist reform along with the quote from the member of the Hartford Union Company, see James P. Delgado, *To California by Sea: A Maritime History of the Gold Rush* (Columbia: University of South Carolina Press, 1990), 28–29; on Connecticut companies, see Francis Alida Hoxie, "Connecticut's Forty-Niners" *Western Historical Quarterly* 5 [1] (January 1974): 17–28.

15. J. S. Holliday, "The Influence of the Family on the California Gold Rush," *Proceedings of the Third Annual Meeting of the Conference of California Historical Societies*, June 20–22 (1957), 157–69, 164–65.

16. William Swain to Sabrina Swain, Buffalo, N.Y., 11 April 1849; Independence, Mo., 5–6 May 1849, 9 May 1849, folder 1, William Swain Collection, Yale.

17. Samuel Adams, "To Philomela," diary, 21 April 1849, CHS.

18. Lucretia Prince to Christopher Prince [in Yorkville, N.Y.], New London, Conn., 8 October 1850, Christopher Prince Collection, NLHS.

19. Enos Christman, *One Man's Gold: The Letters and Journal of a Forty-Niner*, compiled and edited by Florence Morrow Christman (New York: Whittlesley House, 1930), introduction, 89–93.

20. This fact is revealed in one of John's letters home, John H. Beeckman to Margaret Gardiner Beeckman, Sacramento City, 14 November 1849, box 27, Beeckman Collection, CSL; in the letter, John maintained his intention to repay Margaret's mother, and to give her a few thousand dollars as interest.

21. Sarah Staats Bayles [Margaret's mother], diary, La Tourette Collection, Alex.

22. Eri Hulbert to Louise Hulbert, Chicago, 1 January 1852, Eri Baker Hulbert Collection, CSL.

23. "Land of Gold: An Ill-fated Journey to California Via Nicaragua made by Eri B. Hulbert and William W. Walker in 1852," transcription of a letter from Mary Louise Hulbert to her son, by Elizabeth W. Martin, Eri Baker Hulbert Collection, CSL.

24. Karen Lystra, *Searching the Heart: Women, Men, and Romantic Love in Nineteenth-Century America* (New York: Oxford University Press, 1989), 7–11, 42–43, 46–55; see also Ellen K. Rothman, "Sex and Self-Control: Middle Class Courtship in America, 1770–1870," in Michael Gordon, ed., *The American Family in Social Historical Perspective*, 3rd ed. (New York: St. Martin's Press, 1983), 393–410. For a critique of the idea that the love of men might accord women power, see Suzanne Lebsock, *The Free Women of Petersburg: Status and Culture in a Southern Town, 1784–1860* (New York: W. W. Norton, 1984), 48–53.

25. Henry Billington Packer to Mary Elizabeth Judkins [in Griggsville, Ill.], Nauvoo, Ill., 7 June 1849, Packer Papers, Bancroft; background on Packer and Judkins from biographical file in papers.

26. Henry Packer to Mary Judkins, "Lines on the Presentation of a Parasol to a Lady Friend," Nauvoo, Ill., 7 June 1849.

27. Henry Packer to Mary Judkins, Pittsburgh, Van Buren County, Iowa, 4–8 December 1849; Bintensport, Van Buren County, Iowa, 24 January 1850.

28. Rix bio file; Rix Family Diary, entry for 29 July 1849, Rix and Walbridge Families Collection, CHS.

29. Rix Diary, diary entries for 29 February 1850, 12 November 1851, 13 July 1851; the couple frequently complained about money problems. But if their

economic position was tenuous, their middle-class aspirations appear clear. The "adding wheels" that Alfred sold door to door were apparently his own invention. His activity in this self-created business venture, along with his willingness to put new irons into the fire, seems to reflect the energy and optimism of a typical ambitious young man and an ardent desire to arrive at, and ensure, a place of status among the Peacham bourgeoisie.

30. Ibid., 29 May 1850, 1 June 1850.

31. Ibid., 1 August 1850.

32. Ibid., 14 June 1850–1 July 1850.

33. Ibid., Alfred's entry for 22 January 1851.

34. Ibid., Alfred's entry for 4 May 1851; Chastina's entry for 12 June 1851.

35. Ibid., Alfred's entry for 7 July 1851.

36. Ibid., 15 September 1851–2 October 1851.

37. Ibid., Chastina's entry for 4 October 1851.

38. Ibid., Chastina's entries for 7 October 1851, 8 October 1851–20 October 1851. At Alfred's departure the diary was left with Chastina, and for the next two years all the entries are hers.

39. See, for example, Stephen Fender, *Plotting the Golden West: America and the Rhetoric of the California Trail* (London: Cambridge University Press, 1981), 12 and passim.

40. Hiram Clark Gerow, diary [microfilm], postscript, Alex.

41. Jeanne Boydston, *Home and Work: Housework, Wages and the Ideology of Labor in the Early Republic* (New York: Oxford University Press, 1990), 44. This concept did not develop in the nineteenth century, but it may have had its origins in colonial ideals of yeoman competency; see Daniel Vickers, "Competency and Competition: Economic Culture in Early America," *William and Mary Quarterly*, 3rd series, 47 (1990): 3–29. See also John G. Cawelti, *Apostles of the Self-Made Man* (Chicago, 1965); Irvin Wyllie, *The Self-Made Man in America: The Myth of Rags to Riches* (New York, 1966); Loren Baritz, *The Good Life: The Meaning of Success for the American Middle Class* (New York, 1989); E. Anthony Rotundo, *American Manhood: Transformations in Masculinity from the Revolution to the Present* (New York: Basic Books, 1993).

42. Rodney P. Odall Jr., [typescript], diary, undated entry, Odall Collection, Bancroft.

43. Josiah Griswold to Benjamin Hill [in New York City], Rio de Janeiro, 17 May 1849, Benjamin S. Hill Collection, Bancroft.

44. Jared Nash to Leah Rebecca Nash, Monterey Bay, 27 May 1850, in "The Diary and Letters of Jared C. Nash"; William Swain to Sabrina Swain, Independence, Mo., 5–6 May 1849, folder 1, Swain Collection, Yale; J. M. Alexander to Francis Alexander, Jacksonville, Toulomne County, Calif., 24 August 1851; Toulomne City, 21 September 1851; Alexander Correspondence, Bancroft.

45. Sara Jane Pierce to Hiram Pierce, Troy, N.Y., 24–25 May 1849, box 281, Pierce Collection, CSL; Sabrina Swain to William Swain, Youngstown, N.Y., 27 May 1849, Swain Collection, Yale.

46. Elizabeth Martin to Benjamin Martin, Chelsea, Mass., 15 July 1850, Benjamin Thompson Martin Papers, CSL.

47. Linda Peavy and Ursula Smith, *The Gold Rush Widows of Little Falls* (Saint Paul: Minnesota Historical Society Press, 1990), 38–49.

48. William Elder to Sarah Elder, San Francisco, 28 August 1850, Elder Collection, Bancroft.

49. Jonathan Frost Locke to Mary (Adams) Locke, "Five days out from Boston," 15–27 March 1849, San Francisco, 13 January 1850, Jonathan Locke Collection, Bancroft.

50. Jared Nash to Rebecca Nash, San Francisco, 27 May 1850, 29 May 1850, 16 June 1850, in "The Diary and Letters of Jared C. Nash"; J. M. Alexander to Francis Alexander, Jacksonville, Toulomne County, Calif., 24 August 1851, 22 March 1852, Alexander Collection, Bancroft.

51. Park Benjamin, "The California Gold-Seeker to His Mistress," *Godey's Lady's Book* 38 (April 1849): 265.

52. Fanny Fern, *Ruth Hall and Other Writings* (New Brunswick, N.J.: Rutgers University Press, 1986 [1855]), 106–9.

CHAPTER FOUR

1. Reverend Lyman Beecher, *Six Sermons on the Nature, Occasions, Signs, Evils and Remedy of Intemperance* (Boston: T. R. Marvin, 1829), excerpted in David Brion Davis, ed., *Antebellum American Culture* (Lexington: D. C. Heath, 1979), 393–99, scc also pp. 67–73; "California Gold and European Revolution," *Southern Quarterly Review* 17 (July 1850): 298; the idea that these are metaphors for proper manhood comes from Klaus Theweleit, *Male Fantasies: Volume I: Women, Floods, Bodies, History* (Minneapolis: University of Minnesota Press, 1989).

2. "Commerce with California," *[Hunt's] Merchant's Magazine and Commercial Review* 22 [1] (January 1850): 208; James P. Delgado, *To California by Sea: A Maritime History of the California Gold Rush* (Columbia: University of South Carolina Press, 1990). For a record of whaling vessels refitted for the California trade, see Alexander Starbuck's *History of the American Whale Fishery* (Secaucus, N.J.: Castle Books, 1989 [1877]).

3. Reverend Samuel Worcester, *California: Address before the Naumkeag Mutual Trading and Mining Company*, pamphlet reprint of a sermon delivered 14 January 1849, Bancroft.

4. Joseph Augustine Benton, diary, "Outlines Etc of Sermons Etc Preached on Board of the Edward Everett Also in California At Various Times and Places"; "The Glory of Young Men is their Strength," 25 February 1849; "The Desire Accomplished is Sweet to the Soul," 10 June 1849, CSL.

5. Stephen Fender, *Plotting the Golden West: American Literature and the Rhetoric of the California Trail* (London: Cambridge University Press, 1981), 12; Oscar Lewis, *Sea Routes to the Gold Fields: The Migration by Water to California in 1849–1852* (New York: Alfred A. Knopf, 1949), introduction, v–vi; Walton Caughey, *Gold Is the Cornerstone* (Berkeley: University of California Press, 1948), 83.

6. Griffith Meredith, [typescript] "Journal of voyage from New York to California," entry for 2 February 1849, CSL; William Graves, diary [from Salem, Mass., to California aboard the bark *Crescent*], entry for 6 December 1849, Bancroft.

7. David Demerest, [typescript] diary of voyage on board the bark *Norembega* from New York, entry for 8 March 1849, Bancroft.

8. John Rundle to Hannah Rundle, [in Genoa Bay County, N.Y.], "On Board the Bark *Belvidera*," 9 November 1849, John T. Rundle Papers, Bancroft; Jonathan Locke to Mary (Adams) Locke, "Five days out from Boston," 15–27 March 1849, Jonathan Frost Locke Collection, Bancroft.

9. Cited in Delgado, *To California by Sea*, 32.

10. Robert Hutchinson, [typescript] diary [from Cherryfield, Maine, to California], entry for 27 November 1849, NYPL.

11. Henry Hunter Peters, diary [from New York to California], entry for 18 February 1850, box 1, folder 9, Henry Hunter Peters Collection, NYPL.

12. Hubert Hane Bancroft, *California Inter Pocula* (San Francisco: The History Company, 1888), 138–40; John H. Beeckman to Margaret Beeckman, "At Sea," 13 February 1849, box 27, Beeckman Collection, CSL.

13. Garrett Low, *Gold Rush by Sea* (Philadelphia: University of Pennsylvania Press, 1941), 8–9.

14. Bancroft, *California Inter Pocula*, 150; Thomas Williams, diary [from Amesbury, Mass.], undated entries in the form of letters to his wife [Mary Williams], Bancroft.

15. Roger Caillois, *Man, Play and Games* (New York: Schocken Books, 1979), 23–26, 136; Caillois refers to this as "vertiginous play." As a modern example of this type of play, he cites bumper-car rides. Purposefully designed to induce feelings of dizziness and terror, this ride creates a play arena that is a stark alternative to actual driving; the point is to engage repeatedly in stylized versions of violent crashes, to willfully and repeatedly do something that is (fortunately) strictly forbidden on city streets and highways.

16. William Graves, diary [from Boston to California], undated entry, William Graves Papers, Bancroft.

17. Henry Peters, diary, entry for 17 February 1850.

18. Samuel Adams, diary, undated entry [dates of entries are uneven throughout the diary, written partly in the form of an extended letter to his wife], vault MS 1, CHS.

19. Jonathan Locke to Mary (Adams) Locke, "Five days out from Boston," 15–27 March 1849, Jonathan Frost Locke Collection, Bancroft.

20. Robert Hutchinson, [typescript] diary, entry for 28 November 1849, NYPL.

21. William Rowland, "Journal of a voyage to California 1849," see especially entries for 7 June 1849, 9 June 1849, Alex.

22. Thomas Forbes to Hezekiah Branard [in Haddon, Conn.], Rio de Janeiro, 14 April 1849, California Gold Rush Letters Collection, Bancroft.

23. William Graves, diary, undated entry.

24. William Rowland, diary, entry for 21 March 1849.

25. William Graves, diary, entry for 14 January 1849.

26. Octavius Thorndike Howe, *Argonauts of '49: History and Adventures of the Emigrant Companies from Massachusetts, 1849–1850* (Cambridge: Harvard University Press, 1923), 48.

27. John E. Pomfret, ed., *California Gold Rush Voyages, 1848–49* (San Marino, Calif.: Huntington Library Press, 1954), 15–16.

28. Thomas Jefferson Matteson, diary, entries for 27–30 March 1849, 4 July 1849, Sentor Family Collection, Bancroft.

29. Samuel Adams, diary, undated entry [1849].

30. Rodney P. Odall Jr., [typescript] diary [from New York to California], entry for 1 August 1850, Odall Collection, Bancroft; William Elder to Sarah Elder [in Michigan and New York City], San Francisco, 28 August 1850, William Elder Collection, Bancroft.

31. William Rowland, diary, entry for 1 June 1849, New Brunswick and California Mining and Trading Company Papers, Alex; "The Forty Niners—Interesting Letters from Former New Brunswickers," New Brunswick *Daily Times*, 30 April 1879.

32. John M. Cornelison, [typescript] diary, entry for 8 June 1849, NYPL.

33. For an examination of this process, see Sigmund Freud, *Jokes and Their Relation to the Unconscious* (New York: W. W. Norton, 1960).

34. John M. Cornelison, diary, entry for 8 June 1849.

35. Henry Hyde, [MS] "Journal of a Voyage from Boston to California Via Cape Horn," entry for 5 March 1849, Henry Hovey Hyde Collection, CSL.

36. Jared C. Nash, [typescript] diary, entry for 25 December 1849, "Diary and Letters of Jared C. Nash," CSL; Robert Hutchinson, [typescript] diary, entry for 25 December 1849, NYPL.

37. Griffith Meredith, [typescript] diary, entry for 22 February 1849, CSL.

38. Ibid., entries for 26 March 1849, 2 April 1849.

39. Pamphlet of a sermon given in 1848 by Horace Bushnell, pamphlet files, NYPL.

40. Johan Huizinga, *Homo Ludens: A Study of the Play Element in Culture* (New York: Harper and Row, 1970), 26–27; Robert Anchor, "Huizinga and Play: Johan Huizinga and His Critics," *History and Theory* 17 [1] (1978): 63–93. See also Jacques Erhmann, "Homo Ludens Revisited," in Erhmann, ed., *Game, Play, Literature* (Boston: Beacon Press, 1968), 31–57; Francis Hearn, "Toward a Critical Theory of Play," *Telos* 30 (Winter 1976/1977): 145–60; for a modernist critique of Huizinga, see John M. Hoberman, *Sport and Political Ideology* (Austin: University of Texas Press, 1984). See also Daniel Rogers's cogent recognition of play elements within a bourgeois work ethic, in *The Work Ethic in Industrial America* (Chicago: University of Chicago Press, 1978).

41. Francis Hearn, "Toward a Critical Theory of Play," 145–60.

42. See Peter Stallybrass and Allan White, *The Politics and Poetics of Transgression* (Ithaca: Cornell University Press, 1986); A. J. Greimas and F. Rastier, "The Interaction of Semiotic Constraints," in Erhmann, ed., *Game, Play, Literature*, 86–105; the idea that play resists functional analysis is elaborated in T. J. Jackson Lears, "Making Fun of Popular Culture," *American Historical Review*, [no. 5] (December 1992): 1417–26.

43. Griffith Meredith, [typescript] diary, entry for 28 February 1849, CSL.

44. Donald Dale Jackson, *Gold Dust* (New York: Alfred A. Knopf, 1980), 98, 103.

45. "Ourselves," *Petrel*, 26 March 1849, Bancroft.

46. "Sketches by Land and Sea during a voyage from Boston to California in the Ship Duxbury, Captain Varina, in 1849: Chapter 1: The Farewell," *Petrel*, undated, May–June 1849 [the writers of the *Petrel* did not often append dates to the issues of the paper, indicating, in all likelihood, that its publication, which must have been quite time-consuming in that it had to be painstakingly handwritten with pen and ink, was not as regular as its banner professed].

47. "Jack the Giant or the Adventures of the Haverhill Peg Driver," by "Bill-ington," *Petrel*, undated issue, 9? April 1849.

48. "Scenes and Incidents, No. 3: The Storm in the Gulf Stream," *Petrel*, undated issue, July[?] 1849.

49. "Advertisement," *Petrel*, 26 March 1849; "Address to the Washington Lyceum by F. A. Ball," undated issue, April 1849.

50. John M. Cornelison, diary, undated entry, Cornelison Collection, NYPL.

51. Stallybrass and White, *Politics and Poetics of Transgression*, introduction.

52. Charles Ellis, diary, entry for 16 February 1849, in Pomfret, *California Gold Rush Voyages*, 19.

53. Thomas Forbes to Hezekiah Branard, Rio de Janeiro, 14 April 1849, California Gold Rush Letters Collection, Bancroft.

54. Rodney P. Odall Jr., diary, entry for 4 July 1850, Odall Collection, Bancroft; Richard Hale, *The Log of a Forty-Niner* (Boston: B. J. Brimmer, 1923), 26–31, 27.

55. John N. Stone, diary, entries for 3–5 May 1849; 7–9, 23 July 1849, 5–6 June 1849, in Pomfret, ed., *California Gold Rush Voyages*, 114–15, 126–27, 148–51.

56. "Crossing the Line: Old Neptune's Visit to the Green 'uns," *Petrel*, un-dated issue, April 1849.

57. "The Plot Thickens—Varmount's Defense," *Petrel*, undated issue, May–June 1849.

58. Thomas Williams, diary, undated entries [diary runs from 1 March 1849 to 30 September 1849], Bancroft.

59. James L. Tyson, M.D., *Diary of a Physician in California* (Oakland: Biobooks, 1955), 11.

60. David Hewes to his mother, "Panama State of New Grenada," 10 January 1850, Hewes Collection, Bancroft.

61. Henry Hunter Peters, [typescript] diary, entry for 28 February 1850, box 1, folder 9, Peters Collection, NYPL.

62. William Graves, diary, undated entry.

63. John H. Cornelison, diary, undated entry.

64. Richard White, "Discovering Nature in America," *Journal of American History* 79 [3] (December 1992): 878, 882.

65. Tyson, *Physician in California*, 41; Hale, *Log of a Forty-Niner*, 60.

66. Tyson, *Physician in California*, 18–19.

67. Ibid., 19; "Log Book for the Ship Audubon [sailed from New York]," entry [by Captain Winsor] for 14 March 1850, AAS.

68. Charles Ellis, diary, entry for 18 February 1849, in Pomfret, ed., *California Gold Rush Voyages*, 19; Samuel Adams, diary, undated entry.

69. Charles Ellis, diary, entry for 1 March 1849, in Pomfret, ed., *California Gold Rush Voyages*, 23–24.

70. Charles Ellis, diary, entries for 7–30 March 1849; 5 April 1849, in Pomfret, ed., *California Gold Rush Voyages*, 27–28, 31, 38, 43.

CHAPTER FIVE

1. Theodore T. Johnson, *Sights in the Gold Region and Scenes by the Way* (New York: Baker and Scribner, 1849), 6, 8.

2. James P. Delgado, *To California by Sea: A Maritime History of the Gold Rush* (Columbia: University of South Carolina Press, 1990), 7, 18–21; Frances Alida Hoxie, "Connecticut's Forty-Niners," *Western Historical Quarterly* 5 [1] (January 1974): 17–28; John Haskell Kemble, "The Gold Rush by Panama, 1848–1851," *Pacific Historical Review* 18 [1] (February 1949): 45–56; Oscar Lewis, "South American Ports of Call," *Pacific Historical Review* 18 [1] (February 1949): 57–66.

3. For an example of this analysis specifically focused on forty-niner contact with Latin America, see Lewis, "South American Ports of Call"; for an example of this analysis as generally applied to nineteenth- and twentieth-century contacts, see Frederick Pike, *The United States and Latin America: Myths and Stereotypes of Civilization and Nature* (Austin: University of Texas Press, 1992); for a historiographical overview and critique of this approach, see Steve J. Stern, "Paradigms of Conquest: History, Historiography and Politics," *Journal of Latin American Studies* 24 (Quincentenary Supplement, 1992): 1–34; and idem, "Feudalism, Capitalism, and the World System in the Perspective of Latin America and the Caribbean," *American Historical Review* 93 [4] (October 1988): 829–72.

4. On the centrality of social inversions to the history and historiography of the rush, see David Goodman, *Gold Seeking: Victoria and California in the 1850s* (Palo Alto: Stanford University Press, 1994), introduction.

5. John M. Callbreath to his parents, Dry Creek, Calif., 1 October 1850, Callbreath Collection, Bancroft; Alonzo Hill to his sister, San Francisco, 7 April 1850, box 1, Hill Collection, Yale.

6. In addition to Goodman's *Gold Seeking*, my analysis here is informed by the following: Eric Lott, "White Like Me: Racial Cross-Dressing and the Construction of American Whiteness," in Amy Kaplan and Donald E. Pease, eds., *Cultures of United States Imperialism* (Durham: Duke University Press, 1993), 482; Donald E. Pease, "New Perspectives on U.S. Culture and Imperialism," in Kaplan and Pease, *Cultures of United States Imperialism*, 22–40; Edward W. Said, *Orientalism* (New York: Vintage Books, 1979); idem, *Culture and Imperialism* (New York: Alfred A. Knopf, 1993); Marianna Torgovnick, *Gone Primitive: Savage Intellects, Modern Lives* (Chicago: University of Chicago Press, 1990); Tzvetan Todorov, *The Conquest of America: The Question of the Other* (New York: Harper Perennial, 1992); Michel de Certeau, *Heterologies: Discourse on the Other* (Minneapolis: University of Minnesota Press, 1986); Peter Stallybrass and Allon White, *The Politics and Poetics of Transgression* (Ithaca: Cornell University Press, 1986).

7. Bayard Taylor, *Eldorado, or Adventures in the Path of Empire* (New York: George P. Putnam, 1850), 94; John Callbreath to his sister [Grace Callbreath in Sullivan County, N.Y.], Rio de Janeiro, 10 March 1849, Callbreath Collection, Bancroft.

8. Richard Henry Dana, *Two Years Before the Mast: A Narrative of Life at Sea* (New York: Penguin Classics, 1986 [1840]), 236; Francis Parkman, *The Oregon Trail* (New York: Caxton House, n.d.), 226.

9. See William Prescott, *History of the Conquest of Mexico* (Philadelphia: J. B. Lippincott, 1860 [1843]); Inga Clendinnen, " 'Fierce and Unnatural Cruelty':

Cortes and the Conquest of Mexico," *Representations* 33 (Winter 1991): 65–100; R. W. B. Lewis, *The American Adam: Innocence and Tragedy in the Nineteenth Century* (Chicago: University of Chicago Press, 1955), 160–61.

10. Taylor, *Eldorado*, 3.

11. Robert W. Johannsen, *To the Halls of the Montezumas: The Mexican War in the American Imagination* (New York: Oxford University Press, 1985), 12.

12. See Johannsen, *Halls of the Montezumas*, 179–89; Johannsen's survey of this literature includes the following: Timothy Flint, *Francis Berrian; or, The Mexican Patriot* (1826); William Gilmore Simms, *The Vision of Cortes* (1829); Robert Montgomery Bird, *Calavar, or, The Knight of the Conquest: A Romance of Mexico* (1834); Justin Jones [Harry Hazel], *Inez the Beautiful; or, Love on the Rio Grande* (1846); Charles Averill, *The Mexican Ranchero; or, The Maid of the Chapparal* (1847); Lorry Luff, *Antonita, the Female Contrabandista* (1848?); George Lippard, *Legends of Mexico: The Battles of Taylor* (1847); Edward Zane Carroll Judson [Ned Buntline], *Magdalena, the Beautiful Mexican Maid; A Story of Beuna Vista* (1848?).

13. John Callbreath to his sister, Rio de Janeiro, 10 March 1849, Callbreath Collection, Bancroft; George Payson, *Golden Dreams and Leaden Realities* (Upper Saddle River, N.J.: Literature House/Gregg Press, 1970 [1852]), 309.

14. Henry Hunter Peters, [typescript] diary, entries for 5 March 1850, 8 March 1850, box 1, folder 9, Peters Collection, NYPL.

15. Callbreath to his sister, Rio de Janeiro, 10 March 1849; Peters, journal, entry for 5 March 1850; Charles Ross Parke, M.D., *Dreams to Dust* (Lincoln: University of Nebraska Press, 1989), 134; description of Brazil's backwardness cited in Lewis, "South American Ports of Call," 58, 61.

16. John N. Stone, diary entry for 14 April 1849, in Pomfret, ed., *California Gold Rush Voyages*, 108.

17. Log entry of Captain Cleveland Forbes [on the steamer *California*] for 1 November 1849, in Pomfret, ed., *California Gold Rush Voyages*, 195.

18. Garett W. Low, *Gold Rush by Sea* (Philadelphia: University of Pennsylvania Press, 1940), 130; Dore's fascination with Brazil's fruits cited in Lewis, "South American Ports of Call," 59; Taylor, *Eldorado*, 14–15.

19. Daniel B. Woods, *Sixteen Months at the Gold Diggings* (New York: Harper and Brothers, 1852), 32–33; Johnson, *Sights in the Gold Region*, 59–60.

20. William Elder to "Cousin Catherine," Panama, 10 June 1850, Elder Correspondence, Bancroft; Asaph Sawyer, diary entry in Panama City, 1852, NYPL. For the fixed idea that voyagers would find nothing alluring in displays of Catholicism, see Pike, *The United States and Latin America*, 77–85; on Catholic forms as a later source of exotic therapy, see T. J. Jackson Lears, *No Place of Grace: Antimodernism and the Transformation of American Culture 1880–1920* (New York: Pantheon, 1981).

21. Taylor, *Eldorado*, 108, 132, 158; Samuel C. Upham, *Notes of a Voyage to California* (Philadelphia: n.p., 1878), 67, 73–75; Upham's reference to the novels *The Mysteries of Udolpho* and *The Children of the Abbey* suggests a familiarity and fascination with gothic styles contributed to forty-niner perceptions of Latin America. *The Reader's Encyclopedia* describes Mrs. Radcliffe's *Mysteries of Udolpho* (1794) as a gothic novel, "perhaps the most famous . . . of the so-called 'terror school' of English Romanticism."

22. John Beeckman to Margaret Gardiner Beeckman, Rio de Janeiro, 17 March 1849, 27 March 1849, box 27, Beeckman Collection, CSL.

23. Cited in Kemble, "The Gold Rush by Panama," 50; Francis Edward Prevaux, section of a letter—with the date missing—probably written in Panama and sent later from California to his parents in Amesbury, Mass., Prevaux Collection, Bancroft.

24. Reverend Joseph Augustine Benton, *The California Pilgrim: A Series of Lectures* (Sacramento: Solomon Alter, 1853), 44–45.

25. Henry Hunter Peters, [typescript] diary, entry for 2 April 1850 [Mexico], box 1, folder 9, Peters Collection, NYPL; Theodore T. Johnson, *Sights in the Gold Region*, 78; Hale, *The Log of a Forty-Niner* (Boston: B. J. Brimmer, 1923), 134; readers of Mark Twain's *The Innocents Abroad* may see something strikingly familiar in this passage, although Twain places the guide in Italy and Greece.

26. George Payson, *Golden Dreams and Leaden Realities*, 289–90.

27. Peters, diary, entry for 2 April 1850 [Mexico]; Johnson, *Sights in the Gold Region*, 78.

28. The statements of Hall and Coffin are cited in Lewis, "South American Ports of Call," 60, 64.

29. Thomas Jefferson Matteson, [typescript] diary, entries for 15–19 April 1849, Senter Family Papers, Bancroft.

30. Taylor, *Eldorado*, 121–22, 123, 178.

31. Ibid., 33.

32. "Police Court—Before Judge Frank," *Petrel*, undated issue, April–May 1849.

33. "To Rio," *Petrel*, undated issue, April–May 1849; the fact that the poem appeared in the same issue as the report of the trial undoubtedly reflects another ironic touch. The irony here is romantic, however: the passengers of the *Duxbury* do not mind the victory of carnality over morality—as long, that is, as the victory is momentary and offers no sense of resolution or rationalization, and as long as sin and punishment remain in constant oscillation, both forming constituent and equally important elements of the individual.

34. Henry Hovey Hyde, [typescript] "Journal of a Voyage from Boston to California via Cape Horn," CSL.

35. Johnson, *Sights in the Gold Region*, 38; Dana, *Two Years Before the Mast*, 317.

36. Johannsen, *To the Halls of the Montezumas*, 160; Taylor, *Eldorado*, 11, 20; James Tyson, M.D., *Diary of a Physician in California* (Oakland: Biobooks, 1955), 17; Asaph Sawyer, diary, undated entry, Panama City, 1852.

37. Pike, *The United States and Latin America*, 10–13.

38. See: Eugene W. Ridings, "Foreign Predominance among Overseas Traders in Nineteenth Century Latin America," *Latin American Research Review* 20 [2] (1985): 3–27; Barbara Tenenbaum, "Merchants, Money, and Mischief: The British in Mexico, 1821–1862," *The Americas* 25 [3] (January 1979): 317–39; Margaret Creighton and Lisa Norling, eds., *Iron Men, Wooden Women: Gender and Seafaring in the Atlantic World, 1700–1920* (Baltimore: Johns Hopkins University Press, 1996); Margaret S. Creighton, *Rites and Passages: The Experience of American Whaling, 1830–1870* (Cambridge: Cambridge University Press, 1995). On nineteenth-century prostitution in American port cities, see Tim-

othy J. Gilfoyle, *City of Eros: New York City, Prostitution, and the Commercialization of Sex, 1790–1920* (New York: W. W. Norton, 1992).

39. Payson, *Golden Dreams and Leaden Realities*, 55; Lamson's account cited in Lewis, "South American Ports of Call," 63.

40. Josiah Griswold to Benjamin Hill, San Francisco, 29 December 1849, Benjamin Hill Collection, Bancroft.

41. Franklin A. Buck, *A Yankee Trader in the Gold Rush: The Letters of Franklin A. Buck* (Boston and New York: Houghton Mifflin, 1930), 41–42; Upham, *Notes of a Voyage to California*, 55; Parke, *Dreams to Dust*, 129–33.

42. Johnson, *Sights in the Gold Region*, 244; Tyson, *Diary of a Physician in California*, 111.

43. "The Slave Girl at Rio," 17 June 1849; the poem appeared under the pen-name of "Smike," one of the paper's most prolific writers.

44. John H. Cornelison, undated diary entry off the coast of Chile, September 1849, Cornelison Collection, NYPL.

45. Charles Palmer [under the pseudonym Phil Brengle], "A Scene Upon the Pampas," unpublished manuscript sent from San Francisco, 17 May 1851, Bancroft.

46. The statements of Navarro and Rosales are cited in Edwin A. Beilharz and Carlos U. Lopez, eds., *We Were Forty-niners: Chilean Accounts of the California Gold Rush* (Pasadena, Calif.: Ward Ritchie Press, 1976), 109, 103, 23; Mary Seacole, *Wonderful Adventures of Mrs. Seacole in Many Lands* [originally published, 1857], in *The Schomburg Library of Nineteenth-Century Black Women Writers* (New York: Oxford University Press, 1988), 37, 20, 51.

47. For a report on the 1850 riot, see the *New York Herald*, 6 June 1850; Kemble, "The Gold Rush by Panama," 45–56; Stephen Chapin Davis, *California Gold Rush Merchant: The Journal of Stephen Chapin Davis*, Benjamin B. Richards, ed. (San Marino, Calif.: Huntington Library Press, 1956), 38–44.

48. Howard M. Feinstein, *Becoming William James* (Ithaca, N.Y.: Cornell University Press, 1984), 172; on James's voyage to Latin America with Louis Agassiz, see pages 169–81.

CHAPTER SIX

1. Hubert Howe Bancroft, *California Inter Pocula* (San Francisco: The History Company, 1888), 23–24.

2. Theodore T. Johnson, *Sights in the Gold Region and Scenes by the Way* (New York: Baker and Scribner, 1849), 105, 109.

3. Ibid., 157; Stephen Chapin Davis, *California Gold Rush Merchant: The Journal of Stephen Chapin Davis* (San Marino, Calif.: Huntington Library Press, 1956), 73.

4. Elisha Oscar Crosby, *Memoirs: Reminiscences of California and Guatemala from 1849 to 1864*, Charles Albro Barker, ed. (San Marino, Calif.: Huntington Library Press, 1945), 14, 17.

5. See, for example, Paula Mitchell Marks, *Precious Dust: The American Gold Rush Era, 1848–1900* (New York: William Morrow, 1994); Laurence Seidman, *The Fools of '49: The California Gold Rush 1848–1856* (New York: Alfred A. Knopf, 1976); Donald Dale Jackson, *Gold Dust* (New York: Alfred A. Knopf,

1980); George Payson, *Golden Dreams and Leaden Realities* (Upper Saddle River, N.J.: Literature House/Gregg Press, 1970).

6. For examples of this class analysis of the gold rush, see Peter R. Decker, *Fortunes and Failures: White-Collar Mobility in Nineteenth-Century San Francisco* (Cambridge: Harvard University Press, 1978); Ralph Mann, *After the Gold Rush: Society in Grass Valley and Nevada City, California, 1849–1870* (Stanford: Stanford University Press, 1982); Rodman Paul, "After the Gold Rush: San Francisco and Portland," *Pacific Historical Review* 50 [1] (February 1981): 1–21.

7. Susan Lee Johnson, "Bulls, Bears, and Dancing Boys: Race, Gender, and Leisure in the California Gold Rush," *Radical History Review* 60 (1974): 4–37, 8, 12.

8. Samuel C. Upham, *Notes of a Voyage to California* (Philadelphia: n.p., 1878), 222.

9. Frank Marryat, *Mountains and Molehills, or Recollections of a Burnt Journal* (London: Longman, Brown, 1855), 291, 298–99.

10. John McCracken to William G. Webster [in New York City], San Francisco, 4 October 1850, folder 2, California Gold Rush Letters Collection, NYPL; James L. Tyson, M.D., *Diary of a Physician in California* (Oakland: Biobooks, 1955), 90; Henry Hunter Peters, [typescript] diary, entry for 20 March 1850, box 1, folder 9, Peters Collection, NYPL.

11. Leonard Kip, *California Sketches: With Recollections of the Gold Mines* (Los Angeles: N. A. Kovach, 1946), see introduction, 3; Richard Lunt Hale, *The Log of a Forty Niner* (Boston: B. J. Brimmer, 1923), 63–64.

12. Kip, *California Sketches*, 16.

13. Tyson, *Physician in California*, 91.

14. Johnson, *Sights in the Gold Region*, 118, 121, 134; on this tendency, see William H. Goetzmann and William N. Goetzmann, *The West of the Imagination* (New York: W. W. Norton, 1986).

15. On this diverse population, see Robert F. Heizer and Allan J. Almquist, *The Other Californians* (Berkeley: University of California Press, 1971), 149–54.

16. John Swett, "An Evening in the Mines," *Knickerbocker* 43 (June 1854): 635–37; J. Swett, "The Camp-Fire," *Knickerbocker* 47 (March 1856): 245–47.

17. Oscar Bennett to "Brothers" [in Rochester, N.Y.], "Gold Mines on California on the '*North Fork*' of the Sacramento," 15 July 1849, Bennett Letters, CHS.

18. See Heizer and Almquist, *The Other Californians*; Robert F. Heizer, ed., *The Destruction of California Indians* (Santa Barbara: Peregrine Smith, 1974); Alfred Hurtado, *Indian Survival on the California Frontier* (New Haven: Yale University Press, 1988).

19. Marryat, *Mountains and Molehills*, 78; Charles Ross Parke, *Dreams to Dust* (Lincoln: University of Nebraska Press, 1989), 50, 88; Upham, *Voyage to California*, 240.

20. MS statement of Alfred Barstow [1877], Bancroft; MS statement of Henry Louis King [1887], Bancroft.

21. Stephen Wing, MS "Lecture" [based on his journal], Wing Collection, Bancroft.

22. Oscar Bennett to "Brothers," "Gold Mines of California . . . ," 15 July 1849, Bennett Letters, CHS.

23. [Typescript] Rodney P. Odall Jr. to "Parents" [in Rochester, N.Y.], Mariposa, Calif., 25 November 1850, Odall Collection, Bancroft.

24. Hiram Pierce to Sara Jane Pierce, "Mersais" [Merced, Calif.], 28 April 1850, Pierce Collection, box 281, CSL.

25. John M. Callbreath to his parents, "Dry Creek," 20 June 1850, Callbreath Collection, Bancroft.

26. Hurtado, *Indian Survival*, 112–14.

27. Heizer and Almquist, *The Other Californians*, 143, 154; Ping Chiu, *Chinese Labor in California, 1850–1880: An Economic Study* (Madison: State Historical Society of Wisconsin, 1963), 12–13, 142–43; Marlon K. Hom, *Songs of Gold Mountain: Cantonese Rhymes from San Francisco's Chinatown* (Berkeley: University of California Press, 1987), 5, 17.

28. Stephen Wing to his brother [in Yarmouth, Mass.], Dutch Hill, 31 December 1854, Wing Collection, Bancroft.

29. Thomas Forbes to Hezekiah [Brainard?], "N. Fork of the American River," 15 March 1850, Gold Rush Letters Collection, Bancroft; Stephen Wing to "Family," Dutch Hill, 25 June 1854, Wing Collection, Bancroft; J. M. Alexander to Francis Alexander, Jacksonville, Calif., 22 March 1852, Alexander Collection, Bancroft.

30. "Arrival of the Empire City," *Jerseyman* [Morristown, N.J.], 15 November 1849.

31. Hiram Pierce to Sara Jane (Wiswall) Pierce, "Mersais" [Merced], 28 April 1850.

32. Kip, *California Sketches*, 8, 44.

33. Charles Palmer, letter for publication, "Grizzly Den" California, 1850, Palmer Papers, Bancroft.

34. David Demerest, [typescript] diary, entry for 21 January 1850, Bancroft; Bancroft, *California Inter Pocula*, 673.

35. Douglass North, *An Economic History of the United States, 1790–1860* (New York: W. W. Norton, 1966); this formula comes from John Walton Caughy, *Gold Is the Cornerstone* (Berkeley: University of California Press, 1948), 170–71.

36. Henry Hovey Hyde, [typescript] "Journal of a Voyage from Boston to California Via Cape Horn," CSL.

37. Bancroft, *California Inter Pocula*, 197; Henry A. Pierce to Sidney Bartlett [in Boston], San Francisco, 28 August 1849, Sidney Bartlett Papers, NYPL; John Callbreath to his parents, "Dry Creek," 20 June 1850, Callbreath Collection, Bancroft; Oscar Bennett, undated journal entry from the gold mines, CHS.

38. Benjamin Martin to the Chelsea *Pioneer*, original MS headed "Our California Correspondent: Letter Number Six, Sacramento City, California," 19 August 1849, CSL; James Barnes to his family, Sacramento City, 24 November 1850, Barnes Papers, Bancroft.

39. References to California as a "humbug" and the experience as "seeing the elephant" are too frequent to cite; both became running, albeit sometimes bitter, jokes of the rush; William Prentiss to Elizabeth (Gapen) Prentiss, Sacramento City, 27 September 1850, Prentiss Papers, Bancroft; Josiah Griswold to Benjamin Hill, Stockton [Calif.], 1 August 1850, Hill Collection, Bancroft.

40. Charles William Churchill, *Fortunes Are for the Few* (San Diego: San Diego Historical Society, 1977), 95, 99.

41. For the idea that failure created these problems, and that the return of capitalism generated despair and a rise in violence, see Malcolm Rohrbough, *Days of Gold: The California Gold Rush and the American Nation* (Berkeley: University of California Press, 1997), 186–89, 191, 197–98; Leonard Pitt, "The Beginnings of Nativism in California," *Pacific Historical Review* 30 (February 1961): 23–38; Chiu, *Chinese Labor in California*, 16; Josiah Royce, *California* (Boston: Houghton Mifflin, 1886), 307, 356–62.

42. See Charles Howard Shinn, *Mining Camps: A Study in American Frontier Government* (New York: Harper and Row, 1947); *Placer County Record on Mining Laws, Ledgers 1850–1873*, including Eldorado District Mining Rules; *Placer County Mechanics Lein Book, 1850*, Placer County Records, Bancroft.

43. Karen Lystra, *Searching the Heart: Women, Men, and Romantic Love in Nineteenth-Century America* (New York: Oxford University Press, 1989), 7–11; see also Ellen K. Rothman, "Sex and Self-Control: Middle Class Courtship in America, 1770–1870," in Michael Gordon, ed., *The American Family in Social Historical Perspective*, 3rd ed. (New York: St. Martin's Press, 1983).

44. Lystra's analysis avoids the seemingly obvious connections between the intimate letter as exposition of an internal true self and early romantic novelists' use of the letter to provide insights into their protagonists' thoughts; Samuel Richardson's *Pamela* (1740), for example, is just this: a collection of interesting letters. Samuel Adams to Philomela (Johnson) Adams, diary-letters, San Francisco, 7 April 1850, Adams Collection, CHS; Rix family diary, Chastina's entry for 1 April 1852, Rix Collection, CHS. Adams, like many forty-niners, interspersed his journal with letters to his wife. Others wrote their entire journals in the form of long, extended letters to wives or family members. Such writings complicate easy linkage between genre and gender—in effect, diaries cannot be gendered male while letters are gendered female. There were, I would maintain, splits in forty-niner literary voices; but these voices were more frequently overlapped than completely separate.

45. Rose Eyring, "The Portrayal of the California Gold Rush in Imaginative Literature from 1848 to 1875" (Ph.D. diss., University of California, Berkeley, 1944).

46. James L. Tyson, M.D., *Diary of a Physician in California* (Oakland: Biobooks, 1955), 79.

47. Charles F. Dulany to Elizabeth Dulany [staying with family in Clark County, Ill.], Sacramento, 26 February 1849 [misdated 1850], Dulany Family Collection, Bancroft.

48. Isaac Sherwood Halsey, diary, poem titled "I would not live always," "Mokelome [Mokelumne] Hill," 24 October 1850, Bancroft.

49. On the confessional as a vehicle for the discursive production of truth, see Michel Foucault, *The History of Sexuality: Volume I: An Introduction* (New York: Vintage Books, 1980), 53–56, 58–64.

50. Bancroft, *California Inter Pocula*, 274–75.

51. Asaph Sawyer, diary, entry for April 1852, NYPL; Herman R. Le Roy to his sister "Jane" [in New Rochelle, N.Y.], Sacramento City, 22 August 1849, Le Roy Collection, NYHS; Henry Packer to Mary Judkins [in Griggsville, Ill.], "Nauvoo," Ill., 7 June 1849; Sacramento City, 7–13 September 1850, Packer Collection, Bancroft; Harrison L. Allen to Julia Allen [in New Bedford, Mass.],

Merced River, Calif., 24 February 1851, California Gold Rush Letters, box 3, number 139, Bancroft.

52. Stephen Chapin Davis, *California Gold Rush Merchant: The Journal of Stephen Chapin Davis* (San Marino, Calif.: Huntington Library Press, 1956), 20.

53. Julie Roy Jeffrey, *Frontier Women: The Trans-Mississippi West, 1840–1880* (New York: Hill and Wang, 1979).

54. Kip, *California Sketches*, 38; Augustus Fitz Randolph Taylor to the *Fredonian* [New Brunswick, N.J.], reprinted in the New Brunswick *Sunday Times*, 26 January 1930, as "California During the Mad Days of the 1849 California Gold Rush."

55. Benjamin Thompson Martin, "Lecture Del'd Before the Public Ap'l 30th 1851" [at Chelsea, Mass.], Martin Papers, CSL.

56. Kip, *California Sketches*, 38; Asaph Sawyer, diary, entry for March–April 1852.

57. Anonymous, "Tell her she must kiss my children," *Knickerbocker* 37 (April 1851): 381; J. Clement, "The Graves of the Goldseekers," *Knickerbocker* 37 (June 1851): 519; Anonymous, "The Dying Californian," *Knickerbocker* 40 (October 1852): 335.

58. Benjamin Thompson Martin, "Lecture Del'd Before the Public Ap'l 130th 1851" [at Chelsea, Mass.], Martin Papers, CSL.

59. For an analysis of how these conversations confirm male power, see Christopher Newfield, "The Politics of Male Suffering: Masochism and Hegemony in the American Renaissance," *Differences: A Journal of Feminist Critical Studies* 1 [3] (1989): 55–87.

60. Alonzo Hill to his sister [Alvira, in Spencer, Worcester County, Mass.], San Francisco, 7 October 1849; Sacramento City, 27 September 1850, Alonzo A. Hill Papers, box 1, Yale.

61. [Typescript] Frederick Tracy to Emily Tracy, San Francisco—Upper California, 26 August 1849, California Gold Rush Letters Collection, box 2, number 80, Bancroft.

62. James Campbell to Elizabeth Campbell, undated letter, California Gold Rush Letters Collection, box 1, number 20, Bancroft; Samuel Adams, diary-letters, entry for March 1850.

63. Jared C. Nash, [typescript] "The Diary and Letters of Jared C. Nash," entry for 31 January 1850, CSL; Asaph Sawyer, diary, undated entry, NYPL; Samuel Adams, diary, entry for 27 December 1849; log of Captain Cleveland Forbes, entry for 29 November 1848, in John E. Pomfret, ed., *California Gold Rush Voyages, 1848–1849* (San Marino, Calif.: Huntington Library Press, 1954), 205–6.

CHAPTER SEVEN

1. Harriet Dunnel to John Dunnel, Athens, N.Y., 17 June 1849, 13 August 1849, 19 November 1849, Dunnel Collection, folder 8, Bancroft.

2. Henry Dunnel to John Dunnel, New York City, 16 October 1849; Ashley Anne (Baldwin) Racket to John Dunnel (her brother-in-law), New York City, 13 March 1850; Harriet Dunnel to John Dunnel, Athens, 13 August 1849, Dunnel Collection, Bancroft.

3. John Dunnel to Harriet Dunnel, Coloma, Calif., 10 September 1850, Dunnel Collection, folder 25, Bancroft.

4. Hubert Howe Bancroft, *California Inter Pocula* (San Francisco: The History Company, 1888), 228.

5. For analyses of the home as a safe refuge, or a place women might dread leaving, see Carl Degler, *At Odds: Women and the Family in America from the Revolution to the Present* (New York: Oxford University Press, 1980); Christopher Lasch, *Haven in a Heartless World: The Family Besieged* (New York: Basic Books, 1977). For accounts of the creation of the home as apart or private, see Mary Ryan, "American Society and the Cult of Domesticity 1830-1860," Ph.D. diss., University of California, Santa Barbara, 1971; Stephanie Coontz, *The Social Origins of Private Life: A History of American Families 1600-1900* (London: Verso, 1988); Steven Mintz, *Domestic Revolutions: A Social History of American Family Life* (New York: Free Press, 1988). Finally, for an analysis of the ideological components of the home as haven, see Nancy M. Theriot, *Nostalgia on the Right: Historical Roots of the Idealized Family* (Chicago, Midwest Research Pamphlet, 1983).

6. Harrison Allen to Julia Allen [in New Bedford, Mass.], Merced River, Calif., 24 February 1851, California Gold Rush Letters Collection, Bancroft.

7. Christman, *One Man's Gold: The Letters and Journal of a Forty-Niner* (New York: Whittlesley House, 1930), 6–7, Ellen Apple to Enos Christman, West Chester, Penn., 1 July 1849.

8. Julia Allen to Harrison Allen, Freetown, Mass., 25 May 1851, California Gold Rush Letters Collection, Bancroft.

9. Ibid.

10. Sabrina Swain to William Swain, Youngstown, N.Y., 19 September 1849, Swain Family [Uncatalogued] Collection, box 1, Yale.

11. Sabrina Swain to William Swain, Youngstown, N.Y., 22 April 1849.

12. Linda S. Peavy and Ursula Smith, *The Gold Rush Widows of Little Falls: A Story Drawn from the Letters of Pamelia and James Fergus* (St. Paul, Minn.: Minnesota Historical Society Press, 1990), 5, see also pp. 12, 65.

13. Ibid., 79–80.

14. Rix family diary, Chastina's entries for 25 October 1851 through March 1852; quote from entry 14 March 1852, CHS.

15. Ibid., Chastina's entry for 6 November 1851; this was Chastina's birthday and, as she wrote, "a gloomier one I do not ever remember of spending."

16. Ibid., Chastina's entry for 8 November 1851.

17. Ibid., Chastina's entry for 14 November 1851.

18. Sabrina Swain to William Swain, Youngstown, N.Y., 4 November 1849, 7 November 1849.

19. Sabrina Swain to William Swain, Youngstown, N.Y., 7 November 1849.

20. Holliday's transcription of this letter, available in the Swain Family Collection at Beinecke Library, Yale University, contains the passage, but it has been crossed out. Written in the margins is a comment to the effect that it is meaningless ranting.

21. Peter N. Stearns and Carol Z. Stearns, "Emotionology: Clarifying the History of Emotions and Emotional Standards," *American Historical Review* 90 [4] (October 1985): 813–34, 827.

22. Josiah Griswold to Benjamin Hill, San Francisco, 29 December 1849; [San Francisco?], 13 February–[held and added to] 22 May 1850, Benjamin S. Hill Collection, Bancroft.

23. Cornelius La Tourette to Margaret (Staats) (Bayles) La Tourette, Panama, New Granada, 13 April 1849; San Francisco, 3 October 1849; Margaret to Cornelius, Bound Brook, N.J., 10 December 1849, La Tourette Collection, Alex.

24. Margaret La Tourette to Cornelius La Tourette, Bound Brook, 6 February 1851.

25. Margaret La Tourette to Cornelius La Tourette, Bound Brook, 10 December 1849. The death count in her six surviving letters includes members of the New Brunswick Mining and Trading Company; it includes: 1) Voorhies Fisher (died in California), 2) Frederick (their son), 3) Charles (their son), 4) John Lowe (died in Bound Brook), 5) Mrs. Wycoff (a relation), 6) Van Middlesworth (in California), 7) the baby of Mrs. Cox, 8) the two-year-old of the Mollisons, 9) Dr. Dunn (the family doctor who died after falling off a horse), 10) Digby Smith (murdered in California), 11) Daniel La Tourette (a relation who died of cholera, a "wasted skeleton").

26. Ibid.

27. Margaret La Tourette to Cornelius La Tourette, Bound Brook, 6 February 1851, 6 August 1851.

28. On feminine sentimentality and death, see especially chapter 6 of Ann Douglass, *The Feminization of American Culture* (New York: Anchor Press, 1988); also Philippe Aries, *Death in America* (Philadelphia: University of Pennsylvania Press, 1975); idem, *The Hour of Our Death* (New York: Oxford University Press, 1991); Margaret Coffin, *Death in Early America: The History and Folklore of Customs and Superstitions of Early Medicine, Funerals, Burials and Mourning* (Nashville: Nelson Press, 1976); James J. Farrell, *Inventing the American Way of Death 1830–1920* (Philadelphia: Temple University Press, 1980).

29. Mary Louisa Hulbert to Eri Hulbert, Chicago, April 1852; Eri to Mary Louisa, Howard Hotel, New York City, 1 May 1852; New York, 3 May 1852, Hulbert Collection, CSL.

30. [Typescript] "The Land of Gold: An Ill-fated Journey to California Via Nicaragua Made by Eri Hulbert and William W. Walker in 1852," transcription of a letter from Mary Louise Hulbert to her son, Elizabeth W. Martin, Eri Baker Hulbert Collection, CSL.

31. Ibid.

32. Margaret Gardiner Beeckman to John H. Beeckman, "Sherwood Forest" [Tyler Estate], Va., 8 February 1850, John Beeckman Collection, box 27, CSL.

33. Henry Beeckman Livingston to Gilbert L. Beeckman, Fremont, Calif., 27 April 1850, Beeckman Collection, box 27, CSL.

34. Alexander Gardiner to Julia Gardiner Tyler, New York City, 7 June 1850, Beeckman Collection, box 27, CSL.

35. J. A. Lowerey to "Mrs. John H." [Margaret] Beeckman, New York City, 26 July 1851, Beeckman Collection, box 27, CSL.

36. Alexander Beeckman to Henry Beeckman Livingston, New York, 13 June 1850, Beeckman Collection, box 27, CSL. This letter concerns debts owed to Beeckman's business partner, referred to as "Major Bean," who as Alexander

Beeckman wrote "was not as fair in some of his business dealings as he should have been[.]"

37. Cousin Alice [Alice Bradley Haven], *All's Not Gold that Glitters, or, The Young Californian* (New York: Appleton, 1853), 12–13, 26–27, 149, 159; "Graves of Gold Diggers," *Ladies Repository* 2 [12] (1851): 468–69.

38. Jeanne Boydston, *Home and Work: Housework, Wages, and the Ideology of Labor in the Early Republic* (New York: Oxford University Press, 1990), 139–40.

39. Boydston, *Home and Work*, introduction, 44; on the gender system and the ideology of a sexual division of labor, see also Alice Kessler-Harris, *Out to Work: A History of Wage-Earning Women in the United States* (New York: Oxford University Press, 1982); idem, *Women Have Always Worked: A Historical Overview* (New York: McGraw Hill, 1981); W. Elliot Brownlee and Mary Brownlee, *Women in the American Economy: A Documentary History, 1675 to 1929* (New Haven: Yale University Press, 1976); Claudia Dale Goldin, *Understanding the Gender Gap: An Economic History of American Women* (New York: Oxford University Press, 1990). For the legal dimensions of the sexual division of labor and property, see Martha Minow, *Making All the Difference: Inclusion, Exclusion and American Law* (Ithaca: Cornell University Press, 1990).

40. Boydston, *Home and Work*, 6–20; Carroll Smith Rosenberg, *Disorderly Conduct: Visions of Gender in Victorian America* (New York: Oxford University Press, 1985), 62, 74.

41. Johnny Faragher and Christine Stansell, "Women and Their Families on the Overland Trail to California and Oregon, 1842–1867," *Feminist Studies* 2 [2–3] (1975): 150–66, 151. For the same general conclusion, see John Mack Faragher, *Men and Women on the Overland Trail* (New Haven: Yale University Press, 1979); Julie Roy Jeffrey, *Frontier Women: The Trans-Mississippi West, 1840–1880* (New York: Hill and Wang, 1979).

42. Arguments about whether it was the rise of capitalism or the presence of men that relegated women to unpaid labor or to the unseen domestic sphere may be found in Eli Zaretsky, *Capitalism, the Family, and Personal Life* (New York: Harper and Row, 1986); Heidi Hartmann, "The Family as the Locus of Gender, Class and Political Struggle: The Example of Housework," *Signs* 6 (Spring 1981): 366–94; idem, "Capitalism, Patriarchy, and Job Segregation by Sex," *Signs* 1 [3] (Spring 1976): 137–70.

43. Peavy and Smith, *Gold Rush Widows*, 38–49; Holliday, *The World Rushed In*; Jared Nash to Leah Rebecca Nash, San Francisco, 16 June 1850, Nash Collection, CSL; J. M. Alexander to Francis Alexander, "Garota," Calif., 20 January 1852, Alexander Correspondence, Bancroft.

44. Peavy and Smith, *Gold Rush Widows*, 54–55.

45. The idea of kinship as women's work, or even as paid work, is discussed in Michaela Di Leonardo, "The Family World of Cards and Holidays: Women, Families and the Work of Kinship," *Signs* 12 [3] (Spring 1987): 440–53. Other analyses of the relations between kinship and women's work include John Mack Faragher, *Sugar Creek: Life on the Illinois Prairie* (New Haven: Yale University Press, 1986); Laura Thatcher Ulrich, *Goodwives: Image and Reality in the Lives of Women in Northern New England 1500–1800* (New York: Alfred A. Knopf, 1982); David Murry Schneider, *American Kinship: A Cultural Account* (Chicago:

University of Chicago Press, 1980); see also the essays in Jane Fishburne Collier and Sylvia Junko Yanagisako, eds., *Gender and Kinship: Essays Toward a Unified Analysis* (Stanford, Calif.: Stanford University Press, 1987).

46. Diary of Sara Davenport, *Publications of the New Canaan Historical Society* [offprint, n.d.]; Margaret La Tourette to Cornelius La Tourette, Bound Brook, N.J., 6 August 1851, La Tourette Collection, Alex.

47. William Prince to Charlotte Prince, Clinton Hotel, New York City, 19 April 1849, William Robert Prince Collection, Bancroft.

48. Ibid.; "30 Miles South of Cape Lookout," 21 April 1849, Prince Collection, Bancroft.

49. William Prince to Charlotte Prince, on board the steamer *Falcon*, New York Harbor [this was his second letter of the day], 19 April 1849, Prince Collection, Bancroft.

50. William Prince to Charlotte Prince, Toulomne, Calif., 6–10 August 1849 [postscripted 28 August 1849]; San Francisco, 27 September 1849, Prince Collection, Bancroft.

51. William Prince to Charlotte Prince, Sacramento City, 21–30 October 1849, Prince Collection, Bancroft.

52. William Prince to Charlotte Prince, San Francisco, 6 November 1849; Sacramento, 26 December 1849, Prince Collection, Bancroft.

53. Sara Jane Pierce to Hiram Pierce, Troy, N.Y., 24–25 May 1849, box 281, Hiram Dwight Pierce Collection, CSL.

54. Sara Jane Pierce to Hiram Pierce, Troy, 7 June 1849, Pierce Collection, CSL.

55. Hiram Pierce to Sara Jane Pierce, San Francisco—Pleasant Valley, 18 October 1849, Pierce Collection, CSL.

56. Sara Jane Pierce to Hiram Pierce, Troy, 10 December 1849, Pierce Collection, CSL.

57. Sara Jane Pierce to Hiram Pierce, Troy, [no month/day] 1850, 10 March 1850, Pierce Collection, CSL.

58. Sara Jane Pierce to Hiram Pierce, Troy, 7 June 1849, [undated] 1850; Hiram Pierce to Sara Pierce, "Merapusas" [Mariposa], Calif., 21 January 1850, Pierce Collection, CSL.

59. Sara Jane Pierce to Hiram Pierce, Troy, 22 August 1850, Pierce Collection, CSL. Sara's calling in of the debt from Sears elicited the following response from Hiram [from San Francisco, 9 October 1850]: "I don't recollect any man by the name of Sears that owes me anything." Undoubtedly, Sara's letter referred to a debt incurred while he was in California. The fact that he could not immediately conceive of this possibility suggests the strength of the idea that no business could be initiated in men's absence.

60. Hiram Pierce to Sara Pierce, "Meraposa" [Mariposa], 24 February 1850; "Meriposes," 24 March 1850, Pierce Collection, CSL.

61. Sara Jane Pierce to Hiram Pierce, Troy, [undated] 1850, Pierce Collection, CSL.

62. Sara Jane Pierce to Hiram Pierce, Troy, 23 April 1850, 10 March 1850, Pierce Collection, CSL.

63. Sara Jane Pierce to Hiram Pierce, Troy, 22 August 1850, Pierce Collection, CSL.

64. Sara Jane Pierce to Hiram Pierce, Troy, 7 June 1849; Troy, [undated] 1850, Pierce Collection, CSL.

65. Hiram Pierce to Sara Pierce, "Long Canyon, Mersais" [Merced?], Calif., Pierce Collection, CSL.

66. Peavy and Smith, *Gold Rush Widows*, 194.

67. Ibid., 197.

CHAPTER EIGHT

1. George Payson, *Golden Dreams and Leaden Realities* (Upper Saddle River, N.J.: Literature House/Gregg Press, 1970), introduction.

2. Mark Twain, *Roughing It* (New York: Signet, 1980 [1871]), 309–10.

3. John H. Cornelison, diary, entry for 20 December 1849 [1850?], Cornelison Collection, NYPL.

4. Frederick Jackson Turner, *The Frontier in American History* (New York: Henry Holt and Company, 1920), 33n. On this first generation post-Turner, see Warren Susman, "The Frontier Thesis and the American Intellectual," in *Culture as History: The Transformation of American Society in the Twentieth Century* (New York: Pantheon, 1984), 27–38; and, for example, Van Wyck Brooks's 1915 essay "America's Coming of Age," in *Van Wyck Brooks: The Early Years: A Selection of His Works, 1908–1921* (New York: Harper and Row, 1968), 79–158. This second group—alternately dismissed or praised as the "symbol and myth school," would include the following: Henry Nash Smith, *Virgin Land: The American West as Symbol and Myth* (New York: Alfred A. Knopf, 1950); R. W. B. Lewis, *The American Adam: Innocence, Tragedy, and Tradition in the Nineteenth Century* (Chicago: University of Chicago Press, 1955); Leo Marx, *The Machine in the Garden: Technology and the Pastoral Ideal in America* (New York: Oxford University Press, 1964); for its most current statement by its most prolific proponent, see Richard Slotkin, *Gunfighter Nation: The Myth of the Frontier in Twentieth Century America* (New York: Atheneum, 1993). For a brief tour of this final group, "The New Western Historians," see Patricia Nelson Limerick et al., eds., *Trails Toward a New Western History* (Lawrence: University of Kansas Press, 1991).

5. See, for example, Joe B. Frantz, "The Frontier Tradition: An Invitation to Violence," in Hugh Davis Graham and Ted Robert Gurr, eds., *Violence in America: Historical and Comparative Perspectives* (New York: Bantam Books, 1969), 127–54; and Thomas P. Slaughter, *Bloody Dawn: The Christiana Riot and Racial Violence in the Antebellum North* (New York: Oxford University Press, 1991).

6. "The Condition of California," *New York Herald*, 14 March 1849; the wording here echoes Parkman's description of the frontier: "a country where the rifle is the chief arbiter between man and man. . . ." See Francis Parkman, *The Oregon Trail* (New York: Macmillan, 1930 [1849]), 15.

7. Alfred Barstow, "Statement" [1877], Bancroft; Herman Le Roy to his sister [Jane], Sacramento City, 22 August 1849, California Manuscripts Collection, NYHS; Benjamin Martin to Chelsea *Pioneer* [through Elizabeth Martin], Martin Collection, CSL; Hiram Pierce to Sara Pierce, undated, 1849, box 281, Pierce Collection, CSL; David Hewes to his mother, Sacramento City, 24 February 1850, Hewes Collection, Bancroft.

8. Hiram Pierce to Sara Pierce, Pleasant Valley, Calif., 18 October 1849; "Merapusas" [Mariposa, Calif.], 21 January 1850, box 281, Pierce Collection.

9. Payson, *Golden Dreams and Leaden Realities*, 76.

10. Garrett Low, *Gold Rush by Sea* (Philadelphia: University of Pennsylvania Press, 1941), 171–75.

11. Alonzo Hill to his sister [Alvira], San Francisco, 24 September 1849; San Francisco, 7 April 1850, box 1, Hill Collection, Yale; Theodore T. Johnson, *Sights in the Gold Region and Scenes by the Way* (New York: Baker and Scribner, 1849), 181–84. Elisha Crosby noted the anonymity of the mines and that all miners simply referred to themselves as Pikes. "This name," he explained, "was derived from the frequent answer given by early emigrants when asked where they came from, 'Pike County Missouri,' and it soon became a convenient answer by so many who did not care to tell their true state of nativity, they would belch out 'Pike' and pass on." See Elisha Oscar Crosby, *Memoirs: Reminiscences of California and Guatemala from 1849 to 1864*, ed. Charles Albro Barker (San Marino, Calif.: Huntington Library Press, 1945), 20–21.

12. For an example of current historians who state this view, see Paula Mitchell Marks, *Precious Dust: The American Gold Rush Era, 1848–1900* (New York: William Morrow, 1994), 22–23; Eric Lott, *Love and Theft: Blackface Minstrelsy and the American Working Class* (New York: Oxford University Press, 1993), chap. 7; Richard B. Stott, *Workers in the Metropolis: Class, Ethnicity, and Youth in Antebellum New York City* (Ithaca: Cornell University Press, 1990), chap. 9. For examples of historians who come close to stating it, or who imply it, see practically any published analysis of the gold rush, including Malcolm Rohrbough, *Days of Gold: The California Gold Rush and the American Nation* (Berkeley: University of California Press, 1997); and J. S. Holliday, *The World Rushed In: The California Gold Rush Experience* (New York: Simon and Schuster, 1981).

13. Susan Lee Johnson, "Bulls, Bears, and Dancing Boys: Race, Gender, and Leisure in the California Gold Rush," *Radical History Review* 60 (1994): 14, 26.

14. David Reynolds, *Beneath the American Renaissance: The Subversive Imagination in the Age of Emerson and Melville* (Cambridge: Harvard University Press, 1988), 54–91, 169–210.

15. Daniel B. Woods, *Sixteen Months in the Gold Diggings* (New York: Harper and Brothers, 1852), 74; John C. Callbreath to his parents, San Francisco, 30 June 1849, Callbreath Collection, Bancroft; Thomas Jefferson Matteson, [typescript] diary, entries for August 28–30, September 7, 1849; folder 21, Sentor Family Collection, Bancroft.

16. Frank Marryat, *Mountains and Molehills, or, Recollections from a Burnt Journal* (London: Longman, 1855), 33; Charles Ross Parke, *Dreams to Dust* (Lincoln: University of Nebraska Press, 1989), 101; Samuel C. Upham, *Notes of a Voyage to California Via Cape Horn, Together With Scenes in Eldorado* (Philadelphia: n.p., 1878), 226.

17. *Letter From a Gold Miner, Placerville, California, October, 1850* (San Marino, Calif.: Friends of the Huntington Library, 1944), 25; *Personal Recollections of Harvey Wood* (Pasadena, Calif.: n.p., 1955), 22.

18. Marryat, *Mountains and Molehills*, 35.

19. Franklin Buck to his sister, 27 June 1850, in Franklin A. Buck, *A Yankee Trader in the Gold Rush* (Boston: Houghton Mifflin, 1930), 68.

20. Woods, *Sixteen Months at the Gold Diggings*, 74; Marryat, *Mountains and Molehills*, 33.

21. John N. Stone, diary, undated entry in San Francisco, cited in Pomfret, *California Gold Rush Voyages*, 167; David Demerest, diary, entry for 12 January 1850, San Francisco, Demerest Collection, Bancroft; Benton, *The California Pilgrim: A Series of Lectures* (Sacramento: Solomon Alter, 1853), 227.

22. Cited in Edwin A. Beilarz and Carlos V. Lopez, *We Were Forty-niners!: Chilean Accounts of the California Gold Rush* (Pasadena, Calif.: Ward Ritchie Press, 1976), 86–87.

23. Henry Billington Packer to Mary Judkins, "Downeyville" [Calif.], 20 July 1851, Packer Collection, Bancroft.

24. Benton, *The California Pilgrim*, 175–76.

25. Crosby, *Memoirs*, 107–8; J. A. Drinkhouse, MS "Statement" [1878], Bancroft.

26. John M. Callbreath to his parents, Dry Creek [Calif.], 1 October 1850, Callbreath Collection, Bancroft.

27. Henry Hunter Peters to Joe Ellicott [in Boston], San Francisco, 12 August 1852, box 1, folder 1, Peters Collection, NYPL; Oscar Bennett to his family, Sacramento City, 2 January 1850, Bennett Collection, CHS; Crosby, *Memoirs*, 113.

28. Francis Prevaux to "Parents," San Francisco, 2 March 1851, Prevaux Collection, Bancroft.

29. Cited as a real occurrence in Robert F. Heizer and Allan J. Almquist, *The Other Californians: Prejudice and Discrimination under Spain, Mexico, and the United States to 1920* (Berkeley: University of California Press, 1971), 147–48.

30. See Heizer and Almquist, *The Other Californians*, 28; Albert Hurtado, *Indian Survival on the California Frontier* (New Haven: Yale University Press, 1988), 129–35; Robert F. Heizer, *The Destruction of California Indians* (Santa Barbara: Peregrine Smith, 1974), 180, 206, 226–33.

31. See Heizer and Almquist, *The Other Californians*, 145; Bancroft, *California Inter Pocula*, 569–81; Samuel Adams, diary, entry for 24 February 1850, Adams Collection, CHS; Edmund Booth to Mary Ann Booth, "Jacksonville, Tuolomne County, California," 18 August 1850, in "Edmund Booth Forty-Niner: The Life Story of a Deaf Pioneer," *San Joaquin Pioneer and Historical Society* (Stockton, Calif., 3rd pub., 1853), 27.

32. Franklin Buck to Mary Buck Sewell, Weaverville, Calif., 6 June 1852, in Buck, *Yankee Trader*, 103.

33. David Demerest, [typescript] diary, entry for 16 April 1849, Bancroft; [typescript] Rodney Odall to his parents [in Rochester, N.Y.], Mariposa, Calif., 25 November 1850, California Gold Rush Letters Collection, Bancroft; Alfred Barstow, "Statement" [1877], Bancroft.

34. Constance Rourke, *Troupers of the Gold Coast; or, The Rise of Lotta Crabtree* (New York: Harcourt Brace, 1928), 27, 129–30.

35. William B. Lorton, diary, Vol. 6, entry for 14 August 1849; Vol. 8, undated introduction; Bancroft.

36. Stephen Wing, diary, entry for 27 April 1852, Bancroft.

37. Albert Powell to Rachel Powell [at Houston Street, N.Y.], Washington, [Calif.], 25 July 1850, box 282, Powell Collection, CSL.

38. William Swain to his family, 15 March 1850, folder 2, Swain Collection, Yale.

39. Fergus's letter cited in Linda Peavy and Ursula Smith, *The Gold Rush Widows of Little Falls* (Saint Paul: Minnesota Historical Society Press, 1990), 84.

40. Sabrina Swain to William Swain, Youngstown, N.Y., 15 April 1849, folder 1, Swain Collection, Yale; Peavy and Smith, *Gold Rush Widows*, 84. Interestingly, the authors let this clear example of male power within the cycle of suffering pass without comment.

41. Charles Ross Parke, *Dreams to Dust* (Lincoln: University of Nebraska Press, 1989), 101.

42. J. D. Stevenson to James H. Brady [in New York, who sent the letter on to the *New York Herald*], San Francisco, April 1849, cited in Walker D. Wyman, *California Emigrant Letters* (New York: Bookman Associates, 1952), 175–76; Sabrina Swain to William Swain, Youngstown, [N.Y.], 9 June 1850, box 1, uncatalogued Swain Collection, Yale.

43. See W. Eugene Hollon, *Frontier Violence: Another Look* (New York: Oxford University Press, 1974); Brian Dippie, "American Wests: Historiographical Perspectives," in Limerick et al., eds., *Trails Toward a New Western History*, 112–36, 230–45. This legitimization of violence, if it inspired "direct action" undercurrents to a success culture, might also extend frontier ideals to ideologies of national self-assertion: see Slotkin, *Gunfighter Nation*; idem, "Gunfighters and Green Berets: *The Magnificent Seven* and the Myth of Counter-Insurgency," *Radical History Review* 44 (1989): 65–90.

44. Martin Green, *The Great American Adventure: Action Stories from Cooper to Mailer and What They Reveal about American Manhood* (Boston: Beacon Press, 1984), 102.

45. On the relationship between violence and literary realism, see T. J. Jackson Lears, *No Place of Grace: Antimodernism and the Transformation of American Culture, 1880–1920* (New York: Pantheon, 1981), 102–3; Robert Edson Lee, *From West to East: Studies in the Literature of the American West* (Urbana: University of Illinois Press, 1966), 1–3, 69, 159; Eric J. Leed, *The Mind of the Traveler: From Gilgamesh to Global Tourism* (New York: Basic Books, 1991), 221, 230; Leverenz, *Manhood and the American Renaissance*, 6, 73; Richard Slotkin, "Myth and the Production of History," in Sacvan Bercovitch and Myra Jehlen, eds., *Ideology and Classic American Literature* (Cambridge: Cambridge University Press, 1986), 73.

46. On the frequency of slumming in nineteenth-century America, see Leslie A. Fiedler's introduction to George Lippard, *The Monks of Monk Hall [The Quaker City]* (New York: Odyssey Press, 1970), xi–xxi.

CHAPTER NINE

1. *Dictionary of American Biography*, Vol. 3 (New York: Charles Scribners, 1935), 283; Eliza Woodson Farnham, "California Association of American

Women," broadside, 2 February 1849, CHS. Despite the autobiographical nature of Eliza Farnham's writings and her romantic tendency toward morbidity, Thomas Jefferson Farnham's death elicited no recorded emotion. For that matter she almost never mentions her husband at all. On the figure of the redemptive woman in the West, see Peggy Pascoe, *Relations of Rescue* (New York: 1990). For a broader analysis of the redemptive woman as a character central to the market revolution as a whole, see Barbara Cutter, "Devils in Disguise, Angels on the Battlefields, American Womanhood, 1800–1865," Ph.D. diss., Rutgers University, 1999.

2. Madelon Heatherington, "Romance Without Women: The Sterile Fiction of the American West," in Barbara Howard Meldrum, ed., *Under the Sun: Myth and Realism in Western American Literature* (New York: Whitson, 1985), 74–89; Nina Baym, "Melodramas of Beset Manhood: How Theories of American Fiction Exclude Women Authors," *American Quarterly* 33 [2] (Summer 1981): 123–39; David Pugh, *Sons of Liberty: The Masculine Mind in Nineteenth-Century America* (Westport, Conn.: Greenwood Press, 1983), 11–27, 60–61. My analysis here is informed by studies suggesting continuums between a "homosocial" world of a bachelor culture and the heterosocial basis of both patriarchal power and middle-class ethics; see Mary Poovey, *Uneven Developments: The Ideological Work of Gender in Mid-Victorian England* (Chicago: University of Chicago Press, 1988); Gayle Rubin, "The Traffic in Women: Notes Toward a Political Economy of Sex," in Rayna Reiter, ed., *Toward an Anthropology of Women* (New York: Monthly Review Press, 1975); and Eve Kosofsky Sedgwick, *Between Men: English Literature and Male Homosocial Desire* (New York: Columbia University Press, 1985). For a social history example of the way the homosocial confirms patterns of heterosocial gender-power relations, see Elliot Gorn, *The Manly Art: Bare Knuckle Prize Fighting in America* (Ithaca, N.Y.: Cornell University Press, 1986), especially 75, 142; this chapter is also very much informed by the theoretical approaches in Joan W. Scott, "The Evidence of Experience," *Critical Inquiry* 17 (Summer 1991): 773–97.

3. "To the Editor, From His Son, Dated San Francisco . . . ," *Jerseyman* [Morristown, N.J.], 20 October 1849; Kevin Starr, *Americans and the California Dream 1850–1915* (New York: Oxford University Press, 1973), 69–73; William Francis Hanchett Jr., "Religion and the Gold Rush, 1849–1854: The Christian Churches in the California Mines," Ph.D. diss., University of California, Berkeley, 1952; Robert Cleland Mann, "Protestant Missionary Activities in California, 1849–1859," master's thesis, University of California, Berkeley, 1950.

4. Reverend Joseph Augustine Benton, *The California Pilgrim: A Series of Lectures* (Sacramento: Solomon Alter, 1853), 43, 63, 135; Benton began these lectures shortly after arriving in California from Boston aboard the *Edward Everett*. Their publication in book form was a reflection of their popularity in California. Again, such popularity gives evidence of the enjoyment with which men read of their own moral slippage. For the source of Benton's allegories, see John Bunyan, *The Pilgrim's Progress* (New York: Penguin, 1965 [original, 1684]).

5. Benton, *The California Pilgrim*, 66, 101–2, 119–23, 258.

6. These statistics are taken from J. S. Holliday, "The Influence of the Family on the California Gold Rush," *Proceedings of the Third Annual Meeting of the*

Conference of California Historical Societies, June 20–22 (1957), 157–69; see also Malcolm Rohrbough, *Days of Gold: The California Gold Rush and the American Nation* (Berkeley: University of California Press, 1997), 94.

7. Holliday, "The Influence of the Family," 157–69; Hubert Howe Bancroft, *California Inter Pocula* (San Francisco: The History Company, 1888), 308.

8. Cited in: Carey McWilliams, *California: The Great Exception* (Santa Barbara, Calif.: Peregrine Smith, 1979), 79.

9. Cited in Rohrbough, *Days of Gold*, 99.

10. Hinton Helper, *The Land of Gold: Reality Versus Fiction* (Baltimore: Henry Taylor, 1855), 114–15.

11. J. A. Drinkhouse, MS "Statement" [1878], Miscellaneous Statements Collection, Bancroft.

12. Augustus Fitz Randolph Taylor, diary, entry for 28 August 1849, Alex; reprinted in the New Brunswick *Sunday Times*, 26 January 1930, as "California During the Mad Days of the 1849 Gold Rush."

13. Charles F. Dulany to his sister [Elizabeth, in Clark County, Ill.], Sacramento, 26 February 1849 [misdated 1850], Dulany Family Correspondence/Papers, Bancroft. Dulany sent this letter in response to a report that his sister Molly wanted to join him in the gold country. Interestingly, her plans may have been made in response to his complaints.

14. Oscar Bennet to Milton Bennet [in upstate New York], Sacramento City, 2 January 1850, Bennet Collection, CHS.

15. Edmund Booth to Mary Ann Booth, Jacksonville, Tuolumne County, Calif., 18 August 1850, in "Edmund Booth Forty Niner: The Life Story of a Deaf Pioneer," San Joaquin Pioneer and Historical Society, Stockton, Calif., 3rd pub. (1953), 27.

16. Helper, *The Land of Gold*, 115.

17. Felix P. Wierzbicki, *California As It Is & As It May Be; or, A Guide to the Gold Region* (New York: Bart Franklin, 1970 [1849]), 65–66.

18. These perceptions are cited in Albert Hurtado, *Indian Survival on the California Frontier* (New Haven: Yale University Press, 1988), 176–77; Robert F. Heizer, ed., *The Destruction of California Indians* (Santa Barbara, Calif.: Peregrine Smith, 1974); Robert F. Heizer and Alan J. Almquist, *The Other Californians: Prejudice and Discrimination under Spain, Mexico, and the United States to 1920* (Berkeley: University of California Press, 1971), 28, 166–67.

19. Wierzbicki, *California As It Is*, 64, 66.

20. *The National Cyclopaedia of American Biography*, Vol. 3 (New York: James T. White, 1893), 355; *Dictionary of American Biography*, Vol. 3 (New York: Scribners, 1935), 282. The author of the entry for Farnham is listed only as "M. Sh——r."

21. Eliza W. Farnham, *Life in Prairie Land* (Urbana: University of Illinois Press, 1988), 150—see also John Hallwas's "Introduction"; Madeleine B. Stern, "Introduction," to Eliza Farnham, *California Indoors and Out* (Nieuwkoop, Calif.: B. De Graaf, 1972), vi–xli; from her studies in phrenology, Farnham would gather "scientific" evidence for these qualities of kindness and her superior "nature" as a woman—see the studies of her head in *The Phrenological and Physiological Almanac for 1849* (New York: n.d.), 31; and *American Phrenological Journal* (June 1857): 133.

22. John Hallwas, "Introduction," to Farnham, *Life in Prairie Land*; *National Cyclopedia of American Biography*, Vol. 3, 355; *Dictionary of American Biography*, Vol. 3, 282; Thomas Jefferson Farnham's western narratives are examined in Charles B. Churchill, "Thomas Jefferson Farnham: An Exponent of American Empire in Mexican California," *Pacific Historical Review* 60 [4] (November 1991): 517–37.

23. Eliza Farnham and Marmaduke Blake Sampson, *Rationale of Crime and Its Appropriate Treatment* (Montclair, N.J.: Patterson Smith, 1973 [1846]); Helen Beal Woodward, "Biology Triumphant: Eliza Woodson Farnham," in *The Bold Women* (New York: Farrar, Straus, and Young, 1953), 337–56.

24. Georgianna Bruce Kirby, *Years of Experience: An Autobiographical Narrative* (New York: G. P. Putnam's, 1887).

25. Eliza Farnham to William Cullen Bryant, undated, hand-carried letter, letters box 6, William Cullen Bryant—Parke Godwin Collection, NYPL.

26. Farnham, "California Association of American Women."

27. Julie Roy Jeffrey, *Frontier Women: The Trans-Mississippi West 1840–1880* (New York: Hill and Wang, 1979), 109–10, 128; Helen Valeska Bari, *The Course of Empire: First Hand Accounts of California in the Days of the Gold rush of '49* (New York, Coward/McCann, 1931), 217; "The Life and Loves of Eliza W. Farnham," by Peter A. Evans, E Clampus Vitus Pamphlet, Biography Collection, CHS.

28. Mary Kelley, *Private Women, Public Stage: Literary Domesticity in Nineteenth Century America* (New York: Oxford University Press, 1984), passim and 269.

29. See Kelley, *Private Women, Public Stage*; Kathryn Kish Sklar, *Catharine Beecher: A Study in American Domesticity* (New York: W. W. Norton, 1976); Nina Baym, *Woman's Fiction: A Guide to Novels by and about Women in America, 1820–1870* (Ithaca, N.Y.: Cornell University Press, 1978); David Leverenz, *Manhood and the American Renaissance* (Ithaca, N.Y.: Cornell University Press, 1989). Leverenz raises class over gender in outlining this problem, maintaining that domesticity, as a guarantor of middle-class position, could not be abandoned; literary domestics like Harriet Beecher Stowe refused to bond with women across class and racial lines, thus the quandary: their critiques of men sounded like little more than a "genteel [and for Leverenz, easily dismissable] white woman's call to arms."

30. Farnham, *Life in Prairie Land*, see Hallwas introduction, xxi, Farnham's preface, xxxiv; Annette Kolodny, "Mary Austin Holley and Eliza Farnham: Promoting the Prairies," chap. 5 of *The Land Before Her: Fantasy and Experience of the American Frontiers 1630–1860* (Chapel Hill:University of North Carolina Press, 1984), 93–111, 109–11; as suggested by the title of this chapter, Kolodny sees Holley as the other primary example of this radical western fusion. See also *Life in Prairie Land*, 18–23, for Farnham's resultant description of housework, which contrary to the "cult of domesticity" depicts the confinement of women to the home, and to home-bound "chores," as an example of male "brutishness."

31. Eliza Farnham, "On the Subject of Women," *Hesperian* (San Francisco), 5 (December 1860): 451–561.

32. This synopsis of Farnham's thought is taken from a variety of her writings; as for her enjoyment of gardening and reading, see Eliza Farnham, *California,*

Indoors and Out; or, How We Farm, Mine, and Live Generally in the Golden State (New York: Dix, Edwards and Company, 1856), vi–vii.

33. Eliza Farnham, "On the Subject of Woman," *Hesperian* 6 (March 1861): 9–31; This series of articles, written while Farnham was farming in Santa Cruz, later served as the groundwork for *Woman and Her Era* (New York: A. J. Davis, 1864). Certainly, Farnham's defense of Fanny Wright would seem to indicate a radical element to her domestic ideology. For mid-nineteenth-century attitudes toward "Wrightism," see Lori D. Ginzberg, " 'The Hearts of Your Readers Will Shudder': Fanny Wright, Infidelity, and American Freethought," *American Quarterly* 46 [2] (June 1994): 195–226.

34. Cited in Donald Dale Jackson, *Gold Dust* (New York: Alfred A. Knopf, 1980), 87; Woodward, *The Bold Women*, 352–53.

35. Farnham, *California, Indoors and Out*, vi–vii.

36. Ibid., 294, 296, 300–301.

37. Untitled editorial, *Alta California* (San Francisco), 28 June 1849; "Mrs Farnham's Association for California," *New York Herald*, 12 April 1849.

38. Letter printed in the *Adventure*, (Saint Joseph, Mo.), 10 October 1849, reprinted in Walker D. Wyman, ed., *California Emigrant Letters* (New York: Bookman Associates, 1952), 168–69.

39. "Mrs. Farnham off for California," *Alta California* (San Francisco), 19 July 1849; "That Cargo of Ladies," Sacramento *Placer Times*, 1 August 1849.

40. Farnham, *California, Indoors and Out*, 25, 27.

41. In reports of the *Angelique*'s arrival, the captain's name is listed variously as "Wasson" and later "Windsor." Given his actions in regard to Farnham, this confusion may have been purposeful on his part, an effort to avoid prosecution. See: "Arrival of the Ship angelique," *Alta California* (San Francisco), 12 December 1849, 18 January 1850.

42. Farnham, *California, Indoors and Out*, 1–4, 7.

43. Ibid., 5–21.

CHAPTER TEN

1. Donald Dale Jackson, *Gold Dust* (New York: Alfred A. Knopf, 1980), 252; untitled editorial, *Alta California* (San Francisco), 3 November 1851.

2. Samuel Adams, diary, entry for 20 December 1849, CHS; Adams referred to the source of the story about the *Angelique* as simply "a widow." He met the woman while taking a friend to a San Francisco hospital and while Farnham was still stuck in Valparaiso. He also indicated that word of mouth around the town was that she had received help from friends and was "hourly expected."

3. Eliza Farnham, *California, Indoors and Out; or, How We Farm, Mine, and Live Generally in the Golden State* (New York: Dix, Edwards and Company, 1856), 23.

4. "Pioneer Scribes—Santa Cruz's Interesting Literary History: A Circle of Intellect," *Call* (San Francisco), 11 June 1893; "Two Letters from the Sophisticates of Santa Cruz," *The Book Club of California Quarterly Newsletter* (Summer 1968).

5. Samuel Adams, diary, entry for 20 December 1849, CHS.

6. "Arrival of the Angelique," *Alta California* (San Francisco), 14 December 1849.

7. Anonymous, "An Important Lesson, Well Enforced," *Knickerbocker* 37 (April 1851): 381.

8. Perhaps the best list of gold rush "imaginative literature" can be found in Rose Eyring, "The Portrayal of the California Gold Rush in Imaginative Literature from 1848 to 1875," Ph.D. diss., University of California, Berkeley, 1944). Interestingly and despite the male authorship of many or most of these texts, Eyring sticks to the perception that women "sentimentalized" the rush. Complete citations for the above works read Alonzo Delano, *A Live Woman in the Mines; or, Pike County Ahead* (New York: Samuel French, 1857); Albert Brewster, *The Devoted Wife; or, California in '49 and '50* (San Francisco: Alta California Printing House, 1874); John Ballou, *The Lady of the West; or, The Gold Seekers* (Cincinnati: Moore, Wilstock, Keys and Overend, 1855); Mrs. J. Blakeslee Frost, *The Gem of the Mines: A Thrilling Narrative of California Life* (Hartford, Conn.: n.p., 1866); C. W Kenworthy, *Amelia Sherwood; or, Bloody Scenes at the California Gold Mines with a Narrative of the Tragic Incidents of a Voyage to San Francisco* (Richmond, [Va.?]: n.p., 1850).

9. Francis Prevaux and Lydia (Powell) Prevaux to Francis's parents, part of a running-account letter begun August 1849 and sent August 1850 from San Francisco, Bancroft.

10. Mary Ballou, " 'I hear the hogs in My Kitchen': A Woman's View of the Gold Rush," letter from Negro Bar, Calif., 30 October 1852, in Christiane Fischer, ed., *Let Them Speak for Themselves: Women in the American West 1849–1900* (Hamden, Conn.: Archon Books, 1977), 44–47.

11. Julie Roy Jeffrey, *Frontier Women: The Trans-Mississippi West 1840–1880* (New York: Hill and Wang, 1979), 116.

12. Carl Wheat, "Introduction," to Louise Amelia Knapp Smith Clappe, *"Dame Shirley": The Shirley Letters from the California Mines 1851–1852* (New York: Alfred A. Knopf, 1949); Josiah Royce, *California* (Boston: Houghton Mifflin, 1886), 345.

13. Clappe, letters of 13 September 1851, 10 April 1852, *Shirley Letters*, 5.

14. Clappe, letter of 15 March 1852, Indian Bar, *Shirley Letters*, 120–21.

15. Clappe, letter of 13 September 1851, Rich Bar, *Shirley Letters*, 13, 15.

16. Clappe, letters of 15 September 1851, 13 September 1851, *Shirley Letters*, 26–27, 17–18.

17. Clappe, letters of 7 October 1851, 15 March 1852, *Shirley Letters*, 61, 125.

18. Clappe, letter of 20 October 1851, *Shirley Letters*, 68; Beckwourth was a remarkable character, a free black who sought room in the perceptually liberating spaces of the West for adventurist and literary talents inexpressible in the East. Although he portrayed himself—and has been portrayed—as a man who transcended constrictions of race in becoming a frontier hero, Clappe did refer to him as a "mulatto adventurer." His imaginative autobiography has been republished as James Beckwourth, *The Life and Adventures of James P. Beckwourth* (New York: Alfred A. Knopf, 1931).

19. Clappe, letters of 15 December 1851, 1 May 1852, 27 October 1852, *Shirley Letters*, 96, 141, 205.

20. Clappe, letter of 25 November 1851, *Shirley Letters*, 88.

21. Clappe, letter of 27 January 1852, *Shirley Letters*, 104–6.

22. Clappe, letter of 5 July 1852, *Shirley Letters*, 155–56.

23. See Royce, *California*, 354.

24. Clappe, letter of 4 August 1852, *Shirley Letters*, 161–74.

25. Clappe, letters of 4 August 1852, 21 November 1852, *Shirley Letters*, 173, 212.

26. For this confrontation, see Sarah Royce, *A Frontier Lady: Recollections of the Gold Rush and Early California* (New Haven: Yale University Press, 1932), 114; Jacqueline Baker Barnhart, *The Fair but Frail: Prostitution in San Francisco, 1849–1900* (Reno: University of Nevada Press, 1986), 35; Frank Soule and James Nisbett, *The Annals of San Francisco* (Palo Alto, Calif.: Lewis Osborne, 1966 [1855]), 244.

27. Royce, *A Frontier Lady*, 85–86.

28. Charles Theodore Hart Palmer [under the pseudonym "Phil Brengle"] to the *Journal of Commerce* (New York), March–August 1850, "Grizzly Den, Eldorado of California," Palmer Papers, Bancroft.

29. Charles Palmer to his grandmother [in New York City], "Ophir," Calif., 24 September 1852, Palmer Papers, Bancroft.

30. William Swain to "All the Family," San Francisco, 6 November 1850, folder 2, Swain Collection, Yale.

31. Augustus Fitz Randolph Taylor, diary, entry for 25 January 1850, entries for 20 February 1850 to 27 June 1850, diary volumes 2–3, Taylor Collection, Alex; Margaret La Tourrette to Cornelius Wyckoff La Tourrette, Bound Brook, [N.J.], 10 December 1850, La Tourrette Letters, Alex.

32. Hiram Pierce to Sara Jane Pierce [in Troy, N.Y.], Rochester House, San Francisco, 9 October 1850, box 281, Pierce Collection, CSL; Hiram Dwight Pierce, journal-diary, entry for 8 January 1851, Bancroft.

33. Richard L. Hale, *The Log of a Forty-Niner* (Boston: B. J. Brimmer, 1923), 173.

34. Margaret La Tourrette to Cornelius Wyckoff La Tourrette, Bound Brook [N.J.], 6 August 1851, La Tourrette Collection, Alex.

35. Lines written on envelope, George Swain to his family, "Lovejoy House, N.Y.C.," 31 January 1851, Swain Collection, Yale.

36. [T. B. B.?] Dewey to William Prentiss, Davenport, Iowa, 27 March 1853, William Prentiss Papers, Bancroft.

37. Joseph Chaffee to his parents [in New York City], "Salmon Falls," [Calif.], 7 December 1850, Joseph Bennett Chaffee Collection, NYHS.

38. William Elder to Sarah Elder [in Michigan], "Gold Mountain," [Calif.], 6 April 1851, Elder Collection, Bancroft.

39. Rix diary, Chastina's entry for 30 June 1852, Rix Family Collection, CHS.

40. Ibid., Chastina's entries for 16 September 1852, 28 October 1852.

41. Ibid., Alfred's entries for 10 May 1853, 3 February 1857; Mary Ann (Harris) Meredith, [typescript] diary, annotations on transcript from original made by her daughter, Minna M. Mackinder, CSA.

42. Albert Powell to Rachel Powell [in New York City], Washington, [Calif.], 11 July 1850, Albert Powell Collection, CSL.

43. Albert Powell to Rachel Powell, Yolo County, Calif., 28 April 1851, 29 May 1851, Powell Collection, CSL.

44. Enos Christman to Ellen Apple, Herald Office, Sonoma, Cal, 26 October 1851, in Enos Christman, *One Man's Gold: The Letters and Journal of a Forty-Niner*, compiled and edited by Florence Morrow Christman (New York: Whittlesey House, 1930), 242–44, 250.

45. Ellen Apple to Enos Christman, West Chester, Penn., 8 December 1851, Christman, *One Man's Gold*, 278.

46. Hubert Howe Bancroft, *California Inter Pocula* (San Francisco: The History Company, 1888), 173.

47. On the social geography of gender, see Mary Ryan, *Cradle of the Middle Class: The Family in Oneida County, New York, 1790–1865* (New York: Cambridge University Press, 1981), 190–218; and E. Anthony Rotundo, *American Manhood* (New York: Basic Books, 1993), 23–24, 104–5.

48. Hale, *The Log of a Forty-Niner*, 120.

49. "Social Meeting," *Chelsea Pioneer*, 13 September 1850, newspaper clipping from the Benjamin Thompson Martin Papers, CSL.

50. Bancroft, *California Inter Pocula*, 372.

51. Stephen Wing, MS lecture, folder 12, Wing Collection, Bancroft; Wing apparently worked very diligently on this lecture, delivering it with changes from the 1860s through the 1890s.

52. Clipping from the *Pennsylvania Journal*, 9 May 1853, cited in Christman, *One Man's Gold*, appendix-conclusion.

53. Thomas Wentworth Higginson, *Woman and Her Wishes; An Essay Inscribed to the Massachusetts Constitutional Convention* (Boston: Robert F. Wallcut, 1853), 24.

54. Farnham, *California, Indoors and Out*, 258.

55. Georgianna Bruce Kirby, diary for 1852–53, CHS; Kirby's entries are only sporadically dated, suggesting that this version of her diary may have been her own revision of an earlier copy.

56. Eliza Farnham to Parke Godwin, San Jose, Calif., 11 August 1855, William Cullen Bryant—Parke Godwin Collection, Letters 1814–61, NYPL.

57. Farnham, *California, Indoors and Out*, 213–47 (poem, 226).

CONCLUSION

1. Horatio Alger, *Digging for Gold: A Story of California* (New York: Collier Books, 1968 [1891]).

2. On the occult properties of gold, its linkage with preindustrial or anti-bourgeois attitudes toward immediate riches and abundance, see Keith Thomas, *Religion and the Decline of Magic* (New York: Charles Scribner's Sons, 1971); Alan Taylor, "The Early Republic's Supernatural Economy: Treasure Seeking in the American Northeast, 1780–1830," *American Quarterly* 38 [1] (Spring 1986): 7–34; and Jackson Lears, *Fables of Abundance: A Cultural History of Advertising in America* (New York: Basic Books, 1994), chaps. 1–4. The primary gold-seeking cult figure of the time was Joseph Smith, later founder of the Mormon Church.

3. See, for example, Stephen Kern, *The Culture of Time and Space, 1880–1918* (Cambridge: Harvard University Press, 1983), chap. 5; for some historians, it is the dispersal of the time piece that marks the divide between pre-modern and modern work habits and ethics; see Herbert G. Gutman, *Work, Culture and Society in Industrializing America* (New York: Random House/Vintage, 1966), 22–24; Daniel T. Rogers, *The Work Ethic in Industrial America* (Chicago: University of Chicago Press, 1978), 18–19.

4. See especially, Louis Hartz, *The Liberal Tradition in America: An Interpretation of American Political Thought Since the Revolution* (New York: Harvest / Harcourt Brace Jovanovich, 1991 [1955]).

5. Joseph's quote is taken from Albert L. Hurtado and Peter Iverson, eds., *Major Problems in American Indian History* (Lexington, Mass.: D. C. Heath, 1992), 291–92.

6. Maria Amparo Ruiz de Burton, *The Squatter and the Don* (Houston: Arte Publico Press, 1992); the editors of the book seem incapable of dealing with Ruiz de Burton as a member of the Californio aristocracy. They see her only as a victim, perhaps because according to American standards of thought, the aristocrat is always an enemy.

7. As an example of efforts to stress the multiculturalism of the rush, see the special series of commemorative articles in the *Sacramento Bee*, 18 January 1998.

8. "Emigration to California," *New York Herald*, 11 January 1849; Mark Twain, *Roughing It* (New York: Signet, 1980 [1871]), 309–10; Josiah Royce, *California: From the Conquest in 1846 to the Second Vigilance Committee in San Francisco* (Boston: Houghton Mifflin, 1886); Frederick Jackson Turner, *The Frontier in American History* (New York: Henry Holt, 1920), 33n.

9. James M. Hutchings, "The Miners Ten Commandments," broadside, Placerville, Calif., 1853.

Index

Edward Everett (ship), 52, 101
Elder, William, 259
Ellis, Charles, 101, 109, 115–16
Emerson, Ralph Waldo, 39, 56, 232
Emma Isadora (ship), 32
Emotion, 174–75
Environment, destruction of, 168
Erie Canal, 17, 25, 36
Etiquette guides, 28–31; reform contributions by, 29; references to class identity in, 29–30; morality in, 31
Eyewitness accounts, effect on historiography of, 10–11

Failure in California, 156, 158–59, 161, 163, 202
Family as context for forty-niners, 171, 178–79, 181, 187
Fandangos, 134–35
Farnham, Eliza Woodson, 221–23, 247, 248, 255, 267–68; historical interpretations of, 221–22, 233; redemption mission of, 222–23, 230–31, 233, 237–42; background of, 231–32; thought and ideology of, 234–38, 315 (n. 30); forty-niner perceptions of, 243–45; abandonment in Chile of, 316 (nn. 41, 2). See also California, Indoors and Out; Life in Prairie Land; Woman and Her Era
Farnham, Thomas Jefferson, 232, 312–13 (n. 1)
Fergus, James, 173, 216–17
Fergus, Pamelia, 173, 216–17
Finney, Charles Grandison, 13, 46, 121, 133
Fisher, Vorhees, 177
Five Points District (New York City), 27
Flint, Timothy, 124
Forbes, Cleveland, 167
Forbes, Thomas, 100, 109, 153
Foreign Miner's Tax, 158
Forty-niners: mythological dimensions of, 4–6, 198, 271; women as, 7; occupations and economic backgrounds of, 32–37; diaries of, 94–

96; departure for California of, 96; diversity of, 101–2, 108, 158; and nature, 112–15; in Latin America, 120–22; temptations of, 133, 205–10; arrival in California of, 143–44; and work, 154–55; failure of, 156–58, 197, 202–3; weeping, 162–64, 178; and violence, 212–14; return east of, 256–58; lectures and tales of, 265–66
Foster, George, 61–63. See also Three Weeks in the Gold Mines
Foucault, Michel, 279 (n. 15)
Fuller, Margaret, 232, 237

Gambling: as Latin American characteristic, 127, 142; in California, 205–8, 210, 215, 217, 227
Garden of Eden, 68, 86, 113, 141
Garland, Hamlin, 218
Gender, 70–71; ideology, 72–73, 86–87; and duty, 78, 89–90; and power, 78–82, 91–92; and suffering, 170; and class, 263; and frontier, 263–64. See also Separate spheres ideology; Women
George Washington (ship), 131
Gettysburg, Battle of, 268
Godey's Lady's Book (magazine), 47, 91; perspectives on the forty-niners, 6; criticisms of gold seeking, 38, 63; "A Dreamy Hour in the Gold Regions," 38–39
"Going to California" (Rodman), 23–25
Gold: ambivalence toward, 6, 41–42; criticisms of seeking for, 17–18, 37–42, 270; pre-rush attitudes toward discoveries of, 18; early reports of, 19–21; antebellum attitudes toward, 269; and the occult, 319 (n. 2)
Golden Rule, 31, 39, 55, 210
Gold Fever, 3, 17
"Goldometer," 65
Gold rushes: in Georgia and Alabama, 18; imaginative literature on, 317 (n. 8)
Goldsmith, Oliver, 286 (n. 21)